THE RISE AND FALL OF THE NEOLIBERAL ORDER

Praise for *The Rise and Fall of the Neoliberal Order: America and the World in the Free Market Era*

A *New York Times Book Review* Editors' Choice
A *De Tijd* (Belgium) Best Non-Fiction Book of 2022
A *ThePrint* (India) Most Loved Book of 2022
A *Capitalisn't* Best Book of 2022
An Orion Best Book for a Progressive Bookshelf, 2022–2023
A *Majority Report* Best Podcast of 2022 (for discussion of *Neoliberal Order*)

"[A] new political economy epic."

—Fortune.com

"Fascinating."

—Martin Wolf, *Financial Times*

"Magisterial."

—Michael Marmot, *The Lancet*

"A brilliant study of neoliberalism. . . . A heady, enthralling mural of big ideas and revelatory anecdotes, reminiscent of Thomas Piketty's *A Brief History of Inequality*."

—Hamilton Cain, *Oprah Daily*

"Enlightening. . . . Gerstle carefully recreates the new order Reagan wanted. . . . Gerstle emphasizes its market side—the administration's busting of the air-traffic controllers' union, its deregulation of key industries, its dramatic reduction of the wealthiest Americans' tax rate and its attempt to construct a Supreme Court hostile to the New Deal order—which, as it turned out, released the force of greed more than it did the genius of the marketplace. . . . There the neoliberal order remained, all but untouchable in its orthodoxy, until the crash of 2008. In that seismic event Gerstle sees a dynamic much like the one that had shattered the New Deal order. . . . [A] fine book."

—Kevin Boyle, *The New York Times*

"Big economic ideas, political hubris, and tumultuous change feature in this fast-paced and well-written account. Unmissable for its sharp insights into American politics and global supremacy, Gerstle's work is no comfort blanket."

—Shruti Kapila, *ThePrint*

"More than ever, there is a feeling that the world is at a pivotal moment where old certainties crumble to make way for an as yet unknown new order. In his well-timed and elegantly written book, Cambridge professor Gary Gerstle zooms in on the rise and fall of the neoliberal order that the US has embraced in recent decades."

—*De Tijd*

"Gary Gerstle's book, already considered a classic, accurately dissects this economic era that opened in the 1980s."

—Frederic Mas, *Atlantico*

"This book is worthwhile reading for anyone who wants to understand what the word neoliberal means, and why it's become so broadly condemned."

—Bethany McLean, *Capitalisn't*

"Gary Gerstle brilliantly explains the end of the New Deal order and the rise of neoliberalism."

—James Gustave Speth, *Orion: A Progressive's Bookshelf*

"A cogent, erudite historical analysis."

—*Kirkus Reviews*

"Anyone baffled at how the U.S. could possibly have moved over a half-century from embracing a state-centered New Deal to relentlessly unraveling it will be greatly enlightened by Gerstle's beautifully written, engrossing, and powerful telling of the rise of the neoliberal order. And some may take heart from his claim that it too is in free-fall, albeit leaving behind enduring vestiges of free market orthodoxy. I know no better guide to the complex transformations that have shaped our own times."

—Lizabeth Cohen, Howard Mumford Jones Professor of American Studies, Harvard University, and author of *Saving America's Cities*

"*The Rise and Fall of the Neoliberal Order* finds a master historian at the top of his craft. By identifying Clinton as the key facilitator, Gerstle is the first historian to so compellingly show how and why neoliberal ideas were installed in a new political order. With no less acuity, Gerstle also shows the neoliberal order cracking up over the last decade. What happens next? I know of no better political history of our times to help answer that question than this gem of a book."

—Jonathan Levy, Professor of History, University of Chicago

"Expertly synthesizing a vast body of new scholarship—on international trade, the Cold War, race, polarization, Ralph Nader, the labor movement, and the rise of conservatism—Gary Gerstle delivers the most compendious and commanding history of neoliberal America to date. Along the way he opens new windows on the unexpected collaboration between Bill Clinton and Newt Gingrich in deregulating America into the internet future. Gerstle also provides the best account I've read of how 'neoliberal' came to be the word of choice for an order that promises liberation and delivers subjection, that divides our two parties on some issues but conjoins them on others."

—Corey Robin, Distinguished Professor of Political Science, Brooklyn College and the CUNY Graduate Center

"Among the foremost chroniclers of the American past, Gary Gerstle deploys in this bold book the powerful notion of 'political order' to examine our most recent history—the past forty years when the nation fastened its fortunes to marketization, global economic integration, a harsh penal state, and sharpening inequality. By charting the rise and fall of the neoliberal order, this fast-paced account helps us make sense of the arc of American history from Ronald Reagan to Bernie Sanders, from Bill Clinton to Donald Trump. A must read for anyone interested in the world we inhabit today, with all its mortal dangers and yet-to-be fulfilled promises."

—Sven Beckert, Laird Bell Professor of History, Harvard University

"Gary Gerstle offers a brilliant, engaging, and provocative first-draft history of the last half century, a period sorely in need of scrutiny. With characteristic big-think flair, he shows that the neoliberal wisdom of that era—that markets would bring democracy, that the age of big government was over—emerged from specific historical forces and circumstances. He also suggests that many of those ideas can and should now be consigned to the past."

—Beverly Gage, Professor of History & American Studies, Yale University

"Just beneath the surface of our fractured and polarized polity, Gary Gerstle argues that there has been a Neoliberal Order under which both parties worked in the 1990s and early 2000s. Even as they bitterly disagreed, the nation's political debate moved far away from the class-based pillars of the New Deal. In another of his characteristically eye-opening analyses, Gerstle takes readers through the rise and fall of the political order that has shaped our leaders and electorate—that is, until powerful forces over the past decade, on the right and left, have opened the door to a new era."

—Julian Zelizer, author of *Abraham Joshua Heschel*

THE RISE AND FALL OF THE NEOLIBERAL ORDER

AMERICA AND THE WORLD IN THE FREE MARKET ERA

GARY GERSTLE

OXFORD
UNIVERSITY PRESS

OXFORD
UNIVERSITY PRESS

Oxford University Press is a department of the University of Oxford. It furthers
the University's objective of excellence in research, scholarship, and education
by publishing worldwide. Oxford is a registered trade mark of Oxford University
Press in the UK and certain other countries.

Published in the United States of America by Oxford University Press
198 Madison Avenue, New York, NY 10016, United States of America.

© Gary Gerstle 2022

First issued as an Oxford University Press paperback, 2023

CIP data is on file at the Library of Congress

ISBN 978–0–19–767631–8

Paperback printed by Sheridan Books, Inc., United States of America

For the Dinner Crew

CONTENTS

———∞———

ACKNOWLEDGMENTS

———⊙∞∞⊙———

THE IDEA FOR THIS book was born at a 2015 University of California, Santa Barbara, conference to mark the 25th anniversary of *The Rise and Fall of the New Deal Order, 1930–1980*. The book took further shape across a series of Cambridge-Oxford-Harvard workshops on work and inequality in 2016–2017. It acquired depth in a 2018–2019 graduate student–faculty neoliberalism study group at Cambridge. And it received critical inspiration at a 2018 Seattle conference that dared to imagine a politics lying beyond the neoliberal era. I owe a great deal to the organizers of these events—Nelson Lichtenstein, Alice O'Connor, Jennifer Hochschild, Desmond King, Daniel Coleman, Richard Saich, Angus Burgin, Steven Teles, and Heather Boushey (and the Center for Equitable Growth).

I debuted my own thinking on *The Rise and Fall of the Neoliberal Order* in a lecture to the Royal Historical Society in 2017 and then refined that thinking for two keynote addresses, one at Oxford and another at the University of Chicago. The feedback I received from these lectures and on the publications that issued from them was incredibly helpful and encouraging. For that feedback, I wish to thank, in particular, Sven Beckert, Margot Canaday, Liz Clemens, Liz Cohen, Nancy Cott, Gareth Davies, Steve Fraser, Art Goldhammer, Joel Isaac, Alex Jacobs, Ira Katznelson, Russ Kazal, Desmond King, Robert Kuttner,

Jonathan Lear, Jon Levy, Nelson Lichtenstein, Peter Mandler, Lisa McGirr, William Novak, Alice O'Connor, Christopher Phelps, Daniel Rowe, Barbara Savage, Steve Sawyer, Stephen Skowronek, Adam Smith, and Jim Sparrow. I also wish to acknowledge the generous Cambridge University Press policy that has allowed me to reproduce in this book portions of an article that first appeared in the 2018 *Transactions of the Royal Historical Society*.

I intended to debut a key chapter of this book (Chapter 3) at the 2020 Annual Meeting of the Organization of American Historians. When the pandemic made that presentation impossible, three of the commentators who had signed on for the session kindly agreed to carry out a private Zoom workshop with me. Angus Burgin, Melinda Cooper, and Quinn Slobodian delivered commentaries that were learned and penetrating. Margot Canaday and Ira Katznelson later weighed in with their own insightful readings of the chapter. I'm not sure I have addressed all of these readers' concerns, but their comments helped me to lift my thinking on the genealogy of liberalism and neoliberalism to a higher level.

At Cambridge, I have been privileged to be part of a remarkably robust and engaged group of Americanists, including Andrew Preston, Sarah Pearsall (recently departed for Johns Hopkins), Nick Guyatt, Julia Guarneri, Bobby Lee and John Thompson; visiting Pitt professors Margaret Jacobs, Barry Eichengreen, Ira Katznelson, Heather Thompson, Naomi Lamoreaux, Kathleen Brown, and Theresa Singleton; Mellon fellows Stephen Mawdsley, Seth Archer, Emma Teitelman, and Emily Snyder; a talented array of junior research fellows who year-in and year-out enliven and replenish our ranks; and the spirited Cambridge American History Seminar that has persisted through strikes, storms, and a pandemic.

Beyond the ranks of American historians, I wish to thank these Cambridge colleagues: Peter Mandler, my stalwart friend and comrade; Joel Isaac (now at the University of Chicago), Saul Dubow, and Eugenio Biagini, co-editors and co-authors on projects addressing themes similar to those I explore here; David Runciman, Helen Thompson, and Catherine Carr, all of *Talking Politics*, with whom I have spent many stimulating hours puzzling through the mysteries and paradoxes of

American politics; and the fellows and staff of Sidney Sussex College, who have welcomed me into their community these past eight years.

I also wish to salute my Cambridge undergraduate and MPhil students, whose challenging questions and sophisticated writing about American history have kept me on my toes. Every member of my stellar group of past and present Cambridge PhD students deserves to be named: Sveinn Jóhannesson, Katherine Ballantyne, Eric Cervini, Merve Fejzula, Ruth Lawlor, Huw Batts, Rob Bates, Clemency Hinton, Lewis Defrates, Jeanine Quené, Yasmin Dualeh, Richard Saich, Daniel Coleman, Kristian Dekatris, Marie Puységgur, Rob O'Sullivan, Sybill Chen, Fergus Games, and Hugh Wood. Some of these young historians have already begun to make their mark on the profession; more will do so soon. Richard Saich deserves a special thanks for giving me timely and essential help in meeting key publisher deadlines.

My longtime assistant, Jonathan Goodwin, has provided this project with years of indispensable research and feedback. Jonathan, I can't thank you enough for helping me in so many ways, large and small.

At several points in this book's history, Angus Burgin has stepped up in a major way to offer me the benefits of his expertise, insight, and critical acumen. Andrew Preston brought his foreign relations expertise to bear on Chapter 6. A long discussion with Joseph Stiglitz about his time in the Clinton Administration deepened my understanding of politics in 1990s America. I also wish to thank Andrew Marantz of the *New Yorker* and Amana Fortunella-Khan of *The Guardian* for introducing my work on neoliberalism and political orders to a broader public, thus generating valuable commentary that has left its mark on this book.

I am deeply grateful to my agent, Sarah Chalfant. Her professional skills are formidable. Her incisive and thoughtful feedback on my chapters helped me to shrink the distance between what I was writing and what I wanted the book to be. Every phase of this project has benefited from her involvement. Thanks go as well to her associates at Wylie, Rebecca Nagel and Emma Smith.

Dave McBride has been a superb editor. His erudition is immense, his judgment sure, his editorial interventions on the mark. At key moments in the book's gestation and development, he has acted decisively and efficaciously. Dave is a busy man at Oxford, yet his door was always open to me. He has helped me to make this a much better book.

I owe a big thanks, too, to the rest of the transatlantic Oxford team: to production coordinator Emily Benitez, production editor Jeremy Toynbee, copyeditor Patterson Lamb, senior art director Brady McNamara, director of publicity and trade marketing Jocelyn Cordova, and publicists Amy Packard Ferro and Kate Shepherd.

I would be remiss if I didn't register my appreciation for the seven anonymous reviews I received via Oxford—four on the original book proposal and three on a near finished version of the entire manuscript. To the authors of these reviews: I hope that you will discern in this finished book the difference your commentary has made.

Steve Fraser and I first met in 1986 at a midtown Manhattan restaurant; by the time we finished our two-hour lunch and celebrated the fleeting success of our cursed Queens baseball team, we had sketched out the book that would become *The Rise and Fall of the New Deal Order*. Without that meeting, that book, and decades of collaboration and friendship that issued from both, *The Rise and Fall of the Neoliberal Order* would have been much harder to imagine and write.

Several other longtime friends have also made notable contributions to this book. David Casey, Chuck Lane, and Michael Kazin gave me feedback on core ideas, saved me from potentially embarrassing errors, and helped me to push this manuscript across the finish line. I am grateful most of all for their friendship, for the fierceness of their intellects, and for discussions of American history and politics that have spanned decades.

My greatest debt is to my family, or "Gary's Dinner Crew": to my lifelong love Liz (the Crew's irrepressible dynamo), to my sons Danny and Sam, to my daughters-in-law Aimee and Aliza, and to the family pooch, Oliver. During the first terrible year of the pandemic, our summer cottage became a family refuge, a place where we gathered to live, work, talk, hike, watch movies, read, write, cycle, cook and eat, and cook and eat some more. I thank every member of this crew for their love, energy, passion, and insight. And for revealing to me on a daily basis a new world—and a better American future—taking shape. This book is for them and for that future.

THE RISE AND
FALL OF THE
NEOLIBERAL ORDER

Introduction

ACROSS THE SECOND decade of the twenty-first century, the tectonic plates structuring American politics and life began to shift. Even before the pandemic struck, developments that ten years earlier would have seemed inconceivable now dominated politics and popular consciousness: the election of Donald Trump and the launch of a presidency like no other; the rise of Bernie Sanders and the resurrection of a socialist left; the sudden and deep questioning of open borders and free trade; the surge of populism and ethnonationalism and the castigation of once-celebrated globalizing elites; the decline of Barack Obama's stature and the transformational promise that his presidency once embodied for so many; and the widening conviction that the American political system was no longer working, and that American democracy was in crisis—a crisis that the January 6, 2021, assault by a mob on the Capitol so shockingly dramatized.

In this dizzying array of political developments, I discern the fall— or at least the fracturing—of a political order that took shape in the 1970s and 1980s and achieved dominance in the 1990s and first decade of the twenty-first century. I call this political formation a neoliberal order. Ronald Reagan was its ideological architect; Bill Clinton was its key facilitator. This book is a history of this political order's rise and fall. It offers a history of our times.

The phrase "political order" is meant to connote a constellation of ideologies, policies, and constituencies that shape American politics in ways that endure beyond the two-, four-, and six-year election cycles. In the last hundred years, America has had two political orders: the New Deal order that arose in the 1930s and 1940s, crested in the 1950s and 1960s, and fell in the 1970s; and the neoliberal order that arose in the 1970s and 1980s, crested in the 1990s and 2000s, and fell in the 2010s.

At the heart of each of these two political orders stood a distinctive program of political economy. The New Deal order was founded on the conviction that capitalism left to its own devices spelled economic disaster. It had to be managed by a strong central state able to govern the economic system in the public interest. The neoliberal order, by contrast, was grounded in the belief that market forces had to be liberated from government regulatory controls that were stymieing growth, innovation, and freedom. The architects of the neoliberal order set out in the 1980s and 1990s to dismantle everything that the New Deal order had built across its forty-year span. Now it, too, is being dismantled.

Establishing a political order demands far more than winning an election or two. It requires deep-pocketed donors (and political action committees) to invest in promising candidates over the long term; the establishment of think tanks and policy networks to turn political ideas into actionable programs; a rising political party able to consistently win over multiple electoral constituencies; a capacity to shape political opinion both at the highest levels (the Supreme Court) and across popular print and broadcast media; and a moral perspective able to inspire voters with visions of the good life. Political orders, in other words, are complex projects that require advances across a broad front. New ones do not arise very often; usually they appear when an older order founders amid an economic crisis that then precipitates a governing crisis. "Stagflation" precipitated the fall of the New Deal order in the 1970s; the Great Recession of 2008–2009 triggered the fracturing of the neoliberal order in the 2010s.

A key attribute of a political order is the ability of its ideologically dominant party to bend the opposition party to its will. Bending of this sort comes to be perceived as necessary within the ranks of politicians competing for the top prizes in American politics—the presidency and control of Congress. Thus, the Republican Party of Dwight

D. Eisenhower acquiesced to the core principles of the New Deal order in the 1950s, and the Democratic Party of Bill Clinton accepted the central principles of the neoliberal order in the 1990s. Acceptance is never complete; there are always points of tension and vulnerability in a polity as fissiparous as the American one. And yet, the success of a political order depends on its proficiency in shaping what broad majorities of elected officials and voters on both sides of the partisan divide regard as politically possible and desirable. By the same token, losing the capacity to exercise ideological hegemony signals a political order's decline. In these moments of decline, political ideas and programs formerly regarded as radical, heterodox, or unworkable, or dismissed as the product of the overheated imaginations of fringe groups on the right and left, are able to move from the margins into the mainstream. This happened in the 1970s, when the breakup of the New Deal order allowed long-scorned neoliberal ideas for reorganizing the economy to take root; it happened again in the 2010s, when the coming apart of the neoliberal order opened up space for Trump-style authoritarianism and Sanders-style socialism to flourish.

Steve Fraser and I introduced the concept of political order in a 1989 book that we coedited, *The Rise and Fall of the New Deal Order, 1930–1980*. Since that time, the phrase "New Deal order" has become a popular one for underscoring the dominance that the New Deal and the Democratic Party exercised in American politics from the 1930s through the 1960s. I begin this book with an account of how that earlier political order rose to prominence in the 1930s and 1940s, and how it fell apart in the 1960s and 1970s. This is no simple retelling of the history contained in the Fraser-Gerstle collection; rather, this narrative incorporates my own rethinking of key elements of that story. Reaching back to the New Deal order at the beginning of this book also serves the useful purpose of throwing into sharp relief how much the neoliberal order of recent times has differed from what preceded it.[1]

I then turn to the main event itself—the construction of the neoliberal order. This story unfolds in three acts: The first is the rise in the 1970s and 1980s of Ronald Reagan and the free market Republican Party he forced into being; the second is the emergence in the 1990s of Bill Clinton as the Democratic Eisenhower, the man who arranged his party's acquiescence to the neoliberal order; and the third explores

George W. Bush's determination to apply neoliberal principles every-where, in projects as radically dissimilar as building a post–Saddam Hussein Iraq and making America a more racially egalitarian nation. Bush's attempt to universalize the implementation of neoliberal prin-ciples was born more of hubris than of a serious reckoning with the problems at hand and eventually pushed the US economy into its worst crisis since the Great Depression. But Bush's hubris reveals not just the flaws of a man but, also, the unassailable prestige of neoliberal princi-ples, an influence that Barack Obama's election in 2008 initially did little to change. Two final chapters consider the political explosions that issued from the Great Recession of 2008–2009 (the Tea Party, Occupy Wall Street, Black Lives Matter, and the rise of Donald Trump and Bernie Sanders) and that pushed the neoliberal order to its breaking point. The neoliberal order was already fragmenting when the 2020 pandemic delivered the coup de grace. This book tells the whole of the neoliberal order's story from its origins in the 1970s and 1980s, through its dominance in the 1990s and 2000s, and ending with its fragmenta-tion and decline across the 2010s.

Reckoning with Neoliberalism

In the United States, conservatism has long been the preferred term to frame the political developments that are at the heart of this book. Why, then, label the political order that dominated America in the late twentieth and early twenty-first centuries a neoliberal one rather than a conservative one? That choice deserves some explanation.

Conservatism, in the classical sense, signifies respect for tradition, deference to existing institutions and the hierarchies that structure them, and suspicion of change. One can find manifestations of these ideas in American politics across the second half of the twentieth cen-tury, most importantly in a widespread determination among white southerners to maintain racial privilege in the era of civil rights and among Americans throughout the country who, in the name of tradi-tion, were pushing back against liberation movements calling for equal rights for women and gays, and for sexual freedom.[2]

Other beliefs commonly associated with conservatism in America, however, do not fit comfortably under this political label. A celebration of free market capitalism, entrepreneurialism, and economic risk-taking was central to Republican Party politics of the late twentieth century. Yet this politics was not about maintaining tradition or the institutions that buttressed it; rather, it was about disrupting traditions and upending institutions that stood in the way. Neoliberalism is a creed that calls explicitly for unleashing capitalism's power. Invoking this term allows us to shift the focus of political history in the last third of America's twentieth century somewhat away from white southerners and family patriarchs resisting change to venture capitalists, Wall Street "modernizers," and information technology pioneers seeking to push change forward. That shift in emphasis, this book suggests, is long overdue. Central to the politics of the Clinton years were major legislative packages that fundamentally restructured America's information/communication and financial systems and whose influence on twenty-first-century political economy has been decisive. And yet those restructurings have attracted less attention than they deserve, their significance hidden by the smoke generated by the decade's fiery culture wars. Those culture wars cannot be ignored any more than the racial backlash against the civil rights movement can be slighted. But it is time to bring the project of economic transformation more into focus, to give it the kind of careful examination it deserves, and to adjust our views of late twentieth-century America accordingly. A focus on neoliberalism can help us do that.[3]

Neoliberalism is a creed that prizes free trade and the free movement of capital, goods, and people. It celebrates deregulation as an economic good that results when governments can no longer interfere with the operation of markets. It valorizes cosmopolitanism as a cultural achievement, the product of open borders and the consequent voluntary mixing of large numbers of diverse peoples. It hails globalization as a win-win position that both enriches the West (the cockpit of neoliberalism) while also bringing an unprecedented level of prosperity to the rest of the world. These creedal principles deeply shaped American politics during the heyday of the neoliberal order.

Neoliberalism, I argue, sought to infuse political economy with the principles of classical liberalism. Classical liberalism (born in the eighteenth century) discerned in markets extraordinary dynamism and possibilities for generating trade, wealth, and a rising standard of living. It sought to liberate markets from encumbrances: monarchy, mercantilism, bureaucracy, artificial borders, and tariffs. It sought, in other words, to release the economy from the heavy hand of the state in its various guises. It wanted to allow people to move around in pursuit of self-interest and fortune—to truck, barter, and trade as they saw fit. Classical liberalism wanted to let individual talent rise (or fall) to its natural level. It carried within it emancipatory, even utopian, hopes of people freed and a world transformed.

My argument for treating neoliberalism as a descendant of classical liberalism puts me somewhat at odds with those scholars who have emphasized differences between the two. The most common argument for distinction is that neoliberalism, in order to reinvigorate markets, requires far more state intervention than classical liberalism ever did.[4] I agree with the claim that strong states are necessary to organize (vibrant) markets, but I dispute the contention that the turn to strong states was a development that only began with the advent of neoliberalism. The excellent work done these last fifteen years by historians of nineteenth-century US state-building has revealed how the presence of a strong government, with the ability to set down and enforce rules for making contracts and with the capacity to expand and protect markets through law, military force, and tariffs, was critical to the success of classical liberalism in nineteenth-century America. Flourishing markets, then and now, require strong governments that can enforce rules of economic exchange. Markets need structure in order to operate freely. This principle was as intrinsic to classical liberalism as it has been to neoliberalism.[5]

Affixing "neo" to "liberalism," I suggest in the pages that follow, was less about distinguishing this liberalism from classical liberalism than about separating it from what modern liberalism, in the hands of Franklin D. Roosevelt, had become: a version of social democracy that called for a far greater intervention by the government into market mechanisms than what liberals in the classical mode, such as Roosevelt's predecessor as president, Herbert Hoover, could tolerate. Those politicians who supported Hoover would eventually call themselves conservatives. But many intellectuals in their ranks understood that conservatism, with its emphasis on order, hierarchy, and embeddedness of individuals in institutions, was contrary to the liberal spirit of disruption, invention, and innovation that they so admired.[6] Somehow the term liberal had to be re-possessed. Invoking the term "neoliberal" was one way to do it.[7]

Recognizing the close kinship between classical liberalism and neoliberalism allows us to see how some who embraced neoliberal principles sought to resuscitate the promise of emancipation and individuality that was so central to classical liberalism itself. The notion that neoliberalism embodies this promise will arouse skepticism among some. Many regard neoliberalism as the work of elites and their allies aspiring to economic and political power. Those who figure centrally in their imaginations are often influential intellectuals, or deep-pocketed billionaires and the think tanks they support, or financial institutions, domestic (the Federal Reserve) and international (the International Monetary Fund and the World Bank), operating largely free of democratic oversight. Neoliberalism, from this point of view, is configured as the enemy of "the people" and framed as a tool used by elites to subvert democracy and to undercut emancipatory movements. Interpretively, these works are driven by the conviction that elites have been the creators and disseminators of neoliberal thought and practice.[8]

In the pages that follow, I pay careful attention to the harsh elements of neoliberalism, including mechanisms of coercion it advocated in order to impose market discipline on a society; support, sometimes ruthless, for pursuing capitalist accumulation; and an indifference to questions of economic equality and redistribution. But I also insist that an elite-driven model for understanding neoliberalism cannot suffice to account for the popularity that its views achieved in the United States. Ronald Reagan convinced many Americans that joining his political crusade would unshackle the economy from regulation and make them free. He framed that freedom as every American's birthright; the pursuit of that freedom, he told his followers, was the reason the American Revolution had been fought, the reason the American nation had come into existence. Reagan resuscitated the emancipatory language of classical liberalism for a late twentieth-century audience, an act of recovery that helped to make him one of America's most popular political figures. Seeking the sources of his popularity requires moving beyond elite-based understandings of neoliberalism and inquiring into the reasons that individuals up and down the social scale were drawn to Reagan-style neoliberal rhetoric and policies.

If Reagan was a popular figure, he was also a divisive one. He deliberately stoked racial tensions as a way of securing his political base. As his presidency became associated with market freedom on the one hand, it encouraged a revolt against civil rights advances on the other. A disturbing discourse arose in the 1980s depicting poor blacks as part of an "underclass" that was neither capable nor deserving of participation in the market economy that Reagan was so intent on creating. These were the years in which a program of mass incarceration took shape, one intent on removing hundreds of thousands and then millions of individuals, disproportionately minority, from ordinary economic activity and regular processes of market exchange. Successful experiments in freedom, the apostles of Reaganism seemed to be suggesting, depended on the denial of liberty to those unable (allegedly) to handle its privileges and responsibilities. Several chapters in this book explore the spread of unfreedom amid the advance of market freedom. This paradoxical feature of the neoliberal age, like others, turns out to have been rooted in the practices of nineteenth-century liberalism.

If the appeal of neoliberal policies had been confined to Reagan and his supporters, the problem of mass incarceration likely would have been addressed sooner than it was. But, it turns out, support for neoliberalism spilled beyond Reagan and his political precincts and into the districts of the New Left, a constellation of radical liberation movements that emerged in the 1960s.

The New Left's engagement with neoliberal principles can be discerned in the vehemence of its revolt against what it regarded as the over-organization and bureaucratization of American society resulting from New Deal reform and in the desire to multiply the possibilities for personal freedom. This New Left revolt against excessive regulation is apparent in Paul Goodman's cri de coeur, *Growing Up Absurd*; in the 1962 *Port Huron Statement* that defined the early goals of the New Left; in the rhetoric that Mario Savio used to frame the ambitions of Berkeley's 1964 Free Speech movement, an early moment of New Left mass protest; in the early cybernetics movement that inspired the likes of Stewart Brand and Steve Jobs to associate the creation of the personal computer with the quest for individual freedom; and in the determination of Ralph Nader and his political allies to "free" the consumer from repressive corporate and government elites. Freeing the individual and his or her consciousness from the grip of large, stultifying institutions; privileging disruption over order; celebrating cosmopolitanism—and multiculturalism—and the unexpected sorts of mixing and hybridities that emerge under these regimes: All of these beliefs, each of which marinated for years in the political and cultural milieux inspired by the New Left, furthered neoliberal aspirations and helped to make it into a hegemonic ideological force.[9]

Emphasizing the influence of classical liberalism on neoliberalism (and showing how the emancipatory elements of the former resurfaced in the latter) is one way in which this book's account of neoliberalism is distinctive. Broadening our understanding of neoliberalism's rise beyond an elite-centered model of politics to include the way in which popular and left forces spread its appeal is a second way. And then there is a third way: the importance this book ascribes to international politics in creating the circumstances in which neoliberalism moved from political movement to political order.

The international origins and reach of neoliberalism have been well documented by a variety of scholars. The European roots of neoliberalism in post–World War I Vienna, the home of neoliberal economists Friedrich Hayek and Ludwig von Mises, have been ably explored by Angus Burgin and others. Interwar Geneva has emerged as a critical incubator for neoliberal ideas, and Mont Pèlerin (Switzerland) is generally recognized as the place where Hayek and others attempted to turn neoliberalism into a disciplined thought collective. Quinn Slobodian has expertly examined the role of neoliberal policies in shaping relations between the Global North and the Global South in the post–World War II era, especially through organizations such as the International Monetary Fund and the World Bank. Amy Offner has dissected the impact of these policies on Latin America. And David Harvey was way ahead of everyone else in understanding the contributions of neoliberalism to the so-called Washington Consensus that structured US involvement with the world during neoliberalism's 1990s heyday. Their work forms a critical backdrop to this study of the neoliberal order in America.[10]

Generally missing from studies of the international roots and reach of neoliberalism, however, is a reckoning with the Soviet Union and of communism more generally. And yet, this book argues, the Soviet Union and international communism cannot be ignored. Few international events in the twentieth century matched the Russian Revolution of 1917 in importance. In the fifty years after their rise to power in Russia, communists walled off large parts of the world—the vast Soviet Union itself, then half of Europe, and then China—from capitalist economics. For the first third of the Cold War era, communism was a serious threat in western Europe; for the first two thirds of the Cold War it posed a similar threat across innumerable nations emerging in Africa and Asia, and across Latin America. Fascism and Nazism can be understood as radical right responses to communism's rise. Meanwhile, in the United States, from the 1920s forward, communism was regarded as a mortal threat to the American way of life. The Great Depression and the Second World War moderated America's anticommunism, but only temporarily. No other single political force had a comparable influence on the world or American politics across the twentieth century.[11]

The power of—and the fear unleashed by—the communist threat is now largely forgotten. Few accounts of neoliberalism treat the fall of the Soviet Union between 1989 and 1991 or the collapse of communism as capitalism's chief global antagonist as seminal events. But the consequences of that empire's fall and the simultaneous defeat of its legitimating ideology were immense. Together they made possible neoliberalism's American and global triumph.

One consequence of communism's fall is obvious: It opened a large part of the world—Russia and Eastern Europe—to capitalist penetration. It also dramatically widened the willingness of China (still nominally a communist state) to experiment with capitalist economics. Capitalism thus became global in the 1990s in a way it had not been since prior to the First World War. The globalized world that dominated international affairs in the 1990s and 2000s is unimaginable apart from communism's collapse.

Another consequence of communism's fall may be less obvious but is of equal importance: It removed what had been an imperative in America (and in Europe and elsewhere) for class compromise between capitalist elites and the working classes. From the 1930s through the

1960s, communism was understood through the lens of totalitarianism, meaning it was regarded as a totalizing system of rule that once established could never be overthrown. A nation once lost to communism would never be regained for the capitalist world (or so the influential theory of totalitarianism taught).[12] Thus the specter of communist advance required from the United States a policy of military containment unprecedented in its history. It also impelled capitalist elites in advanced industrial countries, including the United States, to compromise with their class antagonists in ways they would not otherwise have done. The fear of communism made possible the class compromise between capital and labor that underwrote the New Deal order. It made possible similar class compromises in many social democracies in Europe after the Second World War.

The collapse of communism, then, cleared the world of capitalism's most ardent opponent. Vast new territories and peoples could now be brought into a single capitalist marketplace. The possibilities for growth and profits seemed boundless. The United States would benefit from this growth, of course. And perhaps the class compromise that had formed the basis of the New Deal order could now be jettisoned. There was no longer a hard left to fear.

The precise timing of the fall of the Soviet Union and of communism more generally—1989–1991—explains why the 1990s was a more decisive decade in neoliberalism's triumph than the 1980s had been, and why Bill Clinton's role in securing neoliberalism's triumph was in some ways more important than that of Reagan himself. After 1991, the pressure on capitalist elites and their supporters to compromise with the working class vanished. The room for political maneuver by class-based progressive forces narrowed dramatically. This was the moment when neoliberalism transitioned from a political movement to a political order. The fall of communism, in short, forms a central part of the story of neoliberalism's triumph.

Putting the fall of communism at the center of the story of neoliberalism's rise requires an understanding of the role of communism in shaping the politics of the United States in the sixty years prior to the 1990s that is different from what is offered in many histories. In these accounts, fear of communism is treated as a limiting force on progressive politics. Countless progressive movements, it has been argued, trimmed their political sails rather than risk being tagged with the kiss-of-death label, "soft on communism."[13] But the threat of communism, I argue, actually worked in a quite different direction: It inclined capitalist elites to compromise so as to avert the worst. American labor was strongest when the threat of communism was greatest. The apogee of America's welfare state, with all its limitations, was coterminous with the height of the Cold War.[14] The dismantling of the welfare state and the labor movement, meanwhile, marched in tandem with communism's collapse.

To argue for communism's importance is not meant to rehabilitate it as a political movement. Communism was an indefensible system of tyranny. Rather, it is meant to help us to understand the role that communism played in the century when it was a feared force, and then to call on us to reckon with the effects of its sudden and complete disappearance from international and national affairs. The very real communist threat in the period from the 1930s to the 1960s facilitated the class compromise between capital and labor that sustained the New Deal order. The disappearance of that threat between 1989 and 1991 facilitated the scuttling of that compromise and the triumph of the neoliberal order. This perspective underscores the importance of situating the history of neoliberalism, and the political order it sustained, in the broader context of the epic seventy-five-year global struggle between capitalism and communism.[15]

"Polarization" and Political Order

Every political order contains ideological contradictions and conflicts among constituencies that it must manage; the neoliberal order was no exception in that regard. One such contradiction has already been noted: that which existed between those who saw neoliberalism as a strategy for enhancing rule by elites and those who saw in it a pathway toward personal emancipation. Another lay in the uneasy coexistence within the neoliberal order of two strikingly different moral perspectives on how to achieve the good life. One, which I label neo-Victorian, celebrated self-reliance, strong families, and disciplined attitudes toward work, sexuality, and consumption. These values were necessary, this moral perspective argued, to gird individuals against market excess—accumulating debt by purchasing more than one could afford and indulging appetites for sex, drugs, alcohol, and other whims that free markets could be construed as sanctioning. Since neoliberalism frowned upon government regulation of private behavior, some other institution had to provide it. Neo-Victorianism found that institution in the traditional family—heterosexual, governed by male patriarchs, with women subordinate but in charge of homemaking and childrearing. Such families, guided by faith in God, would inculcate moral virtue in their members and especially in the young, and prepare the next generation for the rigors of free market life. The intellectual guiding lights of this movement, such as Gertrude Himmelfarb and her husband, Irving Kristol, believed that nineteenth-century Britain under Queen Victoria had achieved this symbiosis of family and market, and that late twentieth-century America could achieve it again under Ronald Reagan and the Republican Party that he was fashioning. This view found a mass base in Jerry Falwell's legions of evangelical Christians, mobilized politically as part of an influential religious organization known as the Moral Majority.[16]

The other moral perspective encouraged by the neoliberal order, which I label cosmopolitan, was a world apart from neo-Victorianism. It saw in market freedom an opportunity to fashion a self or identity that was free of tradition, inheritance, and prescribed social roles. In the United States this moral perspective drew energy from the liberation movements originating in the New Left—black power, feminism, multiculturalism, and gay pride among them—and flourished in the era of the neoliberal order. Cosmopolitanism was deeply egalitarian and pluralistic. It rejected the notion that the patriarchal, heterosexual family should be celebrated as the norm. It embraced globalization and the free movement of people, and the transnational links that the neoliberal order had made possible. It valorized the good that would come from diverse peoples meeting each other, sharing their cultures, and developing new and often hybridized ways of living. It celebrated the cultural exchanges and dynamism that increasingly characterized the global cities—London, Paris, New York, Hong Kong, San Francisco, Toronto, and Miami among them—developing under the aegis of the neoliberal order.

The existence of two such different moral perspectives was both a strength and a weakness for the neoliberal order. The strength lay in the order's ability to accommodate within a common program of political economy very different constituencies with radically divergent perspectives on moral life. The weakness lay in the fact that the cultural battles between these two constituencies might threaten to erode the hegemony of neoliberal economic principles. The cosmopolitans attacked neo-Victorians for discriminating against gays, feminists, and immigrants, and for stigmatizing the black poor for their "culture of poverty." The neo-Victorians attacked the cosmopolitans for tolerating virtually any lifestyle, for excusing deplorable behavior as an exercise in the toleration of difference, and for showing a higher regard for foreign cultures than for America's own. The decade of the neoliberal order's triumph—the 1990s—was also one in which cosmopolitans and neo-Victorians fought each other in a series of battles that became known as the "culture wars." In fact, a focus on these cultural divisions is the preferred way of writing the political history of these years.[17] Many political scientists regard "polarization" as the key phenomenon in American politics and devote themselves to explaining how it arose and how it has shaped—or rather misshaped—American society.[18]

I do not deny the reality of this polarization, which, ultimately, would contribute to the fracturing of the neoliberal order. But this reality should not be allowed to obscure the coexistence of cultural polarization with a broad agreement on principles of political economy. This paradoxical coexistence of cultural division and political economic agreement manifested itself in the complex relationship between Bill Clinton and Newt Gingrich in the 1990s. In the media, they were depicted (and depicted themselves) as opposites, sworn to each other's destruction. Clinton offered himself as the tribune of the New America, one welcoming of racial minorities, feminists, and gays. He was thought to embody the spirit of the 1960s and something of the insurgent, free-spirited character of the New Left. Gingrich presented himself as the guardian of an older and "truer" America, one grounded in faith, patriotism, respect for law and order, and family values. Both men drew immense prestige from major 1990s electoral victories. In 1992, Clinton became the first Democrat in sixteen years to win the

White House; in 1996, he became the first Democratic president since Roosevelt in 1944 to win re-election. In 1994, Gingrich became Speaker of the House when he masterminded the Republicans' first sweep of both houses of Congress since 1952. Gingrich pledged himself and his party to obstructing Clinton at every turn, to defeating him in the 1996 election or, failing that, to removing him from the presidency via impeachment. Gingrich almost succeeded in the latter. Clinton, meanwhile, regarded Gingrich as the unscrupulous leader of a vast right-wing conspiracy to undermine his presidency.

Yet, despite their differences and the hatred for each other they made a point of exhibiting, these two Washington powerbrokers worked together on legislation that would shape America's political economy for a generation. Their behind-the-scenes collaboration made possible the triumph of the neoliberal order. In pulling back the curtain on the 1990s, this book reveals the powerful and coherent economic accord that sustained the neoliberal order across decades of culture wars.

In the history that follows, I aim to show the utility of the concept of political order to the history of the last hundred years. This concept allows us to comprehend the complex array of forces—elite and popular, economic and moral, domestic and international—at work in configuring political life. It broadens our conception of political time and asks us to consider intervals that stretch beyond the election cycles that dominate so much thinking and writing about American politics. It allows us to understand the power that a political ideology, once established, can exercise over a polity. It encourages us to examine in new ways how conflict can exist—even thrive—amid consensus. And it draws our attention to those signal moments, such as the 1970s and the 2010s, when one reigning political order comes apart and another struggles to be born.[19]

The neoliberal order emerged out of the ruins of the New Deal order. Understanding the rise and fall of that earlier order is where our quest to comprehend the neoliberal order begins.

Part I

The New Deal Order, 1930–1980

I

Rise

HERBERT HOOVER WAS an exceptionally talented and accomplished man. Raised in modest and orphaned circumstances in Iowa, he earned a coveted place at Stanford University, trained as a mining engineer, and then rose rapidly to top management positions in globe-spanning mining companies. A gifted and tireless administrator, Hoover won international acclaim for his work as head of the US Food Administration, which saved millions of European civilians and soldiers from starvation in the aftermath of the First World War. In 1921, Hoover became an active and influential secretary of commerce and a contributor to the remarkable prosperity that the United States enjoyed across the "roaring twenties." Campaigning as the Republican nominee for president in 1928, he declared that "we in America today are nearer to the final triumph over poverty than ever before in the history of any land. The poorhouse is vanishing from among us." Sharing Hoover's optimism, the American people gave him a resounding victory in November 1928.[1]

Nothing in Hoover's background, however, prepared him for the catastrophic stock market collapse that struck a mere eight months after he had assumed office. Between October and December 1929, the market lost 50 percent of its value. By 1932, the worst year of the Great Depression, the market had fallen by another 30 percent. More than 100,000 businesses went bankrupt and thousands of banks closed their doors, wiping out the savings of millions. Unemployment soared to 25 percent. Prices collapsed in a deflationary spiral. Farmers began killing their cows and hogs because the costs of raising them and transporting them to market exceeded the prices these livestock fetched. The specter of farmers slaughtering their livestock as millions of undernourished Americans lined up at soup kitchens for a dollop of thin gruel seemed to underscore both the irrationality of America's capitalist system and the incompetence of its political class. Nothing Hoover tried seemed to work. The more he failed, the more he fell back on moral bromides about self-reliance, self-help, and putting one's fiscal house in order. Hoover began to seem hardhearted and out of touch, indifferent to the fate of the common man. By 1932, he had become one of the most reviled presidents in American history and was trounced by his Democratic opponent, Franklin D. Roosevelt (FDR), in the November election of that year.[2]

Roosevelt's success across the next twelve years was as impressive as Hoover's presidential failure. He would be re-elected three times, making his tenure in the White House longer than that of any other president before or since. He devised a set of policies called "a New Deal for the American people," or New Deal for short, that succeeded in reforming American capitalism, restoring prosperity, and securing vastly improved opportunities for the country's economically disadvantaged.[3] The prestige of the New Deal was such that the Republican Party, when it finally regained the White House in 1952, acquiesced to its core principles. As Dwight D. Eisenhower's presidency unfolded, it became apparent that the New Dealers had bent him and other Republicans to their will, structuring the very terrain on which the latter were compelled to fight. The ability of a partisan political movement to define the parameters of American politics in enduring ways indicates the presence of a political order. What were the key elements of this order? And what made it the dominant political formation in American life from the 1930s through the 1960s? These are the questions this chapter addresses.

The New Deal Order

At the heart of the New Deal order stood a powerful Democratic Party, suddenly dominant in its ability to win elections consistently. Urban ethnic workers, primarily of European descent, and an ethnic middle class in the North formed one key constituency; white Protestant voters constituted an equally important constituency in the South. Increasingly, black voters in the South and North joined Democratic ranks, turning away from the party of Lincoln that had engineered their emancipation from slavery. A large and mobilized labor movement provided many of the Democratic Party's shock troops, its members working hard to get out the vote, staff polling stations, and generate enthusiasm for FDR and Democratic candidates up and down the ballot. Labor was matched in influence—and even more so in campaign contributions—by sectors of the business class persuaded that their industries would benefit from the full-employment, mass-consumption system of regulated capitalism that the New Deal promised to create. Moreover, the communist success in the Soviet Union scared American businessmen as did the influence of communists in the ranks of American labor, inclining them (the businessmen) to compromise with more moderate sectors of the labor movement.[4]

The New Deal order gained its power not just from dependable electoral and business constituencies but also from its ability to implant its core ideological principles on the political landscape. One article of faith was that unfettered capitalism had become a destructive force, generating economic instability and inequalities too great for American society to tolerate. The lack of jobs was calamitous; across a decade, the United States struggled with unemployment rates that hovered around and often exceeded 20 percent. This level of market breakdown drove a stake through the ideology of laissez-faire, a shibboleth of American economic life in the late nineteenth and early twentieth centuries. Large majorities of Americans now agreed that some force was necessary to counterbalance the destructive chaos of markets and to manage capitalism's growth in the public interest. Those pushing for change looked to the federal government as the one institution with the size, resources, and will to perform that role.

FDR and the New Dealers unleashed the power of the central state in ways rarely done during peacetime. Some of this work focused on a highly visible overhaul of the country's economic infrastructure. New Dealers built countless roads, bridges, airports, dams, schools, and libraries. One jobs program, the Works Progress Administration, hired 5 million people to work on these and related projects. The commitment to public works was so extensive that the New Deal even enlisted artists to adorn the interiors of hundreds of government buildings. Colorful, often arresting, murals of Americans at work and at play, cooperating and in conflict, began to sprout everywhere on these interiors, from the majestic walls of the Department of Interior in Washington, DC, to innumerable plain post offices and schools in cities and towns across the country. The artists who painted these murals brought the pageant of America vividly to life. Everyone knew that the construction of this pageant, and the celebration of America that it implied, was the work of the New Deal.[5]

As part of its campaign to assume new powers, the federal government placed extensive new controls on the country's financial system. In 1933, Congress passed the Glass-Steagall Act separating commercial from investment banking and establishing the Federal Deposit Insurance Corporation to assure depositors that the federal government would guarantee their savings. The Securities Act of 1933 and the Securities Exchange Act of 1934 reined in buying stocks on margin (i.e., with borrowed money to be paid back from the proceeds of expected increases in stock value) and established the Securities and Exchange Commission to enforce the new kind of financial regulation that the New Deal was imposing. These laws would bring a stability to the stock market that it had never previously enjoyed.[6]

The Roosevelt administration also embraced a vernacular form of Keynesianism in 1935 and 1936. Keynesian theory, so-called because the Cambridge economist John Maynard Keynes was its architect, postulated that expenditures well beyond government revenues were a positive good during the trough of business cycles, as were the deficits they generated. Such deficit spending put money in the hands of consumers that they would not otherwise have had, thereby stimulating them to buy goods. Money in the pockets of the masses could come in various forms: unemployment insurance, old-age pension checks, public employment, efforts to strengthen labor's ability to wrest larger rather than smaller wage increases from their employers, and low interest rates on borrowed money for homes and cars. Once economic recovery was achieved, government expenditures and easy money policies would be rolled back and budgets balanced. By the 1940s, most economists working for the Democrats had formally committed themselves to Keynesian economic ideas and would remain advocates of them for the next three decades.[7]

Keynesianism was not designed to replace capitalism but to sustain it. Those who persisted in arguing that the economy ought to be left to its own devices, that the market ought to be allowed to rebalance itself through the decisions of individual buyers and sellers, were consigned to the periphery of American politics, with little chance of winning an election or a majority in Congress. The fall of Herbert Hoover was paradigmatic in this regard. Friedrich Hayek, an architect of neoliberalism, grasped how marginal laissez-faire liberalism had become, which may explain the isolated Swiss mountain he chose in 1947 to found the Mont Pèlerin Society where classical liberal ideas might survive the new age of Keynesianism and collectivism. There they would regenerate and be repackaged as a new set of commandments that would someday descend from the mountaintop in the hands of a latter-day laissez-faire Moses. But in the 1930s, Hayek's voice, like Hoover's, was scorned.[8]

The New Deal's commitment to arranging a class compromise between the warring forces of capital and labor similarly expressed the imperative of curtailing capitalism's destructive chaos. Strikes abounded in the 1930s, 2,000 in 1934 alone. Some were massive affairs, such as the 400,000 textile workers who struck from Maine to Alabama. Others engulfed entire cities, such as the San Francisco General Strike of that same year. Numerous urban centers, including San Francisco; Minneapolis; Toledo, Ohio; and Woonsocket, Rhode Island, exploded in violence. Employers took to arming themselves. Republic Steel in Chicago, which engaged in a violent confrontation with their workers in 1937, had assembled an arsenal that was greater than all the weapons held by the Chicago police department, an institution charged with maintaining order in a multimillion-person city. Communists were present in multiple sites where the labor movement was militant, deeply involved in organizing strikes and confrontations with employers.[9]

To remedy this situation, the New Deal put in place in 1935 a new labor relations system that compelled employers and unions to negotiate with each other. That system curbed employer power and gave workers more workplace rights than they had previously enjoyed. It set up a mechanism, the National Labor Relations Board, to enforce those rights and to compel employers to enter meaningful negotiations with workers who had voted to join unions. The New Deal thereby shifted leverage from employers to employees and facilitated the growth in the labor movement from fewer than 3 million members in 1932 to more than 15 million in 1945, from less than 10 percent of the industrial work-force to more than 35 percent. Thus strengthened, workers were able to compel employers to share with them a higher percentage of their revenue and profits.[10]

The resistance to this new system among employers was fierce until a radical series of sit-down strikes occurring in late 1936 and early 1937 compelled both employers and the Supreme Court to bow to the New Deal and its supporters. In these strikes, automobile workers occupied factories of General Motors, then one of the most powerful corporations in the world. They stayed for weeks, making it impossible for General Motors to carry on with production and to generate revenue and profit. Neither the state of Michigan nor the federal government did what governments had done in America so many times before in similar situations: send in National Guard or federal troops to break the strike. General Motors capitulated in March 1937, as did the Supreme Court, which voted by the slimmest of margins (5–4) to uphold the constitu-tionality of the congressional act that created the new system of labor relations. At that moment (March 1937), laissez-faire in America lost whatever was left of its moral and jurisprudential hold on American politics.[11]

The result was not socialism. When labor became too aggressive in its demands, the Roosevelt administration pushed back. The same was true of Roosevelt's successor, Harry Truman, who did not sup-port a 1946 United Auto Workers (UAW) strike that aimed to make the union a significant partner in corporate decision-making. Truman's aim, like Roosevelt's, was not workers' control or the nationalization of industry but a compromise between employers and workers over the terms of work and the distribution of revenues between the two groups. The 1950 accord between the UAW and the big three auto-mobile manufacturers—General Motors, Ford, and Chrysler—was paradigmatic in this regard. Unionized workers received a 20 percent wage increase, a defined benefit pension with generous terms, and a re-markably comprehensive health care plan that would continue through the end of each autoworker's life. The car manufacturers received a guarantee of five years of labor peace (and thus of uninterrupted production in a world starved for cars) and a promise from the UAW not to encroach any further on investment and pricing decisions, now seen as the province of management alone. In return for giving up its most radical demands, the UAW received significant returns, most notably opening a door for a million-plus autoworkers and their families to enter the middle class. This labor agreement, increasingly known as the Treaty of Detroit, would be much emulated by other employers, union and non-union. It defined the terms of the class compromise that was foundational to the New Deal order.[12]

New Dealers also forced into existence fiscal and social policies that benefited the poor. A large national welfare state emerged for the first time, much of it funded by the New Deal's commitment to progressive taxation. In 1935, the marginal taxation rate on the wealthiest Americans rose to 75 percent. In World War II, the top marginal rate rose still further, to an astounding 91 percent. This high rate of taxation, in combination with the wage concessions that employers made to unionized workforces, resulted in a significant redistribution of resources from the rich to the working and middle classes of America. Economic inequality fell in the 1940s to its lowest point in the twentieth century, and it stayed there as long the New Deal order prevailed.[13] Paul Krugman, Thomas Piketty, and other economists have labeled this fall in inequality the "great compression."[14] This fall was not a function of impersonal economic forces (which is what the term "great compression" is interpreted by some to mean) but of political struggle that yielded a class compromise between capital and labor. This grand bargain spread America's wealth across a much greater swath of the country's workers and consumers, thus generating and sustaining higher levels of demand and, across the next two decades, an era of impressive affluence. To the poor, the federal government offered a range of welfare programs, from social security to pensions, on the one hand, to aid to dependent children, on the other, that it had not made available before.

If the New Deal order rested on durable electoral constituencies, a class compromise between capital and labor, and a hegemonic belief in the value of government constraining markets, it also brought into politics a distinct moral perspective: first, that public good ought to take precedence over private right; second, that government was the instrument through which public good would be pursued and achieved; and third, that the goal of government action—and a central part of the pursuit of the public good—ought to be to enhance every individual's opportunities for personal fulfillment. Classical liberalism had long made the full flowering of each person's individuality a centerpiece of its agenda. New Dealers did not abandon this age-old liberal goal; they simply argued that government intervention in markets and, to a certain extent, in private life had become necessary to position people to enjoy the full ambit of their freedom.[15]

The broad commitment to the public good, and to the use of government to achieve it, was evident in the determination of New Dealers to regulate private centers of power, such as Wall Street and private corporations, across a broad front. This commitment extended to the new media companies that had arisen to provide the country with telephone and radio service. The Communications Act of 1934 declared the airwaves to be the property of the American people, not of private corporations. As such, this industry had to be regulated in ways that advanced the "public interest." The act established the Federal Communications Commission (FCC) to oversee media corporations and to develop rules of access, competition, and service, where necessary. The FCC was particularly concerned with the threat of media monopolies and put in place policies to forestall this. The good of the American people required a diverse and regulated media landscape.[16]

In their efforts to make possible (and to measure) the pursuit of personal fulfillment, New Dealers increasingly defined the good life in terms of the quantity and variety of consumer goods that citizens were able to purchase. This marketplace orientation entailed more than materialism, however. For one, it carried a strong egalitarian message: Participation in the marketplace was to be made available to all Americans regardless of class, race, gender, religion, or nationality. New Dealers viewed consumption in qualitative terms too, believing that a precocious and alluring marketplace would enhance the possibilities for individual expressiveness.[17] Such expressiveness would compensate for the growing impersonality of public life, now increasingly dominated by large institutions—corporations, centralized labor unions, and big government. New Dealers believed that the personal could be managed as skillfully as the economic. They had great confidence in secular expertise—in the hard sciences, to be sure, but also in soft science: sociology, anthropology, psychiatry, and social work—and in the ability of government to spread the benefits of such expertise through the citizenry.[18] A commitment to the public good over private right; happiness and expressiveness through consumption; the capacity of the marketplace to deliver on America's egalitarian promise; and a faith in the ability of expertise to nurture individuality: These were the components of the New Deal order's moral perspective.

It is worth stating what this moral perspective declined to engage: religion. While Roosevelt thought of himself as a religious man, he did not want to expend much energy imposing his faith on politics. Keeping faith at a distance was in part strategic: Suspicions between northern Catholics and southern Protestants still ran deep, and Democrats needed the support of both groups for their political order to flourish. The best way to satisfy both constituencies was to keep religion out of politics. But the absence of religion from the New Deal order's moral perspective reflected something deeper: a belief that a secular government was superior to one built on faith and that religion was best left to the private realm and individual choice.[19]

The New Deal was also slow to embrace the cause of racial justice and tolerated the system of white supremacy in the South known as Jim Crow. There were plenty of individuals within the ranks of the New Deal who pushed hard for racial equality, but they never succeeded in making this issue central to the New Deal's moral perspective. Here was a case where morality succumbed to *realpolitik*: FDR had calculated that he needed the support of southern white supremacists to create and sustain his New Deal far more than he needed black votes. A generation would pass before the issue of racial equality would move from the periphery to the center of the New Deal order's moral perspective.[20]

The Communist Challenge

When Steve Fraser and I published *The Rise and Fall of the New Deal Order* in 1989, we portrayed the 1940s as a time of retrenchment. The New Deal order survived, we argued, but several of its radical elements had been shorn away. This retreat was evident in a variety of ways: in the articulation of a set of managerial rights held by corporations that unions were not permitted to encroach upon; the abandonment, after World War II, of democratic forms of industrial planning through tripartite boards of corporate executives, union leaders, and representatives of the public; the passage of Taft-Hartley, a measure expressly intended to limit the power of unions by stripping communist-led unions of collective bargaining rights and allowing states to pass "right-to-work" laws that allowed individual workers to refuse to join unions, even where the latter had won elections to represent all the workers in a plant.[21]

The 1940s did witness the rollback of certain worker rights and New Deal ambitions. But our analysis did not take seriously the possibility that things might have gone much worse for the New Deal coalition. The entire New Deal might have been disassembled. There were certainly many conservative Republicans in Congress who wished to pursue this path. Fraser and I did not regard this as a live historical possibility.[22] We partook too much of the view of New Dealers themselves: namely, that conservatism was too out of step with the temper of modern times to mount such an attack. It was an atavism that would be dissolved, one way or another, in thirty years if not ten, by the sands of modernity.

We now know, of course, that we (and many others) were wrong to treat conservatism as a spent ideology. There was power there, and it would soon burst on American society with force. In fact, already in the 1940s, there were signs that it was rebounding robustly. The 1946 election gave majorities to Republicans in the House and Senate for first time since the election of 1930. Under the leadership of Robert Taft, the party's most prominent senator, the Republicans looked primed to do what they had done after World War I: take down the large central state that the Democrats had built for the war effort; spare no effort to repress organized labor; stymie the internationalist ambitions of a Democratic president; return America to isolation, small government, and an economy driven principally by private corporate power.

But the 1920s did not repeat themselves in 1940s America. By 1950, Taft lost his standing as the GOP standard-bearer; his policies came to be seen as sweet anachronisms or worse, as embarrassments. Truman won the 1948 presidential contest that everyone was sure he would lose. In 1952, the Republicans did reclaim the White House for eight years. But the man who pulled off that victory, Dwight D. Eisenhower, seemed as much Democrat as Republican. In the late 1940s, virtually everyone had trouble deciphering which of America's two major political camps had the allegiance of the former supreme commander of Allied Forces in Europe. By 1952, Eisenhower was firmly in the Republican column. But he did not dismantle the New Deal order when he came into office. To the contrary, he secured it. In fact, facilitating the GOP's acquiescence to the New Deal order may have been Eisenhower's most significant domestic political accomplishment.

Why did the GOP under Eisenhower acquiesce to the New Deal? It had far less to do with Eisenhower the man than with the geopolitical situation in which the new president and his party had been thrust. The Cold War was on. The Soviet Union had to be stopped. Partly this had to be accomplished through military means. But partly it had to be done through domestic policy. The leader of the "free world" had to demonstrate that he could take better care of his ordinary citizens than the leaders of Soviet communism could provide for theirs.

Thirty years out from the end of the Cold War, we have forgotten how powerful and prestigious a movement communism once was. Arguably, there was no more important twentieth-century event than the Russian Revolution of 1917.[23] Wherever they came to power—in the Russian empire itself, in Eastern Europe, in China—communists repudiated capitalism. From the 1940s through the 1970s, they were a political force in much of western Europe. Across the same period, they vied for power in Latin America and in the new Asian and African nations emerging from European and Japanese colonialism.[24] Americans regarded communism as an existential threat to economics, politics, and culture. No other single force rivalled the influence of this political movement across the twentieth century.

In a very real sense, the threat posed by communism dissuaded Republicans from dismantling the New Deal when they regained Congress in the 1940s and the presidency in the 1950s. Historians have written extensively about how fear of communism—and specifically the fear of being seen as "soft" on communism—hemmed in the Democratic Party in the 1950s and 1960s.[25] The threat of international communism, I argue, hemmed in the Republicans even more. To understand why, we must first know how this radical political movement came to be seen as such a frightful force capable of dominating the United States and the world, even during the decades—the 1940s and 1950s—of America's greatest triumphs and geopolitical strength.

Communism had a potent message: deliver the poor of the world from their oppression; turn the vast productive system developed under capitalism to public purpose; substitute intelligent planning for market chaos; eliminate all manifestations of inequality. Its striving to create a society in which everyone could be freed from want and domination shared a good deal with its ostensible opponent, classical liberalism. Both communism and liberalism traced their origins back to a common moment of eighteenth-century revolution, with the former tying itself to the French Revolution and the latter to the American. Both camps saw themselves as freeing humanity from old, encrusted social orders marked by privilege, inequality, and widespread misery. Both camps believed in the universalism of their message and sought to carry it to every portion of the globe. President Woodrow Wilson had unleashed a "new liberalism" at home and abroad that, he believed, would be equal to the communist challenge and that would redeem the world in the wake of the barbarism and slaughter that the Great War had unleashed. Arriving in Europe in 1919 to negotiate the Treaty of Versailles, Wilson was greeted in Paris, Milan, and elsewhere by crowds larger than any ever assembled on European soil. Wilson and Vladimir Lenin, the leader of the 1917 communist revolution that was transforming the Russian Empire into the Union of Soviet Socialist Republics (Soviet Union for short), had both become figures of global adulation, each a Messiah promising emancipation and rebirth to suffering millions.[26]

Yet, as both Wilson and Lenin understood so well, liberalism and socialism were radically dissimilar. Liberalism prized private property and individual rights as the cornerstones of the perfect economy and polity. It celebrated markets where buyers and sellers could come together of their own free will to animate the economy. States would nurture and sustain markets but otherwise stay out of economic decision-making. Communism, by contrast, wanted to socialize all private property, by force if necessary, and prioritize the public good—which it defined in terms of the needs of the working class—over individual rights. Communists would emancipate the working class, not individuals. State planning would substitute for markets which, in the eyes of communists, had never really been free sites of exchange. A strong centralized state was a communist imperative; the nationalization of industry and all other private centers of wealth and privilege would be among its first acts. Communists made clear that they were implacable foes of capitalists, and of liberals, old and new, whom they saw as capitalism's handmaidens. They did not hesitate to strip both capitalists and liberals in their midst of wealth, power, and influence.[27]

Communists were also hostile to the internationalist capitalist economy—and to the world of free trade and free movement of people that liberals like Wilson were so eager to see emerge from the carnage of the Great War. They would not hesitate to cut off international capital from access to the Soviet Union or to any other country they controlled. This Joseph Stalin, Lenin's successor, did when he embarked in 1928 on a state-driven industrialization program to transform the Soviet Union overnight into an advanced and self-sufficient industrial country. Stalin's so-called five-year plan set targets for production, prices, and industries and invested state resources accordingly. This program was intended both to give the Soviet Union the strength to resist attacks by its enemies in the world and to demonstrate that industrialization driven by a socialist state was the path that all underdeveloped countries should follow toward a bright future.[28]

Stalin and the Soviet Union remained in the shadow of America in the 1920s. The American capitalist machine seemed to be whirring to perfection, without a breakdown or flaw. The United States supplanted Great Britain as the international engine of manufacturing and finance. The industrial world was awed by American production techniques developed by the likes of Henry Ford and by the disciples of Frederick Winslow Taylor and the principles of scientific management they were deploying. America was turning out cars and consumer durables at an astonishing rate. The abundance of goods and their falling prices appeared so great that Americans, led by Hoover, began dreaming about lifting every American out of poverty. Then the terrible Great Depression struck.[29]

As production plummeted in the United States and the rest of the western capitalist world, it soared in the Soviet Union. Indeed, the Soviet Union more than tripled its share of world manufactured products in the 1930s.[30] And everyone in Russia's industrial sector seemed to have a job. The Soviet Union boasted that the reason for its success lay in its ability to replace chaotic market mechanisms with intelligent government planning.

A steady stream of visitors, including many Americans, arrived in the Soviet Union in the 1930s to see the new world of communist planning in action.[31] One was Walter Reuther, a young tool and die maker from Wheeling, West Virginia, who worked in Detroit's automobile industry. Ten years later, Reuther would become president of the UAW in America and, as such, a prime architect of labor movement and the American welfare state (and of the Treaty of Detroit). In 1933, he and his brother Victor went to the Soviet Union to see this workers' paradise for themselves. They found work as tool and die makers at the newly established Gorky automobile and truck works, an enterprise built in a city, Nizhny Novgorod, located 250 miles east of Moscow in the middle of nowhere. Its scale was meant to rival that of the massive River Rouge complex that Henry Ford, America's leading capitalist, had constructed in Dearborn, Michigan, just outside Detroit. The Soviets had hired Ford's architect for River Rouge, Alfred Kahn, along with legions of American engineers, to design what came to be called the Gorky Automobile Factory. They recruited tens of thousands of workers from the Soviet countryside and trained them in the latest equipment and the most advanced techniques, many of them imported from America. The factories at Gorky were some of the most integrated and fastest production systems in the world. But this Soviet system, unlike the one run by Henry Ford, was under public, rather than private, control. Automobile manufacturing in the Soviet Union had been accomplished at startling speed—in a matter of years—and not by private capitalists responding to market stimuli but by the "enlightened" leaders of a Union of Soviet Socialist Republics (USSR) who had committed themselves, Reuther believed, to society-wide planning and the common good. By 1937, Gorky was producing an impressive 200,000 cars per year.[32]

The productive success of Gorky persuaded Reuther that the communists were capable not just of the most advanced forms of technical mastery but also of what Reuther then approvingly called "proletarian democracy." Reuther would later repudiate his enthusiasm for the Soviet experiment and fight to expel communists from the UAW. But not in the early to mid-1930s, when he thought he had found in the Soviet Union a model for industrial renewal and proletarian justice.[33]

The costs of the Soviet Union's economic rise were only partially understood in the 1930s, even by Reuther himself: the suffering, famine, and death resulting from the socialization of agriculture, especially in Ukraine; the forced nature of industrialization—uprooting rural peoples and concentrating them in cities, often built (as Gorky was) from scratch in isolated areas; the lack on the part of these new workers of rights at the workplace or a voice in their nation's politics; Stalin's determination to concentrate all power in his own hands and to purge government and the party of anyone whom he construed as a threat to his authority.[34] The magnetism exerted by the red star of communism—the belief that this movement would extinguish the brutalities of capitalism—was simply too strong for many of those in its force field to escape. This belief in a communist future was never as strong in the United States as elsewhere, but it was significant. Communist supporters were present in US labor unions, in Hollywood (and by extension other sectors of the culture industry, such as the theater, journalism, book publishing, and the arts), in certain quarters of the New Deal administration (such as the Agricultural Adjustment Administration and the National Labor Relations Board), and in third-party political movements in a number of states, including New York, Wisconsin, Minnesota, and California. The promise of communism gripped the imaginations of quite a few Americans of talent, ambition, and commitment, eager to see a harsh and downtrodden world revolutionized and transformed.[35]

The beginning of World War II initially weakened the force of communist attraction. In 1939, Stalin had secretly negotiated a separate peace with his arch-enemy, Hitler, to spare the Soviet Union from a German attack in the war that he saw coming. Communists around the world were aghast at this deal. They had been taught to see fascism as their most dangerous enemy; indeed, prior to 1939, the communists had been the ones spearheading mobilization against the Nazis and their allies. Stalin was spared a permanent stain on his communist reputation, however, by Hitler's rash 1941 decision to tear up his pact with the Soviet Union and unleash the full fury of his armies on the communist state. Only the vast expanse of the Soviet Union and the frigid character of its winters saved a country unprepared for war from ignominious defeat. Britain and the United States put ideological differences aside and now welcomed the communist state as an ally, rushing support and materiel to the Soviets. There was self-interest at work here: Churchill and Roosevelt were eager for the Soviet Union to take the brunt of the Nazi attack and spare western troops the carnage. This the Soviet Union did, at a frightful cost, with Stalin's distrust of the West's motives mounting steadily as months and then years passed without Britain and the United States opening the promised second front against the Nazis in western Europe. When the second front finally did come in June 1944, in the form of the Normandy invasion, the USSR had been fighting the Nazis largely on its own in northern Europe for three years. The cost was frightful. An estimated 7 million Soviet soldiers died in combat or in German prison camps. A total of 17 to 20 million Russian civilians are thought to have perished during the war, bringing total Soviet World War II losses to a staggering 24 to 27 million.[36]

The scale of suffering and the stoicism with which the Russians endured it restored the prestige that the communists had sacrificed when Stalin struck his deal with Hitler. So, too, did the leadership role that communists took throughout German-occupied Europe in resisting Nazi rule. The iron discipline of communist parties, the long training of its cadres in circumstances of illegality and war, and the passionate nature of their devotion to their ideals served them well in fighting vastly superior enemy forces and in circumstances where exposure yielded imprisonment and execution.

The communists emerged from World War II, as a result, with enormous standing throughout Europe. In France and Italy in 1945, communists formed the largest political party, with 900,000 members in the former and 1.8 million members in the latter. In postwar elections in France and Italy, communists received 29 percent and 19 percent of the vote, respectively. In Finland it was 23 percent, in Belgium 13 percent, and even in Norway, thought to be part of a Scandinavian bloc congenitally hostile to communism (and embracing social democracy), a significant 12 percent.[37] Communists had also been prominently involved in resistance movements against Japanese occupiers in East and South Asia, giving them prestige and influence in the movements for national liberation in countries such as Vietnam that had been European colonies and that were now seeking independence.[38] In both the West and East, communists, and their benefactor, the Soviet Union, were going to be central players in shaping the postwar world. Their leadership role in defeating fascism bathed them in glory and made them models of liberation for many of the world's oppressed.

The Cold War and Republican Acquiescence to the New Deal Order

In the United States, there were some, like FDR and his former vice-president and secretary of agriculture, Henry Wallace, who believed that the Soviet Union could become part of a functioning new world order emerging after 1945.[39] But FDR died in 1945, and Wallace faded after his 1948 presidential campaign on the Progressive Party ticket went awry. They were replaced by leaders such as Harry Truman who viewed the communists as a threat to the American way of life as deadly as the Nazis had been. Truman and others paired Nazism and communism as twin manifestations of a novel and malignant form of dictatorship. This was a tyranny different from that of monarchs, sultans, or small-nation oligarchs. It was modern. It used new technologies of surveillance and media to penetrate every aspect of society, to achieve in the words of Hannah Arendt "total domination." "Totalitarian" regimes needed enemies whom they could castigate, and then conquer, imprison, and kill. They were thus a perpetual source of danger to portions of their own people and to nations beyond their borders. Internally, totalitarian regimes needed to keep their own subjects on edge and thus vulnerable to propaganda about threats, internal and external, to their nation's well-being. In exacerbating fear and vulnerability, these regimes were thought to have robbed those under their control of the ability to distinguish between truth and falsehood, and thus of their will to resist. In works of fiction and in reportage read by millions, writers such as George Orwell and Arthur Koestler portrayed totalitarian regimes as impervious to dissent and protest, despite the enormous crimes that they had committed against their external and internal foes. These regimes could only be conquered by massive war and pressure from the outside. World War II had demonstrated that this could be done (the Allied forces had destroyed Hitler), but only at a staggering cost of life and expenditure of resources.[40]

Officials in the Truman administration worried that conditions for a second totalitarian apocalypse were ripening in western Europe. Hunger and cold were stymieing efforts at economic recovery. A terrible harvest in 1946 had been followed by severe coal shortages. Communist parties in the region, it was feared, would prey on popular hardships and anxieties. Under secretary of state Dean Acheson frightened Congress in February 1947 with reports that French communists controlled the country's largest labor federation and had placed their cadre throughout "government offices, factories, and the armed services," including in four cabinet posts. With communists situated so highly in French government, Acheson warned senators and congressman, the Russians could "pull the plug [on France] any time."[41] Germany would likely follow France, with "the whole of Germany" pushed into the "Soviet sphere of influence."[42]

These fears form the critical backdrop to a massive foreign aid program for Europe, known as the Marshall Plan, announced by secretary of state George Marshall in his Harvard commencement speech of June 1947. The program was unprecedented in peacetime not only in its scale—$13 billion—but in its structure. It was to be administered by the US government rather than by private US bankers. Funds would be offered to European governments as grants rather than loans and thus would never have to be repaid. Recipient governments had to meet a few requirements: They had to be democratic (rendering communist regimes ineligible); they had to relinquish any desire to impose wrathful reparation terms on Germany, as Britain and France had done after World War I; and they were asked to explore with other European governments how they might collaborate with each other in rebuilding infrastructure, industries, and markets. The Marshall Plan was thus an early spur to those who wished to advance European integration. But beyond these rather modest requests, individual national governments were given broad scope to decide how best to use the Marshall aid, with Americans indicating a willingness to tolerate a range of political parties, including socialists and social democrats on the left and Christian democrats on the right. European leaders appreciated the degree of autonomy thus extended to them; it allowed them to sell the plan to their own people as something other than a crude exercise in American imperialism. Neither the generous level of aid nor the freedom given to the recipient countries to use the aid as they saw fit would have occurred absent the fear that western Europe was close to disappearing behind what Winston Churchill had chillingly described as the "Iron Curtain."[43]

The Marshall Plan helped to stabilize western Europe and blunt the appeal of the communists in the region. Plans to formally include western Europe under the US defense umbrella through the establishment of the North Atlantic Treaty Organization (NATO) deepened the region's sense of security. But these developments had barely occurred when the Cold War heated up again. The Soviet Union exploded an atomic bomb in August 1949, years before anyone in the West had expected it would. In October 1949, Mao Tse-tung's communists emerged victorious in China's civil war and immediately established a second communist state, this one also located in a large country with a far bigger population than in the Soviet Union itself. Then, in 1950, communist North Korean troops crashed into South Korea, triggering the Korean War.

The United States responded to these challenges with a global policy of containment, famously embraced in National Security Council memo 68, published in 1950. This memo declared that the United States would meet the communist threat wherever it appeared and use all the weapons in its arsenal—military, economic, political, psychological—to protect the "free world." This aggressive anticommunist foreign stance was matched in the United States by a systematic effort to root out communists where they had established beachheads: in labor unions, in Hollywood, in the government, and in universities and school classrooms. A second Red Scare gathered steam, spearheaded by a coarse, unscrupulous, but immensely influential rookie legislator from Wisconsin, Senator Joseph McCarthy.[44]

For many years, scholars studying the 1940s have emphasized how the quest to defeat the communists abroad and at home derailed New Deal liberalism. Alonzo Hamby framed this interpretation fifty years ago in a seminal piece that tracked the transition from an expansive "popular front liberalism" of the 1930s to a fearful "cold war liberalism" of the 1940s. Cold War liberals, in this telling, sought to purge communists from all public and private institutions. These liberals also sought to expunge from their party platforms and policy initiatives any ideas that could be construed as socialist. Liberals had become far more fearful of being tagged as communistic themselves or, in the language of the age, "soft on communism." According to this line of interpretation, liberalism lost its fighting elan and became much more modest— and much more like conservatism—in its aims. A few commentators hailed the scaling back of liberal expectations as constituting a "vital center," the only defensible path to pursue in an age of communist menace.[45] But a far more numerous brigade of historians saw this turn as giving rise to a dispiriting age of consensus, one in which liberalism sacrificed its grand dreams.[46]

The purging of the communist left from liberal movements and the expunging of "leftist" ideas from liberal ranks did happen. But this focus on liberalism and the left ignores parallel developments on the right. In the late 1940s and early 1950s, hard-line Republicans, in their quest to defeat communism, were faced with a similar set of choices: either make concessions in domestic politics that they detested, or else— if they remained true to their ideals—risk becoming bit players in the major political contests of the day. If we look carefully at the politics of the late 1940s and early 1950s, we can see that the imperative of fighting the communists caused Republicans to make even larger concessions than the Democrats did. To ensure success in the fight against communism, those in the mainstream of the Republican Party actually acquiesced to the core principles of the New Deal, thereby facilitating the New Deal's transition from political movement to political order.[47]

The capitulation of Republicans to the New Deal can best be grasped by a glance at the contrasting fortunes of its two leaders during this time. The first was Robert Taft, senator from Ohio, who desperately wanted to restore laissez-faire and small government to America but could find no way, in a world organized around the Cold War, to persuade enough Republicans and Americans to go along with him. The second was Dwight D. Eisenhower, whose willingness to support the New Deal as president ensured the ascendance of his star as Taft's faded.

Robert Taft, the eldest son of President William Howard Taft, served in the Ohio House of Representatives and Senate between 1921 and 1933, and then in the US Senate from 1939 until his death in 1953. By the 1940s, he was regarded as one of America's leading GOP senators known affectionately simply as "Mr. Republican." Absent the Cold War, he might well have become president in 1948 or 1952 and led the effort to take down the New Deal. But in both elections, he was denied the Republican nomination for the presidency in large part because his brand of politics was perceived to be too reactionary in a world dominated by the threat of communism.[48]

Few Republicans detested the New Deal as much as Taft did. In this he resembled one of his mentors, Herbert Hoover, for whom he had worked in 1919 and 1920 in the Paris headquarters of the US Food Relief Administration. For Taft, as for Hoover, individual liberty was the most prized political value in America. Taft regarded America's federal political system, with a central government sharply limited in its powers and political authority diffused across countless states and municipalities, as the key to maintaining that liberty. From the start, Taft saw the New Deal as a threat to America's liberty-enhancing political system. He denounced the emergency programs Roosevelt had put in place in 1933 and 1934 to save the banks, relieve suffering, and revive industry and agriculture. The "permanent incorporation" of these programs into "our system," Taft warned in 1934, "would politically abandon the whole theory of American government, and inaugurate what is in fact socialism." By 1935, he regarded the New Deal as revolutionary, bent on destroying what in America was most dear. FDR's rhetorical attacks on wealthy Americans could trigger "a redistribution of wealth" that "would soon lead to a Socialistic control of all property and income."[49] Redistribution of wealth could happen only through a vast augmentation of the powers of the central state, which Taft saw as the worst evil of the Roosevelt administration. "History shows," Taft intoned in 1936, "that once power is granted it is impossible for the people to get it back. In Greece republics gave way to tyrannies.

The Roman Republic became an Empire. Medieval republics became monarchies. If we extend Federal power indefinitely, if we concentrate power over the courts and the congress in the executive, it will not be long before we have American fascism."[50]

Even before he took his Senate seat, Taft had become a leader of a movement first to stall, and then to undo, the New Deal. As late as 1940, when German tanks were already rolling through Europe, Taft was still arguing that "excessive Executive authority" amassed by the Roosevelt administration in the United States was a greater danger to American liberty than "armed autocracy in Europe." If that degree of concentrating power in the executive continued, he warned, America would soon "see here a completely totalitarian government."[51] He even declared that "there is a good deal more danger of the infiltration of totalitarian ideas from the New Deal circle in Washington than there will ever be from any activities of the communists or the Nazi bund."[52] Taft never ceased decrying the New Deal for turning America into a "totalitarian state." He applied the same criticism to Truman's 1948 elaboration of a Fair Deal, meant to secure and extend the New Deal.[53] To tar the Democratic reform program with the totalitarian brush was a serious smear, for it cast the New Deal as being no different in its essence than Nazism or communism.

When the Republicans gained control of Congress in 1946, Taft led the charge to roll back the New Deal state. The historic 1947 anti-labor legislation, Taft-Hartley, bears his name. He was also deeply involved in movements to shrink the US military, eliminate the extensive regulatory apparatus that had emerged in World War II, and roll back the high taxation state that the New Dealers had brought into being.

Briefly, Taft's reputation soared. But as the Cold War ramped up again in 1948 and 1949, Taft stumbled. He did not have a convincing response to the Truman declaration that America had to mobilize all its resources, and concentrate power in a central state, in order to contain the communist threat wherever it appeared. Taft adhered to an older view of America in the world, one aligned with those known in the 1930s as isolationists. This group believed that America should do everything it could to avoid foreign entanglements, especially with European powers. Too much time spent on a war footing and too much money expended supporting a large standing army, Taft argued, would eviscerate the foundations of the American republic. Taft believed that geographical isolation, in the form of broad oceans on its east and west borders, gave America a great natural advantage. This dispensation, which Taft and many others regarded as providential, meant that the United States did not have to concern itself unduly with European crises and conflicts.

For an uncomfortably long time after the outbreak of war in Europe, Taft had been willing to sacrifice all of continental Europe to Nazi domination. In the early years of the Cold War, he seemed ready to cede all of continental Europe to the Soviets. He had trouble accepting the foreign policy implications that flowed from the totalitarian theory he had ostensibly embraced: namely, that every muscle had to be turned toward containing totalitarian regimes within their existing borders. He was untroubled by the prospect of additional nations falling to the Soviet Union as long as they were located far away from American shores.[54]

Taft was not wrong about the dangers to America of remaining on a war footing indefinitely, fighting everywhere, and degenerating into what the sociologist Paul Lazarsfeld warned would be a "garrison state."[55] But he never offered his fellow Republicans a convincing alternative policy to the Truman plan for containing Soviet power. His pronouncements on what to do about the communist threats in East Asia—in China and Korea—were particularly muddled. So, by the late 1940s and early 1950s, his star began to fade. Leadership of the GOP passed to a man who was perceived as far more capable than Taft of containing the Soviet threat. His name was Dwight D. Eisenhower.

Eisenhower did not see a strong central state as a force that unduly trammeled American freedoms. His military career had languished under the small government administrations of Coolidge and Hoover, and flourished under the big government regimes of Roosevelt and Truman. A large centralized state able to mobilize massive numbers of men and materiel had won the Second World War and brought Eisenhower the general his coveted fifth star. Eisenhower's command of US and Allied forces in Europe meant that he had sat at the center of an immense public bureaucracy, in this case a military one. Eisenhower came away from that experience with a deep respect for what government—and a well-organized bureaucracy—could do. The

US government, he believed, would be indispensable in winning the Cold War, as it had been in winning the Second World War.

In his first inaugural, delivered in January 1953, Eisenhower made clear that communism was by far the largest threat confronting America. It was a dire threat, and it was global. "Freedom is pitted against slavery," he intoned, "lightness against the dark." It was imperative that "all free peoples" of the world unify to resist. "Destiny had laid upon" the United States "the responsibility of the free world's leadership." This required the United States not just to be strong but to inspire "the hope of free men everywhere."[56] Repeatedly, Eisenhower referred to his and the American people's religious faith as a critical source for this inspiration. The struggle against communism was not just a global chess match; for Americans and many of their allies, it had become a religious crusade to save the world from godlessness and darkness.

Nowhere in Eisenhower's speech about communism and faith can one discern a sympathy for the views that so animated Taft and his colleagues: namely, that the New Deal was evil, that the power of labor had to be rolled back, that government regulation of the economy had to end, that federal budgets had to be slashed and balanced, and that a nineteenth-century conception of liberty had to be restored. Senator Lyndon Johnson, the new Democratic minority leader, was being a bit cheeky when he noted that Eisenhower's inaugural contained "'a very good statement of Democratic programs of the last twenty years.'"[57] In fact, Eisenhower, in his speech, said nothing about his support for or his opposition to domestic reform. But Johnson was right in reading into Eisenhower's silence on domestic politics a repudiation of Taft.

Indeed, Eisenhower's actions in office would soon reveal that he had acquiesced to the core elements of the New Deal. He believed in using Keynesian fiscal and monetary tools to smooth out the highs and lows of the business cycle. The historic contract that the UAW had achieved with America's major car manufacturers in 1950, the Treaty of Detroit, did not trouble him.[58] To the contrary, he accepted that strong unions were necessary to moderate the power of corporations and spread the affluence of American capitalism through the social order. What the UAW and the automobile manufacturers had done in the private sector, Eisenhower wanted to accomplish in the public sector. Thus, rather than curtail or abolish social security, Eisenhower actually worked successfully to expand the number of Americans covered by this welfare program and to increase its benefits. Eisenhower even endorsed the progressive, high taxation regime that the New Deal had put in place across the 1930s and early 1940s. Taft-style Republicans regarded the progressivity of that tax system as a horror, amounting to nothing less than a communistic strategy for confiscating and redistributing private property.

Eisenhower's decision to maintain this high tax regime was driven, in the first instance, by the imperatives of fighting communism everywhere. Eisenhower was well aware that 70 percent of every tax dollar in 1950s America went to support the country's large Cold War military and rapidly growing nuclear arsenal.[59] It is also true, however, that Eisenhower was beginning to discern the good that a high tax regime would generate not simply to contain the Soviet military threat but to improve the lives of millions of Americans. This stance became plain when he spoke to the nation in 1954 about the importance of supporting the omnibus tax bill working its way through Congress, a bill that would maintain the highest marginal rate at more than 90 percent.

In that 1954 speech, Eisenhower did not justify his support for high tax rates simply in terms of the need to maintain a high level of military preparedness. He also shared with the American people his vision of "a great program to build a stronger America for all our people," all of it paid for by a broad and progressive tax regime. "We want to improve and expand our social security program," Eisenhower declared. "We want a broader and stronger system of unemployment insurance. We want more and better homes for our people. We want to do away with slums in our cities. We want to foster a much improved health program." Broadened social security, better unemployment insurance, urban renewal, and national health care—here, in embryo, was the vision that would animate the Great Society, the ambitious legislative program pushed through Congress by Democratic president Lyndon Johnson in the 1960s to complete the welfare state that Roosevelt and the New Deal had launched in the 1930s. Already in the 1950s, this reform vision was being articulated not just by Democrats but rather by a moderate Republican.[60] Eisenhower would soon commit major federal tax dollars to building a massive interstate highway system and overhauling the St. Lawrence Seaway. Over the course of his two terms in office, his administration's expenditures on public works actually exceeded those of FDR and Truman.[61]

Eisenhower was careful to justify this expansion of government activity by reference to national security. The bill authorizing a new interstate highway system was labeled "The National System of Interstate and Defense Highways." Supporters of the legislation argued that building 41,000 miles of new roads would facilitate both the quick transfer of military units to parts of the United States under attack and rapid evacuation of people from areas threatened by atomic bombs.[62]

Likewise, creating a free and bountiful society for all its citizens was now also framed as a Cold War imperative. Fashioning such a society, Eisenhower believed, could no longer be left to the vagaries of the free market. Too many Americans had seen their livelihoods destroyed in the 1930s, the longest period of market failure in American history. National security now required a managed capitalist system; it demanded that the New Deal be maintained, even expanded. Social programs once anathema to Republicans were now legitimate, for they would help to contain the Soviet threat—both at home, so that Americans would have no cause to find communism appealing, and abroad, by demonstrating the success of the American system to the emerging nations of Asia and Africa.

Which system was better at generating a consumer society—filling stores with alluring goods, putting citizens of the two systems in a position to participate fully in those marketplaces—became a central bone of contention between the Cold War adversaries. Hence the slightly comical but deadly serious "Kitchen Debate" involving Nikita Khrushchev and Richard Nixon in Moscow in 1959. This was the third meeting of the first secretary of the Soviet Union and the vice-president of the United States to debate the comparative merits of the communist and capitalist systems. This one occurred inside a cutaway kitchen of an American suburban home whose components had been disassembled for transport to Russia and then reassembled in Moscow just for this occasion. Nixon took pride in showing off a refrigerator, an electric range, and, most enticing of all (because it was a machine yet to become standard in American homes), a dishwasher. Khrushchev thought the

American addiction to gadgets a bit much, even as he understood that the superpower that best provided the common man and woman with a comfortable life might well win the Cold War. Khrushchev playfully told Nixon that the latter's grandchildren would grow up under communism, and Nixon responded in kind, predicting that Khrushchev's grandchildren would know only capitalism.

That Nixon felt compelled to spar with Khrushchev about the comparative virtues of Soviet and American kitchens revealed the geopolitical importance he attached to putting an attractive consumer marketplace within reach of every American. This goal was too important to be left in the hands of "free markets." Nixon and Ike had both come to understand that New Deal policies, specifically Keynesianism, were necessary to sustain aggregate demand and the flow of goods into the much-celebrated suburban utopias in which many Americans now lived.[63]

Perhaps, in his heart, Eisenhower wanted to return America to Taft's imagined pre–New Deal past. But, in his judgment, a politician wanting to succeed in America in the 1950s could not do it. As Eisenhower wrote to his brother in the early 1950s, "Should any political party attempt to abolish social security, unemployment insurance, and eliminate labor laws . . . you would not hear of that party again in our political history."[64] Eisenhower felt the same way about high rates of progressive taxation and about the compression of economic inequality that those high rates had triggered. Under Cold War pressure, Eisenhower made the Republican Party a supporter of Democratic Party programs. This was the moment when the New Deal transitioned from political movement to political order, when all meaningful players in the political arena felt compelled to abide by its principles.

There were, of course, dissenters. The brilliant and iconoclastic Yale graduate William F. Buckley was, at this very moment, assembling a fiercely anti–New Deal group around a new journal, *National Review*.[65] The actor and former New Deal enthusiast Ronald Reagan had become an evangelist for America's free enterprise system, speaking on TV in spots sponsored by General Electric to audiences across the country.[66] Henry Hazlitt, an economics columnist for the popular magazine *Newsweek* was another figure who, like Reagan, had migrated from the center-left (he had once been literary editor of the *Nation*) to the right, entering Hayek's orbit as a member of the Mont Pèlerin Society along the way. He found Eisenhower's politics repellent, a betrayal of Republican Party principles. Early in Eisenhower's presidency, Hazlitt sounded an alarm, calling Ike's policies a "semi–New Deal."[67] Soon after, he declared, with deepening dismay, "that the President had accepted the heart of the Keynesian and New Deal philosophies."[68] After a dissection of Eisenhower's fiscal and monetary policies that revealed how much the president was following Keynesian prescriptions, Hazlitt lamented, "We are all Keynesians now."[69] Milton Friedman, who, in the 1960s and 1970s would lead the ideological assault on the New Deal order, is thought to have been the originator of this lament in a December 1965 column for *Time*, then *Newsweek*'s arch-rival in the newsmagazine business. But Hazlitt beat Friedman to it by a decade, and he made his point about the dominance of Keynesian thinking not in reference to the Democratic politics of the 1960s (as Friedman did) but in reference to the Republican politics of the 1950s.[70] As Hazlitt's commentary about the hegemonic character of Keynesian economics reveals, even in the 1950s under a Republican president, critics of the New Deal order had precious little political space in which to operate.

The Cold War was the engine driving the mainstream Republican Party to the left. Its imperatives forced a political party that loathed a large centralized state and the extensive management of private enterprise in the public interest to accept these very policies as the governing principles of American life. The threat of international communism made possible the transition of the New Deal from political movement to political order and ensured its dominance in American life for thirty years.

The Cold War, then, secured the New Deal order. That order was not as expansive a reform project as it had been in the late 1930s and early 1940s, but it remained the most successful such project that the United States had enacted since the Civil War. Its achievements in terms of managing capitalism, strengthening labor, and establishing a welfare state followed long records of American failure in each of these areas. That the New Deal compelled its political opponents to abide by its principles is a most revealing sign of its power and influence. Those who remained opposed to New Deal politics were pushed to the margins of American politics where they exercised little influence.

In a world dominated by the New Deal order, Herbert Hoover never regained his stature nor the public respect so often bestowed on ex-presidents. His death in 1964 attracted little notice. He would make a comeback of sorts, not through a rehabilitation of his presidential reputation but through a transformation in the nature of the Hoover Institution he established at Stanford in 1919 to house a global collection of documents pertinent to the Great War. In the 1960s, under the direction of W. Glenn Campbell, the Hoover Institution not only widened its collecting to include other subjects having to do with war, revolution, and capitalism. It also embraced a new mission: to become a think tank, and a nerve center, for those committed to taking down the New Deal order. The Hoover Institution would succeed in that mission and, in doing so, perhaps bring a bit of posthumous vindication to its founder. But the Hoover Institution's ultimate success does not alter the reality of Hoover's long period of political exile and the fact that he spent what should have been the best decades of his political life ruled by a political order that he despised. The threat of communism had made Roosevelt's New Deal into a formidable political order.

2

Fall

EVERY POLITICAL ORDER contains within it tensions, contradictions, and vulnerabilities that at a certain point become too difficult to maintain. A political order can also be destabilized by an event exogenous to the order itself, such as war or economic crisis, that reveals limitations to its repertoire of governing strategies that few had previously grasped. Either a political order finds a way to adapt or it loses authority and then hegemony.

The 1960s and 1970s were the New Deal order's moment of reckoning. As race and Vietnam became the two most important issues in American politics, they created divides among Democratic Party constituents that the New Deal order could not bridge. These divisions were followed by the long economic recession of the 1970s, a recession whose consequences endured because they were associated with underlying changes in the world economy. These three forces—race, Vietnam, and economic decline—battered the New Deal order in the 1960s and 1970s beyond a point where it could repair itself.

Race and Vietnam

As the Cold War secured the transition of the New Deal from political movement to political order, it was also giving the cause of civil rights a boost. Across the Great Depression and World War II, New Dealers had done little to promote civil rights, even as the economic egalitarianism of the New Deal was drawing African Americans to the Democratic

Party in large numbers. Some constituencies within the Democratic Party, especially those in the North, had long supported the cause of racial equality, but others never did. These latter constituencies were concentrated in the South, among whites, for whom the Democratic Party had long been the party of states' rights, white supremacy, and Jim Crow. Southern blacks had been disenfranchised early in the twentieth century, effectively eliminating the Republican Party as a force in southern politics. Thereafter, Democratic candidates for Congress from the South rarely had to face serious Republican challenges, meaning that, once elected, they tended to hold their seats for long periods of time. They thus controlled a disproportionate number of committee chairmanships in the House and Senate, through which they exercised influence over Congress. In the 1930s and 1940s, these southern barons were willing to allow a strengthening of the central government for the purposes of alleviating the suffering of America's white poor, but they would not tolerate any legislation that threatened the racial hierarchies of southern life.[1]

Franklin Roosevelt grasped this southern disposition and the congressional arithmetic that resulted from it. Early in his presidency he concluded that the success of his New Deal depended on the continued support of his party's southern wing in Congress; he believed he could not afford to antagonize its members. Civil rights legislation suffered accordingly. Jim Crow was not challenged (except in Washington, DC, government offices), efforts to pass anti-lynching bills in Congress failed, and the World War II army sent to Europe to crush the Nazis and their ideology of racial hatred was a thoroughly segregated institution. Black and white soldiers did not live together, fight together, or even share the army's blood supplies.[2]

This toleration of white supremacy within the Democratic Party, so strong in the 1930s and early 1940s, plummeted after World War II. Truman desegregated the Armed Forces in 1946, the Democratic Party inserted into its 1948 platform a plank committing itself to the cause of racial equality, and the Supreme Court, now populated largely by Roosevelt-appointed justices, declared Jim Crow unconstitutional in its stunning 1954 *Brown v. Board* decision.

International factors played a significant role in this turnaround, just as they had in enhancing the authority of the New Deal. The remarkable sweep of the Japanese military through East and Southeast Asia in 1941–1942 had reduced to rubble the rule of every western power present there—America in the Philippines; the British in Burma, Singapore, and Malaya; the French in Indochina; and the Dutch in the East Indies. Nonwhites everywhere who had long aspired to throw off colonial domination—including African Americans in the United States who wanted to escape the Jim Crow yoke—could now more easily imagine that they could be free and self-governing. Movements for racial equality and national liberation erupted across Asia and Africa. The hardening of Cold War antagonisms in the late 1940s magnified their geopolitical importance. The United States and the Soviet Union stood to be strengthened or weakened depending on how many—or how few—of the national liberation movements and new countries emerging from them could be persuaded to join their camp.[3]

The rivalry between the United States and the Soviet Union for the loyalty of what was coming to be called the Third World was fierce. Both sides understood how much the outcome could turn on race. Already in the 1940s the Soviet Union was taking delight in embarrassing the United States internationally, by showing how the institutions of white supremacy in the southern states contradicted America's professed commitment to the proposition that all men are created equal. The Soviet press was disseminating in Africa and Asia stories about black children in the South being denied adequate schooling, black accident victims dying because no white hospital in the South would admit them, and African diplomats being refused access to white restaurants and washrooms while traveling south of the Mason-Dixon line. The State Department worked hard to counter this image but its efforts would count for little as long as the American South remained segregated. The United States, its foreign policy establishment concluded, had to demonstrate through deeds a commitment to dismantling segregation to achieve racial equality. The Cold War was helping to make civil rights a paramount issue in America.[4]

This may explain why the Supreme Court decision in *Brown v. Board* came as early as it did (1954), with the entire court lined up behind it. In 1954, civil rights social activism in the United States was still episodic. Almost all the key demonstrations and confrontations that would define the movement—the Montgomery Bus Boycott, the Little

Rock School Crisis, the Freedom Rides, the March on Washington, the battle for Birmingham, Freedom Summer, and the northern urban insurrections of 1964 and 1965—lay in the future. Why such an early determination by the Supreme Court, a key element of the American political establishment, to put itself on the side of civil rights? Partly the Court's action reflected the arrival of Chief Justice Earl Warren, former Republican governor of California and Eisenhower's first appointee, who had become far more of a civil libertarian in the decade after World War II than most people in the GOP, Eisenhower included, had realized. Already sitting on the court were many liberal, Roosevelt-appointed justices with whom Warren had to work. But the Court acted not simply because its members had imbibed a progressive race consciousness. They acted because they understood how much the Cold War had thrust the race problem into the center of American politics.

Prior to 1954, the US Justice Department had begun filing amicus curiae briefs in support of NAACP lawsuits challenging the legality of segregation in the South. In these briefs, the government repeatedly stressed the embarrassment that race discrimination was causing America abroad and the damage it was doing to national security. In the amicus brief filed in *Brown*, the Justice Department reproduced a statement from former secretary of state Acheson declaring that "hostile reaction [to American racial practices] among normally friendly peoples . . . is growing in alarming proportions" and jeopardizing the "effective maintenance of our moral leadership of the free and democratic nations of the world."[5]

Many of those writing and reading these briefs had long thought of themselves as liberals on the American race question. They were from the North, by and large, and they looked down on the South for the "primitive" nature of its race relations. But they had not made agitation for civil rights a priority. They did not think they needed to. They regarded Jim Crow as an anachronism that would not long withstand the modernizing forces at work in the United States. The Cold War made this complacent stance untenable. It compelled members of the American establishment to realize that they had to do something on the American race question, not so much because African American citizens deserved equal rights but because the failure to act would harm the country in its life-and-death international struggle with the Soviet Union.[6]

Of course, any serious effort to dismantle the racist structures and institutions of American life needed more than a reorientation within America's political elite that a Supreme Court decision would provide. It required as well a social movement to demand the dismantling of Jim Crow and the rejection of the ideology of white supremacy in all its forms.

By the late 1950s and early 1960s, this movement had taken shape around two salients: first, a church-based and largely southern movement of working-class and middle-class African Americans led by Martin Luther King Jr. and deeply committed to the principles of nonviolent protest; and second, a black student movement, emerging first and most forcefully at historically black colleges in the South. Both movements targeted the institutions of Jim Crow; both undertook marches in the South and thereby provoked confrontations with whites. The students were often more radical in their tactics, occupying spaces—lunch counters, buses, waiting areas in bus terminals, and so on—that had been marked as "white" and also undertaking voter registration campaigns in rural areas where southern whites had long preserved their power through legal and extra-legal terror. Expecting to provoke violent reactions among southern whites, black protesters and their white allies had trained to react to such assaults with superhuman restraint and "the turning of the other cheek." Newspapers and television networks began broadcasting to the entire country visual images, photographs and film clips of whites beating blacks and of southern sheriffs unleashing high-powered water hoses and attack dogs on peaceful columns of black protesters. Photographs of three civil rights volunteers murdered near Philadelphia, Mississippi, for daring to register southern blacks to vote also went national. These images vastly increased the prestige of the civil rights movement among whites as well as blacks. President John Kennedy (JFK), discomfited by the scale of the protest and the violence visited on protesters, in 1963 himself committed to a civil rights bill with an effective enforcement mechanism. "One hundred years of delay have passed since President Lincoln freed the slaves," Kennedy declared to a national television audience on June 11, 1963, "yet their heirs, their grandsons, are not fully free. They are not yet freed from the bonds of injustice. They are not yet free from social and economic oppression." It was time, Kennedy insisted, for "this Nation to fulfill its promise" and to carry through a peaceful revolution in race relations. Kennedy was therefore calling on Congress "to act, to make a commitment it has not fully made in this century to the proposition that race has no place in American life or law." In the next week, he requested Congress to take up a civil rights bill that would bar discrimination on the basis of race and give the federal government the enforcement powers it needed.[7]

We will never know how insistently Kennedy would have pursued this measure, for he was cut down by an assassin's bullet less than six months after he had proposed his legislation. But his successor, Lyndon Baines Johnson (LBJ), long hungering for the presidency and long denied a crack at it, made JFK's civil rights bill central to his presidency. Regarding Franklin Roosevelt as the greatest politician of his lifetime, Johnson intended to secure his place in American history by establishing himself as FDR's foremost heir. This required a legislative program, the Great Society, that would complete the New Deal and earn LBJ a place alongside FDR in the pantheon of heroic Democratic reformers. Through it, Johnson hoped to address the need of those groups left on the margins of the New Deal. He secured congressional support for massive health insurance programs for the elderly, community action programs to empower the poor, and public housing for those in need. Arguably the most skillful parliamentarian in American politics since Woodrow Wilson, LBJ pushed one initiative after another through a Congress disoriented by the scale of civil rights protests, on the one hand, and the assassination of President Kennedy, on the other.[8]

A believer in the Keynesian principles of the New Deal order, LBJ was confident that he could use government to correct the ills of the American economy and society. LBJ also understood that he would need to attack and remedy racial inequality, a task that FDR had scrupulously evaded. Indeed, Johnson's Great Society committed itself both to dismantling Jim Crow and to remedying through affirmative action the institutional racism that coursed its way through so many American institutions, private and public, North as well as South. In two landmark pieces of legislation, the Civil Rights Act of 1964 and the

Voting Rights Act of 1965, Johnson delivered the strongest measures of their kind since Reconstruction. His executive order 11246 committed his administration and subsequent ones to a vast project of social engineering: the elimination of racial, religious, and sexual bias from all institutions, public and private, that received significant amounts of federal funds. This program came to be known as affirmative action. Johnson did all this knowing that such an ambitious program of racial remediation, entirely deserving of the name "Second Reconstruction," would probably cost the Democratic Party the white South, one of the key constituencies on which the New Deal order had built its power. That constituency included Democrats in Johnson's home state, Texas, who had propelled him into public life and had facilitated his ascent to the presidency.[9]

If he perceived this outcome presciently, Johnson was also distracted from thinking about it by a war in Vietnam that he inherited from Eisenhower and Kennedy. Here too the Cold War had influenced American domestic politics in significant ways. Given the willingness to improve the condition of African Americans in the 1950s, one might have thought that elements of the American establishment would have been equally willing to help the Vietnamese people, another group of nonwhites, to assert their rights, in this case against French colonial power. FDR, indeed, had been sympathetic to the efforts of the Vietnamese, led by Ho Chi Minh, to free themselves from French domination, but Truman was not. The latter's administration had decided that the country's primary goal in international affairs was to secure the survival of France (and the rest of Europe) as part of the Free World. American policymakers worried that the Marshall Plan assistance might not be enough. The French desperately wanted their empire back. The United States pledged to France that it would support France in this endeavor. France was soon fighting Ho's liberation movement, known as the Viet Minh, now supported by the Soviets. The Truman administration and then the Eisenhower administration no longer saw the Vietnamese as a nation struggling to be free of France but as a client of the Soviet Union, advancing communism into the heart of Southeast Asia. Thus, when France failed to hold its Dien Bien Phu fortress in 1954, the United States took over its fight. Vietnam had little intrinsic importance to America: It possessed no essential raw materials, and it offered the United States little in the way of trade. But the Cold War demanded that a non-communist France be defended, and that communists be fought wherever they appeared.[10]

LBJ's expertise in domestic policy did not extend to foreign affairs. To him, foreign policy always mattered less; he hoped his actions in this realm would preserve the priority of domestic initiatives. Yet LBJ was very much a product of the Cold War, believing its shibboleths about communist conquest being irreversible and requiring worldwide containment even when a country, such as Vietnam, that might be falling to the communists did not threaten US national interests. Johnson was hostage to the domino theory; he was spooked by how well Republicans had been able to wield the charge that Democrats were soft on communism. He worried day and night about being cast as an appeaser like the weak-willed British prime minister Neville Chamberlain, whose concessions to Hitler in Munich in the 1930s had opened the door to continent-wide domination by the Nazis. And thus, Johnson could not absorb the advice that key aides laid before him in 1965: The Vietnam War had taken a bad turn and the United States should consider withdrawing or limiting its involvement. Instead, Johnson doubled down on America's involvement, vastly expanding the commitment of troops and weaponry, while at the same time seeking to hide from the American public the true state of the war, the weakness and corruption of the South Vietnamese regime that the United States was supporting, and the strength of the Viet Cong (the successor movement to the Viet Minh) and their North Vietnamese allies.[11]

The scale of the American escalation, the revival of a World War II–era conscription policy that intended to draft many middle-class white boys into the military, and the shading of the truth about the war sparked an anti-war protest of a scale unprecedented in US history. It also made a small New Left into a mass movement with hundreds of thousands of members and followers. Within three short years, the war and the protests it sparked had destroyed Johnson's career, impelling him to announce in spring 1968 that he would not even seek re-election. Having to service demands for both guns and butter, the US economy began to overheat; inflation ensued. Many Great Society initiatives were rolled back or abandoned. Meanwhile, the racial reforms that Johnson had secured in 1964 and 1965 had sparked as much racial conflict as harmony, inclining some blacks toward urban insurrections and causing many whites, fearing for their safety, to flee the Democratic Party and embrace Republicans, now offering themselves as the protectors of law and order and, in the South, of white supremacy.[12]

If racial remediation and a war gone wrong had been the only forces at work, the Democrats might have recovered and sustained their New Deal order. Richard Nixon, the Republican candidate for president in 1968, did not defeat his Democratic opponent, Hubert Humphrey, by much. Majorities of Democrats had ruled the House of Representatives and Senate since 1955 and continued to do so after Nixon was elected. But other forces at work, namely, the changing circumstances of the world economy, were undermining the political conviction most precious to the New Deal order: the notion that government power could be wielded effectively to manage the economy in the public interest.

Economic Trouble

From the mid-1940s to the mid-1960s, the New Deal order rode a wave of global power unlike anything America had experienced before. On the eve of World War II, the United States was already producing more than a fifth of global gross domestic product (GDP), with the second and third biggest economies, Germany and Great Britain, together producing 16 percent. By the late 1940s, the United States was generating more than a quarter of the world's GDP, its share exceeding the output of the next eight economies combined.[13]

Having little to fear from foreign competition, US corporations competed mostly against each other. Where domestic oligopoly had been achieved, as was the case, for example, in iron and steel and in automobiles, the three or four major players in each industry forestalled genuine competition through informal market-sharing agreements. The privileged position of these American manufacturers made it easier for capital and labor to sustain the class compromise on which the New Deal order been founded. The limits on competition meant that individual employers could tolerate higher wage and benefit costs. The clearest manifestation of that compromise was the landmark 1950 Treaty of Detroit in which automobile employers agreed to share a significant portion of their resources with autoworkers in return for labor peace. This collective bargaining agreement, much emulated across sectors of the American economy where organized labor was strong, had been made possible in the first instance by a federal government willing to support the right of workers to organize and willing to punish employers who violated that right. It had been made possible in the second instance by the extraordinary preeminence of American industry in the world. American automobile manufacturers did not have to worry about competition from German and Japanese cars.

The global preeminence of American industry explains decisions made in the late 1940s that otherwise appear foolish: individual corporations, for example, assuming responsibility for the cost of health insurance of their employees, a commitment that, if the employees were unionized, often extended into retirement and old age. These costs would balloon as workforces aged, and would impose huge penalties on American employers when, beginning in the 1970s, they found themselves in competition with agile foreign car manufacturers unburdened by the health care insurance costs that American corporations had taken on. But in the late 1940s and early 1950s, American manufacturers could not imagine that they would one day be threatened by an internationally competitive marketplace. They behaved as though their global economic supremacy was going to last forever.[14]

Yet, even as the US government was underwriting the class compromise on which the New Deal order rested, it was also pursuing policies in the international arena that were designed to restore international competition and make the domestic compromise between capital and labor more difficult to sustain. US government officials across the 1940s and 1950s still feared the return of the kind of market saturation and exhaustion that had prolonged the 1930s depression; they worried, too, that foreign nations might become advocates once again of the protectionist policies embraced by governments around the world in the depression decade. It was thus imperative to tie as many countries as possible to a well-lubricated and US-centered system of international trade. This imperative required generous aid packages to foreign countries so that they could recover their older economic robustness or, if they were new nations, generate markets that would involve them in trade with the United States. Strengthening trading relationships also required the worldwide containment of communism; if containment failed, countries such as Vietnam that were thereby "lost" to communism would be lost (it was thought) forever to the US-led international capitalist order. The Marshall Plan, as noted, was the template for this new kind of American foreign policy, combining generous aid packages with security arrangements—the North Atlantic Treaty Organization (NATO) in the case of Europe—to keep countries with populations tempted by communism in America's capitalist orbit. The United States also created the World Bank (WB) and International Monetary Fund (IMF) in the 1940s to make additional funds available to recovering and developing countries. The WB and IMF immediately began investing resources in ports and roads and other infrastructural items that private investors were reluctant to fund. Finally, the United States brought into existence the General Agreement on Tariffs and Trade (GATT) in 1947 to keep tariff walls at tolerably low levels, another effort to make sure that 1930s autarky would not resurge.[15]

Ideologically, the United States preached the virtues of free trade throughout its "free world" zone. In practice, however, it often allowed countries to protect their domestic markets with tariffs (and thus keep American imports out), even as it granted European and Japanese manufacturers privileged access to US markets. The United States not only dispensed with most tariffs on its borders, but it also tolerated "dumping," a trade practice in which foreign governments either subsidized their countries' exports to America or permitted these exports to be sold in the United States below manufacturing cost. The United States tolerated this asymmetry (these same governments did not permit the dumping of American goods in their lands) for economic and geopolitical reasons. Economically, American superiority seemed unassailable.[16] Geopolitically, the rapid recovery of the western European and Japanese economies was seen as vital to the stalling and then reversal of communism's expansion. The United States needed these countries to become productive and then affluent so as to undercut the Soviet Union's assertion that only communism could deliver peoples from poverty and injustice. Thus, economic policies that could be construed as inimical to the United States' material interests were nevertheless embraced because, as a Bureau of Budget report declared in 1950, "'foreign economic policies . . . must be subordinated . . . to our politico-security objectives.'"[17]

At a certain point, of course, competition from abroad would begin to challenge American supremacy. Made complacent by their apparent invincibility, many American manufacturers were slow in the 1950s and 1960s to invest in innovation and new plants, a reluctance that began to show up in declining rates of productivity increases. European and Japanese competitors, meanwhile, were working with the newest machinery and plants, as so much of the old machinery and plants in their lands had been destroyed by war. By the early 1970s, they had become serious rivals. The Japanese emerged as a force in several American industries—automobiles, motorcycles, office machines, and electronics—where ten years earlier they had had no presence.[18]

The United States was also hurt during these years by the need to divert a huge portion of its resources to its military, much of it, in the era of Vietnam, being spent abroad, worsening America's balance of payments ledger. The country began running trade deficits in 1970; in 1976, for the first time since 1945, it imported more goods and services than it exported.[19] Meanwhile, American corporations, frustrated by their inability to crack protectionist regimes in other countries, began tunneling under foreign tariff walls by building more manufacturing facilities abroad. By the 1970s, they were coming to see themselves more and more as multinational entities rather than national ones, their opportunities and investment wagers shaped as much by international as by national markets. Their loyalty to the American nation and people began to ebb.[20] As these corporations prospered, the country in which their headquarters resided began to suffer. As early as 1971, a blue-ribbon panel appointed by Nixon reported that "the nation's economic superiority was gone."[21]

The decline of America's competitive advantage also became apparent through a second major change in international economic relations occurring in the 1960s and 1970s: the rising political and economic power of commodity-producing nations. Petroleum producers were the paradigmatic case. Cheap energy had underwritten the New Deal order's economic robustness from the start. The flow of cheap oil had also fueled the West's and Japan's economic recovery from the Great Depression and Second World War. "Free world" oil production nearly quintupled between 1948 and 1972, from less than 9 million to more than 42 million barrels a day. None of the world's leading capitalist countries in the Global North could service their share of oil consumption from domestic wells. The United States, the world's largest producer of oil throughout this period, was generating by the 1970s only 65 percent of the 17.4 million barrels it consumed every day. The gap between domestic production and consumption had to be closed through the importation of foreign oil.[22] Europe and Japan were almost completely dependent on oil imports. Saudi Arabia, Kuwait, Iran, Iraq, and Venezuela made up the shortfall for the world's industrial heartlands, producing far more than they could consume. Libya, Algeria, Qatar, Nigeria, Mexico, and Norway, meanwhile, had ramped up their drilling and the export of oil thus extracted to the world's industrial core.

Western companies such as Aramco, a joint British-American venture, had for decades done the drilling and refining of oil in, and shipping from, Saudi Arabia, which possessed the largest known reserves in the world. For a long time, these private companies, in consultation with their British and American home governments, decided how much oil to extract, refine, and ship, and what prices to charge. Governments in oil-producing nations, however, increasingly grasped the immense economic power that control of these oil reserves could place in their hands, and they intended to seize it.[23] Their decision in 1960 to launch the Organization of Petroleum Exporting Countries (OPEC) signaled this desire for change.

The trigger for the actual deployment of OPEC's power was the Yom Kippur War of 1973, the fourth Arab Israeli war in twenty-five years. In this one, the Arab armies had surprised an unprepared Israel with a well-coordinated attack on the holiest day in the Jewish calendar, Yom Kippur, when most Jewish Israelis were in synagogue or at home with family. Israel was slow to mobilize its military, and then had to fight in unfavorable settings, causing its forces to suffer heavy losses. When the Soviet Union began resupplying Arab armies, Israel pleaded with the United States to replenish its military with tanks and planes, and when it did so, Saudi Arabia terminated oil shipments to America.

Suddenly, and for the first moment in the nation's petroleum age, Americans could not get enough gasoline. Long lines formed at service stations. By December 1973 the price of crude oil had nearly quintupled, crashing financial markets. The Dow Jones Industrial Average lost more than 40 percent of its value within a year.[24] In early 1974, the United States did work out an agreement with Saudi Arabia and other major oil-producing nations to resume the smooth flow of oil to industrial districts of the Global North. But that flow was now governed by radically different terms of trade. OPEC dictated the volume of oil exports and the prices to be charged to companies and consumers. Oil-exporting countries overnight became immensely rich and powerful. In the words of historian Steven Schneider, they "had secured the greatest nonviolent transfer of wealth in human history."[25]

The postwar American economy and way of life were both built on the belief that cheap oil would last forever. This belief had made America the land of large, heavy, high-powered, and gas-guzzling automobiles. It had underwritten a vast postwar project of road building and sprawling suburbanization that aimed to make every American man a homeowner with a garage large enough to accommodate two, and sometimes even three, family cars. If these homes sat in bucolic countrysides at long distances from urban centers where work was concentrated, so much the better. American (and mostly male) breadwinners who trekked into and back from the city every day could make believe that ownership of their piece of green suburban land allowed them to re-enact the Jeffersonian dream. They imagined themselves as a new yeomanry, affluent and independent, pillars of the republic. The stratospheric rise in oil prices radically disrupted this world. Other commodity-producing nations could not duplicate the overnight success of OPEC—no other commodity was as critical as oil was to the economy and life of the United States, Europe, and Japan. But in the 1970s and 1980s, the nations that controlled raw materials prized by the Global North made those materials much more expensive to procure.

The effects of this 1970s oil crisis were stark. Real gross national product in the United States fell by 2 percent in 1974 and almost 3 percent in 1975. In the latter year unemployment shot up beyond 8 percent. The simultaneous rise in inflation beyond a rate of 10 percent baffled Keynesian policymakers. Richard Nixon and his successor Gerald Ford, both coming of age politically under the aegis of the New Deal order, faithfully deployed the various Keynesian instruments available in their toolkit.[26] They lowered interest rates to make borrowing easier and cut taxes to put more money in the hands of consumers. Some stability returned in 1976 and 1977. Then came a second oil shock, triggered by a 1978–1979 Iranian revolution that deposed the shah, a close friend of the West, and brought to power the Middle East's first radical Islamic regime. This regime followed Saudi Arabia's 1973 lead in shutting off the flow of Iran's petroleum to the United States, spiking oil prices once again, this time by 50 percent.[27]

Major American industries, dealing with softness in demand since 1973, now cratered. By 1980, the US steel industry, operating at only 50 percent capacity, had laid off 20,000 steel workers; most would never get their jobs back.[28] Domestic automobile production plunged from 9.3 million in 1978 to 6.5 million in 1980, the worst level of sales since 1930. Car companies shuttered forty assembly plants and 1,500 dealerships and laid off more than 700,000 autoworkers.[29] The federal government saved Chrysler Corporation, the country's third largest car manufacturing company, with a 1979–1980 bailout package worth $1.5 billion. Part of the auto industry's crisis stemmed from Americans delaying purchases of new cars until oil prices stabilized. But another part signaled something far more ominous: Many consumers had decided to shift from American gas guzzlers to Japanese gas misers. By 1980, Japan and other foreign car manufacturers had cornered more than 25 percent of the US market. In that year, Japan actually sold more of its cars in the United States than it did at home. The American share of global car production had declined from 80 percent in 1950 to less than 30 percent.[30] The era of unassailable US global dominance in its greatest industry had ended.

Rather than invest in new facilities at home, American manufacturers followed the lead of the auto industry in building new factories abroad, either to get underneath high tariff walls in Europe or to take advantage of the cheap labor costs in the developing economies of Mexico and East Asia. During the recession of the mid-1970s, the flow of foreign investment, much of it American, into South Korea, Taiwan, Mexico, and Brazil allowed those countries to increase their industrial production by 8 percent.[31] These patterns would continue to intensify over the next fifteen years.

Meanwhile, economic suffering spread across the United States. American manufacturers shuttered hundreds, even thousands, of plants. The consequent elimination of millions of well-paying factory jobs began to rip the economic heart out of American manufacturing, especially in the northeast quadrant of the country where so much of that activity was concentrated. This area stretched from Boston and Philadelphia in the East, through Cleveland and Pittsburgh and then on to the automobile districts of southern Michigan and the industrial centers of Chicago, Gary (Indiana), St. Louis, and Cincinnati in the Midwest. Fewer jobs meant fewer taxpayers in once thriving municipalities, now struggling to meet their payroll, infrastructural, and welfare commitments. Unable to pay its bills or to raise money in credit markets, New York City veered dangerously close to bankruptcy in 1975. The federal government, now led by Republican president Gerald Ford, initially declined to come to the city's rescue. The most notorious headline ever to the grace the front page of a New York tabloid simply read: "Ford to City: Drop Dead."[32]

Four hundred fifty miles away, in the far northwest corner of New York State, the heretofore vigorous steel center of Buffalo was hemorrhaging jobs and people at an alarming rate. Twenty years later its factories were largely gone and its population halved. Scholars coined a new phrase, "deindustrialization," to denote such developments in Buffalo and elsewhere. Many residents of these areas began to think about pulling up stakes and moving to the South or West, where the economy seemed more robust. But the poorest citizens of these urban districts were generally not mobile. With plunging tax revenues and land values, municipal governments had fewer and fewer resources with which to address urgent social welfare needs. Shrinking urban resources also meant fewer police and thus more danger for law-abiding urban citizens. Life across America's urban centers became markedly less safe during the 1970s and 1980s.[33]

In the cities of America's industrial core, the crisis frequently pitted working-class and lower-middle-class whites, many of them of European origin, against working-class blacks. White ethnics who had scrambled to get a piece of the American dream now felt as though their future was imperiled. Blacks, by and large, had never gotten a part of that dream; they understood all too well that the heaviest consequences of deindustrialization would fall on them. The conflict between white ethnics and blacks would erupt in fierce fights over housing, employment, and the busing of schoolchildren. Violence always lay just beneath the surface and would occasionally break through. A long night of urban crisis descended on America's once proud cities of the Northeast and Midwest.[34]

As blacks and white ethnics fought out their battles in urban politics and sometimes on city streets, economists were struggling to understand the nature of the economic crisis. Keynesian counter-cyclical policies were not working. Inflation and unemployment were rising at the same time. Pundits and some economists began referring to the Misery Index—a number resulting from adding together the rate of inflation and the rate of unemployment. In the late 1970s, this figure was in the high teens; in 1980, with inflation running 13 percent (and then higher) and unemployment rising to 7 percent, it breached the 20 percent barrier.[35] This index had no real economic meaning, but the mere circulation of a statistic purporting to claim that more than a fifth of the economy was malfunctioning inclined observers to think that the hard times of the 1930s had returned. These changing economic circumstances, coming on the heels of the divisions over race and Vietnam, broke apart the New Deal order.

A Transitional Presidency

Trying to manage this crisis was a well-intentioned but inexperienced and ultimately failed president, Jimmy Carter. Americans have long had a love affair with upstart presidential candidates, those thought to be untainted by the business of politics and its temptations, riding into Washington to save the republic. In the 1970s, America was hungering for such a candidate in the aftermath of the Watergate fiasco, when Richard Nixon was forced to resign from office in 1974 for his role in covering up a break-in at the offices of the Democratic National Committee by members of his (Nixon's) own re-election committee. Democratic and Republican Americans alike were aghast at Nixon's abuse of power; this abuse, coming on the heels of the protests and deep divisions of the 1960s, made many thirst for an honest and ethical man who could restore dignity to the office of the presidency and integrity to America's political system. They thought they had found such a man in Jimmy Carter, a successful small businessman from Plains, Georgia, an engineer trained at the US Naval Academy, and a deeply religious man who strove to live a good and moral life. He was still a political novice, having served only one term as governor of Georgia. But the distance he cultivated from the normal business of American politics was precisely what made him so appealing.[36]

Carter scored some successes as president. His evident integrity and strong ethical core went a long way toward restoring dignity to the presidential office he now occupied. His engineering background made him a good problem solver, as he demonstrated in twelve extraordinary days at Camp David in 1978 when he induced the Israelis and the Egyptians to make peace with each other. His insistence on enforcing the 1975 Helsinki Accords, specifically the affirmation that all the peoples living behind the Iron Curtain possessed inalienable human rights, marked him as a visionary, someone who believed that the nightmare of communist domination would one day end.[37] But, in economic matters, Carter could not find his way. To be fair, it is not clear if anyone ascending to the presidency in 1977 would have.

Carter did, however, accelerate the search for ideas and strategies that would move beyond Keynesian orthodoxy and the principles governing the New Deal order. Carter had no particular affection for Franklin Roosevelt. He did not partake of Lyndon Johnson's passion for completing the New Deal. As he contemplated the federal government over which he presided, he saw an institution that had grown too large, too opaque, and too unaccountable to the American people. Government regulation might have been necessary during the Great Depression, Carter conceded; but now America had too much of it, and it was harming both American business and the American consumer. During his 1976 campaign for the presidency, Carter returned to the theme of bloated and undemocratic government again and again. If elected, he boasted, he would reduce the number of federal agencies from 1,900 to 200.[38] A shrinkage on that scale was fantastical. Nevertheless, the steps Carter took to "deregulate" the economy may have been the most significant domestic accomplishment of his presidency.

Unlike Reagan, Carter had not spent his spare time reading Friedrich Hayek. Unlike economist Alan Greenspan, who began a long public career as chairman of the Council of Economic Advisers under Gerald Ford, he did not grow up entranced by the novels of Ayn Rand. But Carter did have a muse of his own who filled his ears with thoughts about the need to rethink the relationship between government and the economy. This muse was left-leaning. His name was Ralph Nader. Nader and Carter had first met in the 1960s when Nader gained national visibility with his attack on automobile manufacturers for their indifference to the safety of the cars they were selling. Carter had been attempting unsuccessfully to implement Nader-like policies of consumer protection in the state of Georgia. The two men stayed in touch, and by the time of Carter's election, they had become close. Nader advised Carter at several moments during his presidency. Nader's disciples, known as Nader's Raiders, populated Carter's administration for a time, beginning with James Fallows, hired by Carter as a speechwriter. By the time Carter's presidency had ended, more than sixty consumer activists, many of them with ties to Nader or his organizations, had served in the Carter administration.[39]

Though not formally part of the New Left, Nader partook of its spirit. He was deeply anti-corporate. Like many New Leftists, he had come to see government not as a tool for restoring democracy but as an instrument of corporate domination and bureaucratic drift. Both corporations and government regulators, in Nader's eyes, were part of a "system" that had served the people poorly. The flaws of this "system" had to be exposed and reformed. Only after such exposure and reform would "the people" be restored to their sovereign perch. Consumers were at the center of Nader's vision of popular democracy; they, not workers, were the ones whom he wanted to empower.

Neither Nader nor Carter worshipped the private sector in the manner of neoliberals such as Milton Friedman or Alan Greenspan. However, their determination to strengthen consumers meant that they, too, began to give priority to improving markets. This meant attacking corporate oligopoly, on the one hand, and excessive and counterproductive government regulation, on the other. Their shared goal was to make consumers sovereign in the marketplace. In Nader's thinking, and in his policies, we can detect a point of origin for neoliberalism on the left.[40] We shall encounter more such points in Chapter 3.

The anti-government dimensions of Carter's incipient neoliberalism dominated his presidential rhetoric. "There is a limit to the role and the function of government," he declared in his 1978 State of the Union address. "Government cannot solve our problems, it can't set our goals, it cannot define our vision. Government cannot eliminate poverty or provide a bountiful economy or reduce inflation or save our cities or cure illiteracy or provide energy. And government cannot mandate goodness."[41] These declarations constituted a quite extraordinary rejection of the pro-government creed that lay at the heart of the New Deal order. Carter was giving voice to neoliberal stirrings. In concrete terms, they manifested themselves in the deregulatory legislation aimed at the airline, trucking, and railroad industries that Carter pushed through Congress. These laws removed restrictions that had hampered the entry of new providers into these sectors, thereby intensifying competition and stimulating innovation. The changes were most immediately visible in the airline industry, where Congress shifted regulatory responsibility from a lumbering Civil Aeronautics Board (CAB) to a Federal Aviation Administration far more open than the CAB had been to licensing new carriers, to reducing costs, and to expanding service.

One of the first upstart airlines to appear under this new regime was People's Express, based at a then little-used airport in New Jersey (Newark), which quickly became famous for its $19 flights to other northeastern cities and its $149 flights to London. Southwest Airlines appeared shortly thereafter in the region of the country diametrically opposite the Northeast. Many of the new airlines did not survive, of course, or they got swallowed up by larger carriers. Multiple established carriers, such as Pan Am and Eastern Air Lines, meanwhile, went under, driven out of business by the new competition. But across the ensuing quarter century, the deregulatory effort of the 1970s put many more planes in the air and made many more seats available at lower cost. Airline travel became available to masses of Americans in ways it had not been before. Changes of similar import restructured the trucking industry. The Carter administration also supported the initiative, begun under Gerald Ford, to dismantle American Telephone and Telegraph (AT&T), which held a monopoly over phone service. In 1982, a consent decree between AT&T and the Justice Department broke that mammoth corporation into smaller entities and allowed new providers to enter the industry. The termination of AT&T's government-sanctioned monopoly was the first step in a series of reforms that would revolutionize the nation's telecommunications system across the next two decades.[42]

Carter never succeeded in making deregulation a central message of his presidency, as Reagan would shortly do. He did not articulate a sense that America was on the cusp of a historic change in its political economy, one that would restore the country's greatness, as Reagan insisted it was. To the contrary, as Carter moved ahead with deregulation, he also sought to placate old-style Democrats who wanted to meet the crisis of the 1970s with an expansive regulatory response, one that would revive the spirit of the New Deal. These old-style Democrats were Keynesians; the New Deal order, they believed, could be reinvigorated. They fought hard for labor law reform meant to reanimate the labor movement and the capital-labor compromise on which the New Deal for so long had rested. They hoped that the passage of the Humphrey-Hawkins Full Employment and Balanced Growth Act of 1978 would impel the government to use its fiscal and monetary resources to encourage job creation in the private sector and to launch public-sector jobs programs. In 1979 and 1980, New Deal order stalwarts within the Democratic Party also drew Carter into deep discussions about creating tripartite boards of labor leaders, corporate heads, and representatives of the public of the sort that had flourished in the 1930s and 1940s. These boards, it was thought, would push the government to move beyond the mere deployment of fiscal and monetary powers and to contemplate direct interventions into the affairs of particular industries that were ailing. Perhaps they would lay the foundation for an industrial policy that harkened back to the halcyon days of the New Deal order.[43]

Carter tacked back and forth between his deregulators, on the one side, and his Keynesian, industrial policy constituencies, on the other. One month he drew close to the supporters of the labor movement and industrial planning. The next month he appointed Paul Volcker, a financial economist who had become a hardnosed monetarist, to chair the Federal Reserve.[44] Carter sought to create common ground between his inflation-licking and jobs-creating constituencies. He did not find it. This futile search made Carter seem indecisive, unable to chart a clear road ahead, far more buffeted than in command. He would be repudiated by the American people in 1980. But, in retrospect, we can see that he began preparing the country to move beyond the New Deal order by creating a political environment conducive to the elaboration of new ideas, new vectors of political mobilization, and new networks of policymakers.[45]

The Soviet Union was unable to capitalize on America's 1970s economic distress as it had done in the 1930s. In the 1950s, Khrushchev wanted to debate a leader of the "free world" about the comparative economic strengths of the two systems. The Soviet economy was then expanding at a rate equal to and sometimes greater than the pace of advanced economies of the West and of Japan. This rapid growth stopped at some point in the 1960s; by the 1970s, the Soviet system as well as the other command economies of the communist bloc were falling behind the economies of the West and of Japan. No Soviet leader in the 1970s was eager for a 1950s Khrushchev-type debate with a western leader, even with the economies of the West ailing and with the rise in petroleum prices bringing a windfall to the oil- and gas-rich Soviet Union. No communist nation was enjoying a degree of economic growth that rivaled the economic miracles under way in West Germany and Japan—soon to be followed by Taiwan, South Korea, and Singapore. A few communist nations, such as Yugoslavia and China, having removed themselves from the Soviet Union's orbit, were engaging in some promising economic experimentation. But it was too early in the 1970s to know where those experiments would lead.[46]

The stagnation that had overtaken most of the communist world deepened the conviction of those in the United States who wanted to free their own nation from the "command economy" of the New Deal order. America's economic decline, they believed, was happening for the same reasons that a decline was occurring in the Soviet world: Government was strangling free enterprise. The New Deal order, in their eyes, had stifled free markets, technological and managerial innovation, and economic growth.[47] The neoliberal moment was at hand.

Part II

The Neoliberal Order, 1970–2020

3

Beginnings

MOST HISTORIES OF neoliberalism locate its origins in Europe in the interwar years, specifically in Vienna, the cosmopolitan capital of a once-great Austro-Hungarian empire brought to its knees first by its World War I defeat and then by revolutionary movements of the left and right that ripped through its streets. Neoliberalism's key founders, most notably economists Friedrich Hayek and Ludwig von Mises, were distressed by revolutionary movements of the left, and by the collectivism that "Red Vienna"—the left's Austrian incarnation—sought to impose on their country's economic and political life. Because classical, or what they called laissez-faire, liberalism had, in their eyes, failed in its attempts after World War I to reorganize European life, they sought to design a new, reformed, and hardened liberalism to point a way toward a better future. This new liberalism is what they began to call neoliberalism, a term that others embraced at two convocations usually regarded as the founding moments of the movement—the Colloque Lippmann held in Paris in 1938, and the first meeting of the Mont Pèlerin Society in Switzerland in 1947. Accounts of neoliberalism's history customarily shift from Europe to America from the 1940s onward, tracking the movement as it transited the Atlantic and found homes at several US universities, most prominently in the economics department of the University of Chicago, branching out from there into public policy and politics.

Hayek, von Mises, and other pioneering neoliberals wanted to be seen as the creators of a disciplined "thought collective" with the ability to unleash a singularly fresh and coherent liberal ideology on the world.[1] Their myth of a new, powerful, and monolithic creed has shaped the writing of a good deal of the history of neoliberalism. But the actual origins are rather messier. Neoliberalism had to contend from the very beginning with an inconvenient fact: namely, that it was not the first "new liberalism" to appear on the historical stage, but the second. The first new liberalism was the New Deal liberalism of FDR, declaring (as neoliberalism wanted to claim for itself) that it offered a novel third way between laissez-faire on the right and collectivism on the left. Neoliberalism would come to define itself in opposition to this first new liberalism, proclaiming its third way as true and the New Deal's as false. But it was never as easy in practice as in theory for self-proclaimed neoliberals to disentangle their ideology from other liberalisms that were swirling around them.

This disentangling was an especially challenging project in the United States where, as Michel Foucault once observed, liberalism has always been everywhere, never confined to one party or school. Liberalism in America, Foucault remarked in lectures he gave at the Collège de France in 1978 and 1979, was "many sided, ambiguous," with roots and influence on the left as well as on the right.[2] This chapter takes Foucault's insight as inspiration.[3] It argues that neoliberalism's career in America was marked as much by heterodoxy as by orthodoxy, by its capacity to make individuals as different as tech hippies and Ronald Reagan, as dissimilar as Barry Goldwater and long-haired university students who wanted to bring down "the system," feel as though they held the keys to unlocking a future of untrammeled personal freedom.

The lack of a singular message does not render the rise of neoliberalism in the middle decades of the twentieth century less portentous. To the contrary, neoliberalism's protean character, this chapter suggests, enhanced its appeal, allowing its proponents to move in directions both new and old, right and left. It offered novel approaches to solving economic and social problems while also resuscitating the emancipatory spirit that had been central to classical liberalism's popularity in the late eighteenth and early nineteenth centuries.

Throughout this analysis, I have been guided by historical geographer Jamie Peck's argument regarding the perpetually incomplete and contested nature of neoliberalism. " 'Finding neoliberalism,' " Peck has written, "is . . . not about locating some essential center from which all else flows; it is about following flows, backflows, and undercurrents across and between . . . ideational, ideological, and institutional moments, over time and between places."[4] What Peck says about neoliberalism might also be said about the older ideology—liberalism—from which neoliberalism emerged. Liberalism itself is best understood as a series of ideational and institutional moments varying in form and meaning across its 250-year history.[5]

Neoliberalism is part of that longer history. To properly understand it, we must comprehend something about the arc of liberalism itself: the movement from classical liberalism in the eighteenth and nineteenth centuries to New Deal liberalism in the twentieth, and then from New Deal liberalism to neoliberalism. And that means we must begin our story of neoliberalism's emergence not in interwar Europe, but 150 years earlier, in British North America, when an anticolonial war for independence made a relatively marginal political ideology—liberalism—into a force of world historical importance.

Classical Liberalism

"All men are created equal and endowed by their creator with unalienable rights to life, liberty, and the pursuit of happiness," proclaimed the American revolutionaries when they gathered in Philadelphia on July 4, 1776, to sign the document proclaiming the independence of thirteen North American colonies from Great Britain. The revolutionaries went on to detail their grievances against their king, George III: He had trampled on their rights, stolen their liberty, and put the entire British Empire on the road to tyranny. This oppression had become intolerable, justifying the drastic act of separation that the American colonists were undertaking. Liberty was a critical word in revolutionary discourse, invoked repeatedly, urgently, and in a wide array of contexts. What did it mean?[6]

Politically, liberty signified a determination to limit government and thereby to maximize individual freedom. In the twenty years following 1776, it became fundamental to American political thought and integral to the system of government set up under the US Constitution, ratified in 1789. That system fragmented the authority of the central government into three branches—the executive, the legislative, and the judicial—so as to prevent any one of them from accumulating sufficient power to reproduce the tyranny of George III. The first ten amendments to the Constitution, adopted in 1791, further strengthened the liberal character of American governance by elaborating a set of individual rights—to freedom of speech, assembly, and religion; to petition the government without fear of reprisal; to a swift and fair trial if charged with a crime—that could not be abrogated except under extreme circumstances. The rights enumerated in these ten amendments came to be known as the Bill of Rights and arguably they constitute the greatest liberal document ever produced by the United States. This bill identified a core area of human freedom, asserted its inviolability, and protected it from the exercise of arbitrary government power. This emphasis on human freedom and its protection was foundational to classical liberalism—and to the American republic.[7]

The Bill of Rights spoke to the political dimension of classical liberalism. An economic dimension of liberalism drew on the thought of Adam Smith, the Scottish political economist and philosopher who had published his magnum opus, *An Inquiry into the Nature and Causes of the Wealth of Nations*, in the same year that the Americans had declared their independence from Britain. In *Wealth of Nations*, Smith stressed the imperative of creating an economy in which people would be free to pursue their economic interests and advantage. Smith believed that individuals so blessed with freedom would work hard and inject into the economy commercial and creative energy. The invisible hand of the market would coordinate the myriad individual pursuits and channel the economic energy generated, thus ensuring that the pursuit of individual well-being would contribute to the common good. Producers would be inventive and innovative, applying the principle that Smith labeled the "division of labor" to break down production processes into their simplest parts, each to be performed by one group of workers performing a single task. Efficiency would spring from such specialization, increasing the quantity of production while decreasing the price of each manufactured unit, thus enhancing opportunities for market exchange. This specialization and differentiation of labor would also occur on a macro level between sectors of the economy and between nations, increasing domestic and international trade, all accruing to the "wealth of nations." The proponents of this dimension of liberalism, what they celebrated as market freedom, argued that it would trigger extraordinary economic growth. Economic liberalism also carried within it an emancipatory current, since creating a world of free exchange required liberating national economies from the state controls that monarchs and mercantilists had everywhere imposed and that Smith despised. In this context, Smith's simple call to allow people to "truck, barter, and exchange" as they saw fit could have, and did have, revolutionary implications.[8]

A cultural dimension of liberalism encouraged an emphasis on individuality and its cultivation. Individuality called for something more than the pursuit of economic self-interest. It focused attention instead on the full achievement of the individual's potential. Liberals speaking in this register called for a commitment to a rational inspection of the world and the jettisoning of beliefs grounded in superstition and unthinking tradition. They put a premium on education. They stressed moral improvement, the cultivation of conscience and of responsibility for one's fellow human beings, and, ultimately, a belief in progress. This emphasis on conscience, moral improvement, and progress gave rise in liberal ranks to humanitarian dreams of emancipation—for religious minorities, for women, for the enslaved, and for impoverished workers. A century later it would encourage dreams of pluralism and cosmopolitanism, of humanity enriched by the encounters between people of different faiths, traditions, and nationalities.[9]

If we grasp classical liberalism in these three dimensions—political, economic, and cultural—we can begin to understand the magnitude of its challenge to prevailing eighteenth-century ways of organizing the world. Liberalism promised new forms of government, new ways of organizing the economy, and new possibilities for cultivating the self. It was profoundly dynamic, emancipatory, and transformative in its ambitions. Surveying the dreams unleashed by liberalism in the nineteenth century, the prominent twentieth-century journalist and cultural critic Walter Lippmann, writing from the perspective of the 1930s, declared that liberalism had been nothing short of revolutionary. Liberalism changed "the condition in which men lived," Lippmann declared. "It was no accident that the century which followed" liberalism's appearance, Lippmann argued, "was the great century of human emancipation. In that period, chattel slavery and serfdom, the subjection of women, the patriarchal domination of children, caste and legalized class privileges, the exploitation of backwards peoples, autocracy in government, the disfranchisement of the masses and their compulsory illiteracy . . . were outlawed in the human conscience, and in a very substantial degree they were abolished in fact." Lippmann followed Smith in arguing that this march of human freedom was grounded, first and foremost, in the progress of economic freedom. The advance of economic freedom was rooted, in turn, in liberalism's success in lifting barriers to individual initiative and in unshackling Smith's division of labor dynamic, triggering both economic growth and new confidence in the scope of human individuality.[10]

We will attend shortly to the problems that Lippmann's encomium to classical liberalism elided. But first let us take stock of the three decades—the 1840s to 1870s—when the promise of this liberalism seemed on its way to fulfillment, both in the United States and in Europe. In the United States, this moment was marked by the emergence of a new political party (the Republican Party) from the ranks of American Whigs, calling for "free soil, free labor, and free men," the abolition of slavery, and the re-founding of the American republic on a racially egalitarian basis. The Liberal Party emerged in Great Britain simultaneously from the ranks of British Whigs, committing itself to a global project of free trade and the enfranchisement of the working classes. The path toward liberalism was more circuitous in France, as the hopes generated by the revolutions of 1848 shattered when Napoleon III made himself emperor in 1852, inaugurating the Second French Empire. But Bonaparte and autocracy fell in 1870; soon after, France's liberals succeeded in breathing life into the country's Third, and most enduring, Republic. This was also the era when the campaign for women's emancipation gained traction in the United States, when the English philosopher John Stuart Mill published his classic work, *On Liberty*, and when the French built a mammoth Statue of Liberty for America to honor Lincoln's work in emancipating the enslaved and thus, they believed, in strengthening liberty and liberalism everywhere.[11]

From Classical Liberalism to the "New Liberalism" of the New Deal

Even at the height of its achievements, however, classical liberalism was beset by problems. From the very start, America's liberal constitution had suffered from a fundamental contradiction: It had permitted slavery, the most basic form of unfreedom. The Civil War, emancipation, and the constitutional amendments prohibiting a return to slavery and outlawing discrimination on the basis of race had ostensibly eliminated this contradiction and given America, in Lincoln's memorable phrase, "a new birth of freedom." But this liberal revolution was followed by a conservative counter-revolution, one in which white southerners, through their state legislatures, implemented policies that subordinated blacks to whites and betrayed the liberal promise imbedded in the North's Civil War triumph. The subjection and terrorizing of southern blacks were often justified by appeals to order. Ex-slaves, white southerners charged, did not know how to handle their freedom responsibly, and, indeed, interpreted liberty as license to corrupt political institutions, pursue their sexual interest in white women, and evade honest labor. Where blacks had been in power during the years of Reconstruction, white southerners alleged, anarchy had reigned. Regimes of order, including that of Jim Crow, were now necessary to rein in the "mobs" of the once enslaved.[12]

The late nineteenth-century obsession with order was not just a white southern or racial affliction. The Paris Commune of 1871, which had broken out in the midst of the Franco-Prussian war, saw workers barricading themselves in sections of the city, establishing a short-lived working-class republic, and engaging in armed battles with regiments of the French Army. In the 1870s and 1880s, it was not hard to imagine that American workers might emulate the communards and establish their own radical republics. Bitter and often violent strikes were convulsing centers of northern industry, with battles spreading from manufacturing sites and railroad depots through city streets, destroying property and sometimes life itself. The trigger for these confrontations was often a financial crisis or a trough in the business cycle, causing layoffs and wage cuts. But the deeper issue was the growing conviction among American workers that the freedom promised to them by the

American Revolution and reaffirmed by the Civil War had produced only counterfeit liberty—thus, the growing appeal in working-class ranks of various forms of radicalism, including socialism, and the increasing resort to strikes and armed confrontations.[13]

The turn toward insurgency and violence terrified elite and middle-class groups in Europe and America. Many liberals had come to fear the left, the alleged carrier of anarchy, as much as the right. They wanted to distinguish themselves from the left by delineating orderly and constitutional paths of political development. As they turned toward order, some liberals also began to suggest that not all peoples were equipped with the tools necessary to cultivate their individuality, and thus, that they were not ready for full participation in liberal projects. Modern peoples, the prominent English liberal, Herbert Spencer, argued, were engaged in a Darwinian struggle for freedom in which only the fittest would survive. Not every nation and race, therefore, would succeed in constructing a liberal polity and in handling freedom responsibly. Those who were deemed unfit for such freedom were to be excluded from polities or denied full participation in them. Some liberals did develop conceptions of civilizing missions to bring enlightenment, rationality, and individuality to those races and groups judged to be deficient in them, producing by the end of the nineteenth century liberal forms of imperialism that sought to extend hope to "benighted" peoples that they could eventually be part of liberal uplift. But the behavior of the British in South Africa in the Boer Wars and of the Americans in the Filipino Wars revealed the mailed fist that stood ready to enforce a liberal imperial order on unwilling subjects.[14]

The growing inclination of liberals to privilege order over freedom—and to become, in the caustic words of Walter Lippmann, "apologists for miseries and injustices that were intolerable to the conscience"—is what prompted many dissenters to forsake liberalism altogether for new and more radical ideologies. Lippmann was among those who, as youth, immersed themselves in socialist thought and politics.[15] The perceived failure of liberalism is what would make socialism, and later communism, one of the most prominent creeds of the twentieth century.

Equally important, however, was the determination of many within the liberal fold not to abandon the field but to rethink and refashion

the content of their liberalism. This rethinking happened simultaneously in the United Kingdom and the United States. In the United
Kingdom, reformers L. T. Hobhouse and J. A. Hobson elaborated what
they called a "new liberalism" that, in the first two decades of the twentieth century, transformed the politics of Britain's Liberal Party. In the
United States, a similar new liberalism was bubbling up in both the
Democratic and Republican parties, its adherents increasingly calling
themselves "progressives." Their intellectual leaders included Herbert
Croly, author of the 1909 manifesto *The Promise of American Life*,
which set forth a program for a new liberalism in the United States that
paralleled what Hobhouse's treatise, *Liberalism* (1911), had proposed in
the United Kingdom. Croly influenced Theodore Roosevelt who, by
1910, had adopted Croly's label, "new nationalism," as his own. Jane
Addams, of Chicago settlement house fame, was as influential as Croly
in the ranks of the new liberals. In 1912, the two of them, along with
other reform-minded liberals, joined forces to found the Progressive
Party, making Theodore Roosevelt their tribune. This third-party effort
was short-lived, like most that preceded and succeeded it in America.
But before flaming out, it influenced Roosevelt's principal rival for the
1912 presidency, the Democrat Woodrow Wilson who, by 1914, as president, had given himself over almost entirely to the principles of the
Progressive Party. That was the year in which Croly and colleagues
founded the *New Republic*, soon to become the most influential magazine of liberal opinion in the United States.[16]

Both Roosevelt and Wilson rejected the notion that the free market
constituted a natural order whose energies were beyond the capacity of
humans to manage or redirect. They believed that unregulated markets
had produced an intolerable imbalance in power and wealth between
employers and employees. The human casualties of a capitalist system
had grown too numerous, their injuries too disabling. The time had
come for a strong central state to intervene in economic processes, to
create a level playing field in which workers and employers could engage each other on more or less equal terms, and to provide a cushion
for those who, through injury, unemployment, and poverty, had been
cast aside. The Progressive era (1900–1920) was defined by efforts to
curb corporate power, to grant labor unions rights to collective bargaining, to inaugurate schemes of social insurance, and to establish a

welfare state. Herbert Croly had laid out a comprehensive program of this sort in *The Promise of American Life*, and Theodore Roosevelt had distilled it into this pithy and powerful sentence that stood at the heart of the epoch-defining oration he had given at Osawatomie, Kansas, in 1910, the place where, in the 1850s, the fiery abolitionist John Brown and his supporters had held off a large group of pro-slavery settlers in a fierce gun battle: "The man who wrongly holds that every human right is secondary to his profit," Roosevelt declared, "must now give way to the advocate of human welfare, who rightly maintains that every man holds his property subject to the general right of the community to regulate its use to whatever degree the public welfare may require it."[17]

In 1917, Wilson became the first president to attach the word "liberal" to the view expressed by Theodore Roosevelt in 1910. But many "liberals" in America were still not comfortable with this naming exercise, since this new liberalism seemed to stand in stark contradiction to classical liberalism. Thus, the term "progressive" continued to compete with "liberal" as the most appropriate word to frame this new philosophy. This competition ended in the 1930s when the Great Depression vaulted Franklin Roosevelt into the White House.

FDR was heir to both Theodore Roosevelt and to Wilson. He had long modeled his own career on that of his illustrious cousin Teddy; and he had drawn close to Wilson and the Democratic Party when he served Wilson's administration as assistant secretary of the navy across the World War I years. FDR made liberalism the defining label of his New Deal politics and the exclusive property of the Democratic Party. His success at the polls gave him the authority to do this. Shortly after becoming the first president in American history to win a third term of office in 1940, FDR declared that the Democratic Party was America's "liberal party." The label stuck. The New Deal order that Roosevelt built was heretofore to be known as a liberal order.[18]

The specter of radicalism in its anarchist, socialist, and communist hues shadowed this ideological transformation. Theodore Roosevelt's New Nationalist politics had arisen in an era when anarchists were assassinating prominent politicians (one had killed Roosevelt's predecessor, William McKinley, in 1901, clearing the way for Roosevelt to assume office) and in which a credible socialist presidential candidate, Eugene Debs, shaped political debate during the pivotal 1912 election.

Woodrow Wilson had been acutely conscious of the challenge posed by the Russian Revolution in 1917. By the time he sailed for Europe in late 1918 to negotiate a treaty to end the Great War, Wilson regarded Lenin as his chief international rival. Wilson's plans for world reconstruction were motivated from the start by a determination to thwart and defeat the communist challenge. Several of the enduring elements of Roosevelt's New Deal program, meanwhile, took shape only in 1935 and 1936, when mass insurgencies in the United States, often led by radicals, were posing a threat to FDR's 1936 re-election. Theodore Roosevelt, Wilson, and FDR were all looking for a third way between what each regarded as the "soul-crushing" collectivism of the left and the discredited "laissez-faire" ways of the right.[19]

Racism likewise shadowed this new liberalism, apparent especially in Theodore Roosevelt's and Wilson's low opinion of most people of color, and their reluctance—and sometimes outright refusal—to regard them as full rights-bearing individuals deserving of full inclusion in the new liberal polities they were intent on creating. Their racism manifested itself at home, as when Theodore Roosevelt refused to allow black delegations from southern states to participate in the Progressive Party's founding 1912 convention and when Wilson resegregated Washington and the federal civil service soon after taking office in 1913. Racism also manifested itself abroad when Wilson, at the 1919 Paris Peace conference, largely denied nonwhite peoples living beyond Europe's borders the right to self-determination and self-governance. The threat of Lenin and communism preoccupied Wilson far more than race did; hence he and his fellow new liberals defined their manifest challenge in terms of finding a third way between laissez faire and collectivism. As president, FDR would frame his mission similarly. But from the 1910s to the 1940s, racial prejudice permeated this new liberalism in ways large and small; a reckoning with it could be delayed but not ultimately escaped.[20]

Neoliberalism Struggles to Be Born

From the start, challengers arose to contest FDR's claim that his new liberalism offered the best hope for finding a third way between laissez-faire and collectivism. Herbert Hoover led the charge, even after his

1932 defeat. Hoover did not see himself as a reactionary, as others often portrayed him at the time. To the contrary, he saw himself as the true new liberal, one who had found the authentic middle path between the dreaded extremes. Roosevelt, on the other hand, was not just an imposter in calling himself a liberal; worse, he was a dangerous deceiver. His New Deal would not forestall socialism but hasten its arrival. It would grant the government of the United States control of economic life and individuality similar to what had already triumphed in Soviet Russia and Nazi Germany. "There are some principles that cannot be compromised," Hoover intoned in 1936. "Either we shall have a society based upon ordered liberty and the initiative of the individual, or we shall have a planned society that means dictation no matter what you call it or who does it. There is no half-way ground. They cannot be mixed. Government must either release the powers of the individual for honest achievement or the very forces it creates will drive it inexorably to lay its paralyzing hand more and more heavily upon individual effort."[21]

Hoover refused to call himself a conservative; he was the true new liberal! But filling his new liberalism with content was easier said than done. Because it was the second new liberalism to appear on the historical stage, it was always being squeezed in its early years by the first one, that elaborated by Roosevelt as the New Deal. Hoover found a kindred spirit in Lippmann, who had abandoned his youthful socialist proclivities for a reconstructed liberalism that, he hoped, would triumph both over its laissez-faire and New Deal rivals. Like Hoover, Lippmann was withering in his criticism of laissez-faire supporters and their claim that markets existed in nature and, as such, were beyond the capacity of humans to control through state action. "The rugged individualist may have imagined that in economic life he was the person that God and his own will had made," Lippmann wrote in 1937. "But in fact he was a juristic creature of the law that happened to prevail in his epoch."[22] Because markets were created by humans and protected by law, Lippmann argued, they could be improved by human agency— and by state intervention. What, then, was the proper relation of government to markets? Hoover, in a major address in the 1930s, argued that in America only "government-regulated business" would work as a formula for liberal politics.

What did Hoover mean by government-regulated business? He was adamant that it was fundamentally different from the New Deal, which he viewed as "government-dictated business." Yet, trying to distinguish between government-dictated and government-regulated business seemed, at times, like splitting hairs. Indeed, the more Hoover outlined his plan for the latter, the more it began to sound like the New Deal itself. It called for regulating banking, finance, and markets; for extending to labor the right to collective bargaining; for providing workers with government insurance against unemployment; for imposing income and inheritance taxes to limit the accumulation of private wealth; for eliminating "slums, child labor, sweated hours, and sweated wages."[23] Hoover attempted to distinguish his regulatory scheme from that of the New Deal by focusing on the latter's determination to give America a "planned economy" that would kill private enterprise.[24] The New Deal did incorporate some such planning—the Tennessee Valley Authority is one example—but it was hardly in the mainstream of New Deal reform. In truth, by the mid-1930s, there was little to differentiate Hoover's scheme for government regulating business, or what he also called the "American system of regulation," from Roosevelt's New Deal.

Lippmann also tried his hand in the 1930s at defining a second new liberalism, and it was as muddled as Hoover's effort. Lippmann called for the regulation of capital markets, elimination of corporate monopolies, and government-initiated programs to help "farmers, workingmen, and consumers . . . increase their strength in the marketplace." A steeply graduated income tax system would recover the unearned income of the rich. These tax revenues would be used to fund social insurance programs for the disadvantaged and promote "a great equalization of incomes" across American society. Lippmann also called for public works to improve infrastructure and to conserve land and resources. To be sure, he objected to the dole and to government handouts. But that was because he wanted structural change that would eliminate "the conditions that made the poor."[25] Lippmann's concrete program, like Hoover's, looked like a version of the New Deal, even as he repeatedly told his readers that he abhorred New Deal "collectivism."[26]

The convergence between the reforms advocated by Roosevelt, on the one hand, and by Hoover and Lippmann, on the other, points to the underlying problem facing anyone seeking to construct a second new liberalism in the 1930s: How exactly would it distinguish itself from the first new liberalism? Through minor revisions of a New Deal–inspired regulatory scheme, which is what Hoover and Lippmann seemed to be offering in the 1930s? This hardly made for a compelling alternative to the New Deal; most voters could only have scratched their heads attempting to parse the differences. This lack of differentiation between the first and second new liberalisms may explain why Lippmann would soon largely abandon his interest in domestic reform and why Hoover would become, as noted, an irrelevant player in American politics.

Most scholars who have written about the origins of neoliberalism in Europe have ignored the difficulty encountered by Hoover and Lippmann in implementing a home-grown neoliberalism in America. This is strange given how profoundly Lippmann's 1937 book, *The Good Society*, was bound up with neoliberalism's official European launch in 1938. The French philosopher of science Louis Rougier organized the launch by gathering twenty-six people in Paris that year for the Colloque Lippmann, a workshop to discuss *The Good Society*, the book in which Lippmann had offered both a comprehensive history of liberalism and a road map for making liberalism an appealing and successful politics for the twentieth century's middle decades. What drew Rougier to *The Good Society* was Lippmann's condemnation of laissez-faire, which Lippmann and many others held responsible for liberalism's early twentieth-century decline. In Lippmann's eyes, the fatal mistake made by laissez-faire advocates was to think that markets were founded in nature and needed no superintending. To the contrary, Lippmann insisted, markets had never existed in the natural world. They had to be built by human hands and actively maintained. Market malfunctions would inevitably occur and require repair. By insisting that markets were natural creations and in need of no superintendence, laissez-faire dogmatists, Lippmann charged, had unwittingly freed up political space for the superficially attractive but actually wicked collectivisms of the right and left to take hold.[27]

Rougier found Lippmann's condemnation of laissez-faire invigorating. The task of Colloque Lippmann, as he saw it, was to build an active political program based on Lippmann's insight that markets had to be properly nurtured and superintended. Defining an active role for the state in stimulating and controlling markets would, in Rougier's eyes, define a new liberalism, a project that he and several of his European colleagues had begun to call "neoliberalism." Most participants in Colloque Lippmann shared Rougier's enthusiasm for Lippmann's insistence that markets were human creations that needed to be adjusted, fine-tuned, and transformed. But if they set as their task defining a program for managing markets, they reached no agreement on how to do it. The individuals who attended the Colloque harbored very different views about the degree and nature of state intervention. Several, such as Raymond Aron, Wilhelm Röpke, and Lionel Robbins, proposed projects that, in their calls for robust state intervention into the economy, looked a lot like the New Deal. The former Italian prime minister Francesco Saverio Nitti went further, calling explicitly for a fusion of liberalism and socialism. At the other end was Ludwig von Mises, who was suspicious of any Third Way and who wanted the purest market economy possible unleashed or restored. The cacophony of voices on the nature of this second new liberalism became the Colloque's defining feature, the participants united far more by what they disliked than what they thought should be done.[28]

The difficulty of defining the content of neoliberalism also shaped the second quasi-official founding moment of neoliberalism, the Mont Pèlerin, Switzerland, gathering in 1947, this one organized by Friedrich Hayek. The participants at Mont Pèlerin, under Hayek's leadership, were aware of the difficulty and intended to overcome it by making the Mont Pèlerin Society into an exceptionally disciplined and focused network of thinkers. Membership in the society was by invitation only; invitees were to be carefully vetted; new members were expected to pledge their affinity to market-based approaches to political economy. This emphasis on subscribing to certain principles of political economy and to developing and disseminating coherent policies for advancing these principles gave rise to the notion that neoliberals constituted a "thought collective."[29] But aspiring to being a thought collective and actually becoming one were two different matters. The 1947 Mont Pèlerin meeting was better organized and more productive than Colloque Lippmann had been, and it would succeed in giving its participants the tools to implant neoliberalism across western Europe and the United States. The neoliberal seeds sown in the United States by Chicago economist Milton Friedman and other American participants at Mont Pèlerin did sprout in the postwar era. These plantings grew tall and would bear fruit, especially once Hayek and von Mises arrived in the United States in the years after Mont Pèlerin to nourish them. But these Mont Pèlerin Society crusaders would never succeed in imparting to American neoliberalism a singular shape or meaning.[30]

For that reason, it may be better to understand postwar neoliberalism in America not as having a singular meaning but rather as having several. In fact, we can discern in American neoliberalism three quite distinct strategies of reform, or clusters of policy initiatives, each crystallizing in the twenty years between the first meeting of the Mont Pèlerin Society and the late 1960s, when the crackup of the New Deal order gave neoliberal reformers their opportunity to gain influence in American politics. The first strategy of reform was to encase free markets in rules governing property and exchange and the circulation of money and credit. Encasement required strong government interventions in economic life, both domestically and internationally. The second strategy was to apply market principles not just to those two areas traditionally identified as market driven (work and production, on the one hand, and income and consumption, on the other) but to all areas of human endeavor. Some neoliberals began extending market analysis into the private realm of family and morality, reimagining these spheres not, in Smithian terms, as preserves of human association and sensibility located at a safe distance from market forces, but as behavior best understood in economistic terms of inputs and outputs, investments and returns. The third strategy sought to recuperate the utopian promise of personal freedom embedded in classical liberalism. This strand privileged not order and control and the analysis of inputs and outputs, as did the first two strategies, but the thrill and adventure of throwing off constraints from one's person and one's work. Foucault had argued in his 1978–1979 Collège de France lectures on neoliberalism that this last strategy became particularly influential in America, drawing support from the left as well as the right, its "utopian focus . . . always being revived."[31] Let us look more closely at each of these neoliberal strategies.

The first strategy sought to construct an economic order that nourished markets both domestically and internationally. This strategy flowed from Lippmann's insight that markets were not naturally occurring phenomena but the product of human agency and organization. Markets had to be built and maintained by rules of property and exchange codified into law. The rules periodically required adjustment and sometimes, to use Lippmann's word, reconstruction, as unanticipated economic and social problems arose. Adjustment became central to the neoliberal creed: Markets needed monitoring and periodic correction to function properly. This work in turn required an active state, or a state strong in its ability to shape markets, domestic and international, and ultimately, the field of play on which workers and employers, buyers and sellers, encountered each other. Thus, neoliberalism, in this incarnation, cannot be adequately understood in terms of its desire simply to free economic activity from the heavy hand of the state. Neoliberals were clear that government interventions in the economy had gone too far in the 1930s and 1940s, and they were adamant in their efforts to liberate industry and capital from the grips of national legislatures that had become, in their eyes, overly indulgent of demands by organized labor and the poor. But neoliberals were committed to strengthening the state in other areas—by awarding it, for example, exclusive control of the money supply through a central bank or a kindred institution, such as the Federal Reserve. Neoliberals readily justified giving the government powers it had formerly lacked if such power could be demonstrated to ensure the smooth operation of markets.

This strategy was built on a paradox: namely, that government intervention was necessary to free individuals from the encroachments of government. Another way of framing the paradox is to note that the establishment of economic order, or what Hayek called a "constitution of liberty," was a prerequisite for making possible liberty of individuals from government.[32] To conceptualize the paradox in this way and, in particular, to introduce the word "order" as a critical dimension of a government's campaign to establish a liberal society is to reveal how much this "new" strategy of neoliberalism resembled an approach that classical liberals had embraced almost from the start. As Lippmann understood so well, liberals stretching back into the nineteenth century believed that the enjoyment of liberty required a certain level of political and economic order. And these liberals were willing to empower governments to impose order, economic and social, when and where it was perceived to be lacking.[33]

The second neoliberal strategy was more genuinely innovative: expand the terrain of human activities subject to market principles. In classical liberalism, *homo economicus*, "economic man," was defined as a man of exchange, who swapped his labor for a wage. The resulting income he then exchanged for goods in the marketplace that he either needed or desired. Much economic analysis revolved around how the two economic spheres of "production" and "consumption" were to be structured on both a micro and macro scale. Other realms of human existence—the family, religion, and politics—were thought to stand apart from these two major arenas of economic exchange and outside the realm of activity encompassed by *homo economicus*.

Neoliberals, however, began to argue that economic man could not be comprehended in such narrow terms. Rather, economic man was himself a repository of capital. He was the producer of his own wants and needs; he was what Foucault would later call "an entrepreneur of himself," "being . . . his own capital."[34] The concept of *homo economicus*, therefore, had to be expanded to include the various investments that such a man and others had made in his personhood. A capitalist of the self, *homo economicus* was always being called on to make decisions about how to deploy his capital so as to satisfy his needs and wants.

The elaborators of this approach organized their insights into what came to be called a theory of human capital. Those working with this approach who were interested in public policy took it upon themselves to dissect the human capital at each person's disposal: what it was, where it came from, to what ends it could be deployed. Acquiring such knowledge meant bringing into economic discourse aspects of human existence at one point considered separate from economic calculation: marriage, family, morality, education, even sports. Already in the 1940s, a group of neoliberals, based in Freiburg, Germany, and calling themselves ordo-liberals, were pioneering this form of analysis. They would become influential in setting social and government policy in postwar West Germany.[35] In the 1950s and 1960s, this kind of thinking spread to the United States and in particular to elements of that part of the Chicago School of Economics developing under the leadership of Gary Becker. Becker was among the first to subject to economic analysis aspects of human existence, most famously the family, that until that time were thought to belong to a private sphere of life insulated from the hurly-burly character and contractual imperatives of the marketplace.[36]

Not surprisingly, turning private life into a branch of behavioral economics divided scholars and critics. A libertarian French-Canadian economist, Jean-Luc Migué, wrote excitedly in 1976 about the potential of this development, using a human capital analysis of household relations as an example of the large dividends it could yield. "One of the great recent contributions to economic analysis," he wrote, "has been the full application to the domestic sector of the analytical framework traditionally reserved for the firm and the consumer." It was fitting to treat the household in the same way as one would treat a classical firm, Migué argued, for "what is the household, if not the contractual engagement of two parties to furnish specific 'inputs' and to share, in given proportions, the benefits of the combined 'output?'" Just as firms benefited from ordering relations between employers and employees through contracts, Migué wrote, so too "the two parties [of a household] settle the general terms of the exchange in a long-term contract." The alternative was to engage "incessantly and expensively [in] renegotiating and supervising the innumerable contracts inherent in the exchanges of everyday domestic life."[37]

The political theorist, Wendy Brown, surveying the spread of behavioral economics across the forty years after Migué wrote these words, came to a much less sanguine conclusion about the effects of this neoliberal governing strategy. "Neoliberalism," she wrote in 2015, "transmogrifies every human domain and endeavor, along with humans themselves, according to a specific image of the economic. All conduct is economic conduct; all spheres of existence are framed and measured by economic terms and metrics, even when those spheres are not directly monetized." Brown abhorred the transformation of all human encounters and aspirations into questions of capital. She condemned as oppressive the *homo economicus* "tasked with improving and leveraging its competitive positioning and with enhancing its (monetary and nonmonetary) portfolio value across all of its endeavors and venues."[38] Understanding individuals in this way, Brown charged, privileged instrumental living of the crudest sort. The human aspirations that Brown treasured the most—justice, equality, democracy, and fairness, among them—suffered accordingly.

One can find prefigurations of broad-based economistic thinking in the nineteenth-century writings of Jeremy Bentham and his followers in Britain, but of a rudimentary sort. We might designate Bentham's calculus of increasing pleasure and minimizing pain as an early form of this economizing. Bentham, however, did not have the tools for collecting data that would be available to the neoliberals 150 years later; nor did his conception of man as a rather simple pleasure-pain machine come anywhere near the sophistication of Becker's notion of the individual as an entrepreneur of the self, always looking to balance inputs and outputs for the sake of maximizing his capital and return on it.[39] This strategy of neoliberalism really did mark a new departure.

The German ordo-liberals who were among the pioneers of this economistic analysis recognized early on the amoralism imbedded within it. Extending economic analysis across the entire terrain of human existence and subjecting the most intimate aspects of household and private life to input-output analysis might well undercut the place of love, virtue, and compassion in the understanding of human affairs. The German ordo-liberals believed they could parry this threat by encasing their pioneering economic analyses in a proper "political and moral framework."[40] Wilhelm Röpke, a prominent figure in their ranks, outlined such a framework, calling on fellow ordo-liberals to be guided by community and cooperation, and to privilege integration over individualism. Embedding ordo-liberalism in a moral frame capable of influencing individuals' decision-making, however, turned out to be hard work. Ordinary Germans, Röpke believed, could handle this responsibility, as could most other European peoples, because all of them were heirs to a rich western, Christian, and moral civilization. But Röpke increasingly doubted the ability of the races and nations beyond Europe's borders to flourish in the kind of liberal market-economy he was so intent on creating. By the 1960s, he had become a notorious supporter of apartheid in Rhodesia and South Africa, declaring black Africans unsuited for the "free" yet morally disciplined society he was so intent on creating. Only the Calvinist-descended Afrikaners and their white supporters were capable, in Röpke's eyes, of generating the required discipline in that portion of the African continent.[41]

The American neoliberals around Becker were less troubled by moral dilemmas that the economizing of social life was likely to generate. Thus, they were less consumed in the 1960s by the contradictions in which Röpke found himself ensnared, and they were more radical in their determination to analyze every human relationship in economistic terms. The United States became the undisputed home of the human capital revolution at this time. But as the construction of a neoliberal economy in the United States advanced across the 1970s and 1980s, and as deregulation privileged market forces and weakened the social ties that had been so important to establishing a "good society," American neoliberals themselves had to reckon with the problem of moral corrosion that had preoccupied Röpke and other ordo-liberals. By the 1980s and 1990s, the color line began to loom as large in the reckoning of some in their ranks as it had for Röpke in South Africa.[42]

The first two strategies of neoliberalism emphasized order, control, encasement, technocracy, and manipulation. The third strategy promised something else: recuperation of the promise of personal freedom that had so undergirded classical liberalism. This strand privileged not order and control but the thrill and adventure of throwing off constraints from one's person. Classical liberals had discerned in markets extraordinary dynamism and sought to liberate them from encumbrances, especially those imposed by governments. They wanted to endow individuals with the freedom to pursue their self-interest and fortune. They regarded their motivations as emancipatory; they aspired to a world transformed by personal liberty and by a system of "free" economic exchange.

As neoliberal thinking began to migrate from the salons of the Mont Pèlerin Society and the University of Chicago into districts of American politics, this dimension of neoliberal reform loomed larger and larger. Those who embraced it imagined that they were reconnecting their nation to the promise of freedom embodied in the American Revolution. They called for releasing American individuals from constraints and encouraging them to pursue opportunity and reinvention. This strategy of neoliberal reform promised wealth to the entrepreneurially minded, of course; but it also promised to make available to everyone a special kind of freedom, one that would allow individuals the liberty to structure their lives independent of the heavy hand either of large corporations or of a large regulatory state. The Cold War gave this pursuit of freedom both priority and urgency. The struggle could not wait; Americans were cautioned not to be deluded by the affluence that the prosperous but overly managed US economy of the 1950s had put within their grasp. Communism was a dire threat to American liberty; the regulated capitalism of the New Deal, now supported by a Republican president (Eisenhower), was the Trojan Horse through which communism would enter the United States and destroy the liberty-loving civilization that generations of Americans had painstakingly built there.

These were the arguments that Henry Hazlitt, the *Newsweek* columnist and Mont Pèlerin Society member, was making in the 1950s.[43] These were also the claims that Milton Friedman was circulating through his writings, especially his celebrated treatise *Capitalism and Freedom*, first published in 1962.[44] The politicians who most insistently sounded this alarm were Barry Goldwater and Ronald Reagan. In the early 1950s, they were marginal figures in American politics. Goldwater was a department store owner and US senator from the thinly populated state of Arizona who had become convinced that the New Deal, with Eisenhower's acquiescence, was destroying American freedom. Reagan was rescued from his stalled acting career by General Electric, which hired him to host *General Electric Theatre*, a TV show that aired every Sunday night from 1954 to 1962. This theater variety show was not itself political, but GE also asked Reagan to be its goodwill ambassador for twelve weeks a year, with the aim of visiting all of its 125-plus facilities in the United States and engaging with most of the corporation's 250,000 employees. Reagan was still a Democrat when he started working for GE, but his perception of the Soviet Union's aggression, his reading of Hayek and Hazlitt on the long train rides from one GE facility to another (he did not like to fly), and his interaction with all kinds of GE middle managers pulled him further and further to the libertarian right. Goldwater and Reagan vaulted to the forefront of American politics in 1964 when Goldwater shockingly bested moderate Republican Nelson Rockefeller for the GOP nomination in July of that year and when Reagan was conscripted three months later to deliver a nationally televised speech to bolster the Goldwater campaign when it began to flag.[45]

Goldwater's ascent is often framed in terms of his opposition to the Civil Rights Act of 1964 and his consequent ability to capture the votes of the white George Wallace legions who wanted to preserve rather than destroy white supremacy in America. No doubt there is truth to this framing. But it also slights the actual content of Goldwater's nomination acceptance speech to the GOP, in which he focused not on race but on restoring to America the creative, entrepreneurial spirit that Goldwater regarded as the nation's birthright. In this speech, Goldwater targeted not civil rights protesters or rioters but the New Dealers, abetted by Republicans like Eisenhower, who had created a society of regulatory excess suffocating to the human spirit. "Our Republican cause," Goldwater declared, was "not to level out the world to make its people conform in computer regimented sameness. Our Republican cause is to free our people and light the way of liberty throughout the world." What was the content of Goldwater's imagined "way of liberty?" The Arizona senator's key words were "diversity" and "creativity." Goldwater's diversity was not a forerunner of the multiculturalism that, within a decade, would become a Democratic Party shibboleth. But neither was it simply a code word for allowing the southern states to retain their "divergent" Jim Crow regimes, though that is undoubtedly what some white southerners in his audience heard. In Goldwater's mind, diversity mattered because it stimulated individuality and innovation. One had to allow individuals the liberty to follow their own inclinations; this license would trigger "an emancipation of creative differences." Goldwater understood that some individual roads to creativity would lead nowhere. But overall, a commitment to unleashing individual creativity would allow the nation to "again thrive upon the greatness of all those things which we, as individual citizens, can and should do." Men and women would once again "pursue the truth, strive to cure disease, subdue and make fruitful our natural environment, and produce the inventive engines of production, science, and technology."[46]

Worries about conformism in American society were widespread at the time, of course. Indeed, it had become the major motif of cultural critics, evident in such epoch-defining works as William H. Whyte, *The*

Organization Man; David Reisman, *The Lonely Crowd*; C. Wright Mills, *White Collar*; Richard Hofstadter, *The American Political Tradition*; and Paul Goodman, *Growing Up Absurd*.[47] But such worries are usually associated with New Deal liberals and incipient New Leftists; the degree to which they had penetrated districts of the Republican Party is not well understood, nor have we grasped how much the Goldwater insurgency was bound up with emancipating the self from New Deal–imposed conformism. In other words, we can detect in Goldwater's words what Lippmann had called the "intoxicating promise" of classical liberalism.

It was a note that Reagan was striking as well. In a 1957 commencement speech at his alma mater, Eureka College in Illinois, he criticized New Deal liberals who were obsessed "with placing an economic floor beneath all of us so that no one shall exist below a certain level or standard of living." Reagan's quarrel was not with the construction of a bottom floor, per se, but with the determination of these same "well-meaning people" to build "a ceiling above which no one shall be permitted to climb." Reagan also bemoaned the fact that between the floor and ceiling, all Americans were being pressed "into conformity, into a mold of standardized mediocrity." Such pressures threatened to negate the "rare qualities of courage and imagination" that had nourished generations of American pioneers.[48]

It mattered that both Goldwater and Reagan identified so strongly as Westerners, Goldwater as a native son and Reagan as an adopted son. The West in their imagination was a place where a man could throw off convention and pursue individuality without constraint; where he could create a society where there had been none; where American liberty and democracy were constantly being replenished and reborn. This way of thinking, of course, has been exposed as a myth. The West was not empty space. To the contrary, it was occupied by indigenous peoples and rival European empires. And its settlement required a lot more than the pluck of courageous individuals; it required as well large subsidies from the central government to build railroads and highways, to fund a military capable of defeating the Indians, and to develop water and energy infrastructure sufficient to support economic development. During the New Deal, the West received per capita government appropriations that exceeded those bestowed on any other region.[49] Yet, we should not forget Benedict Anderson's insight into myths: What matters is not simply whether they are true or false, but also the intensity with which they are believed.[50] The belief in the West as a frontier, as a place of freedom and reinvention, was and remains a powerful cultural and political force in America. And it was a force that propelled Goldwater's and Reagan's beliefs in the capacity of Americans to rediscover their freedom and cultivate their individuality. John F. Kennedy sought to appropriate this mythology for himself and his party when he famously declared in his 1960 acceptance speech to the Democratic Party Convention that "we stand today on the edge of a New Frontier."[51]

Friedrich Hayek was himself interested in cultivating freedom and individuality, even as this cultured central European never warmed to the idea of frontier living. Hayek had come to America in 1950 to take up a post in economics at the University of Chicago. Between 1950 and 1960, he wrote and published his magnum opus, *The Constitution of Liberty*, a rigorous analysis of the building blocks that had to be in place to create and nourish liberal regimes. Throughout the book, Hayek emphasized the importance of establishing a constitutional order, by which he meant "a government of law not men," one in which rights to free speech, assembly, and mobility, to own private property, and to choose one's line of work were sacred. But Hayek also stressed again and again that a constitutional order must create a society in which individuals acquired the freedom to be unscripted, to create, and to innovate. Many efforts at innovation, Hayek conceded, would fail. But some would succeed, and through their success would yield advances of great importance for both economic growth and personal fulfillment. Which future creations would yield the most dividends, Hayek made clear, were unknowable in any human present. The unknowability and unpredictability of the future explain why Hayek had set his face so determinedly against the planned economy. Humans could only plan for what they already knew; they could not plan for what was not yet knowable.[52]

Cultivation of what Hayek called "spontaneity" was, in his eyes, the only way to prepare for the unknowable future—that, and cultivating a market economy that would reward acts of spontaneity. Hayek sprinkled the word "spontaneity" throughout *The Constitution of Liberty.* He called it "the essence of liberty." It speaks to the same phenomenon that Goldwater highlighted through his emphasis on creativity and diversity. Hayek never developed much interest in the American West; he never would have joined Theodore Roosevelt for a restorative visit to a "dude ranch." In fact, he never really adjusted to life in America; in 1962, he would return to Mittel Europa. Yet his discomfort in America never dented his admiration for what he called the "Anglican theory of liberty," originating in England and then traveling to America with legions of British settlers. This ideology, more than any other, he believed, had done the most to nurture spontaneity.[53]

Hayek also regarded the US Constitution of 1789 as the governing framework that, of all those then in existence in the world, best nurtured freedom. The American experiment in freedom had acquired its foundation the moment the Constitution was ratified; it was to be cherished and celebrated.[54] In this regard, Hayek, Reagan, and Goldwater were all singing from the same hymn book. This third strategy of neoliberal reform differed from the first two strategies, which had emphasized control, political and ideological. If we want to understand the power of the neoliberal ideology, we must grasp its desire not just for control but to re-inject freedom, spontaneity, and unpredictability into politics, society, and economics. This desire is what Hayek meant when he talked about creating the conditions in which the unexpected, the brilliant, and the revelatory could occur.

This third strategy of neoliberal reform helps us to see what scholars have largely ignored: neoliberalism's appeal in America to the left, specifically the New Left. Allen Ginsberg had sounded the tocsin for rescuing humanity from the deadening hand of modernity, which he saw in terms of capitalism, materialism, and monotony, each contributing to the crushing of the human spirit. He inveighed against these enemies in his startling 1956–1957 poem, *Howl,* especially where he described the worship of the false god Moloch that had so undermined the possibility of human existence: "Moloch whose mind is pure machinery! . . . Moloch whose love is endless oil and stone! Moloch whose soul is electricity and banks! . . . Moloch! Moloch! Robot apartments! invisible suburbs!"[55] Paul Goodman, expressed similar sentiments, albeit in more restrained prose, in his 1960 book, *Growing Up Absurd,* which would become an inspirational text to America's left-leaning youth. "In our society,"

Goodman declaimed, "bright, lively children, with the potentiality for knowledge, noble ideals, honest effort, and some kind of worth-while achievement, are transformed into useless and cynical bipeds, or decent young men trapped or resigned early, whether in or out of the organized system." This deterioration among the youth had occurred, Goodman went on, "by the mutual accommodation of both 'liberals' and 'conservatives' in the interests of creating our present coalition of semimonopolies, trade unions, government, Madison Avenue, etc."[56] America's over-regulated society was deadening the human spirit. Like Reagan, Goldwater, and Friedman, Goodman pined for "the heroic age of capitalist enterprise" when young men could aspire to being something other than an organization man, and to land "a real job that you could risk your soul in and make good or be damned."[57]

A similar dismay with the present was a central feature of the *Port Huron Statement*, the manifesto composed by a group of radical university students who had gathered on the shores of Lake Michigan in 1962 to establish a New Left. "The decline of utopia and hope," the student authors declared, "is in fact one of the defining features of social life today. The reasons are various[:] the congressional stalemate makes men narrow their view of the possible; the specialization of human activity leaves little room for sweeping thought; the horrors of the twentieth century, symbolized in the gas ovens and concentration camps and atom bombs, have blasted hopefulness. To be idealistic is to be considered apocalyptic, deluded. To have no serious aspirations, on the contrary, is to be 'tough-minded.'"[58] The aim of the New Left was to rekindle serious human aspirations, to recover the capacity to imagine and then strive for utopia, and to render American society both genuinely democratic and alive.

There was far more in the *Port Huron Statement* on the horrors of war and of the atomic bomb than one would find in the treatises of the neoliberal right. And there was no pining, as there was in Goodman, Reagan, and Friedman, for the swashbuckling days of nineteenth-century free market capitalism. Capitalism had to be superseded, not restored. But both left and right, in their new incarnations, shared a deep conviction that the organized and bureaucratized society—what the New Left would come to label and condemn as "The System"—had become the signature feature of the New Deal order and that it was suffocating the human spirit. Many New Leftists increasingly equated New Deal liberalism with what they now called "corporate liberalism"—a liberalism dominated by the very corporations that the New Deal had promised to bring to heel. In the demonstrations surrounding the Free Speech Movement at the University of California, Berkeley, 1964, one of the first events to bring this New Left national attention, a popular placard slogan declared, "I will not be folded, spindled, or mutilated." This was a riff on the signature—"Do not fold, spindle, or mutilate"—that appeared on every $7^3/_8$ by $3^1/_4$ inch punch card, thousands of which were then required to run even the simplest programs on every IBM mainframe computer. Berkeley students were expressing their anger at being mere cogs in a giant machine, as undifferentiated in the eyes of university administrators and professors as a stack of 1,000 indistinguishable punch cards. IBM, fancying itself the most modern and most innovative of American corporations, now stood accused of undermining individuality through regimentation of the most tyrannical sort.[59]

As with those who were leading the insurgency in the Republican Party, much of the earliest noise surrounding the New Left came out of the West, and especially California, the Bay Area in particular. Berkeley, of course, was an institution critical to the incubation of the New Left; so was Haight-Ashbury, the district of San Francisco in which hippie culture was born and flourished. California, for the left as well as for the right, was a place for dreaming, for shedding past identities, and for reinvention.[60]

Given that similar sentiments were percolating in districts both of GOP rebellion, soon to be styled the New Right, and of New Left insurgency, it is fair to ask: Was there any cross-pollination or coordination between the two groups? Not much, not even on campuses, where a vehicle for GOP insurgency, the Young Americans for Freedom, was as large a force in the early 1960s as Students for a Democratic Society, the organization founded shortly after Port Huron to fight for New Left goals. But there were at least three points of intersection.

The first were the novels of Ayn Rand. A refugee from the Soviet Union whose life had been upended by the Bolshevik Revolution of 1917, Ayn Rand (nee Alyssa Rosenbaum) dedicated her life to fighting not just communism but all government-sponsored reforms, such as those embodied in the New Deal and the welfare state, that (in her view) threatened to impose the tyranny of collectivism on America. Rand's fame rested on her literary success, notably two novels she published in 1943 and 1957, *The Fountainhead* and *Atlas Shrugged*. By the 1960s, the novels had sold millions of copies.[61]

At the heart of each novel was a singular male character, architect Howard Roark in *The Fountainhead* and engineer John Galt in *Atlas Shrugged*, of uncommon ability, drive, vision, and with soaring levels of testosterone. Rand portrayed Roark and Galt as gifted individuals who, left to their own devices, would have achieved greatness both for themselves and for the American nation in which they lived. But both, in Rand's telling, had been stymied by "second raters" and their enablers—corporate and government elites among them, who preferred a regimented, predictable, and soul-stifling society to the pursuit of genius, adventure, and innovation.

Rand's formal political affiliations were firmly on the right. Across the 1940s and 1950s, she sought out and was invited into coalescing neoliberal and libertarian circles, connecting, for example, with Henry Hazlitt, the *Newsweek* columnist who had become a sharp critic of Eisenhower's acquiescence to the New Deal, and von Mises himself, who liked her politics and her fiction.[62] But Rand's constant railing in her novels against what the New Left called "the system," for its alleged role in suffocating the talents and aspirations of individuals, also intrigued many who regarded their politics as lying closer to the center or to the left side of America's political spectrum.

Rand's novels spoke as well to the quest for sexual liberation coursing its way through the ranks of the young. Rand's writing was sexually charged. Her "masters of the universe" were marked not just by the brilliance of their minds but by the unstoppable force of their libidos. Sexual encounters between main characters were always on the verge of breaking out. Rand cast her male leads as tall, square-jawed, Protestant men: powerful, irresistible, dominant. She had assimilated this sexist (and white Anglo-Saxon Protestant) vision of male prowess into her way of thinking during her years working as a screenwriter in 1930s Hollywood and had transposed it to her 1940s and 1950s fiction. Rand's female characters were no simple replicas of 1930s cinematic stereotypes, however. Though women in Rand's novels were expected, in the final analysis, to submit to male power, they were granted a level of sexual desire and a freedom from the obligations of marriage, monogamy, and domesticity that received little expression elsewhere in 1930s, 1940s, and 1950s popular or middlebrow culture. Rand granted the women of her novels the sort of independence she ardently sought for herself.

Some female as well as male readers, then, were able to find in Rand's fiction affirmation for their quest for individuality and freedom in a world that appeared to be suffocating their talents and aspirations. Affirmation of this sort was especially attractive to adolescents and young adults, themselves brimming with irrepressible sexual energy, much of it now sanctioned by the New Left's commitment to "sexual liberation."

Thus, Rand's parables celebrating the subversion of societal roles deemed injurious to the human spirit could be mobilized to support positions on the left as well as on the right. The cultural studies scholar Lisa Duggan has written about the "voluminous correspondence" testifying "to the appeal of Rand's novels" across a broad range of adolescents, including in later decades, those seeking a feminist and queer politics. The legal scholar and Obama administration official Cass Sunstein has confessed his own enchantment with Rand when he encountered her fiction in the 1960s as a teenager. Sunstein's Rand attraction did not last long. The transitory nature of Rand's appeal probably describes a lot of teenage encounters with her fiction. Rand was a "mean girl," to use Duggan's language, whose contempt for ordinary people, amply displayed in her novels, could begin to grate. Nevertheless, Rand's literature opened a door for young people of various political orientations struggling to find meaningful individuality in a world they perceived as overly regulated and stultifying.[63]

The second point of intersection between the New Left and the New Right in the 1960s was a journal, *Left and Right: A Journal of Libertarian Thought*, launched by Murray N. Rothbard in 1965. Rothbard was a New York–born thinker who grew up in the 1930s and 1940s immersed in the currents of socialist and communist thought then coursing through his extended Jewish immigrant family. As an adult, Rothbard repudiated his leftist upbringing, making himself a disciple of von Mises (and for a brief period one of Rand's as well, before he fell out with her) and a relentless advocate for establishing a market economy free of government meddling of any sort. Rothbard became a self-proclaimed libertarian, a diehard opponent of the organized economy and military-industrial complex that the New Deal order and the Cold War had spawned, and an architect (in the 1970s) of the Koch brothers–supported Cato Institute. His chief aim was to shrink to Lilliputian size the American Leviathan that had made possible the New Deal order. Only then would America's great tradition of liberty, forced by the New Deal to gasp for air, revive.[64]

In the 1960s, Rothbard found interlocuters in the ranks of the New Left who shared his antipathy to the centralized state both for its alleged role in allowing corporations to dominate economic policy and for the military adventurism that both the New Left and the libertarian New Right saw as a product of the country's military-industrial complex. He persuaded only a few New Leftists to write for his journal before it folded in 1968. But one of these New Right-New Left collaborations endured: a book that Rothbard coedited with then New Leftist Ronald Radosh, *A New History of Leviathan: Essays on the Rise of the American Corporate State*.[65] In this book, published by a large commercial house in 1972, Rothbard and Radosh brought together a glittering constellation of first-generation New Left scholars—William Appleman Williams, Martin Sklar, and James Gilbert among them—with Rothbard-style libertarians. The resulting volume of essays became a foundational text for a new vector of interpretation, labeled the "corporate liberal school," that would significantly influence the writing of American political history across the next quarter century.[66]

The third point of intersection would be slower to materialize but more consequential than the first two: one that began to take shape in Silicon Valley, where new forms of venture capitalism were linking up with young engineers imbued with a New Left, and sometimes New Age, belief in the liberating and transformative power of cyberspace. Steve Jobs's career as a communard and "(apple) tree-hugging" hippie at Reed College is well known, an experience seen as a crucial prelude to his capacity to imagine a new world of freedom arising out of the personal computer. Stewart Brand, the man who invented the phrase "personal computer" and who is credited with helping generations of nerds and hackers to imagine the full potential—and freedom—of cyberspace, spent time in the 1960s alternating between two enthusiasms: first hanging out with Ken Kesey's group of crazed "merry pranksters" and participating in the psychedelic parties Kesey was hosting at his home near the Stanford University campus; and second, publishing the *Whole Earth Catalog*, a paperback book of giant dimensions, each page packed with products and how-to information needed by individuals who were fleeing Moloch for communes where they could lead autarchic and self-sufficient lives.[67] The *Whole Earth Catalog* eliminated the advertising, brand promotion, and mindless captions that filled the pages of just about every other catalogue and magazine in the United States at the time. It abandoned the "Madison Avenue sell" and reification of commodities that such hard selling entailed. It rejected "the system" that had given rise to Madison Avenue. It consecrated itself instead to utility and to giving individual readers the knowledge they needed to advance their freedom. On the first page of the first *Whole Earth Catalog*, Brand had written these words: "A realm of intimate, personal power is developing—power of the individual to conduct his own education, find his own inspiration, shape his own environment, and share his adventure with whoever is interested."[68] Brand was then a man of the left; but Reagan, Goldwater, Hayek, and Friedman would have been hard-pressed to improve on Brand's articulation of this dimension of the neoliberal creed. Steve Jobs would later salute Brand—the libertarian, one-time hippie—as a crucial influence on him and would celebrate the *Whole Earth Catalog* as "Google in paperback form, thirty-five years before Google came along."[69]

The personal computer revolution was still incubating in the 1960s and would not begin breaking on American society with force until the late 1970s and early 1980s. But many of its architects considered themselves rebels inspired by 1960s political and cultural insurgency. They also understood that their success would depend on their ability not just to free their consciousness and ways of thinking from the dreaded IBM mainframe way of doing things but also to raise large amounts of cash from deep-pocketed venture capitalists. The resulting unions of hackers and capitalists would bring together the left and right versions of neoliberal ideology in particularly powerful ways. They would give Silicon Valley its character and showcase it as a demonstration of how classical liberalism's original promise to set men free to transform the world could be made concrete. The Silicon Valley story provides a window on many of the characteristics, anticipated and unanticipated, of the coming neoliberal order.

Fulfilling the potential of classical liberalism was only one strand of neoliberal thought. The others emphasized order, on the one hand, and careful management of the self as a vessel for human capital inputs and outputs, on the other. It was precisely this protean character of American neoliberalism that would give this creed extraordinary sway, able to operate on a broad terrain and assemble under its canopy diverse sets of actors.

Terminology will be something of a problem as we go forward, because so many of the advocates of free markets in America would end up calling themselves conservatives, largely a result of the theft of the liberal label by the Rooseveltian New Dealers fifty years earlier. That theft qualifies as one of history's great terminological heists.[70] Many of the principals in the story of neoliberalism's rise, as a result of the heist, ended up identifying themselves as conservatives. But *conservative* is not a good descriptor of the commitment to free market capitalism that lay at the heart of their worldview. Free market capitalism connotes dynamism, creative destruction, irreverence toward institutions, and the complex web of relations that imbed individuals in those institutions. This sort of capitalism, in other words, is the enemy of what conservatives in the classical sense value: order, hierarchy, tradition, embeddedness, continuity.

The principals in the neoliberal story understood all too well the poor fit between their worldview and a conservative worldview. "Because of the corruption of the term liberalism," Friedman wrote in 1962, "the views that formerly went under that name are now often labeled conservative. But this is not a satisfactory alternative. The nineteenth century liberal was a radical, both in the etymological sense of going to the root of the matter, and in the political sense of favoring major changes in social institutions. So too must be his modern heir."[71] Even as more and more people called Friedman a conservative, he refused the label, insisting throughout his career that he be considered either liberal or radical.

Hayek expressed similar discomfort. "It is necessary to recognize," he wrote in 1961, that what I have called 'liberalism,' has little to do with any political movement that goes under that name today [in America]." That term could no longer be repossessed, Hayek conceded, forcing true liberals like himself to scavenge for a different label. "What I should want is a word which describes the party of life, the party that favors free growth and spontaneous evolution. But I have wracked my brain unsuccessfully to find a descriptive term that commends itself." He rejected the alternative of "libertarian" as carrying the flavor of "a manufactured term and of a substitute."[72] And he rejected emphatically the term conservative.

This terminological rejection was not something that those active in American politics could afford. Goldwater and Reagan embraced the label conservative. But we should not mistake that embrace for an affiliation with classical conservative values of order, hierarchy, tradition, embeddedness, and continuity. They, like other neoliberals, wanted to shake things up. Neoliberalism is not a perfect term to describe their worldview. It had never been thus; from its origins in the 1930s and 1940s, those who took on the term were hemmed in by the success of the first group of new liberals—those led by Franklin Roosevelt to create the New Deal in America. But if neoliberals struggled with terminology, they would nevertheless be successful in pushing into the public eye ideas that would take down the vaunted New Deal order in the 1970s and 1980s and usher in what we must call the neoliberal age.

4

Ascent

BY THE EARLY 1970s, neoliberals had been laboring for decades to spread their gospel. But except for some breakout figures—Milton Friedman, Ronald Reagan, and Barry Goldwater among them—they had remained on the margins. And even the aforementioned individuals were seen as outliers, too isolated and extreme to constitute a majority political movement, let alone a political order. All that began to change across the 1970s, as the long economic recession generated frustration and fear. Wealthy donors imbued with neoliberal conviction found each other and candidates to whom they were willing to donate millions. They also established well-funded think tanks and charged them with developing policymaking muscle as quickly as possible. In Ronald Reagan they discovered a candidate who could carry their message to the American people with a popular touch that matched FDR's appeal. Powered to the presidency in 1980 by constituencies he had peeled away from the Democrats (whites in the South and white urban ethnics in the North), Reagan began to implement his neoliberal vision for American life across a broad front: deregulating the economy; stripping the government of power and resources; reshaping the courts and their jurisprudence; establishing new rules to "free" political conversation from the grip of establishment, and allegedly, New Deal–oriented, media; and cultivating a neo-Victorian moral code to gird Americans against the temptations of excess that were forever present in an economy given over to market freedom. Reagan's two terms were not sufficient to transform everything. But by the time he left office in 1989, he had profoundly altered the landscape of American politics. Money, votes, policies, jurisprudence, media influence, and a strong moral stance: These were all part of the architecture of an ascending neoliberal order. They came together under the presidency of Ronald Reagan.

A Neoliberal Call to Arms

The neoliberal ascent began innocuously enough. In 1971, Lewis Powell, then a successful corporate lawyer in Virginia, issued a call to arms in the form of a private memo he had sent to the head of the US Chamber of Commerce. Entitled "The Attack on the Free Enterprise System," the memo described as tyranny the comprehensive regulatory edifice that the New Deal order had built to manage capital, labor, finance, retirement, poverty, and the environment. "We in America already have moved very far indeed toward some aspects of state socialism," Powell lamented. "The experience of the socialist and totalitarian states demonstrates," he continued, that "the contraction and denial of economic freedom is followed inevitably by governmental restrictions on other cherished rights."[1]

The failure of the natural defenders of economic freedom in America, especially in the business community, to fight back upset Powell most of all. While the New Left was capturing the imagination of university students and their professors, and then the nation's media, corporate leaders had remained largely silent and supine. Such complacency, Powell insisted, had to end. Businesspeople and their allies had to become more outspoken, build organizations and campaigns to promote their values, and then vie for political power. "Such power," Powell declared, "must be assiduously cultivated; and . . . when necessary . . . used aggressively and with determination—without embarrassment." If businessmen failed in this endeavor, they might lose the fight for capitalism altogether.

At first, Powell's memo circulated only privately among select members of the business community. But Powell could not keep it private once Richard Nixon nominated him in 1971 to the Supreme Court. Soon after, a *Washington Post* columnist shared the content of Powell's memo with his readers. Liberally minded Americans were incensed that a jurist who presented himself as a moderate in the Senate confirmation hearings had "secretly" issued such a radical call to arms. But the public release of the Powell memo was a gift to the neoliberal movement for it served as a rallying point for the many businesspeople, intellectuals, and would-be policymakers who wanted to restore free enterprise and free markets to the center of American life. John M. Olin, a onetime chemical magnate who had established the Olin Foundation in 1953, now redoubled the efforts through his foundation to mount ideological defenses for free market capitalism. "The Powell memorandum," he wrote, "gives reason for a well organized effort to re-establish the validity and importance of the American free enterprise system."[2] Joseph Coors Jr., part of a team of brothers who owned the Colorado-based Coors Brewery Company, was also inspired by the Powell memo.[3] In 1973, he, along with Paul Weyrich, founded the Heritage Foundation as a think tank charged with promoting free market principles and policies. Heritage quickly developed ties to Mont Pèlerin circles through Edwin Feulner, a Hayekian acolyte and Mont Pèlerin Society member who would succeed Weyrich as Heritage president in 1977. Heritage established a reputation as the most politically aggressive think tank in the neoliberal firmament.[4]

Another neoliberal (and former Mont Pèlerin member), Murray Rothbard, was instrumental in founding the Charles Koch Foundation in 1974, soon to be rechristened the Cato Institute. Charles Koch was one of the four sons of Fred Koch, who had built his Kansas-based oil refining business, Koch Industries, into one of the country's largest and wealthiest corporate entities. Fred Koch was also a founding member of the John Birch Society and bequeathed the intensity of his right-wing political commitments to his sons. No think tank would outdo the Cato Institute in terms of its hostility to the New Deal order and the fierceness of its belief in libertarian principles.[5] Yet another think tank, the Manhattan Institute, founded in 1977, began supporting the work of George Gilder, whose celebration of free market capitalism, *Wealth and Poverty*, became one of the bibles of the Reagan administration and the emerging neoliberal order on its publication in 1981.

Liberals and leftists were slow to recognize the size and coordinated nature of this counter-offensive, in part because it was taking shape outside the districts in which they lived and worked. These districts included universities (and the college towns surrounding them), Georgetown salons, labor unions, institutions such as Brookings and the Ford and Carnegie foundations, newspapers such as the *New York Times* and the three television networks—ABC, CBS, and NBC—that dominated national broadcast media. They constituted a kind of New Deal order establishment, now pushed to the left by radical student movements. Powell's memo had, in essence, instructed supporters of the free market system to bypass this policy-media formation, thought to be contaminated by New Deal Keynesianism, on the one hand, and New Left "liberation," on the other. The call to arms was to build what the journalist Sidney Blumenthal long ago identified as a "counter establishment": think tanks that would rival the best universities as incubators of new ideas; newspapers, such as the newly free market–fierce *Wall Street Journal*, that would take on the *New York Times*; new forms of media, such as direct mail techniques pioneered by Richard Viguerie (and later, talk radio and cable TV), to counter the influence of the mainstream media, especially the three dominant television stations, seen as reflexively and dangerously liberal; and new forms of corporate political mobilization both to influence public policy and to raise money for pro-capitalist candidates.[6]

The Business Roundtable represented one novel form of corporate mobilization. Founded in 1972, it was meant to encourage the nation's largest and most respected corporations to develop a common political voice and to intervene in policy matters of urgent concern. In 1978, the Business Roundtable played a major role in defeating a labor law designed to strengthen unions in their organizing campaigns. The defeat came as a shock to organized labor, which thought it had the advantage in Congress. The labor movement had yet to take a full measure of Business Roundtable or the intensifying anti-labor corporate coalition readying itself for battle.[7]

Corporate political action committees (PACs) constituted a second new form of business mobilization. Campaign finance law changes in the 1970s had made it possible for individual corporations to ask their employees to contribute to a company's PAC, with decisions about which policies and political campaigns to support left in the hands of firm owners and executives. This rule change dramatically increased the potential for corporate influence, as the ceiling on the size of PAC contributions permitted by law was much higher than the amount a single wealthy individual could donate to a candidate. Justin Dart, owner of Dart Industries, a nationwide chain of drugstores based in southern California, grasped the financial punch that corporate PACs could deliver. He undertook a campaign that propelled almost 750 PACs into existence in less than five years (1974–1978), nearly a tenfold increase.[8]

For forty years, Dart had detested FDR and his enduring influence on American politics. Most of Dart's efforts since the 1930s to rid America of its New Deal order, however, had failed. But in Ronald Reagan he thought he had found a man who might succeed in doing so. Dart raised large amounts of money for Reagan's two gubernatorial victories in California, earning him a seat at Reagan's kitchen cabinet table. In the 1970s, he redoubled his efforts to get his man to the White House. Dart's ability to open corporate sluicegates and flood the GOP with PAC money contributed critically to sustaining Reagan during his long march to the White House.[9]

Dart's corporate organizing drew other businessmen and financiers to the banner of Reagan and neoliberalism. Among them was William Simon, a onetime partner in the Wall Street firm of Salomon Brothers, secretary of the treasury under Nixon and Ford, and longtime Ayn Rand devotee. In terms that closely echoed the challenge that Powell had laid down in 1971, Simon's 1978 manifesto, *A Time for Truth*, called for " 'a massive and unprecedented mobilization of the moral, intellectual and financial resources' of business to 'aid the intellectuals and writers' who were fighting on the side of capitalism." Neoliberal fingerprints were all over Simon's book. Ayn Rand disciple Edith Efron had ghostwritten it. Milton Friedman had supplied the preface, in which he hailed the book as "brilliant and passionate." Hayek had contributed the foreword, in which he declared that he "got so fascinated" by the book— high praise from the dour Viennese sage—that he read it from start to finish in one sitting.[10] Simon was explicit about his desire to bring Hayekian and Friedmanite ideas into American politics. "The alliance between the theorists and men of action in the capitalist world is long overdue," he declaimed. The National Association of Manufacturers and the National Federation of Independent Business delivered tens of thousands of copies of *A Time for Truth* to their members. The book also succeeded in the retail marketplace, elevated by the *Reader's Digest's* distribution network into a national bestseller. Simon would emerge as a key figure in the executive advisory committee of prominent businessmen formed to support Reagan's 1980 presidential run.[11]

Many businessmen who were intrigued with Reagan were not as radical as Simon and not bent, initially at least, on upending the New Deal order. Quite a number of them had long benefited from the rich set of government-business relations that the New Deal order had engendered. What, then, made them willing to consider the more radical path advocated by Reagan? Three factors stand out. First, the American economy performed poorly for much of the 1970s, its reputation for global preeminence now tarnished, the instruments in the Keynesian toolkit stiff and rusty. Second, the sharp escalation of foreign goods invading the US marketplace made many in corporate ranks less willing to tolerate the power of organized labor. Signing on to high wages and benefits as a matter of course, the precedent set by the 1950 Treaty of Detroit, had become a more costly venture in the age of renewed international competition and minuscule productivity increases.[12] Growing suspicions that the Soviet economy was in decline, and thus that the communist system perhaps posed less of a threat, may also have signaled to the corporate titans of America they were now freer to adopt a more antagonistic stance toward labor unions. Indeed, the Business Roundtable's mobilization to defeat the labor reform act of 1977 was a novel, even shocking, move by corporate America in an industrial relations system still ostensibly governed by the rules hammered out in the Treaty of Detroit thirty years earlier.[13]

The third reason propelling businessmen toward Reagan was their unhappiness about the steady creep of government regulations that neither the recession of the 1970s nor the political leadership of America, Republican or Democratic, seemed capable of stalling or reversing. In 1970, a Republican president, Nixon, had signed into law the Occupational Health and Safety Act, giving the federal government unprecedented power to monitor workplaces. That same year Nixon signed into law the Environmental Protection Act, giving the federal government vast new powers to regulate air, water, and soil quality. Nixon was very much still Eisenhower's lieutenant, acquiescing, as his boss had done previously, to the regulatory economic principles of the New Deal order.

The most consequential effort to extend government regulation occurred in matters of race. The effort to achieve racial equality arguably was the greatest social engineering project undertaken by the US central state in the second half of the twentieth century. Schools and public accommodations had to be integrated, states had to be stripped of long-held powers that had allowed them to discriminate against racial minorities in employment, and poverty, which had disproportionately affected minorities, had to be reduced. To this already formidable list, we must add an effort that hit businessmen, large and small, in the solar plexus: a systematic effort on the part of government to eliminate racial and other forms of discrimination from the workplace.

The crucial initiative in this regard was President Lyndon Johnson's executive order 11246, little noticed when it was issued in 1965, which barred employers from "discrimination in employment decisions . . . on the basis of race, color, religion, sex, or national origin." The executive order affected contractors with fifty-one or more employees and doing business with the federal government worth more than $50,000 per year; they were required to develop affirmative action plans, based on whether analysis of their hiring practices showed disparities between the percentages of qualified minority and female applicants and the percentages actually hired. These new rules applied to thousands of employers who together (in the 1960s) employed 23 million workers spread out among 73,000 work sites. The federal government had never before subjected so many employers to such intense scrutiny on matters involving racial or sex discrimination. A number of subsequent laws, including the Equal Opportunity Employment Act of 1972 and the Age Discrimination in Employment Act of 1974 (also signed into law by Nixon), significantly widened the range of discriminatory behavior subject to federal government oversight.[14]

Altering hiring patterns necessitated counting and categorizing individuals by their race, gender, and other descriptive characteristics. Not surprisingly, counting schemes proliferated, prompting the Office of Management and Budget in 1977 to issue Statistical Directive 15, which instructed all federal agencies to employ five racial categories: white, black, American Indian, Asian and Pacific Islander, and Hispanic, the so-called ethnoracial pentagon.[15] Penalties for non-compliance were substantial enough to persuade private institutions receiving federal funds to overhaul their hiring practices to ensure, at the least, the appearance of compliance.

While many corporations were not enthusiastic about this racial engineering project, they adjusted to its imperatives quite well. As hiring and performance review systems became necessarily more formal and more complex, corporations increasingly turned to human relations experts who, grouped into discrete human relations (HR) departments, professionalized the drive to standardize racial classification and anti-discrimination practices in industry. This new system had sunk such deep roots into corporate America by the early 1980s that Business Roundtable and their allies actually rebuffed Reagan's radically libertarian 1985 proposal to tear it up and rescind the original 1965 executive order that had first given it life.[16]

Smaller corporations and small businessmen, however, found the adjustment to this new regime much tougher. Their margins for profit were smaller, and the resources available to make a success of this new regime were more limited. Smaller businessmen could not afford human relations experts or HR departments. Meanwhile, a certain segment of the business community, particularly company owners who regarded their enterprises as family-run firms (even in instances when those firms had become huge or largely passed into the hands of non-family stockholders), were simply outraged by the numbers of federal regulators coming at them in the 1970s from so many different directions. The Koch brothers who ran Koch Industries fit this profile of the family-led firm, as did the Coors brothers who were in charge of the Coors Brewery Company, and Joseph Olin who ran Olin Industries. Barry Goldwater himself had regarded the ownership of his chain of department stores headquartered in Phoenix (Goldwater's Department Stores) in similarly proprietary terms.

These individuals viewed their businesses as having been built with family blood, sweat, and tears. They interpreted their economic success as a reflection of their gumption, talent, and forbearance, on the one hand, and of America's commitment to free enterprise, on the other. The notion that great reward awaited those taking great risk was central to their understanding of the American dream. They regarded the inspectors of the National Labor Relations Board, the Occupational Health and Safety Administration, the Environmental Protection Agency, and the Equal Employment Opportunity Commission who came knocking on their doors as a fifth column of communist agents seeking to destroy their freedom. They saw these government officials as the leading edge of communist tyranny or, in Lewis Powell's words, of "state socialism."[17]

The anger among these proprietary capitalists at government and the New Deal order gave the Reagan revolution its radical edge. Its members never ceased being inspired by Barry Goldwater's declaration in his 1964 acceptance speech that "extremism in defense of liberty is no vice." No expense was to be spared in mounting this defense, which is why the Kochs, the Coorses, and their ilk were investing large sums from their personal fortunes into foundations, PACs, and candidates that, in their eyes, might save their enterprises and the American system of freedom that had made them possible.[18]

Electoral Triumph

The historian Steve Fraser once observed that the New Deal order had existed as an ideology, as a distinct political formation, and as a series of interlocking relationships bringing together activists, intellectuals, politicians, and donors long before it came to power in the 1930s.[19] We might say something similar about the neoliberal order: The constituent parts of this order—the capitalist donors, the intellectuals, the think tanks, the politicians, the media, and the personal networks linking them together—were all visible in the 1970s. The speed with which the neoliberal order implanted itself on politics in the 1980s is inconceivable without what we might call the "silent phase" of its construction.

Yet there is nothing predetermined about a potential order's triumph, nothing that says that because a leadership team has been groomed, coffers filled with funds, and think-tank file cabinets stuffed with ambitious policy plans, a general staff thus assembled would triumph once given the chance to fight. That chance depends on a president and a party able to marshal an army and lead it to victory at the polls.

In Reagan, the leadership staff had found its general. New Deal America had not taken Reagan's rise seriously. In retrospect, this appears puzzling. Reagan was not a Carter-like figure, a man who at some point in the middle of life decided to dabble in politics. Reagan had been preoccupied with politics since the late 1940s. He had immersed himself in Hayek in the 1950s. He had soared to national prominence in 1964 on the basis of his nationally televised speech giving full-throated support to Barry Goldwater. He had become governor of California in 1966, putting him on the front lines of resistance to the California anti-war, New Left, and black nationalist movements that he despised. He also used his two terms as California governor to experiment with welfare reform, stripping away benefits going to those he regarded as the "undeserving poor" and forcing them to become more responsible, he claimed, for their own economic well-being. He viewed all this work as a rehearsal for the prize he most ardently sought for himself and his party—to make himself president and to make his neoliberal philosophy the dominant one in America.[20]

Unlike Carter, Reagan was not indifferent to Franklin Roosevelt. To the contrary, he regarded FDR as the greatest president of his lifetime. As much as he had come to loathe the New Deal, Reagan urgently wanted to create a political order that could rival the New Deal in its power, appeal, and durability. FDR's presidency had been the country's first rendezvous with destiny; Reagan imagined that his would be the second.[21]

Reagan's surprising success in challenging a sitting president (Gerald Ford) in the 1976 Republican Party primaries should have served notice about the fire and energy gathering around him. And yet, Reagan's critics among the Democrats consistently belittled the seriousness of the man and his politics. Millions believed that Reagan's temperament and background as an actor (and a B-list actor at that) rendered him unfit for high office. He was widely disparaged as an intellectual lightweight. He was thought to be dim because he had trouble identifying a book he had read. He appeared to compensate for his ignorance with an extraordinary capacity to make things up: seeing the world as he imagined it should be rather than as it was. In the 1980 election campaign, he encouraged what looked like a reckless, nuclear brinkmanship with the Soviets.

Even after he became president, he could not stop himself from name-calling, even when those names insulted powerful nations.

People were alarmed when Reagan hurled the epithet "evil empire" at the Soviet Union or talked about arming NATO forces in Germany with tactical nuclear weapons. Did Reagan have any idea what he was doing? Or was he just playing out the narrative of *Star Wars*—Luke Skywalker versus Darth Vader—in real life? When he was not stirring up trouble in world affairs, he indulged his love for old world ceremony, much of it directed toward re-styling the White House to resemble the court of Marie Antoinette. And where did he get his idea of what the court of Marie Antoinette ought to look like? From the movie *Singing in the Rain*, of course. Reagan, not Trump, was the first fabulist to sit in the White House.[22]

But Reagan was also a serious man. Reagan really did want to bring the Soviet Union down, and he believed he could. He really did believe that the New Deal was a form of collectivist tyranny, and he thought he could bring that order down too. And electorally, he had a magic touch, couching his ambitions, political and personal, in compelling parables about American freedom and about imbuing the promise of American life with new vigor.

By 1980, the GOP had been a minority party in Congress for almost fifty years. Only two Republicans were elected president during that half century, Dwight Eisenhower and Richard Nixon, and both subscribed to the principles of the New Deal order.[23] In only two elections after 1932 did the party gain control of both Houses of Congress (1946 and 1952). Since the New Deal order had taken hold, Republican constituencies were not usually sizable enough to bring the GOP to national power. Reagan changed the party's political arithmetic by adding two new constituencies to the Republican base: white (and often evangelical) voters in the South and white ethnics in the North.

Until the 1960s, white southerners had been a pillar of the Democratic Party. They regarded the Republican Party as the party of slave emancipation and racial equality, both of which had brought ruin (in their eyes) to the antebellum southern society that their ancestors had so cherished. But the Democratic Party's pivot toward civil rights, beginning with the Truman administration in the late 1940s and culminating with the Johnson administration in the 1960s, caused many white southerners to forsake their Democratic loyalties. Some had turned to Strom Thurmond's Dixiecrats in 1948; many more turned to George

Wallace's defiantly segregationist campaign for the Democratic Party presidential nomination in 1964. Wallace's insurgency lasted long enough (he ran as the nominee of the American Independent Party in 1968) and enjoyed enough success to alert Republican Party operatives to a large white constituency in the South that might be looking for a new political home. Nixon crafted a political campaign to draw them to the GOP. He framed the Republicans as strong on law and order (and thus able to put down the racial insurrections then ripping through many American cities) and committed to states' rights and local control. While Nixon generally refused to call for a return to segregation in the South, his emphasis on states' rights signaled to white southerners that the GOP would look kindly on their desire to organize political and social life in their towns and states as they saw fit, irrespective of what federal bureaucrats might tell them to do.[24]

Religious resentment further contributed to the alienation of white southerners from the Democratic Party. The New Deal order had always leaned secular. Democratic administrations were stuffed with social scientists—university-trained and often university-employed economists, sociologists, political scientists, historians, lawyers—who put their stamp on Democratic Party policy. Many of these individuals were not anti-religious; they simply believed that science was a better guide to public policy than the Bible. And they also believed, as noted in Chapter 1, that the success of the Democratic Party depended on religion being kept out of the public sphere. This determination to keep religion at a distance from politics surfaced again and again in politics during the decades when the New Deal order ruled. One can even discern this mindset in Eisenhower when he declared in 1952 that America was a land of multiple faiths, all of them legitimate. All he asked of every American was that he or she walk in the path carved out by his or her god. Eisenhower, himself, was effectively urging Americans to make religion a private, and not a political, matter.[25]

A similar strategy informed the Warren Court's decision in *Engel v. Vitale* (1962) that state governments could no longer mandate prayer in public schools. Americans were to be free to worship at a church, synagogue, or mosque of their choice, the Court argued. But they were no longer to bring prayer into the schools where it would, the Court observed, lead to political conflict, with one faith trying to impose its tenets on those students adhering to other religions. The plaintiffs who brought the case were not atheists; rather they were Catholic and Jewish groups who believed that school prayer would invariably favor Protestants and their King James Bible. Better, in their eyes, to eliminate religion from public institutions altogether and consign it to the private sphere where faith in all its forms could flourish. The plaintiffs found in the First Amendment stipulation that government could pass no law "respecting an establishment of religion" the sanction to do so. The Supreme Court agreed.[26]

White evangelical Protestants were astounded by this decision. Schooling for them had always entailed educating the young in the ways of the divine. To now be barred from all such instruction was not just a sin against children and their parents; it was a sin against God himself. The *Engel* decision spurred anger at the Democrats; at the Court for interfering unconstitutionally with the operation of public schools, long seen as the province of local or state governments; and ultimately at the federal government for aggrandizing itself. George Wallace, newly elected governor of Alabama in 1962, condemned "this group of men on the Supreme Court," allegedly influenced by communist ideology, for "forbidding little school children to say a prayer."[27] Preacher Billy James Hargis later recalled feeling that "this was really the beginning of the end of America, that the country had turned its back on God, and that any country that did that couldn't stand."[28]

The anger generated by *Engel* festered across the 1960s and 1970s, little noticed at a time when the nation was preoccupied by racial division. As he geared up his campaign for the presidency, Reagan tapped into its existence and power. He understood that those who were angry about the exclusion of religion from public life were often the same people who were resentful of the changes in race relations being imposed on them from afar.

Reagan's greatest political achievement was to reconcile a politics focused on restoring white supremacy and godliness with his own neoliberal market orientation, with its emphasis on personal freedom and antagonism to the New Deal state. He did so by telling white southerners that the changes in American life that they loathed had been facilitated by a party of big government—the Democrats—that was strangling the cherished liberties of white Americans. In Reagan's telling, a cabal of liberal Washington institutions—the presidency under Johnson, Congress desperate for redemption in the wake of President John F. Kennedy's assassination, the Supreme Court under Earl Warren—had stripped the southern states of their customary way of life. Johnson's Great Society, Reagan alleged, had interfered with long-standing patterns of hiring in the South and North, both in private industries such as construction and in the police, fire, and other sectors of municipal employment. Worst of all, the Supreme Court had deprived religious Americans of the liberty to pray to God at the beginning of each school day.[29]

Reagan's genius was to hang a giant scarlet letter around the neck of the federal government, identifying it as a tyrannical force that had violated the freedoms Americans regarded as their birthright: to worship God in public; to hire the employees they desired; to live among people of their own race; and to send their children to the neighborhood school without fear that they would be bussed, for the sake of racial justice, to another school many miles away. Take away the regulatory power that the central state had amassed to itself during the over-reaching days of the New Deal and the Great Society, Reagan argued, and the social engineering initiatives of the federal government would simply collapse. The God-given liberties of Americans on matters of race, religion, and employment would then be quickly restored. Reagan, seemingly, had found a way to draw on conservative racial and religious fury to propel his anti-government, neoliberal agenda. That was quite a feat.

He found a partner in Jerry Falwell, who founded the Moral Majority in 1979 to promote Christian values in American politics and to help propel Reagan into the White House. Falwell had long immersed himself in Milton Friedman's writings; by 1980, he was willing to make the case that the Bible had instructed Christians to embrace free market capitalism. "The free-enterprise system is clearly outlined . . . in the Bible," Falwell declared. "Jesus Christ made it clear that the work ethic was a part of His plan for man. Ambitious and successful business management is clearly outlined as a part of God's plan for His People." Just as clearly, Falwell believed, big government was not only ruinous to the economy and religious liberty but contrary to biblical precepts.

Falwell was conscripting his evangelical followers into a major political campaign to take down the New Deal order.[30]

In 1980, Reagan crushed Carter both in the popular vote and in the electoral college, winning forty-four out of fifty states, almost as many as Reagan's hero Roosevelt had carried in the epic election of 1936.[31] Americans had never elected a president so hostile to the New Deal. White southerners flocked to Reagan. So, too, did many urban white ethnics in the North, locked in turf wars over jobs, homes, and political power with African Americans in deindustrializing manufacturing cities. These white ethnics would style themselves "Reagan Democrats." White southerners and white northern ethnics had been groups long devoted to the Democratic Party, pillars of the New Deal order. Their shift to Reagan in 1980 pushed him over the top. If the Republicans were to find a way to make these switches in party loyalty permanent, they would possess an electoral formula for making the GOP the majority party for a long time to come.[32]

Neoliberalism, Reagan-Style

Upon becoming president, Reagan quickly deployed neoliberal policies that had long been marinating in counter-establishment think tanks. One core policy was deregulation: removing government from the business of overseeing private industry. Jimmy Carter had already taken the first steps in this direction, rolling back the government's regulation of telecommunications, the airlines, and trucking. Reagan immediately targeted two pillars of the New Deal for deregulatory treatment: federal government support for collective bargaining and progressive taxation. In 1981, he fired more than 10,000 air traffic controllers who had gone on strike for better pay and improved working conditions. Reagan's bold move stunned the union, the Professional Air Traffic Controllers Organization, which had endorsed Reagan in the 1980 election. It signaled to all public and private employers that he would support a tougher stance toward unions than any administration had since the 1920s. In symbolic terms, his act carried as much significance as the refusal of the Democratic governor of Michigan and President Franklin Roosevelt in 1937 to send National Guard or federal troops to Flint to oust the autoworkers occupying the plants of General Motors.

This 1930s refusal signaled that a president and his party were serious about compelling corporations to reach fair agreements with unions that had organized their workers. Similarly, Reagan's firing of an entire workforce for going on strike was the equivalent of a president sending in the troops to break a strike. It served notice that the president and the dominant party were now ready to eviscerate labor's power. From that time forward, American workers who went on strike knew that they might well pay for their actions with the loss of their jobs. The American labor movement hemorrhaged members in the 1980s. The decline in labor membership is often not included in accounts of deregulation and neoliberal success. But, in fact, there is no more powerful form of market deregulation than stripping government of its ability to strengthen workers in their negotiations with employers.[33]

The Reagan administration was equally committed to undercutting America's high tax regime put in place by FDR and his supporters in the 1930s and 1940s and sustained by every president, Democrat and Republican, since. In 1981, Congress, under Reagan's prodding, passed the Economic Recovery Tax Act, which reduced federal income taxes by an average of 23 percent and that cut the highest marginal rate from 70 percent to 50 percent. A second tax bill, passed during Reagan's second term, further reduced the highest rate to 28 percent. In five years, then, Reagan and his congressional allies slashed the tax burden on America's highest income earners by a remarkable 60 percent. These were the opening acts of a GOP initiative to both dramatically reduce the progressivity of the taxation system and deny the federal government the revenue on which its size and future growth depended. Reagan believed that unions and a government bent on using tax revenues for purposes of redistribution harmed the operation of a free market, the productive use of capital, and thus the generation of growth and wealth. The American economy would flourish only when unions and a tax-rich government were brought to heel and, if possible, eliminated. A more direct assault on the principles of the New Deal order could scarcely be imagined.[34]

To further constrain the federal government, Reagan, on entering office, froze hiring at all civilian federal agencies and ordered them to refrain from issuing new regulatory rules. He appointed individuals known for their anti-government zeal to one federal department after another. Reagan authorized these administrators to curb rather than extend the federal government's regulatory reach. Donald Regan, Reagan's secretary of the treasury from 1981 to 1985, offers one example of the deregulatory work undertaken by Reagan appointees. Regan persuaded the Federal Home Loan Bank to allow savings and loan "thrift" associations, traditionally the most regulated sector of the financial industry, to redirect capital resources away from investments that were safe to risky ones that promised the highest yields. This experiment in freeing up the market did not go well. The savings and loans invested irresponsibly, leading by 1987 to a cascade of failures that required a $370 billion government bailout.[35]

Reagan was too much of a believer to be deterred by these failures or by the rough economic conditions that characterized his first two years. By 1983 and 1984, the economy showed improvement and Reagan won re-election in 1984.[36] His second term was notable less for legislation than for a determination to reconfigure key institutions, notably the courts and the media, in ways that would benefit the neoliberal revolution he had launched.

Reagan's attorney general, Edwin Meese, led the campaign to reshape the courts. A lawyer by training, Meese first came to Reagan's attention when he was working in the Alameda County (California) district attorney's office. Appointed as Governor Reagan's legal affairs secretary in 1967, Meese became Reagan's chief of staff in 1969, a position he held through the end of Reagan's governorship in 1975. Reagan chose Meese to chair his election campaign in 1980 and then to head his presidential transition team. Once in the Oval Office, Reagan appointed him special counselor to the president and, in 1985, attorney general. By the time he retired from public service in 1987, Meese had worked closely with Reagan for nearly twenty years.[37]

Shortly after becoming attorney general, Meese launched a jurisprudential assault on the Supreme Court. Meese charged that the Court under Earl Warren (1954–1969) had taken too many liberties in its interpretation of the Constitution in order to justify a "rights revolution" on the one hand and vast growth in the regulatory power of the central state on the other. The Constitution, Meese alleged, did not contain an implied right to privacy granting women access to birth control (and abortion); nor could the constitutional clause giving the federal government the right to control interstate commerce be interpreted to mean that it also endowed the central state with the authority to regulate every aspect of the economy, from manufacturing to civil rights, and from agriculture to the environment. In these instances, Meese charged, liberal judges were no longer ruling on whether or not legislation was constitutional. They were instead making law, thus usurping power that the Constitution had vested exclusively in Congress and in state legislatures. To counteract these tendencies, Meese called in 1985 for a "jurisprudence of original intention" that would require judges to abide by the actual meaning imparted to laws and constitutional articles by their framers.[38]

This emphasis on a strict construction of the Constitution had originated with a Yale law professor, Robert Bork, in the early 1970s. It then migrated to the University of Chicago, where another law professor, Antonin Scalia, became a supporter. Reagan's elevation of both Bork and Scalia to the US Court of Appeals for the DC Circuit in 1985, appointments often recognized as a stepping stone to the Supreme Court, signified the rising prestige of their views with Meese and other ideological architects of the Reagan revolution.[39]

Bork and Scalia initially were most perturbed by the Warren Court's use of rights language to sanction the goals of the liberation movements of the 1960s—especially civil rights and feminism. But as their critique of the Warren Court mixed with neoliberal currents at the University of Chicago, an even more radical challenge to liberal jurisprudence emerged, this one directed at the legal underpinning of the entire New Deal order. The full import of this challenge became apparent in the writing of Richard Epstein, a law professor at Chicago deeply enmeshed in the neoliberal networks dominant in the university's Department of Economics.

Epstein argued that the expansion of federal government power throughout the years of the New Deal order had rested on far too loose an interpretation of the Constitution's commerce clause. Since the late 1930s and early 1940s, liberal Supreme Court majorities had found in the federal government's power to control interstate commerce the authority to regulate not just commerce but manufacturing, industrial relations, social welfare, civil rights, and the environment. Epstein alleged, however, that the *original* regulatory import of the commerce clause, and one that jurists were obligated to respect, was far narrower. Properly construed, this clause limited the central government's regulatory authority to the realms of "interstate transportation, navigation, and sales," and nothing more. Epstein did not mince words: The expansive regulatory uses that New Deal judges and then Warren Court judges had made of the commerce clause were "extravagant" and constitutionally indefensible.

The logic of Epstein's position dictated that many of the regulatory institutions installed under the aegis of the commerce clause, from the National Labor Relations Act of 1935 to the Civil Rights Act of 1964 to the Environmental Protection Act of 1970, were jurisprudentially invalid. If America restored to the Constitution its proper meaning, much of the nation's regulatory state would need to be dismantled; in the process, market freedom would be restored. Epstein had fashioned a bomb to blow up the New Deal order and institute a neoliberal one.[40]

No single bomb, of course, could blow up forty years of court rulings, not in a system with respect for precedent. Moreover, this system was in the hands of layers and layers of federal judges who had built their careers on elastic interpretations of the commerce clause. But the originalist rebels were deadly serious in their intent to undo poor precedents and undermine Warren-style jurisprudence. These rebels mobilized themselves in an organization, the Federalist Society, to recruit hundreds of originalist judges to their banner and to get them placed, via Meese, on the federal judicial bench. Meese scored a big victory with William Rehnquist's appointment as chief justice to the Supreme Court in 1986 and the appointment of Scalia that same year to take Rehnquist's seat as associate justice. Meese lost a bruising battle over Bork's appointment to the Supreme Court in 1987; Bork's replacement, Anthony Kennedy, was not an originalist firebrand in the manner of Bork or Epstein. But the originalists expected defeats of this sort. They understood that a takeover of the federal judiciary would entail reverses along the way. Nevertheless, the very act of readying troops for a long march through the courts reveals the scale and ambition of the Reagan insurgency to topple the New Deal order, in this case by striking at its legal foundations.[41]

Equally ambitious was Reagan's campaign, unfolding simultaneously with the fight for originalism, to "liberate" broadcast media from public regulation. Freedom of the press had been one of America's most cherished freedoms, enshrined in the First Amendment's guarantee of free speech. For nearly a century after the First Amendment became law in 1792, print instruments—newspapers, pamphlets, and books—were thought to constitute the entirety of the press. This print orientation changed with the advent of the telegraph and telephone and then with the coming of radio and television. These new media had a potential reach and power greater than newspapers. Access to them, however, was limited from the start. Because of finite bandwidth, only a limited number of stations could go "on the air" at the same time. Thus, these new media came to be regarded, in ways that newspapers never were, as public utilities that government had a right and duty to regulate. In fact, New Dealers, through the Communications Act of 1934, made the regulation of the new media in the public interest a pillar of their political order. The Federal Communications Commission (FCC) established by the act made sure that no single media company became too powerful or too biased in its political views. Indeed, in 1949, the FCC adopted the "Fairness Doctrine" stipulating that a media company (radio or TV) that aired controversial views had to attempt to make "facilities available for the expression of contrasting viewpoints held by responsible elements with respect to the controversial issues presented."[42] If the company declined to do so, it would be subject to FCC sanctions and could even be taken off the air.

Though never easy to enforce, the Fairness Doctrine compelled private media to strive for objectivity in their news reporting. It was grounded in a belief that public regulation of the broadcast media was essential to ensuring that America's citizenry had the balanced information necessary to make informed political decisions.

The Reagan neoliberals were outraged by this regulation, which they regarded as an assault on free speech. Ed Feulner, head of the Heritage Foundation and member of the Mont Pèlerin Society, declared that government had no right to tell broadcast media what they should air. The Constitution, Feulner argued, had intended that the press constitute a free market for ideas, an aspiration that could never be realized as long as the government was setting guidelines for what could and could not be broadcast. Mark Fowler, the man appointed by Reagan to head the FCC, concurred. Known among his critics as the "mad monk of deregulation" (because of his intense and unswerving dedication to freeing up the communications market), Fowler laid out a case for the Fairness Doctrine's repeal in a detailed 1985 FCC report. In 1986, the Court of Appeals for the DC Circuit (on which Scalia and Bork were sitting) ruled that the doctrine was "regulatory standard rather than a law," meaning that the FCC could repeal it anytime, regardless of whether it had congressional approval to do so.[43] As FCC head Fowler edged the Fairness Doctrine toward extinction in 1987, concerned bipartisan majorities in Congress scrambled to stop him, incorporating its principles into a piece of legislation known as the Fairness in Broadcasting Act. This bill would have compelled the FCC to continue to abide by Fairness Doctrine principles. But Fowler had Reagan in his corner and had already persuaded the president to veto the legislation when it arrived on his desk for signature. "History has shown," Reagan noted in his veto message, "that the dangers of an overly timid or biased press cannot be averted through bureaucratic regulation, but only through the freedom and competition that the First Amendment sought to guarantee." The Fairness in Broadcasting Act "simply cannot be reconciled with the freedom of speech and the press secured by our Constitution. It is, in my judgment, unconstitutional."[44] The Fairness in Broadcasting Act died with that veto; the Fairness Doctrine ceased to guide FCC oversight shortly thereafter.

The repeal of the Fairness Doctrine was a major neoliberal victory. It freed radio and television stations from an obligation to present news that strove for objectivity and balance. It made possible the rise of a new generation of radio "shock jockeys" whose strategy was to cultivate audiences with provocative and one-sided commentary. It launched Rush Limbaugh, the right-wing radio bulldog, on a remarkable thirty-year scorched-earth odyssey across the terrain of American media and politics. Limbaugh's talk radio show went into national syndication only months after the Fairness Doctrine's repeal. His defiantly unbalanced political commentary and his delight in provoking outrage among his liberal critics made his show one of the most popular, colorful, and influential on radio across the 1990s and 2000s. It became a pillar of the Reagan counter-establishment.

Limbaugh himself always believed that the repeal of the Fairness Doctrine had made his rise and influence possible. He cleverly labeled efforts across the next two decades to restore the Fairness Doctrine as the "Hush Rush" movement. When the rare caller challenged him on his biases, Limbaugh defended his approach to politics in free market terms. His radio show was just one voice among many, he declared; his views were essential to balance the far more pronounced biases of the alleged liberal media—the *New York Times*, CNN, and the three long-established broadcast networks. Those who didn't like what he had to say were free to switch the frequency on their radio dial. Let the people, meaning the market, be the arbiter of the success or failure of media programs, not the government.[45]

The success of Rush Limbaugh on radio would soon be matched by the success of Fox News on television. Launched in 1996, Fox would rocket to success and eventually surpass each of its four main rivals—ABC, CBS, NBC, and CNN—in numbers of viewers. Its dedication to mocking the liberal, New Deal establishment was similar to Limbaugh's, as was its devotion to carrying forward the message of the more radical elements of the GOP. It constantly poked its finger in the eyes of its opponents and of the legions mourning the passing of the Fairness Doctrine, by declaring its own approach to the news as "fair and balanced."[46] In fact, cultivating controversy through unbalanced reporting was its *raison d'être*. The Fox News that Rupert Murdoch and Roger Ailes built would not have been possible in a world still governed by the New Deal order belief that media companies were public utilities obligated to serve the public interest.[47]

The telecommunications revolution that began in the 1980s would have forced any political order, Republican or Democrat, to adjust to its imperatives. But the repeal of the Fairness Doctrine, and its justification by reference to the freedom of the press guarantees lodged in the First Amendment, made meaningful public regulation of powerful media institutions in the rapidly changing telecommunications universe much more difficult to accomplish. This repeal had been orchestrated by Ed Feulner, Mark Fowler, and other deregulators who seized the opportunity that Reagan had given them to spread the good word of America's free market paradise.

Military and Carceral Statebuilding in the Neoliberal Age

Much of the neoliberal firepower deployed by the Reaganites fits the parameters described in Chapter 3 as the third strategy of neoliberalism, deregulation, which entailed liberating the market and individuals from government control. Little of the second strategy—expanding market relations into realms considered non-market realms such as family, marriage, and education—yielded much of consequence during the Reagan era. But the Reaganites did deploy the first strategy, amassing state power to increase government's ability to shape markets, in two significant ways: building up the military and expanding the nation's prison system.

Reagan loathed the Soviet state and the communist ideology on which it was based. He was prepared to spare no expense in building a military that would overwhelm this mortal enemy. In his first year in office, Reagan persuaded Congress to increase the military's budget by 20 percent, arguably the largest such increase in US history except in those moments when the nation was engaged in all-out war. By the end of his first term, defense appropriations had risen 34 percent, from $171 to $229 billion. Reagan matched this increased defense spending with an escalating rhetoric of confrontation with the Soviet Union. Reagan made clear that the era of détente and accommodation was over. Sensing the Soviets' growing economic weakness, Reagan declared that the United States would undertake an arms race and military buildup that the Soviet Union could not possibly match, triggering a "great revolutionary crisis" in the communist homeland that would "leave Marxism-Leninism on the ash-heap of history." The United States would throw all its resources into this last, climactic battle with what Reagan liked to call the "evil empire."[48]

Most small government ideologues within the GOP had little trouble justifying the massive expansion of the state required by this military buildup. The ultimate goal was to make every nation in the world safe for capitalism and free markets. And since the American aim in the Cold War was no longer containment but "rollback," those who supported the buildup could imagine its duration as brief and the dramatic expansion in the size of the US military under Reagan as temporary. The lure of Reagan's much derided Strategic Defense

Initiative lay precisely in the hope that it might open a quick path to American victory in a seemingly endless Cold War. If the United States really succeeded in designing a "digital dome" that would protect the homeland from every attacking nuclear bomber and missile, then the doctrine of Mutually Assured Destruction, a strategy that had rendered the Cold War a stalemate for forty years, could be jettisoned. A newly vulnerable Soviet Union could be compelled to surrender or face the threat of unspeakable destruction from unstoppable American missiles. Tellingly, even as Reagan's critics ridiculed the notion that a digital dome would ever succeed in destroying 100 percent of incoming Soviet bombs, missiles, and projectiles, the Soviet Union's leadership itself, like the Reagan administration, regarded America's "star wars" initiative as a game changer. If it did in fact render the Soviet Union vulnerable, then its cost, and the big state required to implement it, could be justified. The end goal was not statism but a world made safe for free markets.

If the military buildup abroad can be understood as an effort to expand international capitalist markets, then mass incarceration can be understood as an effort to strengthen domestic ones. The forces unleashed in the 1970s by the American economy's decline, and the consequent hollowing out of manufacturing districts in the country's urban industrial core, haunted America throughout the years of the Reagan presidency. Unemployment in minority communities was high, reaching levels often in excess of 50 percent among young black males. Many in their ranks turned to employment opportunities in the country's metastasizing underground drug economy. This subterranean economy was itself built on entrepreneurial, market principles, but its goods facilitated the expansion of drug use and exacted a severe toll on users: ill health, inability to hold down jobs, and a turn to petty crime in desperate attempts to find the cash necessary to ensure a steady flow of fixes. Crime rates soared; many urban areas became unsafe, parts of them desperately so. With no major public works program under consideration (this would have been regarded by the Reaganites as an unacceptable Keynesian-style intrusion into the market) and with welfare for the poor dismissed by the GOP as a failed policy, the Reagan administration embraced a strategy of discipline and punish: expand police forces, increase the volume of arrests, and imprison convicted offenders for long periods of time.

Democrats as well as Republicans supported two tough-on-crime bills passed in 1986 and 1988 that would, by the 1990s, swell the numbers of Americans behind bars and give the United States the largest incarcerated population of any nation in the world (in both absolute and relative terms). One of these bills stipulated that harsh mandatory jail sentences would be triggered by the possession of even small amounts of crack cocaine, the drug of choice among the black poor. Those in possession of powdered cocaine, used mostly by middle-class whites, were to be treated with far greater leniency. The percentage of young black males serving time became shockingly high. Meanwhile, most white users of powdered cocaine, viewed as a minor threat to public order, were allowed to remain beyond the reach of the carceral state.[49]

This discrepancy in the treatment of white and black users of cocaine would not have been possible but for a popular discourse of the time that depicted poor blacks as having drifted beyond the reach of both social policy and market discipline. Those operating within this discourse believed that mass incarceration of blacks had become the sole remaining remedy.

The critical word in this discourse was that of the "underclass." *Time* magazine introduced this concept in a 1977 cover story, arguing that a new term was necessary to describe these allegedly new kinds of poor people in America. These poor were "more intractable, more socially alien and more hostile than almost anyone had imagined. They are the unreachables." They existed on the edges of civilization. "The bleak environment" of concentrated poverty in which they lived "nurtured values" in them that were "often at odds with those of the majority— even the majority of the poor." This underclass was producing "a highly disproportionate number of the nation's juvenile delinquents, school dropouts, drug addicts and welfare mothers, and much of the adult crime, family disruption, urban decay and demand for social expenditures."[50]

Technically the term "underclass" could be used to describe the poor of any color. Ken Auletta tried strenuously in his bestselling 1982 book, *The Underclass*, to deploy it in racially neutral ways. But its usage in the United States in the 1980s was coded black. It carried a powerfully racist connotation of urban blacks as less than human and unfit for inclusion in any "normal" community of men and women. Many white Americans believed that not much could be done to redeem these poor; best, then, simply to lock up African Americans who had broken the law and offended civilization and throw away the key. With this population removed from the economy, with criminality and physical insecurity thus purged from urban life, neoliberals could get on with the business of building a successful market economy.[51]

It may seem incongruous to talk about market freedom and mass incarceration as being products of the same moment. But classical liberals and neoliberals had long argued for the need to ringfence free markets, limiting participation to those who could handle its rigors. Nineteenth-century liberals had made such arguments, as had Röpke and his band of German ordo-liberal neoliberals in the 1950s and 1960s. Reagan neoliberals were following in these predecessors' footsteps. Markets had to be "ordered" so that they could function "freely." Policymakers were obligated to undertake this work.

Neoliberalism's Moral Code

Sealing off young black males from normal social intercourse might make cities safer and opportunities to truck, barter, and exchange greater, but it could not entirely insulate "mainstream" America from worries about the ill effects of a free market economy. How to ensure that whites themselves would not fall victim to "underclass" temptation—drugs, alcohol, debt, family breakdown—in a society that elevated personal freedom and indulgence of the marketplace above all other values? Many Reagan supporters increasingly found an answer to this troubling question in a neo-Victorian moral code meant to inoculate the market's most vigorous participants against market peril.

Public intellectuals Gertrude Himmelfarb and her husband, Irving Kristol, were key figures in elaborating this moral code.[52] Himmelfarb's studies of nineteenth-century Britain had led her to conclude that a complete embrace of the market could be corrosive, meaning that an individual's encounter with it had to be regulated in some way. If the state was not going to provide that regulation, then who would? To this question Himmelfarb replied: The individual must regulate himself. She had in mind not Margaret Thatcher's individual, alone in society, but one appropriately nestled in congeries of institutions—in family and church, of course, but also in the vast archipelago of voluntary organizations that Tocqueville had identified as America's most hopeful characteristic. Thus nestled, an individual would acquire the character necessary to engage profitably and responsibly with the market. He (and I am using the male pronoun deliberately) would acquire self-discipline and self-control, and thus self-respect, "a pre-condition for the respect and approbation of others," Himmelfarb wrote.[53] Such an individual would not consume mindlessly or beyond his means; nor would he indulge in an excess of alcohol, drugs, or sex. He would live by the golden rule; he would infuse his own life and the world beyond with "moral and civic virtue." This is what the British Victorians had done so successfully in the late nineteenth century, according to Himmelfarb, to counteract the destructive effects of the laissez-faire economy they had built. And it is what Americans of the late twentieth century needed to do themselves if their market society was going to flourish.

Himmelfarb, Kristol, and their band of neo-Victorians were small in number; they were secular, East Coast urban, and disproportionately Jewish. And yet they articulated a set of beliefs that resonated with millions of Americans from other regions and religions. These mostly Protestant and Catholic Americans shared with neo-Victorian East Coast intellectuals a sentiment that the liberation movements of the sixties and seventies—civil rights, feminism, and gay rights—had turned their country and its moral codes upside down. Husbands and fathers had lost authority in their families. Excessively generous welfare schemes were rewarding idleness and indulgence. Criminals were being coddled, relieved of responsibility for their actions. Permissiveness had allegedly permeated all corners of civil society, rendering every lifestyle—including those of single-parent families, mothers having and raising children out of wedlock, and people living openly as homosexuals—the equal of every other.

To contain this slide into the worst forms of moral relativism, the neo-Victorians and the evangelical movement to which they were linked counterposed a moral traditionalism. They wanted to restore the authority of the father and husband (in her social circles, Gertrude Himmelfarb preferred to be known as Mrs. Irving Kristol); end welfare; punish criminals; suppress homosexuality; and rehabilitate families and thereby restore their capacity to nurture self-reliant, disciplined, and virtuous individuals. Could all Americans benefit from this program? Sometimes the neo-Victorians said yes: Many were religious men and women who had accepted the Bible's teaching that all human beings were God's children. Within the intellectual vanguard of this movement, both George Gilder and Thomas Sowell were adamant in their belief that the moral traditionalism they were advocating—and the economic success that would result from individuals living by a robust moral code—was accessible to all of America's peoples, irrespective of their race or ethnicity. Sowell, one of the few African American intellectuals who embraced the free market movement, insisted again and again that blacks were as capable as Jews, Italians, Poles, and the Chinese of pulling themselves up by their bootstraps.[54]

Sowell emphasized this point not only to critique Great Society welfare policies that, in his eyes, had backfired, producing dysfunctional behaviors among the black poor. He also wanted to fend off moral traditionalists who were inclined to believe that some races and genders were better equipped than others to handle the rigors of independent selfhood, and thus that opening up America to all races, religions, and cultures could spell trouble. Nineteenth-century Victorianism had rested on a set of racial hierarchies; some in the ranks of the twentieth-century neo-Victorians had begun to wonder whether they, too, ought to distinguish between "higher" races that were capable of a morally disciplined life and "lower" ones that were not. This sentiment had begun to surface in the thought of libertarian social critic Charles Murray, especially as he shifted from a focus on the destructive effects of welfare policy on the lives of the poor to alleged divergences in the distribution of intelligence across racial groups. And it informed pundit Patrick Buchanan's increasingly vituperative attacks on Latin American immigrants, whom he regarded as posing a threat to America much like the "barbarians" of the ancient world who had sacked Rome.[55]

The neo-Victorian moral perspective of the Reagan years was fundamental to the emerging neoliberal order. It provided the architects of Reagan's neoliberal America assurance that America could handle the rigors of a free market economy. It bound together the white poor with white Republican Party elites, articulating an ideal of strenuous self-improvement that flowed powerfully across class lines.[56] It preyed opportunistically and powerfully on the racist undercurrents coursing their way through American life. This was not the only moral code that the neoliberal order made possible. As we shall see (in Chapter 5), the neoliberal free market orientation also encouraged a moral code among Democrats grounded in the principles of pluralism and cosmopolitanism. But the neo-Victorian moral code was dominant within the Republican Party, the institution most responsible for the neoliberal order's 1980s ascent.[57]

Democratic Acquiescence and Resistance

By the mid-1980s, Reagan's new political order was already bending Democrats to its will, much as the New Deal order had corralled Eisenhower and other Republicans in the 1950s. Calls for reorienting the Democratic Party toward free market ideology that had first appeared during Jimmy Carter's presidency intensified across the 1980s. Self-styled "Atari Democrats" were among the vanguard of Democrats arguing that their party had to reorient. They regarded information technology industries as the future and were alarmed that the United States might cede its advantages in this critical economic sector to the Japanese (Atari was then a leading American manufacturer of video games). These Democrats were more interested in building America's high-tech prowess than in saving declining industries such as steel and textiles. They talked about the importance of innovation and global trade and were impatient with labor unions insisting on protectionism and job security for workers in "yesterday's" industries. They wanted subsidies and incentives for high-tech entrepreneurs, extensive retraining of American workers to equip them to excel in the kinds of skills—engineering, computer programming, math—required by high-tech industries, and economic growth that would lift all boats rather than a redistribution of societal resources from the rich to the poor.[58]

The left-leaning economist Robert Lekachman used the term "neoliberal" to describe these new Democrats, in part because it was one that some of these new Democrats, such as Charles Peters, used to describe themselves. Intriguingly, few of these homegrown American *neoliberals* (who often inserted a hyphen into this label when describing themselves) seemed to know much about the *neoliberals* who had gathered at Colloque Lippmann and the Mont Pèlerin Society in Paris and Switzerland forty to fifty years earlier. Yet the choice of this term to define themselves seems to have been driven by the same imperative that had produced the original terminological invention: the desire to create a new liberalism that was both different from laissez-faire and from the liberalism embodied in the New Deal order itself.[59]

Lekachman did not like what he observed in these neo-liberals. He criticized them for accepting "private enterprise's primacy as fully as Citibank's Walter Wriston or Ronald Reagan's official family." They "pay small heed," he disapprovingly observed, "to maldistribution of income and wealth." The aims of these neo-liberals were "not to be confused," he alleged, with "traditional, highly honorable liberal aspirations for full employment, universal health coverage, tax equity, adequate housing, urban rehabilitation, integration of minorities into the labor force, and the mild redistribution of income, wealth and power." The neo-liberal ideal, Lekachman concluded, "appears to be more intelligent behavior by capitalists under the gentle tutelage of Government, which stimulates corporations with increased rewards."[60]

Lekachman's portrait of Democratic neo-liberals aptly described Paul E. Tsongas, senator and formerly congressman from Massachusetts. Born and raised in the Massachusetts city of Lowell, Tsongas had grown up amid the abandoned factory hulks of America's original declining industry, cotton textiles. He was transfixed by the economic miracle that Wang Laboratories, an early high-tech manufacturing powerhouse with 30,000 employees, had wrought in his depressed hometown. The embrace of high-tech would, Tsongas believed, revive other declining manufacturing centers in America much as it had Lowell. To propel America into this new world, Democrats had to privilege private industry in ways they were not used to doing. "Our proposals," Tsongas wrote, "presuppose that the economy will work best when private industry leads the way." There was still an important role for government to play, Tsongas conceded, especially in terms of ensuring "an ample supply of trained people and technology industry needs." But Tsongas also insisted that government intervention must be "limited" and "triggered by private industry signals."[61]

Other young Democrats responding to the high-tech siren call included senators Gary Hart of Colorado and Bill Bradley of New Jersey, governors Michael Dukakis of Massachusetts and Bill Clinton of Arkansas, and congressman and then senator Al Gore Jr. of Tennessee. With Lester Thurow, an economist at MIT, and other university-based social scientists, they began to gain a toehold in academia.[62] When Walter Mondale, a traditional New Deal liberal (and disciple of New Deal standard-bearer Hubert Humphrey) lost by a wide margin to Reagan in the presidential election of 1984, the Atari Democrats joined a larger group of frustrated Democratic officials to found the Democratic Leadership Council (DLC). The DLC's intent was to put distance between the 1980s Democratic Party and its 1930s and 1960s forebears by looking favorably on business, free markets, and high tech.

Losing the presidency in 1988 (when George H. W. Bush bested Michael Dukakis) for the fifth time in the last six contests confirmed the DLC in its views. "Old politics must give way to new realities," intoned the preamble to the DLC's New Orleans Declaration of 1990. "The political ideas and passions of the 1930s and 1960s cannot guide us into the 1990s." The "Democratic Party's fundamental mission" must become "to expand opportunity, not government." Democrats needed to recognize that "the free market, regulated in the public interest, is the best engine of general prosperity." The DLC also proclaimed its desire to move the Democratic Party closer to Republican positions on questions of social policy and moral traditionalism. "Our leaders must reject demands" on government "that are less worthy." The DLC called on Democrats to prioritize "preventing crime and punishing criminals" over "explaining away their behavior." Democrats had to work "to bring the poor into the nation's economic mainstream not maintain them in their dependence."[63]

To be sure, the DLC continued to subscribe to basic Democratic Party beliefs in "the politics of inclusion," "equal rights and full citizenship," and making sure that government "respect[s] individual liberty and stay[s] out of our private lives and personal decisions." But discourse about free markets, expanding economic opportunity, punishing criminals, and ending welfare dependence had all been taken from Reagan's GOP playbook. The man chairing the Democratic Leadership Council in 1990 and hoping to lead the Democratic Party to its own neo-liberal future was Arkansas governor Bill Clinton.[64] Clinton had agreed to take on this role once Al From, a key figure in the DLC, convinced him that it would open a path toward winning the 1992 Democratic Party nomination for president.[65]

The growing strength of the DLC should not be interpreted to mean that neoliberalism had conquered all of the Democratic Party by 1990. African Americans, now one of the Democratic Party's most loyal constituencies, made it clear they would not tolerate backtracking on civil rights, affirmative action, or welfare. When Reagan in 1987 had nominated to the Supreme Court a man (Robert Bork) who appeared to threaten all that the Warren Court had done for civil rights (and women's reproductive rights), the opposition deployed by Democratic senators was fierce and successful. Organized labor was another key Democratic Party constituency; even as its membership declined, it kept up a steady stream of donations to the Democratic Party and conducted major voter turnout initiatives on election days. Unionized autoworkers, steelworkers, and electrical workers were not ready to turn their backs on the industries that had long given them good livelihoods or to sign up for suspect retraining programs that the high-tech enthusiasts were touting.

These workers and their union leaders argued that America needed to maintain a manufacturing base with well-paying jobs and that it should impose tariffs, if necessary, to do so. Prominent in the ranks of these Democrats was Tip O'Neill, Speaker of the House for much of the 1980s, and increasingly Senator Ted Kennedy, both from Massachusetts. The surprising early success of Jesse Jackson's campaign for the 1988 Democratic Party presidential nomination demonstrated that a labor union-civil rights alliance might offer a promising way to push New Deal-style politics back to the fore.[66]

Some of the intellectuals who had gathered around these men believed that the future of America's poorer citizens would be best served not by embracing deregulation but emulating the Japanese economy, which prized not free domestic markets but heavily protected ones, and which had triumphed not through neoliberal policies but through thorough-going regulation of corporations by the state. Japan's management of its economy looked a lot more like New Deal–era market regulation than anything the Reagan administration was advocating. Those in America who looked toward Japan wanted to re-establish the business-labor-government partnerships that had guided industrial policy during the 1930s and 1940s, not cede to private enterprise the primacy that Tsongas and other Democratic neo-liberals thought was imperative. Felix Rohatyn, a New York City–based financier radicalized by his role in New York City's 1970s rescue from bankruptcy, had concluded that an excessive regard for the market and its operations was going to consign too many old urban and industrial areas like New York to penury, misery, and social dysfunction. To spare America such a fate, Rohatyn advocated reviving a form of planning once associated with the Reconstruction Finance Corporation, which had executed many successful interventions in 1930s America.[67]

The reservoir of support that Tip O'Neill and Ted Kennedy had in the House and Senate was deep enough to slow the progress of the Reagan revolution and to keep hope alive for an alternative economic future. Moreover, the Reagan revolution lost some momentum as the president's mental acuity declined during his last two years in office, and as the administration had to defend itself against charges that its foreign policy adventurism in Third World countries had broken numerous laws. Reagan's international ambitions were stymied as well by the continuing geopolitical power of the Soviet Union; though weakened by a poorly performing economy, this communist state was still strong enough to deny American capitalists entry into markets they ardently wanted to access.

And yet the consequences of Reagan's move against the New Deal order were undeniable. A new order, one prizing free markets, had taken root. An impressive array of donors, foundations, think tanks, and new political leaders had assembled under its banner. The cultivation of new voting constituencies demonstrated that the GOP might be emerging as America's new majority party. Sweeping victories in the 1980 and 1984 presidential elections prompted GOP leaders to launch bold deregulatory initiatives across a broad terrain. The Reaganite neoliberals overhauled legal thought and judicial appointments to make sure that their policies would survive challenges in American courts. Jettisoning the Fairness Doctrine allowed them to open new fronts in the war for public opinion. And the elaboration of a neo-Victorian moral code relocated responsibility for well-being from the state to the individual, where neoliberals thought it should reside.

That a new generation of Democrats had begun adopting neoliberal principles as their own was a sure sign of this ideology's ascent. The Soviet Union itself felt increasingly under siege as its leaders proved themselves unable to match the economic performance and the technological advances of the United States. The neoliberal order had not yet triumphed. But it had enjoyed a remarkable decade of advance.

5

Triumph

AS LATE AS 1989, the Soviet Union was one of the world's two superpowers. It dwarfed all other land empires in size. It possessed a formidable nuclear arsenal and the largest army on the planet. Its power and influence extended well beyond its borders into Vietnam in East Asia, East Germany in western Europe, Iraq and Syria in the Middle East, portions of southern Africa, and Cuba and Central America in the Western Hemisphere. Internally, across the seventy-plus years of its existence, it had engaged in what historian Ian Kershaw has called "the most remarkable political experiment in modern times," replacing capitalism with communism, private property with publicly run enterprises, and *homo economicus* with "Soviet man."[1] For most of that period, its power, its communist ideology, its atheism, and its appeal to the Third World struck fear in the hearts of US policymakers. Millions of Americans regarded the communist system as an existential threat to their way of life. In their eyes, to be a communist in the post–World War II era was to be an enemy of the American state, a mortal threat to America's tradition of liberty and free enterprise, and a violator of all that was decent and moral in American life.

And then, in December 1991, in a move almost unprecedented in recorded human history, the Soviet Union, communism's home base, dissolved itself quickly and peacefully. Several former Soviet republics became independent nations and the rest banded together in a new polity called the Commonwealth of Independent States (CIS). Whatever CIS was, it was not communist. Before it swept itself into the dustbin of history, the Soviet Union had freed its colonies in Eastern Europe with hardly a shot being fired. Without a fight, it gave up its share of Berlin—the precious prize awarded the Red Army for its World War II years of life-and-death struggle against the Nazi war machine. A young KGB colonel stationed in Dresden at the time would come to regard the Soviet Union's voluntary retreat from Germany and Eastern Europe and its self-dissolution as the most shameful and humiliating moment in Russian history. His name was Vladimir Putin.[2]

Putin desperately wanted the Soviet Union to fight for its life at all costs. Across history, this is what most empires in decline had done. Some went to war. Others tried to save themselves through internal reform, and then repressed their subjects when the reforms unleashed forces of change that no one had anticipated. The Soviet Union could have survived in this manner for decades beyond 1991, especially since no one, outside the mujahideen in Afghanistan, really wanted to fight it. With 500,000 troops in Eastern Europe as late as 1989, and tens of thousands of nuclear warheads spread throughout the country and capable of reaching any destination on earth in an interval ranging from minutes to hours, the USSR still possessed formidable capacity to rain mayhem and destruction on its enemies.

The Soviet Union had been ailing in the 1970s and 1980s, to be sure. It had had trouble keeping economic pace with the capitalist West, especially in delivering to its people the quantity and quality of consumer goods that were becoming the hallmarks of successful societies. Moreover, matching Ronald Reagan's military expansion and budget and developing its own anti-nuclear shield to negate the impact of America's Strategic Defensive Initiative strained the Soviet Union's finances and its technological capacity. Technical advances were stymied not by a shortage of scientists (the Soviet Union had plenty) but by the state's refusal to allow the free flow of information and innovation among them that was required for advances in the IT revolution. At a time in the 1980s when the number of personal computers in the United States was crossing the 25 million threshold, the Soviet Union possessed a paltry 200,000, less than 1 percent of the American total.[3]

The Soviet Union was also undergoing a leadership crisis. It had no effective mechanism for transferring power to a new generation. Its ancient leaders in the 1970s and 1980s hung on as long as they could, with some of the last ones—Leonid Brezhnev, Yuri Andropov, and Konstantin Chernenko in particular—becoming "dead men walking." In Andropov's last months of life in 1984, the only organ of his body that seemed to be functioning properly was his brain. Chernenko, his replacement, lasted only thirteen months before he died in 1985. Their successor, Mikhail Gorbachev, had demonstrated an uncanny ability to interpret the wishes of bosses who could barely issue orders anymore, an ability that helped him to win their favor and to be chosen (in 1985) premier of the Soviet Union and general secretary of the Soviet Communist Party.[4]

Gorbachev was a party insider, steadily and cleverly climbing through the ranks. Somehow, he had kept alive a genuine faith in socialism, one of the last in top Soviet leadership echelons to do so. An heir to the Khrushchev semi-revolution of 1956, Gorbachev ardently believed that communism really could be reformed and socialism with a human face enacted. This stance informed his embrace of the reform policies of glasnost (openness) and perestroika (economic reconstruction allowing marketization and privatization) to reinvigorate the politics and economy of his nation. And when these policies triggered unexpected consequences—the eruption of secessionist nationalisms and popular democracy in both the Soviet republics and the Soviet satellite colonies in Eastern Europe—Gorbachev repeatedly declined to curb reform or to unleash repression.[5]

Gorbachev could have pivoted toward the latter in 1989, as his Chinese communist counterparts were doing at precisely that moment when they attacked the Chinese democracy movement assembled in Beijing's Tiananmen Square with tanks, troops, and bullets. Surveying his country's chaotic state in 1989, the Chinese premier, Deng Xiaoping, concluded that the Chinese ruling elites would successfully manage the transition from communism to capitalism only if they repudiated aspirations for democratic reform. Deng was brutally practical in his determination to preserve the power of the Chinese Communist Party at all costs. Gorbachev was not. The last of the socialist utopians, Gorbachev had decided that if socialism could not be saved in a democratic manner, then it did not deserve to be saved at all.[6]

That conviction explains why Gorbachev did not act on several opportunities between 1989 and 1991 to restore the power of communists within his nation and that of the Soviet Union in world affairs. He could have sent his country's tanks into Eastern Europe in 1989 to crush popular revolts against communist rule there, as his predecessors had done in 1956 in Hungary and 1968 in Czechoslovakia. He did not. He also could have generated mischief for the West in 1990 and 1991 when America, with United Nations backing, landed a massive force in Saudi Arabia to push Iraq's leader Saddam Hussein out of Kuwait and secure that small country's petroleum reserves for western Europe, Japan, and the United States. Gorbachev could have threatened military retaliation in 1990 when the West broke its pledges first to keep a reuniting Germany out of NATO and then to keep NATO from encroaching on the Soviet Union's western border.[7] As late as August 1991, a group of high-ranking Soviet officials showed up at Gorbachev's Crimean hideaway to plead with him to crack down on the country's democratic reformers and to re-establish communist authority. Had he done so, thousands of elite Soviet officials, military and civilian, backed by hundreds of thousands of troops, would likely have rallied to his side. But again, Gorbachev declined to take any action that would undercut glasnost and perestroika. An attempted coup occurring without his support failed. Shortly afterward, Gorbachev resigned from office. The Soviet Union, one of the most powerful empires the world had ever known, slipped quietly into history.[8]

America, in turn, might have shown some appreciation for a Soviet leader who spared the world the violence, both internal and external, that could well have accompanied the Soviet Union's demise. Here and there it did, especially in the occasional utterances of Reagan's successor as president, George H. W. Bush, who grasped the volatility imbedded in this moment of transition and how easily events could have spiraled into devastating internal and external wars. But overall, such appreciation and humility were in short supply on the American side. Instead, Americans congratulated themselves for having vanquished the mightiest foe their country had ever faced. Republicans argued that Reagan's tough policies—rhetorical bluntness, unlimited military buildup, and the unshackling of free market capitalism—had brought the Soviet Union to its knees. Reagan supporters alleged that Democrats, and Republicans too, prior to Reagan's presidency, had been far too soft on communism. Their man had taken the gloves off, denouncing the

Soviet Union as "the evil empire," expanding US military power, and threatening war, even a nuclear-driven one, against communist aggression. Reagan had brought victory to America, to the American way of life, and, last but not least, to the neoliberal way. "The basis of the communist doctrine is dead," exclaimed national security hawk Paul Nitze in 1989. "The *West* has won an ideological victory of tremendous dimensions."[9] The future lay with everything that Reagan's America embodied and that communism was not: free markets, deregulated economies, political freedom, individualism, religious faith.[10]

If the Reaganites were too quick to take credit for the Soviet Union's dissolution, they were not wrong about the enormous implications of its breakup. The immediate shock waves generated by the events of 1989–1991 were not as seismic as those caused by the Russian Revolution of 1917, but they were equally consequential and enduring. One result of communism's fall is obvious: It opened a large part of the world—the former Soviet Union and Eastern Europe in particular—to capitalist penetration. After 1991, capitalists and capital poured into Eastern Europe, along with phalanxes of economists from the West, many of them preaching free market shock therapy as the best way to implant capitalist principles quickly and powerfully. Poland, Estonia, Lithuania, Latvia, Hungary, Czechoslovakia, and Russia itself were among those nations now eager to embrace capitalism of the free market sort. Not so the Chinese, who were much more careful to meld market practices with the Chinese Communist Party's control of state power. Still, capitalism took a giant leap forward in China as well after the 1991 Soviet Union's collapse, with startling economic growth rates vindicating Deng's belief that capitalist development could occur within an authoritarian political framework. Across the 1990s, Deng's communist government laid off 20 million workers in state industries to make them available to private or hybrid public-private enterprises. Western and Japanese corporations rushed in to take advantage of the economic opportunities that Deng had dangled before them, which included a huge number of Chinese laborers now in need of jobs and willing to work for a pittance of what parallel groups of employees in Japan, Europe, and the United States were earning. Across the 1990s alone, China's exports quintupled, making its manufacturing sector a critical part of global supply chains. World trade in manufactured goods doubled in the 1990s and doubled again in the 2000s. Everywhere, except in Cuba, North Korea, and perhaps Albania, the once impenetrable Iron Curtain was disintegrating. Capitalism had become aggressively global in a way it had not been since before the First World War.[11]

Another consequence of communism's fall may be less obvious but is of equal importance: It removed what remained in America of the imperative for class compromise. A compromise between capital and labor had been foundational to the New Deal order. Labor had gained progressive taxation, social security, unemployment insurance, the right to organize, a national commitment to full employment, government backing for collective bargaining, and limits on the inequality between rich and poor. Capital had gained assurances that government would act to smooth out the business cycle, maintain a fiscal and monetary environment that would assure reasonable profits, and contain labor's power.

In the 1990s, capital still wanted the US government's assistance in ordering markets. But in a world cleared of communism, long its most ardent opponent, it felt the need to compromise with labor less and less. After 1991, no country or movement in the world was in a position (so it seemed) to challenge the capitalist way of organizing economic life. Perhaps, then, there was no longer a need for capitalists to purchase insurance against such challenges by paying American workers the high wages that the New Deal order demanded. To the contrary, high wage insurance policies could be dropped and labor protests against wage cuts ignored or met by threats to ship production abroad. The defenders of this hyper-globalized capitalist order argued that whatever American workers lost in wages would be counter-balanced by falls in the cost of consumer products now manufactured abroad for a fraction of their former cost.

The offensive against organized labor in America actually had been under way since the 1970s, its fortunes given a boost by Reagan's decision in 1981 to fire the thousands of air traffic controllers who had gone on strike. By the early 1990s, membership in trade unions had almost halved since the Nixon presidency, from 29 to 16 percent of the non-agricultural workforce.[12] Young, innovative public-sector unions were able to hold their own across the 1990s, helped along by municipal and state governments that were locked in place, unable to take their operations elsewhere in pursuit of cheaper labor supplies.[13] But private employers were not so constrained. The ease with which they could shift production abroad in this post-communist global capitalist world emboldened them to resist their workers' demands for better wages and working conditions. By the turn of the millennium, the percentage of workers in the private sector belonging to unions had sunk to a level—9 percent—last seen in the United States in the early 1930s, a time prior to the great labor rebellion of the mid-1930s that had propelled the New Deal order into existence.[14] By 2000, the institutional matrix that had brought labor such important gains during the New Deal order had been largely wiped out.

It is hardly surprising that economic inequality rose sharply in these circumstances, to pre–New Deal levels. Between 1980 and 2005, the top 1 percent of income earners received more than 80 percent of the nation's increase in income, doubling their share of the nation's overall wealth. The ratio of CEO annual earnings to average worker earnings had roughly tripled in the quarter century between the mid-1960s and 1989. In the ten years after the fall of communism, it more than tripled again, until the average CEO was earning in a year an estimated 368 times what the average worker was bringing home in his or her paycheck. In 1965 that ratio had been a mere 20.[15] As we shall see, there were benefits to the labor market of the 1990s, especially in terms of job creation and declining unemployment. But the increases in the number of jobs was not matched by corresponding increases in pay. The inadequacy of wages forced more and more households to depend on the earnings of two or more members, with women joining men in the workforce in large numbers. In multiple quarters, the increase in percentages of women working was hailed as a feminist advance, signaling employment opportunities for women that had not been there before. But most women did not have a choice about whether they wanted to work; their families required the income. Moreover, many jobs had become much less secure than they had once been, with the portion of households suffering an income decline of 25 percent or more a year from job losses rising steadily across the decade.[16]

The decline of labor was not just evident in shrinking union membership rolls, erosion of political power, and increasing economic inequality. It was also evident in a decline in the very ability to imagine organizing a world on something other than capitalist principles. This was the point powerfully made by the social theorist and philosopher Francis Fukuyama in *The End of History and the Last Man*, the bestselling book he published in 1992. A fierce critic of communism, Fukuyama nevertheless respected the radicalism of communism's critique of liberal democracy (the political system most conducive, Fukuyama argued, to capitalism's flourishing) and the passions that it had long elicited among its supporters. Communism, he argued, had created spaces—geopolitical and ideological—in which capitalism could be challenged. Communists, like capitalists, made their creed available to people around the globe irrespective of nationality, ethnicity, religion, or race. The fall of communism, in his eyes, not only eliminated actual space where alternatives to capitalism were being practiced and implanted on everyday life. It also meant that the last *universal* alternative to capitalism and liberal democracy as a way of organizing economic and political life had passed from the world.[17]

Fukuyama stood outside the left. Those inside the left had to grapple with a second 1990s challenge: namely, that communism had fallen at least in part because it had long before poisoned the dream of socialist emancipation. In most parts of the world, socialism, in any form, had lost its capacity to move masses. Of course, citizens in many countries, and especially in western Europe, continued to vote for social democratic parties that were committed to strong welfare states, limits on the inequalities between rich and poor, and investments in public goods—parks, the arts, strong public transport systems, and the like. These parties had themselves once been socialist. But by the 1990s they were increasingly reformist and technocratic in orientation, seen as maintainers of the status quo and no longer able to inspire the masses with dreams of secular emancipation, as parties of the left had been doing for 200 years since the French Revolution.[18]

The corrosion of this dream of secular emancipation, a disintegrative process most advanced in the Soviet Union and its satellites, lay at the root of Gorbachev's failure to resuscitate socialist passions among the Soviet masses. The same process was eating away at the socialism of radicals outside the Soviet orbit, which is why those who insisted on calling themselves leftists in the West increasingly sought to put their radicalism on a foundation different from the Marxist one. In

America, many were turning to identity politics, where powerful new dreams of liberation—for women, for people of color, for gays—had been incubating. Liberation struggles broke out everywhere in 1990s America, with the partisans of gender, racial, and sexual equality reigniting the passions that had once been the hallmark of socialist movements. But while these struggles over identity generated considerable conflict, they did not threaten regimes of capital accumulation as communism had done. As we shall see, multiculturalism and cosmopolitanism could and did thrive under conditions of neoliberalism, even as pressure on capitalist elites and their supporters to compromise with the working class was vanishing.[19]

The collapse of communism, then, opened the entire world to capitalist penetration, shrank the imaginative and ideological space in which opposition to capitalist thought and practices might incubate, and impelled those who remained leftists to redefine their radicalism in alternative terms, which turned out to be those that capitalist systems could more, rather than less, easily manage. This was the moment when neoliberalism in the United States went from being a political movement to a political order.

An Unlucky President

George H. W. Bush was president during the years when the Soviet Union and communism collapsed. The world may well have been fortunate, as historian Jeffrey Engel has argued, to have a man such as Bush occupying the Oval Office during this transition. Bush grasped the dangers present in the volatility of the moment and the imperative of the United States not to make a misstep as geopolitics was undergoing dramatic change. Bush understood that there still must be some limits on American power.[20]

But there were also reasons that Bush was never adored by the American public nor gained the respect that might have accrued to a head of state who safely steered his nation's ship through dangerous passages. In public utterances, Bush's words usually lacked eloquence and the capacity to inspire; they sometimes failed him altogether. Hardcore Reaganites never warmed to him. When he had run against Reagan in the 1980 GOP primaries, Bush had labeled as "voodoo economics" the kind of tax-cutting, deregulatory regime and disdain for balancing budgets that Reagan was setting forth. Across the eight years he served as Reagan's vice-president, he had never marshaled the zeal of the convert for "supply side" economics or for the belief that releasing the market from all restraint was the key to restoring American greatness.

Bush remained in critical ways the scion of the elite Connecticut Republican family into which he had been born. Old New England Republican families like the Bushes had long believed that economic growth required not just free enterprise but fiscal discipline, that government expenditures and revenues had to be brought into balance. Thus, when, as president, Bush confronted a federal debt that had ballooned from the combination of Reagan-era tax cuts and military expenditures, he supported a modest congressional effort to raise taxes. That move incensed the Reaganite supply-siders and convinced them that Bush never had been and never would be one of them.[21]

Bush had also suffered in American electoral politics from his inability to shed his reputation as a northeastern blueblood. Despite moving his family to Texas and into the oil business in the late 1940s, Bush had never mastered the populist or demagogic touch that might have endeared him to southern voters. Nor did he connect to the Reagan Democrats of the North. The long-standing Bush family compound in Kennebunkport, Maine, to which Bush repaired every summer, was so beautiful and so insulated from the gritty manufacturing districts of New England—and indeed, of the entire Northeast—that Bush was slow to recognize the economic dislocation that was upending the lives of increasing numbers of white working-class and middle-class workers in this stretch of America's industrial heartland.[22]

The short-term problem that Bush faced in 1990–1991 was a recession, which had cost 4.5 million Americans their jobs and raised unemployment to 7.8 percent, its highest level in nearly a decade.[23] But the deeper problem was not a cyclical downturn but the long-term erosion of America's manufacturing base. What good would Bush's victory over the Soviet Union and against Saddam Hussein be if America failed to turn those triumphs into economic prosperity at home? What if it turned out, as the former Democratic senator from Massachusetts Paul Tsongas quipped, that the true winner of the Cold War was not the United States but Japan, still seemingly besting America in one economic sector after another?[24]

Concerns over the sputtering of America's economic machine came to a head over the North American Free Trade Agreement (NAFTA), a Bush administration initiative to turn the entire continent into a single common market by eliminating tariffs on most goods passing between the United States and Mexico and the United States and Canada. Though discussions about this initiative began under Reagan before 1989, planning for it accelerated dramatically after the Soviet Union dissolved. NAFTA expressed the post-communist ambition to turn the entire world into a single marketplace; regional free trade zones were imagined as stepping stones to that destination. This was the moment when the European Union was forming on the other side of the Atlantic and when plans for transnational free trade federations were advancing as well along the western edge of the Pacific rim. NAFTA would promote a similar goal in North America. In his determination to remove unnecessary trade barriers, Bush was being true to the Reaganite inheritance. But Bush and his policy aides failed to grasp the depths of economic hardship in American manufacturing and the fear that NAFTA would dramatically worsen it if American employers rushed to shift their operations south of the Rio Grande where Mexican labor was plentiful and cheap.[25]

The emergence of a challenger to Bush in the 1992 Republican primaries was the first sign that the continental free trade zone that Bush was promising had become controversial. Patrick Buchanan, a former Nixon speechwriter, was running the kind of populist and ethnonationalist campaign that Bush declined to embrace himself. Buchanan declared that NAFTA would be a disaster for the United States, both economically and culturally. Jobs would dash south of the border, causing "tough hearty [white] men" in America to lose good employment and thus their pride and their ability to support their families. One such man, a paper mill worker in New Hampshire whom Buchanan had met on the campaign trail, pleaded with him to "save our jobs."[26] Buchanan was touched by this plea, which motivated him to deepen his opposition to NAFTA.

Buchanan was equally concerned about the high volume of Mexicans that a free trade agreement would allow to move north, taking a disproportionate number of jobs in the remaining sectors of the American manufacturing economy. Buchanan despised Mexicans both for their willingness to work for low wages and for their allegedly inferior racial character. America, in Buchanan's eyes, was meant to be a land for superior European races and their descendants. Buchanan fancied himself an expert on ancient history and especially on the fall of Rome. Just as the "barbarian hordes" invading from the north had ruined Rome, Buchanan believed that Mexican migrants, if allowed to flow freely into the United States from the south, would destroy the great civilization that Europeans had built in North America.[27]

Bush turned back Buchanan's primary challenge, only to confront in the general election a third-party candidate in the person of Ross Perot, a scrappy Texas billionaire with a populist touch, willing to spend unlimited amounts of his own money to attack NAFTA and Bush. Perot amplified Buchanan's economic critique of NAFTA, nowhere more powerfully than in his reiteration, on the stump, of the "giant sucking sound" that would result when NAFTA caused corporations in America to move millions of manufacturing jobs to Mexico. That kind of free trade, Perot argued, would destroy economic opportunity for America's working and lower-middle classes. Perot never had a chance of winning—third-party challengers in America rarely do. But just as Theodore Roosevelt's third-party campaign against William Howard Taft in the 1912 election denied a Republican sitting president re-election and elevated a Democrat, Woodrow Wilson, to the presidency, Ross Perot's Reform Party campaign fractured the majority that otherwise would have re-elected Bush and allowed a little-known Arkansas governor, and a Democrat, to slip into the White House instead. Thus, did Perot's presidential campaign ensure that William Jefferson Clinton would be the man to guide America through the first decade of the nation's post–Cold War era.[28]

Arkansas Boy, Democratic Eisenhower

Clinton was an Arkansas boy raised in modest and chaotic circumstances. He was intellectually gifted, blessed with inexhaustible energy, and driven by a steely ambition to transcend the world in which he had been born and raised. His academic achievements cleared a path that pointed toward Georgetown University, then Oxford, where he spent two years as a Rhodes Scholar, and then Yale Law School. Lawyering was never his goal, however; political office was. An encounter with John F. Kennedy while he was in high school caused him to set his sights high, though he resolved to launch his political career closer to home, by running for Arkansas attorney general in 1976 and governor in 1978, winning both times. When he entered the governor's mansion in 1979, he was only thirty-two, making him something of a political *wunderkind*. But then he stumbled, losing his re-election bid for the governorship in 1980, before regaining his footing and winning a second term in 1982. This time he held the governorship for ten years, until he entered the White House in 1993.

Clinton's early Arkansas falter occurred in part because he was perceived as too progressive and too countercultural for the state's voters. In his 1982 comeback campaign, Clinton went to great lengths to demonstrate that he was a moderate Democrat. Still, despite his subsequent success, some flaws endured. One was a tendency to lose himself in the weeds of programs and agencies. Another was his involvement in extra-marital affairs. As early as 1977, Clinton had a tryst with Gennifer Flowers, then a little-known Little Rock nightclub singer.

If given enough prodding, Clinton was usually able to pull himself out of the nitty-gritty of policy and to frame for voters the big issue at stake. And, for much of the 1980s, Clinton kept news of his sexual affairs under wraps, helped along by admiring journalists, on the one hand, and discreet Arkansas state police officers, on the other. But conservative journalists broke the story of his affair with Flowers in the midst of Clinton's 1992 campaign for the presidency, forcing him and his wife, Hillary, to go on *60 Minutes* both to deny Flowers's charges and to acknowledge that their own marriage had been a troubled one. The earnestness of the Clintons and their ability to demonstrate how dedicated they still were to each other salvaged Bill's race for the presidency. But it would not be the last time that an affair would threaten Clinton's political future and require extraordinary measures to save both his career and his marriage.[29]

Clinton's personal failings should not distract us from an appreciation of his political gifts. He possessed a remarkable intellect. He was an indefatigable campaigner who loved to hunt for votes, press the flesh, and connect with voters, officeholders, and intellectuals on a personal and visceral level. He was magnetic one-on-one, especially once he grabbed your hand or elbow or put his hand on your shoulder and looked you in the eye. He also bridged worlds, an indispensable skill for anyone trying to manage the large and fractious assembly of disparate political constituencies better known as the Democratic Party. Clinton knew and maintained a lifelong affection for the small-town Arkansas world in which he had been reared—he relished being called Bubba—and delighted in opportunities that campaigning gave him to reconnect with places like it. Meanwhile, his years at Georgetown, Oxford, and Yale had prepared him well for the rarified districts of the East Coast intelligentsia, on the one hand, and for the legions of political climbers who swarmed through DC think tanks and lobbying groups looking for their next big chance, on the other. He could hold his own in any intellectual debate and with any group of policy wonks. Indeed, he prided himself on his own "wonkishness" and became famous (or notorious) for policy discussions in the White House that carried on into the wee hours of the morning.[30]

Politically, Clinton had come to consciousness in the outer districts of the New Left. In the late 1960s, he had grown his hair long, smoked weed, and immersed himself in the counterculture, and especially its music. He had opposed the war in Vietnam, was resolute in his support for civil rights, and co-directed Texas operations for George McGovern's 1972 presidential run. The suspicion on the part of many Americans that greeted him when he took possession of the White House in January 1993 was in part wariness about his New Left persona. He was the first left-leaning, pot-smoking, and free-loving baby boomer, after all, to ascend to the most powerful position in American life. But Clinton was never as principled a rebel as his girlfriend and then wife Hillary Rodham, or as Robert Reich, a fellow Rhodes Scholar who would become a lifelong friend (and Clinton's secretary of labor). From the start, Clinton had his eye trained on political advancement and was always willing to make the compromises necessary to climb that slippery pole. Rising in Arkansas politics required him to listen to and bend toward conservative Democrats and Republicans. His largest political ambition was less to accomplish a particular project—such as, for example, completing the New Deal, LBJ's lifelong dream—than to

exert a transformational impact on American life. His political malleability gave him the freedom to shift ideological gears, if *realpolitik*
demanded it. He did so in Arkansas in 1982 and he would do so again
as president in 1995, in both cases after he or his party suffered a shat-
tering political defeat. His lack of political constancy led some to ac-
cuse him of being a "shapeshifter." Those who disliked him disparaged
him as "slick Willie."[31]

A more generous evaluation of these shifts would credit Clinton
with having finely tuned his political antennae and thus with being
able to pick up and make use of signals that others were slower to receive and decipher. In this context, it is not surprising that Clinton had
joined the phalanx of New (Atari) Democrats of the 1980s that organized itself in the aftermath of Walter Mondale's 1984 defeat at the hands
of Reagan. Clinton embraced the New Democrats' conviction that in
the Age of Reagan, the party had no choice but to move toward the
political center. Clinton argued for more market freedom and less government regulation than what New Deal Democrats had traditionally
embraced. He supported NAFTA and the campaign to open the world
to free trade and other neoliberal policies.

However, when Clinton launched his presidency in January 1993,
he was not yet the resolute enforcer of a neoliberal approach to politics
that he would soon become. He intended instead to make an ambitious
national health insurance plan the signature project of his first term.
Pushing this program through Congress, Clinton believed, would result in the biggest expansion of the welfare state since the 1960s and
perhaps since the 1930s. Clinton was betting that he could deliver
on what both Franklin Roosevelt and Lyndon Johnson had so con-
spicuously failed to do, and thus he would get his name up in lights
alongside the two greatest Democratic reformers of the twentieth century. But Clinton's health care reform failed spectacularly, owing to
his administration's gross mishandling of the design and rollout of the
policy, on the one hand, and to the lack of a popular mandate for it, on
the other.[32] Then came a second stunning defeat: Popular anger at Bill
(and at Hillary, too, whom Bill had appointed head of the Health Care
Reform Task Force) allowed Republicans to seize the initiative in the
1994 congressional elections. Under the leadership of Newt Gingrich, a
fiery, insurgent, and loquacious Republican congressman from Atlanta,

the GOP actually reclaimed both houses of Congress, a feat that it had last accomplished in 1954 when Clinton was a mere eight years old. Rarely had a sitting president suffered a repudiation as sharp as Clinton experienced when he became the first Democratic denizen of the White House since Truman (1946) to lose both houses of Congress.[33]

The sting of the 1994 defeat was so sharp in part because it reminded Clinton of others. It brought to mind the rout of McGovern in the 1972 presidential election. It recalled his own loss of the Arkansas governorship in 1980 and the thrashing of Mondale by Reagan in 1984. And now this. Clinton resolved that he would never again experience a defeat of this magnitude. He brought back into his inner circle an old and trusted consultant, Dick Morris, who had orchestrated Clinton's Arkansas gubernatorial comeback in 1982. Morris was not a man inclined to take a stand on political principle. He was a political operative for whom winning was everything. He was brought onto the team to restore Clinton's power and influence.[34]

Morris devised a strategy that he labeled "triangulation." It entailed having Clinton appropriate Republican ideas and rework them into Democratic proposals. The resulting politics would be neither Republican nor traditionally Democratic; rather, they would occupy an independent place, the third leg of the triangle, so to speak. "Acquiescence" is a better term than "triangulation" for what Morris was engineering in 1995 and 1996. The core Republican ideas regarding the economy, Clinton and Morris had concluded, were so powerful that no Democrat could succeed by running against them. Instead, a Democrat had to run with them, and appropriate them. The true test of a political order, I have been suggesting, is when the opposition acquiesces to an order's ideological and policy imperatives. Clinton facilitated that acquiescence. From 1994 forward, he became the Democratic Eisenhower, America's neoliberal president par excellence.

The extent to which Clinton's administration from 1994 forward implemented neoliberal principles is rather stunning. In 1993, in a sign of things to come, Clinton had already signed NAFTA, turning all of North America into a single common market. In 1994, he endorsed the World Trade Organization and its plan to implement neoliberal principles internationally, a project that became known as the "Washington Consensus." In 1996, Clinton, working with Congress, deregulated the exploding telecommunication industry, now including not just phones and television but the cable and satellite sub-industries so important to the new information economy. Soon after, he did the same with the electrical generation industry that sustained (literally) the new economy. And then, in 1999, he supported Congress's repeal of the Glass-Steagall Act, the New Deal law that had done more than any other to end speculation, corruption, and the boom-bust cycle in America's financial sector.[35]

Clinton had come to regard markets as something akin to natural law. Upon signing NAFTA in December 1993, he remarked that the United States really had no choice in the matter. "We cannot stop global change," he declared. "We cannot repeal the economic competition that is everywhere. We can only harness the energy to our benefit." The lesson that Clinton drew from communism's collapse was that there would be no future for a nation seeking to resist market forces. "The institutions built by Truman and Acheson, by Marshall and Vandenberg have accomplished their task," he observed. But now, Clinton argued, the institutions designed to contain communism had to be retired or repurposed, for "the cold war is over. The grim certitude of the contest with communism has been replaced by the exuberant uncertainty of international economic competition."[36] To the extent to which government involved itself with the economy, Clinton argued, it should be to improve and direct markets, not to constrain them. Across his two terms, Clinton may have done more to free markets from regulation than even Reagan himself had done.

Robert Rubin, formerly co-chair of Goldman Sachs, one of Wall Street's leading investment houses, masterminded Clinton's neoliberalization of the economy. Clinton brought Rubin into his administration in 1993 to chair the newly created National Economic Council. Rubin's star was rising even before the Clinton health care initiative collapsed in 1994. For Rubin, the key to unlocking economic growth was to put America's fiscal house in order, a fix that would assure Wall Street about Washington's intentions under Democratic leadership and unleash a torrent of business investment. Thus, Rubin along with Treasury Secretary Lloyd Bentsen (formerly US senator from Texas) and Federal Reserve chair Alan Greenspan, a Reagan-Bush appointee and still an Ayn Rand acolyte, led a campaign to cut the deficit and to balance the budget. The plan they devised proposed shrinking the federal debt by $500 billion over five years through a combination of spending cuts, on the one hand, and increases in taxes on corporations (a 1 percent increase in the top corporate marginal rate) and the wealthy (to 39.6 percent of personal income on those earning more than $250,000), on the other. This was a tough sell to Congress, both to Reagan supply-siders in GOP ranks who were opposed to tax increases of any sort, and to New Deal liberals who expected the first Democratic president elected in sixteen years to expand rather than shrink spending on the party's cherished programs. The Rubin plan slipped through Congress in August 1993 by the narrowest of margins, 218–216 in the House and 51–50 in the Senate, with Vice-President Al Gore casting the tie-breaking vote.[37]

Initially, it was not clear how significant this budget agreement would be; the Clinton health care initiative was still in development and receiving most press attention. But when health care reform plans were shelved in August 1994 and as the economy simultaneously began to improve, the Rubin deficit reduction began to receive post-facto plaudits. Between 1994 and 2000, federal expenditures as a percentage of GDP fell to 17.6 percent, the lowest since the late 1960s. Meanwhile federal revenues rose steadily due to increased employment and the tax hike, bringing the federal government a surplus, also for first time since the late 1960s.[38] Economically, this balancing of the budget proved to be an engine of growth. Stock market values rose dramatically and millions of new jobs were created between 1994 and 2000.

The success of this economic expansion elevated the neoliberal phalanx of the Clinton team into a dominant position in his administration, a perch they would never relinquish. Clinton appointed Rubin secretary of the treasury in 1995 and reappointed the neoliberal Republican Greenspan to a third term as chair of the Federal Reserve in 1996. Clinton had also appointed the onetime Republican and longtime budget hawk, Leon Panetta, as his chief of staff in 1994. The influence on economic policy of this troika of high administration officials proved impossible for the insurgents in Clinton's administration, such as Robert Reich and Joseph Stiglitz, to overcome. Freeing market forces was the animating spirit of the Clinton administration. Everyone was expected to fall into line. One of Rubin's lieutenants,

Lawrence Summers, who would later re-emerge as a key player in the early Obama administration, had this to say about the journey during the Clinton years of ostensibly Democratic Party economists: "Not so long ago, we were all Keynesians. . . . Equally, any honest Democrat will admit that we are now all Friedmanites."[39]

Clinton was as much the instrument as the mastermind of this transformation. The neoliberal reorientation of the Democratic Party had been in the works for a long time. Part of it dated back to the 1960s, when Great Society and New Left activists alike had tilted against the statism of the New Deal order. Both the attacks by Community Action Programs on big city machines and the New Left's antipathy to bureaucracy (private and public) had encouraged Democratic Party interest in market-based social policies.[40] Ralph Nader and his supporters had embraced the "capture thesis" developed by political scientists, the phrase referring to corporate interests "capturing" the very government agencies meant to regulate their behavior. Rather than battling to free government regulatory bodies from corporate control, many Naderites chose to focus instead on enhancing "consumer sovereignty." This meant stripping established corporations of government-protected privilege and making markets more responsive to the desire of consumers both for choice and for high-quality goods. Naderites often preferred deregulation to regulation, at least in those industries where the suffocation of competitive pressures had led to poor products and services, on the one hand, and high prices, on the other. These were the kinds of messages that Nader began transmitting to Jimmy Carter in the 1970s, as well as to some left-of-center forces in the Democratic Party. Nader and his supporters did not believe in the perfectibility of markets as neoliberals did. They remained critics of capitalism. Nevertheless, their efforts to make consumers sovereign over both industrialists and government regulators allowed them to make common cause with Republicans celebrating the virtues of markets that were genuinely free.[41]

A second part of the reorientation of the Democrats emerged more slowly out of a series of painful political calculations, as the conviction grew among them that they would not win the presidency again unless they accepted at least a portion of Republican Party market fundamentalism. McGovern's devastating defeat in 1972 at the hands of

Richard Nixon had sent the first shudder down Democratic spines. The next moment of truth came in 1984, when Reagan triumphed in a landslide over the Democratic nominee Walter Mondale. And then the 1988 Democratic candidate, Michael Dukakis, lost to George H. W. Bush, even as the latter was widely regarded as a weak candidate. As these losses mounted, Democratic Party officeholders formed the Democratic Leadership Council to move the party away from its New Deal past and toward a Republican future. Clinton was at the center of these discussions and plans for party reorientation.[42]

A third part of the reorientation of the Democrats emerged not from the pain of losing elections but from the giddiness that accompanied the information technology (IT) revolution. The 1990s were the decade of IT's extraordinary triumph. The first web browser, Mosaic, launched in 1993; Netscape, the forerunner of Google, debuted in 1994. Jeff Bezos founded Amazon in 1994 and Peter Thiel and his colleagues established PayPal in 1998, which was also the year Google appeared. This was the decade as well in which prodigal son Steve Jobs returned to Apple (in 1996) and put it on the path toward its early twenty-first-century globe-straddling dominance. When Clinton took office in January 1993, an upstart stock exchange, the National Association of Securities Dealers Automated Quotations (NASDAQ), heavily weighted toward these and other technology companies, stood at 670. When Clinton began his last year in office in 2000, the NASDAQ composite average had reached 4,100, more than a sixfold increase in a mere seven years. Meanwhile, unemployment had shrunk to 3.8 percent, the lowest in more than a generation.[43] "Never before," the president exulted in his 2000 State of the Union address, "has our nation enjoyed, at once, so much prosperity and social progress with so little internal crisis and so few external threats."[44] High tech was the straw stirring the American economy's resurgence. Stewart Brand and his band of tech hipsters had completed the journey from acid-besotted merry pranksters to cybernetic masters of the universe, increasingly toasted at gatherings of the world's economic and governmental elites at Aspen and Davos.[45] This internet revolution was closely tied ideologically to visions of market freedom.

Four cyberspace enthusiasts—Esther Dyson, George Gilder, George Keyworth, and Alvin Toffler—encased their IT vision in a manifesto, "Cyberspace and the American Dream: A Magna Carta for the Knowledge Age," which they circulated in 1994. The title of the manifesto said it all: Cyberspace represented an opportunity to renew "the American Dream" and to adapt ancient and revered traditions of Anglo-American liberty for a new century. The manifesto was utopian in its conviction that the cybernetic revolution represented a chance to start the world anew and to free humanity from past shackles. Drawing on the work of the acclaimed futurist in their ranks, Alvin Toffler, it framed the revolution in terms of "Third Wave" innovation.[46] The First Wave had made land and labor "the main 'factors of production'; the Second Wave had 'massified' [labor] around machines and larger industries. In a Third Wave economy, the central resource . . . is actionable knowledge."[47]

The shift in the mainsprings of the economy from material to cerebral resources, the authors declared, signaled nothing less than a fundamental transition in human history. Everything about society and civilization had to be rethought, including the "meaning of freedom, structures of self-government, definition of property, nature of competition, conditions for cooperation, sense of community and nature of progress."[48]

Such hyperbole had long been characteristic of political manifestos of all sorts, as their architects sought to unleash and then harness revolutionary passions for their causes. But hyperbole aside, this manifesto articulated well the vision of individual freedom, deeply associated with market freedom, that made the neoliberal revolution so compelling to so many people, on the left as well as on the right. "We are at the end of a century dominated by the mass institutions of the industrial age," the authors wrote in words that could have been pulled from the New Left's *Port Huron Statement* of 1962 and that reflected Toffler's own roots on the left. This age had "encouraged conformity and relied on standardization. And the institutions of the day—corporate and government bureaucracies, huge civilian and military administrations, schools of all types—reflected these priorities." Such constraints had been necessary in societies built on the Second Wave. Nevertheless, manifesto authors argued, "individual liberty suffered."[49]

Communism (and the Soviet Union) went unmentioned in "Cyberspace and the American Dream," but no ideology did more than it had to push a world of government planning, conformity, and stand-ardization into existence. Many of those in America who hated the New Deal (including George Gilder) did so because they viewed the latter as one step below the centralized planning nightmare imbedded in the Five-Year Plans long adored in the Soviet Union. Both systems (the Soviet one and the New Deal one) allegedly were crushing to in-dividual liberty. Now the cybernetic revolution had given America and the world not just the opportunity but also the technological means to break away from these systems of unfreedom.

Dyson and her co-authors asserted that America was the natural home of this revolution, for it had long been the nation most stead-fast in its opposition to state-centered tyranny, its resolve forged across "more than 150 years of intellectual and political ferment, from the Mayflower Compact to the U.S. Constitution," all of it dedicated to-ward making people free. It was no accident, the manifesto authors further argued, that the [computer] hacker was "a uniquely American phenomenon," the latest incarnation of the freedom-loving fron-tiersman, "who ignored every social pressure and violated every rule to develop a set of skills" that would first explore and then tame the cy-bernetic wilderness. Hackers could not thrive "in the more formalized and regulated democracies of Europe and Japan." Only in America had they "become vital for economic growth and trade leadership. Why? Because Americans still celebrate individuality over conformity, re-ward achievement over consensus and militantly protect the right to be different."[50]

The institution that had to be most radically rethought in the cyber-netic age was government itself. "The mass institutions of the Second Wave required us to give up freedom [to government] in order for the system to 'work.'" The Third Wave spelled trouble for all large, bu-reaucratic organizations. But government was particularly vulnerable, for it was "the last great redoubt of bureaucratic power on the face of the planet, and the coming change" was already challenging it at every turn.[51]

The manifesto's focus on the obsolescence of government must be seen for what it was: ideological assertion rather than proven fact. Such emphatic insistence on this ideologically driven view of govern-ment reflects how deeply market libertarianism shaped the views of its

authors. Gilder and Keyworth had been market libertarians long before they discovered the wonders of cybernetics. Gilder had published
Wealth and Poverty, the market fundamentalist tract of the Reagan
era, in 1981, and Keyworth had been Reagan's science advisor. They
thus had standing among those Republicans who had done the most to
push the GOP into the neoliberal era. Esther Dyson was a key figure
at *Wired*, an upstart technolibertarian journal that presented itself as
the oracle of the Third Wave. Toffler was the country's most famous
futurist, long a prophet of the coming transformation of humanity. It
was a formidable group.[52]

And they had political support. Newt Gingrich was an early pa-
tron. He had helped to organize the Progress and Freedom Foundation
(PFF), the institution sponsoring the writing of "Cyberspace and the
American Dream," hoping to use it to mobilize GOP support for the
technological revolution under way. The conference to discuss the manifesto was held in Gingrich's backyard (Atlanta) in 1994, with Gingrich
in attendance.[53] Until this time, cybernauts had eyed Gingrich with
suspicion. Dyson, who interviewed him for *Wired* in 1995, revealed
that she and many other cybernauts regarded him as the "antichrist"
because of his closeness to the Moral Majority and his own willingness, expressed on numerous occasions, to enforce cultural norms on
individuals, by government regulation if necessary. Such morals regulation was anathema to technolibertarians like Dyson. But Gingrich,
long a futurist himself (as Dyson learned in the course of her interview
with him), had embraced the emancipatory promise of cyberspace and
believed, fervently, that only a cyberspace free of regulation would deliver on that promise. When he became Speaker of the House in 1995
and, for a time, the most influential member of Congress, Gingrich
made it his mission to deliver unregulated cyberspace to America.[54]

Clinton and Gingrich were adversaries on many issues. Gingrich had
framed his campaign for congressional control in the 1994 elections in
terms of the need to check and then override Clinton's power and influence. But on cyberspace, these two enemies shared common ground.
Clinton and his crucial aide, Vice-President Al Gore, like Gingrich,
believed that advances in IT had brought the world to the cusp of
technological, economic, and political revolution. All three men were
borne aloft by the exuberance of the moment, in all its promise and

uncertainty. They themselves were convinced that the IT revolution would sweep all before it, and that Americans had to jump on the train—or more accurately get on the ramp toward the "information superhighway," as Gore had called it, or see their nation left behind.[55]

Initially, Silicon Valley was drawn more to Gingrich than to Clinton. He was the one talking in loudest terms about releasing the creative spirits of the market economy and of ensuring that cyberspace would be free of regulation. But the high-flying high-tech wizards of Silicon Valley had themselves never been entirely comfortable with the Republicans' emphasis on morals and their willingness to use government to enforce them. The wizards believed that an individual should be able to make decisions about his or her own religiosity, sexuality, and entertainment without having to get permission slips from Jerry Falwell–like moral overlords; that was part of the hacker's creed. This emphasis on personal freedom overlapped with Clinton's "live-and-let-live" attitude and made the Democratic Party a more congenial cultural home than the GOP for the West Coast high-tech vanguard.[56]

But would the Democrats, still generally perceived as the party of government regulation, deliver on the economic front? Would they keep their hands off the entrepreneurs, innovators, and corporations seeking to invent the new economy? From 1994–1995 onward, under Clinton's stewardship, the Democrats' answer was a resounding yes. First, Clinton and his administration implemented a regime of fiscal discipline that pleased Wall Street, which was already far along in underwriting the high-tech boom. Second, they committed themselves, under Gore's leadership, to a multi-year campaign to reinvent government, making it smaller, less intrusive, and more flexible—more suitable, in other words, for a third-wave economy.[57] And finally, and most important, they gave their assent to the Telecommunications Act of 1996, reform legislation that would make it possible for Silicon Valley to capitalize fully on its technical innovations. The telecom bill often receives less attention than other Clinton initiatives, such as welfare reform. But it needs to be rescued from this neglect, for it did more than any other piece of legislation in the 1990s to free the most dynamic sector of the economy from regulation and dramatically accelerate the building of a new economy based on neoliberal principles.

Telecom Reform

The Communications Act of 1934 had long ago established a framework for regulating mass media in the United States. Though criticized by some at the time for handing over too much control of the airwaves to private, commercial broadcasters, the legislation actually put telephony and the airwaves under serious public control. An integral element of the New Deal order, the act declared the airwaves to be the property of the American people, not of private corporations. As such, this industry had to be regulated in ways that advanced the public good. The act established the Federal Communications Commission (FCC) to oversee media corporations and to develop rules of access, competition, and service, where necessary. The FCC was particularly concerned with forestalling the rise of media monopolies. It therefore limited the number of radio (and later of television) stations that any one corporation could own. It accepted the prevailing division between telephone and telegraph, on the one hand, and broadcasting, on the other, and prohibited each sector from entering the other's turf. The corporations in question readily accepted this division, as the physical infrastructures each sector used to do its work—copper wires in the case of telephony and equipment to broadcast electronic signals through the air in the case of radio—were then very different.[58]

This divide between the telephone/telegraph and broadcast sectors of the industry was driven not just by technological realities but also by political imperatives, in this case the conviction that no media corporation should be allowed to become too powerful. Excessive concentrations of economic might were thought to be corrosive to the American republic. Media corporations in the early twentieth century had begun to draw particular scrutiny because of the belief that they would saturate the citizenry with "propaganda" and thus make it impossible for individual citizens to make the kinds of informed decisions necessary to make democracy work. As the influence of media corporations rose in the 1920s, it was thought, danger to democracy deepened.[59] Thus, the power of these corporations had to be limited either through regulation of rates and content or through rules compelling them to operate in a competitive environment.

The FCC followed the first route in regard to American Telephone and Telegraph (AT&T), declaring it to be a "natural monopoly" and thus not in need of competition. In return for being accorded this privileged status, AT&T was required to provide universal and reliable service at reasonable rates. Though privately owned, it became in effect a public utility. The FCC, by contrast, sought to nurture a competitive environment for radio, building on an industry pattern that saw hundreds of local stations spring up in the interwar years. As the rise of three national networks (the National Broadcasting Company, the Columbia Broadcasting System, and the American Broadcasting Company, soon to be known as NBC, CBS, and ABC) consolidated the industry in the 1930s and 1940s, the FCC curbed the networks' sway by limiting the number of local radio stations each could own outright. Local stations could choose to affiliate with one of the networks so as to gain access to the latter's rich menus of programs. But the former retained autonomy, which put them (local stations) in a position to control some of what they aired and also to improve their bargaining position relative to the national broadcasting companies. The same rules were applied to the television networks that grew out of the radio networks in the 1950s and 1960s. The Fairness Doctrine that prevailed from the late 1940s to the late 1980s and that required a broadcaster to give equal time to both sides of a political debate also expressed the FCC's desire to regulate the communications market.[60]

By the 1970s and 1980s, however, dissatisfaction with this regulatory regime was mounting. As proposals for designing new technologies began to percolate in the telecommunications industry, AT&T was increasingly criticized for its slow pace of innovation. A court order broke up this state-sanctioned monopoly in the early 1980s. Cable television emerged at the same time, threatening to swamp the carefully regulated world of network TV and its three major providers with hundreds of new channels. Reagan's FCC repealed the Fairness Doctrine in the late 1980s, arguing that the new age of communication had made it possible not only for everyone to speak but also for everyone to be heard; regulation no longer served the public interest. Tellingly, the Clinton administration made no effort to restore the Fairness Doctrine when it moved into the White House in 1993. To the contrary, it wanted to accelerate the IT revolution already under way by modernizing the Communications Act of 1934.

Vice-President Al Gore, who had already embraced the possibilities of high tech in the 1980s, headed up a high-level White House working group on telecommunications reform. After the 1994 election, control of the reform process passed to the Republican Party. But it turned out that it didn't matter much which party was driving reform, given that the Gingrinchites and the Clintonites shared the same passion for deregulation. They agreed on the need to remove the New Deal regulatory shackles, even if that meant stripping away the anti-monopoly provisions of the 1934 act. If hundreds of cable channels would soon be available, why limit the number that any one cable corporation could own or offer? Why confine communications companies to one sector of the industry—telephony, broadcast TV, cable TV, satellite TV, film—instead of letting them engage each other in competition across the entire telecommunications frontier? Such broad competition was thought to be especially important because no one knew exactly where the IT revolution was heading or what benefits might accrue from unexpected collaborations and synergies. Startups were all the rage. All the more reason, then, to let the telecommunications companies compete without restriction. Let the innovations that hackers and their venture capitalist supporters were generating travel to every corner of the media economy and let American consumers determine, through purchases, which of the new products and services delighted them the most.[61]

Excitement about the internet deepened the sense that America, indeed the world, was on the cusp of a market-powered transformation. Observers searching for a precedent for a communications revolution of this magnitude reached back to the invention of the printing press half a millennium before. The internet, some asserted, would do even more than the advent of printed books had once accomplished. Patricia Aufderheide, a hard-headed media critic, herself marveled in the 1990s at how the net "was equally good at sending and receiving in any direction, making every user a potential producer as much as a potential consumer. It could be endlessly recombinant and open at any point to new users and service providers who wanted to hook up."[62] No single corporation would be able to control such a dynamic platform, accessible at all hours of the day and night to so many users as both producers and consumers. The internet was inherently, restlessly, and relentlessly democratic. Monopolies once ruled the world; but, to paraphrase Karl Marx, their once solid control of markets was now melting into air.

Getting the most out of this remarkable digital platform drove the Telecommunications Act of 1996. Signed into law in February, it swept away rules that had long prevented corporations from crossing over from one sector of the industry to another. Phone companies, cable companies, satellite companies, television networks, movie studios, and data providers could all now compete with each other. Restriction on the number of stations or subsidiaries that one company could own was dramatically weakened. The very act of throwing so many corporations from different sectors into competition with each other would make it impossible, it was thought, for any one or two providers to control the industry. Internet innovation would rapidly undercut any media provider lucky or ruthless enough to corner a portion of the market for a time.[63]

Some critics tried to warn Americans that not every aspect of the internet age was new and beautiful. The era of the Gilded Age (1870s–1890s) offered a cautionary tale of stunning technological breakthrough and industrial creativity giving way to monopoly, corruption, and inequality. One of those who tried to sound this alarm in the 1990s was Marvin Kitman, a media columnist for *Newsday*, then a major New York City–Long Island newspaper daily. As he tried to get his mind around the complex bill taking shape in Congress in summer 1995, Kitman's thoughts kept flashing back to what he had learned in school about the Gilded Age, when a previous generation of innovators was transforming America, in this case (to use Alvin Toffler's terminology) from an agrarian first-wave to an urban-industrial second-wave economy.[64] Then the innovators had been the captains of the railroads, the lords of telephone and telegraph services, and the masters of steel production, petroleum refining, electrical machine manufacture, and the creation of chemical compounds. For all the brilliance of their work in generating capital, jobs, and new products, these corporate innovators were also ruthless in their pursuit of economic and then political power. Ida Tarbell, Lincoln Steffens, and fellow "muckraking" journalists were indefatigable in their efforts to expose the unsavory practices of John D. Rockefeller, Cornelius Vanderbilt, and other "robber barons," laying bare for reading publics these men's insatiable drives for power and profits, and their single-minded determination to crush all competition.

Kitman argued that the titans of the 1990s telecommunications industry had more in common with "Johnny Rockefeller and Andy Carnegie and all the other robber barons of Ida Tarbell's day" than anyone thought. "This is land-rush time again," Kitman declared. "Everybody sits around commenting about the coming of the new telecommunications age. It's not new. It's the same old plundering of public resources. Only we have funny-looking real estate now, real estate that can't be seen."[65]

The law that actually passed Congress in early 1996 did nothing to ease Kitman's concerns. A few multimedia giants "are going to wind up owning everything," he declared. "And why not? That's what Time and Warner said when they merged [in 1990]. 'Someday,' as Time Warner CEO Gerry Levin had already predicted, 'there are going to be five companies that own all the media on planet Earth, and we plan to be one.' "[66] It may have sounded like a great idea to make the airwaves free for all, but the media companies didn't really want to compete. The merger movement in their ranks had begun before, indeed in anticipation of, the Telecom Act passing. Kitman fully expected it to continue. The bill, he charged, was going to facilitate precisely the kind of corporate consolidation in critical industries that had occurred a hundred years earlier.

The power of the telecommunication corporations was the theme that Kitman returned to again and again. He did not find anything in the bill that he thought would curb it. To the contrary, Kitman argued, corporate interests succeeded in drafting a bill that served their interests. The regulatory imperative that had done so much to shape popular responses to corporate power a hundred years before didn't seem to exist anymore. Kitman did not have faith that the FCC, as constituted, would have the tools or the authority to take on a telecom industry in full-scale consolidation mode.[67]

To be sure, constituencies other than corporations got something in the bill. Moral traditionalists got the Communications Decency Act to control the spread of pornography on the internet (though it would soon be declared unconstitutional). And progressives got both universal service—the industry was obligated to connect every home, school, and public place to the net—and a tax on cable providers to pay for it. Clinton, Gore, and their allies considered this a big victory, and it was. It enhanced the Naderite vision of making the consumer sovereign, in this case by developing an infrastructure that would put unlimited amounts of information at the user's disposal. Soon, Bill Clinton exclaimed in 1996, "every person will have the opportunity to make the most of his or her life." Technology was "going to liberate Americans and bring them together."[68] But there was nothing in the bill that facilitated putting a brake on corporate power—except for a blind faith first in the ability of the market itself to impose such limits and second in the ability of the FCC, if needed, to rise to the occasion, supported by a Congress willing to give it new powers to enforce the public's will on the private sector.[69]

The 1996 Telecom Act also explicitly relieved corporations controlling the telecommunications network from the obligation to police content flowing across their domains if it originated with independent users or promoters. This exemption held even if such content was deemed to be hateful, false, or incendiary. Internet providers thus acquired broad immunity against suits that might be filed regarding the damage that such content might cause individuals, groups, or institutions. This was Section 509 of the Telecommunications Act, later incorporated as Section 230 of the revised Communications Act of 1934.[70]

Throughout the legislative effort to reform telecommunications, virtually no one of influence in either the Democratic or Republican party dared suggest that the broadcast/cable/satellite spectrum was a public good owned by the American people, or that corporations seeking access to it ought to be regarded (and regulated) as public utilities. To suggest as much in the 1990s—or even to raise the "fairness" of the mass media as value worth pursuing—was to be stigmatized as a seriously out-of-touch Grandpa, someone who simply could not embrace the revolutionary potential of the moment. Most Republicans and Democrats believed that government could not possibly succeed in managing the telecommunications industry's development. The forces of the private sector had to be unleashed, competition had to be intensified, the opportunity to spread internet freedom encouraged at every step. This was the nature of the Third Wave. A belief in the value, indeed the imperative, of deregulation had become hegemonic.

Joseph Stiglitz, the Nobel Prize–winning economist and prolific author, has written revealingly about how he and other like-minded progressives themselves drank too much in the 1990s from the jug of free market Kool-Aid. As a member and then chair of the Council of Economic Advisers, and as a participant in Al Gore's working party on telecom reform, Stiglitz played an important role in the Clinton administration. Democrats like him, he would later observe, "had always provided a check on the mindless pursuit of deregulation. Now, we joined the fray—sometimes pushing things even further than the Reagan Administration. . . . 'We are all Berliners' was the sentiment of President Kennedy's declaration" when he visited Berlin in 1961. "Thirty years later," Stiglitz declared, "we were all deregulators. . . . By adopting deregulation language [ourselves], we had in fact conceded the battle."[71] This concession, this participation on the part of progressive Democrats in the market intoxication of the 1990s, is yet another sign that neoliberalism had become dominant, its advocates compelling all political players to work within its ideological matrix.

A month after signing the telecom reform bill, Clinton and Gore flew to California to celebrate their victory with the leaders of Silicon Valley. The tech companies had chosen this date, which they called "Netday," as the occasion to send their technicians into public schools across the state to lay cable and install routers. Clinton and Gore went to Concord, a town on the eastern part of San Francisco Bay, fancying themselves "technicians for a day," doing their bit to run cable wires through classroom ceiling tiles (Clinton arrived at the school dressed in khakis, ready to get to work). Of course, Clinton had his re-election in mind, with the 1996 primary season already in full swing. It was time for the Democrats to lock down Silicon Valley support, now that Clinton had demonstrated, through the Telecommunications Act, his commitment to the industry.[72]

Clinton didn't quite clinch the tech lobby's support that day, but he did five months later when he returned to California to tell tech leaders that he supported their opposition to the state's Proposition 211, a referendum that would have made these executives and their board members personally liable in lawsuits brought by investors against startups that had improperly squandered resources. The defeat of Proposition 211 was second only to the passage of telecom reform on Silicon Valley's wish list for 1996. Clinton's support gave the opponents of the proposition the assistance they needed. Less than a month after Clinton's visit, industry leaders announced their satisfaction with the Clinton-Gore regime. Steve Jobs put it well: "The past four years have been the best Silicon Valley has ever seen."[73] The message was clear: Silicon Valley wanted another four years of Clinton-Gore. High-tech contributions to the Democrats' 1996 campaign surged. Clinton sailed to victory in November, and California Proposition 211 was defeated.

Media industry consolidation, meanwhile, proceeded apace. Time Warner acquired the Turner Broadcasting System in 1996, bringing it control of the first all-news cable station, CNN. It also acquired two independent film companies, Castle Rock Entertainment and New Line Cinema, and it owned HBO, the first digitally transmitted television movie service. In 2000, Time Warner merged with AOL, and in 2016, this behemoth was gobbled up by an even larger beast, an AT&T long since freed from its public utility constraints.

The Disney Corporation was not far behind Time Warner. Just days after Clinton signed telecom reform into law in 1996, Disney merged with Capital Cities/ABC, which also brought the premier cable sports station, ESPN, into the Disney stable. Amusement parks, professional sports teams, cruise lines, and other sectors of the entertainment industry came and went, part of the Disney empire one day, traded away the next. General Electric, long America's most prominent electrical equipment manufacturer, made itself part of the media company land rush by acquiring NBC and RCA. Another giant electrical manufacturing company, Westinghouse, purchased CBS in 1995 and then merged with Viacom in 1999. The 1996 act had indeed created opportunities for corporations seeking media influence and money to move in any direction almost without restraint. This was the meaning of deregulation in the era of the internet.[74]

It was not all about consolidation of course. It was also about startups, many of which dazzled Silicon Valley (and Wall Street) between 1996 and 2001. Google emerged during this time, and Facebook and Twitter would follow shortly thereafter. A disproportionate number of the key innovators in the global cybernetics industry were located in the United

States; there *was* something about the American economic and political environment that enabled the IT revolution to flourish. Nevertheless, the hoary capitalist principle of innovation and competition leading to consolidation and monopoly still operated. Thus, the phenomenal success of Google's search engine would allow it to control, by 2016, 90 percent of the market. Barely a question had been raised about whether it was good for one unregulated media corporation to have so much influence over how 300-million-plus Americans acquired information.[75] Kitman had been right in predicting that the Telecommunications Act of 1996 would bring a new generation of robber barons to life. Gerald Levin turns out not to have been far off in his prediction that five media companies would one day rule the world. The Clinton administration made it possible for that prediction to come true.

Wall Street Reform

The campaign to unshackle the telecommunications industry marched hand in hand with the campaign to unshackle finance; only then would full free market capitalism be achieved. During the Clinton years, this unshackling went under the name of "financial modernization."[76] As with the media industry, the finance industry was seen by groups on both sides of the political aisle as hobbled by an outdated regulatory regime, this one also established during the halcyon early days of the New Deal order. The relevant legislation in this case was the Glass-Steagall Act of 1933, which had imposed a regime of regulation on Wall Street in order to prevent a recurrence of the wild speculation and trades that had sparked the Great Crash of 1929.

Separating investment and commercial banking stood at the heart of Glass-Steagall. Investment banks were to underwrite loans to corporations looking to expand their business, handle stock offerings, trade securities, and process mergers and acquisitions. They were banned from the retail, or commercial, banking sector—the institutions where ordinary people had their checking and savings accounts and obtained home mortgages and equity loans.

Investment banks were explicitly barred from gaining controlling interests in commercial banks or from using money from commercial bank depositors' accounts for their corporate investments and underwriting. The Federal Reserve was given the authority to regulate commercial banking, and the Federal Deposit Insurance Corporation was set up to guarantee the savings of commercial bank customers. Commercial banks had to be chartered in particular states and were not allowed to do business in other states, a regulation that also prevented consolidation and monopolies from developing in this sector. These commercial banks, moreover, were allowed to invest only 10 percent of their reserves in private securities. They were permitted to trade in government securities, which were deemed to be safe instruments, backed by federal government guarantees. Interest on checking accounts was non-existent, and interest on savings accounts was low. Money market funds did not exist.

Glass-Steagall along with other regulatory legislation in the 1930s restored confidence in the US banking sector and put it on a much more stable footing. These laws structured the New Deal order's financial regime through the entirety of that order's existence. During this era, banks took a back seat to the corporate giants of manufacturing— General Motors, Ford, US Steel, Standard Oil of Ohio (and later Exxon), DuPont, Boeing, and Lockheed-Martin—in driving the economy. Banks provided essential services to these corporations, but they were not the economy's leading edge. This was the era of "bankers' hours"— gentlemanly 10–4 workdays—and of cozy and cordial relationships among the various Wall Street firms that underwrote loans and public offerings for corporations. Within the savings and loan industry, the source of many home mortgages, the "algorithm" dominating work life was not 10–4, but 3–6–3: give depositors 3 percent interest on their savings, use those deposits as the basis of loans issued at 6 percent to homebuyers, and then be on the golf course by 3 in the afternoon. It was a comfortable, and comparatively leisurely, life.[77]

As with telecommunications, dissatisfaction with this regulatory regime was percolating by the 1970s. Deregulatory finance reformers achieved their first big success in the pension industry. This industry itself was a by-product of the New Deal order, a consequence of labor unions compelling employers to set aside funds that would be doled out to employees after their retirement. Huge pools of investable capital sprang up as successful unions spread these pension plans to more and more sectors of the economy, and as non-union employers sought to forestall unionization by voluntarily giving workers union-grade pension plans of their own.

More and more banks, commercial and investment, wanted to get their hands on these funds, upping the pressures for deregulating finance in the process. Then in the 1970s another critical change occurred: Employers won legislation in Congress allowing them to replace "defined benefit" plans with "defined contribution" ones. The former had promised every employee a set monthly payment upon retirement, continuing until death. The latter promised every employee something else: a monthly supplement to his or her paycheck, paid into an individual retirement account (IRA). Upon retirement, these supplements would serve as the employee's pension, with the retiree obligated to withdraw a minimum amount annually for living expenses, to continue until the fund was exhausted or the pensioner died. Employers much preferred the defined contribution scheme to the defined benefit plan, for this scheme made pensioners dependent on their own funds, unable to make claims on the employer for monthly checks that could continue for twenty to thirty and even forty years after retirement.

As a result of these 1970s changes, millions of American employees began to accumulate IRA funds. The cumulative size of this dollar pot grew from millions to billions to trillions. Both commercial and investment banks cast their eyes covetously on this vast investment chest; calls to dismantle Glass-Steagall began to mount. The Reagan administration, as we have seen, responded to this clamor by freeing a portion of the commercial banking industry (the savings and loan sector) from its prior constraints. It did so without eliminating federal deposit insurance, a scheme also put in place in the 1930s through which the federal government promised to bail out any individual depositor whose bank had collapsed. Secure in the knowledge that the federal government would have to save them if they failed, savings and loans took excessive risks, which contributed to the financial crash of 1987–1988.

This setback stalled but did not end the movement for financial deregulation. The IT revolution had convinced many that this movement had to resume, for tech transformation was thought to have changed in fundamental ways the relationship between risk and reward. Highly trained finance experts (as opposed to the "amateurs" who ran savings and loans) allegedly possessed the ability to manage risk in ways that had not been possible before. The fullness and instantaneity of information that computers had served up had put market perfection within human grasp. New information technology made it possible to shrink and even to eliminate risk, and to smooth out the highs and lows of the business cycle. Much existing government regulation was therefore superfluous—or worse, an actual impediment to economic growth and development. Hence, it would be best, market evangelists argued, if governments would just get out of the way. Glass-Steagall had been a necessary part of Democratic politics earlier in the century, but it was no longer needed. Indeed, it was doing more to impede rather than to encourage economic growth. Banking "modernization" was not only still desirable but essential. A new discipline, financial engineering, attracted many of the best and brightest at America's top universities. By the 1990s, they were flooding into Wall Street, intrigued by the challenge of designing complex financial instruments, on the one hand, and by the opportunity to pursue big paydays, on the other.[78] All these forces converged to produce what many scholars have labeled the "financialization" of the economy, manifest in the size, wealth, and power of investment houses and brokerage firms, now seen as the principal drivers of capital generation, innovation, and profit.[79]

Plans for reform developed more slowly than with telecommunications; there was more resistance to be overcome, especially in light of the 1980s savings-and-loan debacle. But in 1999, Clinton signed the Gramm-Leach bill repealing Glass-Steagall's separation of commercial and investment banks. All banks were now free to compete across the entirety of the financial marketplace, just as media companies were free to do across the entirety of their marketplace. A Democratic president had struck down another once indispensable regulatory pillar of the New Deal order. With the stock market soaring, the repeal of Glass-Steagall was generally hailed as another milestone in the construction of Clinton's "bridge toward tomorrow."[80]

Telecom reform and financial modernization tied the West Coast to the East Coast, Silicon Valley to Wall Street, San Francisco to New York. Both coasts, industries, and megalopolises had become integral to Clinton's reconfigured Democratic Party. But the success of America into the twenty-first century depended on more than binding together east coast and west coast elites. It depended as well on the continued international supremacy of the United States. Events in the world across the 1990s had strengthened the US hand. The prestige of US economics and ideas benefited not just from the collapse of the Soviet Union but from the rise of Margaret Thatcher in 1980s Great Britain, and her decision to subject the United Kingdom to a deregulation project even more drastic than what the United States itself had undertaken. Labour leader Tony Blair supported that project in the 1990s once he ascended to power, much as Clinton carried through the revolution that Reagan had started.[81]

Meanwhile, Chancellor Helmut Kohl was reuniting Germany and then Europe under terms that the United States found satisfactory. The European Union (EU) came into existence in 1993 as a single market allowing free movement of goods, services, people, and capital throughout the territory controlled by member states. Its establishment could be interpreted as an achievement for the deregulatory impulse. The EU also laid plans in the early 1990s for a currency union in 1999 and then a single currency, the euro, that would bind together a large subset of EU members. At Germany's insistence, fiscal discipline would be mandated to sustain this currency unification. National governments would have to balance their budgets, and loans to member states would be limited to what they could reasonably hope to repay. These principles converged with those that Robert Rubin had laid down in the United States through his budget agreement of 1993 and later through the Washington Consensus as expressed through the policies of the World Trade Organization and the International Monetary Fund. The United States could plausibly claim to be carrying Europe along with its neoliberal revolution. Kohl contemplated aloud the day when a "United States of Europe" would emerge with a scheme for economic and political integration—and a wise blend of market freedom and market discipline—closely modeled on that of the 1990s American republic.[82]

And yet, neoliberal advances in Britain and the EU also threatened international US financial dominance. Thatcher's 1986 deregulation of banking in the UK, sweeping aside local and national regulation and increasing the appeal of the UK's financial services to investors and dealmakers throughout the world, went beyond what was then going on in the United States. European and American banks rushed to set up branches in Britain, allowing London to rival New York as the premier site for innovative and high-paced financial transactions. The Labour Party, when it returned to power in 1997 under Blair, advanced these trends, further eviscerating the country's regulatory regime by downsizing nine regulatory agencies into one and instructing it not to do anything that would damage "the competitive position of the United Kingdom."[83] Germany also threatened United States primacy now that Kohl had reunited its two halves and transformed this re-integrated nation into Europe's economic juggernaut. Frankfurt emerged as a global financial hub in its own right, with its banks flexing their muscles and flooding both London and New York with their money.

Democratic lawmakers such as Senator Charles Schumer of New York felt the competition of London and Frankfurt keenly. Though he represented the state in which ideas of the New Deal order had incubated under Governor Franklin Roosevelt's stewardship, he, too, was now ready to release America from the financial regulatory system that FDR had put in place. Neoliberalism appeared to be a force too powerful for anyone to stop. The decision by Clinton, Schumer, and others to deregulate finance further wrapped the Democrats in the embrace of elites that were driving the new economy.[84]

In 1997, Robert Reich, who had recently left his post as secretary of labor in the Clinton administration, raised trenchant questions about the political implications of this embrace. Describing an elaborate head-of-state luncheon that the Clinton White House hosted for President Zedillo of Mexico in late 1995, Reich recalled a time when the invited guests would have been "diplomats, artists, and Nobel Prize winners." But now their places had been taken by "executives of global corporations and Wall Street bankers." Heads of state, Reich observed, had "become traveling salesmen, eagerly hawking their countries to anyone large enough to buy them." "Global money," he intoned, was "the new sovereign."[85] Increasingly, central banks and the vast constellations of private financial institutions over which they presided seemed to rule the world.

Political Dissent and Culture in a Neoliberal Age

Though Clinton and Reich had been good friends since Rhodes Scholar days at Oxford, the latter's tenure as labor secretary was not a happy one. To read his memoir of those years, *Locked in the Cabinet*, is to feel the sting experienced by this talented, innovative, and principled small "d" democrat as he was repeatedly shoved aside on economic issues by Rubin, Bentsen, Panetta, and, of course, the grand vizier himself, Alan Greenspan. The latter were all major policymakers in the Clinton administration in ways that Reich was not. Reich's account of being summoned to a one-on-one lunch with Greenspan in the latter's private dining room at the Federal Reserve is chilling, with the atmosphere, as described by Reich, more redolent of an audience with a king than of two officials, both representing a proud democratic republic, sitting down with each other to break bread.[86]

It did not help that Reich was labor secretary, a post never accorded the prestige of secretary of state or secretary of the treasury, or that his principal constituency, the labor movement, was in decline and disarray. Reich's early efforts to reach out to labor leaders failed. Reich's father had been a shopkeeper who had loathed Roosevelt and the New Deal—its taxation, its social welfare, and its labor unions. An academic superstar, Reich's world after he left home had been defined by universities and public policy think tanks, institutions laced with suspicion of labor unions as being small-minded and reflexively defensive in their demands. Reich had been an early proponent of global free trade. He wanted to help workers not by preserving jobs that could not withstand foreign competition but through major commitments to education and retraining. America's workforce, he had long argued, had to adapt to the imperatives of a global economy.[87]

But Reich was a quick study, and his encounters with labor leaders soon persuaded him that education and training were not enough. Workers had to be guaranteed the right to strike; and that right could only be satisfactorily protected if workers who went on strike did not have to worry about being fired from their jobs. NAFTA had increased this worry in the ranks of labor. Reich pleaded with Clinton to support a measure to outlaw firings by employers of workers for strike-related reasons. The president came around, but even his support was not enough to push this law through Congress.[88]

Reich's proposed measure was itself modest; it demanded much less of employers than a full-scale reform of laws governing labor organizing would have entailed. The important package of such laws defeated during the years of Jimmy Carter's administration was never revived during the Clinton years in the White House, not even by Reich himself. As Clinton's Democratic Party was turning its face more and more to Wall Street and Silicon Valley, it was turning its back on the movement that had propelled the party to power in the 1930s and 1940s.[89]

Reich did not give up on his insurgent campaign. He now pivoted to a different but related cause: redressing the growing imbalance of power between the rich and poor that had become a hallmark of America during its neoliberal age. In another bipartisan effort with Gingrich's Republicans, Clinton was already in 1994 designing legislation to pare welfare rolls, limit the number of years that any individual or family could receive benefits, and develop more effective mechanisms for moving the poor from welfare to work. These efforts would eventuate in the Personal Responsibility and Work Opportunity Reconciliation Act of 1996, yet another piece of legislation that struck at a principle of the New Deal order.[90]

Reich was not deeply involved in drafting this bill or the negotiations surrounding it, but he did seize the rhetorical opportunity offered by the prominence of the welfare issue to begin talking about equality of sacrifice. If the poor were being asked to give up their welfare, Reich argued, then the same should be asked of corporations. "Since we are committed to moving the disadvantaged from welfare to work," Reich told a Democratic Leadership Council audience in late 1994, "why not target corporate welfare as well and use the savings to help all Americans get better work? Ending corporate welfare is a worthy goal."[91] Reich did not regard these rather measured two sentences as the words of a militant, but they exploded across the national media the next day as though they were. Corporate leaders were irate. The head of the National Association of Manufacturers bellowed at Michael Kingsley, a host of the popular TV debate show, *Crossfire*: "Corporations are not like welfare mothers. The Secretary has no right to criticize American companies in that way." Over the next two weeks, Reich was repeatedly dressed down for these remarks by the power troika of Rubin, Bentsen, and Panetta.[92]

Reich did, however, get a positive reaction from Clinton, which encouraged the labor secretary to continue his campaign. He altered his language to replace the negative phrase, "corporate welfare," with a positive one, "corporate responsibility." By invoking this latter slogan, Reich was asking corporations to take responsibility not just for their shareholders but for their employees and for the communities in which their plants were located. He uttered the phrase "corporate responsibility," in early 1996 on *Nightline*, then a popular late-night TV news show, only to be excoriated again. This time Rubin delivered the reprimand solo. Reich recalled the conversation as being cordial on the surface, with Rubin barely raising his voice. But Rubin's words were harsh, as he accused Reich of using "inflammatory" language to incite "class warfare" and to undercut Clinton's campaign to win Wall Street to the Democrats' side.[93]

This time Clinton did not come to Reich's rescue. The president's campaign for Wall Street support had recently intensified. He had just signed the Telecommunications Act. He was about to travel to California to get Silicon Valley on board his 1996 presidential campaign. He could not afford to have Reich leading a corporate responsibility campaign from inside his administration. Clinton did not fire his old friend. But over the next six months, Reich came to understand that there would be no future for his kind of politics in the Clinton administration. Soon after Clinton's re-election in November, Reich told his boss that he had decided to resign. Joseph Stiglitz, another left-leaning member of the Clinton administration, resigned shortly thereafter.[94]

The issue of corporate welfare did not die. Ralph Nader made it one of his refrains. Appearing before Congress in 1999, Nader offered a staggeringly long and detailed report on the extent and variety of benefits that the federal government was bestowing on corporations.[95] But Nader, too, got nowhere. His frustration and anger with Clinton, with his anointed successor, Gore, and with the neoliberal order that the two men were putting in place informed Nader's decision to run for the presidency as a third-party candidate in 2000. The votes he would attract would be a factor contributing to Gore's defeat.

Republicans loathed Clinton, despite all the work that Clinton, the Democratic Eisenhower, had done to secure the triumph of the neoliberal order. In part, their hatred simply reflected frustration at having been bested by Clinton in multiple contests. The 1990s, in Republican eyes, were to be the decade of GOP political triumph. The party of Reagan, after all, had been the one that had forced the Soviet Union to its knees and then oversaw its dismemberment. The partisan political rewards from that victory should have been substantial. But everything, as Republicans saw it, had gone awry during the 1990s. First, Ross Perot, a forerunner of Trump, ran a surprisingly successful right-wing populist campaign in 1992 to deny George H. W. Bush re-election and to elevate an obscure small-state Democratic governor to the White House. When the GOP recovered from its 1992 presidential defeat to deliver to Clinton and his fiery feminist wife a shellacking in the 1994 election, the wily Arkansan outwitted the GOP again by stealing their neoliberal program of deregulation (and budget balancing) and implementing enough of it to win re-election as president in 1996. Then, justices such as Sandra Day O'Connor and David Souter, appointed to the Supreme Court by GOP presidents, turned out to be reluctant about implementing the originalist vision laid out by Meese and other Reagan firebrands in the 1980s. What should have been a decade of unqualified GOP electoral triumph had instead become an unending GOP nightmare.

Then, as if to rub salt into the party's wounds, Clinton also demonstrated how much a neoliberal order was compatible with a multicultural republic of many colors, religions, and creeds. In Clinton's hands, multiculturalism had ceased to be what it had been in the 1970s and 1980s: a radical creed that had insisted on the ineradicability of racism from American society. Now it carried a message of racial reconciliation and patriotism. It celebrated diversity as the essence of Americanism. Clinton grasped that his version of the multicultural creed was perfectly suited to a neoliberal vision of a world without borders, one in which peoples of different countries mixed freely with each other, indifferent to the hierarchies of race, religion, and nationality into which they had been born. In Clinton's eyes, multiculturalism was synonymous with cosmopolitanism, a way of living that celebrated robust exchanges not just of goods but of cultures across various racial, ethnic, religious, and national divides.[96] Clinton deployed his cosmopolitanism in the international arena, too, bringing together antagonists (Protestants and Catholics in Northern Ireland, Jews and Arabs in the Middle East) whose differences were long thought to be irreconcilable.[97]

In America, Clinton celebrated this way of living, confident that the diversity and hybridity it was engendering was strengthening the nation. It was no accident that California, the center of the IT revolution, was also a cockpit of this cosmopolitanism. In his 2000 State of the Union address, Clinton saluted America's most populous state for leading the country to its multicultural future: "Within 10 years, just 10 years, there will be no majority race in our largest state of California. In a little more than 50 years, there'll be no majority race in America." Clinton celebrated these developments as being in America's best interests. "In a more interconnected world, this diversity can be our greatest strength. Just look around this chamber," Clinton exulted. "We have members in this Congress from virtually every racial, ethnic and religious background. And I think you would agree that America is stronger for it."[98]

Global cities were the natural homes of this diversity and the global neoliberal networks that nurtured it. California had two such sprawling megalopolises: San Francisco, reaching down to Silicon Valley and San Jose in the South and up to Berkeley and Marin County in the North; and Los Angeles, extending the tentacles of its economy and cosmopolitan culture throughout southern California. Those cities had their counterparts across the United States in Seattle, Chicago, Boston, New York, Miami, Atlanta, and Houston, and internationally in London, Paris, Frankfurt, Hong Kong, Mumbai, and Toronto. All these cities acquired allure as places peopled by individuals from everywhere, drawn to them both to make a good living and to rejoice in life invigorated by exceptional cross-cultural pollination. These were places where prior constraints of culture, identity, and normative sexuality could be tossed aside. Identity politics proved compatible with, and were often nourished by, the urban moral code of the ascendant neoliberal order.

To link identity politics and neoliberalism is not meant to discredit the former, which embodied profound aspirations to personal freedom, even emancipation. It is rather to underscore the positive dimension of the neoliberal order and to understand how it sustained such aspirations. It was no accident that two crucial nerve centers for America's neoliberal order—Silicon Valley and Wall Street—were imbedded in San Francisco and New York City, arguably the most culturally liberal—one might even say culturally radical—cities in the country.

There was an underside to the emergence of these glittering cosmopolitan meccas. Their dramatic growth in population and employment drained resources, human and physical, from other parts of the country, small towns and rural areas most of all. The economic inequality that was so much a hallmark of the neoliberal order had a spatial dimension: Jobs and wealth were concentrated in the big cities and the cosmopolitan corridors that issued from them, with barrenness of economic opportunity increasingly the lot of those who resided beyond these metropolitan borders.[99]

There was a racial dimension to this inequality as well. The clearing of millions of poor, black Americans from city streets through mass incarceration, begun in the 1980s under Republican administrations, continued in the 1990s under Clinton. Clinton prided himself for being tough on crime and for assembling the funds to put 100,000 more police on the streets. The Department of Defense, meanwhile, was accelerating the militarization of local police forces by distributing to them at little or no cost vast supplies of now redundant Cold War–era military equipment. The 1990s was also the decade in which more and more urban police forces adopted the "broken windows" theory of crime articulated in the early 1980s by social scientist James Q. Wilson. The theory posited that the slightest infractions of the law, such as vandalism, loitering, and subway fare evasion, had to be treated with the same seriousness as egregious infractions; minor crimes, left unpunished, inevitably led to a culture of permissiveness that encouraged major ones.[100]

The same philosophy governed the approach to the war on drugs, with possession of small amounts increasingly punished with tough sentences once reserved for the possession and dealing of large amounts. Police acquired the license to roam through cities, deploying "stop and frisk" dragnets, hauling off all kinds of "criminals" to jail. Reform in sentencing protocols had deprived prosecutors of the discretion they had previously possessed to let first time or petty offenders off lightly, with a brief jail term or simply a warning. Now more and more of those arrested went to jail, filling penitentiaries to the point that the United States acquired the largest incarcerated population, in both absolute and relative terms, of any nation on earth.[101]

This war on crime did make cities safer than they had been in the 1970s and 1980s, drawing legions of young people to them to work in finance, in the creative industries, and soon in flourishing and multiplying restaurant and cultural districts. The value of urban real estate soared.[102] New York City's ascent as a center of global finance and cosmopolitanism occurred under the mayoralty of a law-and-order Republican, Rudolph Giuliani, who ran the city from 1994 to 2001. Before becoming mayor, Giuliani had been federal attorney for the powerful Southern District of New York, where he built a reputation as the nation's toughest prosecutor, sending Wall Street charlatans, Mafia bosses, and drug lords to jail. As mayor, he and his police commissioner, William Bratton, became the country's most enthusiastic implementers of Wilson's broken windows theory. Criticism of Giuliani for his pros-ecutorial and police excesses was rife, but he was also a popular figure among New Yorkers, who re-elected him to a second term.[103]

Liberty, as we have seen, had long been closely associated with order in the imagination of both classical liberals of the nineteenth century and neoliberals of the twentieth century. This association stemmed from the conviction that one could not enjoy one's liberty without order. As Walter Lippmann had observed sixty years earlier, well-functioning markets were not part of nature. They had to be built and managed, and governed by contracts and law. Those liberals and neoliberals who stressed the importance of order had also long ago identified groups thought to be lacking in the intellect or discipline necessary to handle the rigors of a market economy; groups so identified were to be excluded from politics, or restricted in their rights, or, in a worst-case scenario, locked up or barred from entering the country.

Across the history of liberalism and neoliberalism, there had been moments when a preoccupation with order had undermined the pur-suit of liberty altogether. The 1990s were not such a moment. Rather, this was a time in which the imperative to lock up those thought unfit for the market economy coexisted powerfully and intimately with the desire to set the American economy and people free. Clinton himself was not troubled by the contradiction between liberty and order that characterized his administration's economic and social policies. Nor were many members of the Democratic or Republican parties, nor the legions of young urban professionals—increasingly known (and mocked) as "Yuppies"—flocking to big cities to enjoy economic opportunity and cosmopolitan culture.[104] Across the exuberant neoliberal 1990s, the mass incarceration of America's young black men commanded remarkably little attention.

Nevertheless, the scale of mass incarceration introduced a stress point into the neoliberal order. All political orders have contradictions built into them, all possess vulnerabilities that need to be managed. Neoliberals "managed" the mass incarceration problem across the 1990s. But managing a contradiction is not the same as resolving it. How many people could be excluded from a life of market freedom before the celebration of that market freedom would come to be tarnished, and perhaps repudiated?

What did upset Republicans (and some Democrats) in the 1990s was the damage that Clinton's celebration of cosmopolitanism (and, by implication, of identity politics) was allegedly doing to American culture. Substantial groups of Republican neoliberals had always been far more comfortable with the free movement of trade and capital than with the free movement and mixing of people. Clinton's multicultural cosmopolitanism scared them; they were not mollified by Clinton's efforts to crack down on welfare cheats or petty criminals. They did not regard his neo-Victorianism as sincere. Only Republicans, they believed, could be trusted truly to reinvigorate the hoary principle of self-reliance; only they could be relied on to re-establish the traditional social hierarchies on which American greatness had, they believed, always rested. They depicted Bill and Hillary Clinton as avatars of free love, as moral relativists, and as inveterate liars who were leading the country to moral ruin. And they resolved to do everything in their power to bring the Clintons down.[105]

Clinton's time in office was dominated by scandals, real and fabricated, in which he had become embroiled: affairs with Gennifer Flowers, Paula Jones, and other women from his Arkansas past; a land development debacle known as Whitewater in which Bill and

Hillary had invested money in the 1980s; the death of Clinton aide Vince Foster, which police concluded was a suicide but which many Republicans believed was a murder ordered by someone high up in the Clinton chain of command; Clinton's lying about an affair with White House intern Monica Lewinsky that caused him to become only the second president in American history to be impeached (his trial in the Senate ended in acquittal). The prominence of these scandals and the bitter enmities that they generated have impelled many observers and chroniclers of the 1990s to view the decade as one ruled by culture wars and by deep polarization between left and right. The decade's culture wars were real; the conflicts they engendered were intense. But to make them the focal point of the 1990s decade is to overlook the broad agreement that Democrats and Republicans reached during those years on matters of political economy.[106]

Large majorities in both parties now supported the neoliberal order. The contrasting cultures embraced by the two parties—cosmopolitanism in the case of the Democrats, neo-Victorianism in the case of the Republicans—were both compatible with the ascendant political economy. One celebrated the diversity, exchange, hybridity, and identity malleability that a global market encouraged. The other emphasized the importance of creating disciplined individuals able to handle the rigors and temptations of market life. Clinton stood for one culture, Gingrich stood for the other. Enemies, of course, but collaborators, too, in securing the triumph of America's neoliberal order. The contradiction between the cosmopolitan and neo-Victorian moral codes might someday weaken the neoliberal order and imperil its survival. But this was not the case in the 1990s.

Culture wars focus attention inward on a polity. But the most important event driving politics in America in the 1990s arguably was not internal but external: the collapse of communism and the Soviet Union. We thus need to end this account of the triumph of the neoliberal order by circling back to the point at which we began, with one more set of reflections on the magnitude of the changes set in motion by the Soviet reformer, Mikhail Gorbachev. Fancy, for a moment, an alternative history for eastern and central Europe during this time. Imagine that Gorbachev had been a different man, more like Deng Xiaoping in China, a right-wing communist reformer rather than a left-wing one. This right-wing version of Gorbachev, whom we might call "alt-Gorbachev," would still have embraced glasnost and pe-restroika in 1985; but he would have repudiated the former in 1989 and 1990, once it became clear that a continued commitment to democracy would lead to the destruction of the Communist Party's power and then to the dissolution of the Soviet Union.

Thus, alt-Gorbachev would have opted in 1990 and 1991 for capi-talist development within an authoritarian political framework, much as Deng was then doing in China. The Soviet democratic dissidents would have been crushed, as the Chinese ones were in Tiananmen Square, and the Soviet Union would have remained intact. The Soviet Union also would have held onto its Eastern European colonies. And in a move that would have pleased the young Putin stationed in the German Democratic Republic, alt-Gorbachev would have refused to countenance the reunification of Germany. Too much Russian blood had been spilled in warring against the Nazis to allow for a reunifi-cation that might one day be seen as a stepping stone to the forma-tion of a Fourth Reich. The establishment of the EU might still have gone forward, but it would have been a less consequential global event, confined to western Europe and involving only part of Germany. Everywhere, international opposition to capitalism's global reach would have been fiercer; the Wall Street–City of London–Frankfurt axis that was to shape so much of global political economy in the 1990s and beyond would have been weaker. The neoliberal revolution would have proceeded more slowly and encountered considerably more do-mestic protest along the way. The Republicans would have remained mired in their decades-long fight against communism, still battling the Cold War as much as the culture war, and Clinton may have felt less compelled to play the role of the Democratic Eisenhower. A different future, in other words, might have unfolded for the United States. The future that did unfold, centered on the triumph of a neoliberal order, had been facilitated in the first instance by the sudden and unexpected collapse of communism and the Soviet Union. The consequences of that collapse still reverberate.

6

Hubris

ONE UPHEAVAL AFTER another jolted America in the first decade of its new century. The first was a bitterly contested presidential election in 2000 that many Americans believed had been stolen. The second was a spectacular terrorist attack on September 11, 2001, that caused the nation to involve itself in two unwinnable wars in Afghanistan and Iraq. The third was the onset in 2008 of the worst economic crash since the Great Depression. The fourth was the election, also in 2008, of the first African American president in American history. Each of these events, on its own, would have been enough to define a decade. Together, they profoundly unsettled the nation. Their cumulative effect would be to hasten the unraveling of America's neoliberal order. But for much of the decade, this unraveling was far from evident, as the order proved resilient and the links between the Clinton and Bush-Obama eras strong. America's neoliberal order was not going to go quietly.

The decade began innocuously enough. A much-hyped threat to America's digital infrastructure—a "Y2K" bug allegedly built into America's IT system that was going to darken every computer in the country and the world at the stroke of millennium midnight (December 31, 1999)—turned out to be a dud. All computers continued to operate as they had done.[1] The race for president, meanwhile, lacked luster. Al Gore, Jr., the Democratic candidate, was Clinton's stolid heir; George W. Bush, the Republican governor of Texas, was widely perceived as the privileged and unfocused son of a former president who had not done enough to earn a shot at the White House. Neither candidate generated much excitement. The turnout on election day barely broke 50 percent of eligible voters. But, then, on election night, all hell broke loose.

The networks first called the election for Gore; then they reversed themselves and called the election for Bush. Then they reversed themselves again, saying the race was too close to call. The problem was Florida. Both candidates needed to win the Sunshine State to put them over the 270-vote victory threshold in the Electoral College. By the morning after the election, it appeared as though Bush had bested Gore by a razor-thin margin of 500-plus votes out of nearly 6 million cast. But there were so many charges of voting irregularities, of ballots improperly counted or improperly thrown out, that the Gore campaign immediately challenged the Bush victory in the courts.

Overturning the initial count in Florida through a legal appeals route was not going to be easy. The GOP controlled both houses of the Florida legislature and the governorship, where the GOP nominee's own brother, Jeb Bush, resided. Its people, in other words, were in charge of the state's electoral machinery. Having suffered through eight years of Clinton, the state and national GOPs had resolved that nothing would stop them from vaulting their man into the White House. As recounts in several Democratic-leaning counties began to erode Bush's minuscule lead, the GOP dispatched squadrons of operatives to storm courthouses where litigation about the election was still proceeding. Then the Supreme Court itself weighed in. In a shockingly partisan and peremptory decision handed down on December 12, 2000, five judges appointed by Republican presidents halted the selective recount of ballots in several Florida counties. The GOP Supreme Court majority might have worked together with Democratic justices to fashion something close to a unanimous judgment—for example, by authorizing a recount of all Florida votes. Instead, the majority simply ordered the recount stopped altogether, thus preserving Bush's victory. For the sake of a smooth transition of power, Gore magnanimously accepted defeat. Millions of Democrats regarded the election as stolen and Bush as an illegitimate president. But there was to be no storming of the Capitol to halt the certification of Electoral College votes.[2]

Anger over the election worsened already fraught party relations. The two sides girded for battle. The first erupted over a massive tax cut that the Bush administration introduced, meant to wipe out the tax hike that Clinton had put in place in 1994. Bush prevailed. But before the two sides could maneuver for the next battle, terrorism struck.

The Towers Fall

September 11, 2001, began as a glorious day in the American Northeast. The air was crisp, the sky a stunning shade of blue. Around 9:00 AM, vague news began to circulate about a plane having flown into one of the World Trade Center towers in lower Manhattan. Initial rumors suggested the plane was small, the pilot lost or unskilled or both, likely a tragic but small loss of life. But when reports came of second plane having struck the other World Trade Center tower, Americans rushed to turn on their TVs. This had to be some of kind of attack.

Across the previous eighteen months, nineteen members of the Middle Eastern terrorist group Al Qaeda, most of them Saudi nationals, had slipped into the United States, carefully separating themselves into sleeper cells of four or five, living unremarkably as ordinary immigrants. Some took flying lessons. Others honed their skills on their home computers via flight simulator programs; a few simply played endless hours of video games. When Al Qaeda leader Osama bin Laden sent the signal to activate, they traveled to New York and Boston, where, on September 11, they boarded four separate airplanes. Armed only with box cutters and knives, they broke into the cockpits, killed the pilots, and seized the controls. None of the hijackers had flown planes of this size and sophistication before. But they were good enough not only to keep the planes aloft but also to guide them to the World Trade Center Towers in New York and the Pentagon just outside Washington, DC. Only one of the four failed to reach its destination, presumably the Capitol Building, because brave passengers on board, having gotten word of the earlier attacks through desperate talks with loved ones over phones, stormed the cockpit and forced the plane to crash in an isolated Pennsylvania field. All those on board died.

Two planes full of fuel hitting the World Trade Center Towers ignited enormous fires, with heat reaching such temperatures that the metal frameworks of the buildings began to buckle. Large numbers of people were trapped in the upper floors and never made it out; some leaped to their deaths to escape death by fire. Heroic New York City firemen entered the burning buildings to evacuate as many as could be saved. But there was not enough time to scale up and down a hundred-plus stories. The collapse of the towers, when it came, was quick. It was as if the entirety of the two buildings had been rigged with explosives, all set to go off simultaneously with the touch of a button. Within minutes of an imaginary switch having been flipped, the buildings collapsed. By 10:30 AM, little was left of either tower except mountains of debris and immense and intense clouds of toxic smoke from fires that were still burning. Bin Laden, the attack's mastermind, had orchestrated an extraordinary act of destruction. Its success likely exceeded his wildest dreams.[3]

Al Qaeda's 9/11 attack was the deadliest assault on American soil since Pearl Harbor. In terms of numbers of civilians killed in a single day, it may have been the deadliest ever. It crashed America's sense of invincibility and impregnability—sentiments that had governed the nation's sense of itself since its victory over the Soviet Union in the Cold War. The attackers confounded the country. They represented no nation-state; they were instead networks of Islamic radicals based in multiple Middle Eastern countries and beyond. They had nothing resembling a conventional army that could be attacked on a field of battle. They had no capital city that could be overrun. Defending one's own land from these attackers was problematic as well. Enemy combatants who had infiltrated America did not wear uniforms or travel in regiments. They moved around as individuals and civilians, guerilla fighters on US soil rendering themselves invisible except in the moment of attack. Their willingness to turn airliners into kamikaze missiles, to don suicide vests and blow themselves up, and to release chemical weapons among crowded populations made them exceptionally dangerous. US administration officials in the aftermath of 9/11, poring over intelligence reports at the beginning of every day, worried constantly that a terrorist cell would get its hands on a portable nuclear device or release an equally deadly chemical into some part of the country's air or water supply.[4]

This unseen and unpredictable foe gripped Americans with fear for days, weeks, and months after 9/11, even in areas far away from New York and Washington, DC. Individuals were loath to venture out from their homes into public places. No one knew where the next suicide bomber might strike. This fear allowed the president, his advisors, and Congress to push through a draconian act permitting the government to justify almost any infringement on civil liberties in order to protect what was coming to be called homeland security.[5] And this intense fear was accompanied by an equally intense desire for revenge, a desire that would destabilize and seriously compromise decision-making at the highest levels of the US government.

One target of revenge was clear from the start: Afghanistan, home of the Taliban, a radical Islamist group that controlled much of the country and had given refuge to bin Laden and Al Qaeda after they had been expelled from Saudi Arabia. By late September, Congress had authorized the use of military force against all those who had played a role in the 9/11 attacks. The United States, supported by a broad coalition of North Atlantic Treaty Organization forces, attacked Taliban strongholds in Afghanistan in October. By late December 2001, the Taliban had been routed, their fighters fleeing either to the Afghan mountains or to Pakistan. This initial campaign failed to capture or kill bin Laden himself, however.[6]

This victory was not enough for Bush and his advisors, who decided to use this crisis to bring down Saddam Hussein, Iraq's head of state. Hussein was an easy target. He was a brutal ruler who had jailed and killed tens of thousands of his own people. Without justification, he had invaded Kuwait ten years earlier, an act that required a massive effort by the West under the leadership of George H. W. Bush to force him out. Hussein had slaughtered Kurds in the Iraqi north and elements of the majority Shiite population in the south when they rose up against him in the war's aftermath. Hussein possessed chemical weapons, which he had deployed both in a 1980s war against Iran and against his own people. Bush and his advisors feared that Hussein would turn these banned chemicals into weapons of mass destruction (WMDs), thereby causing thousands and perhaps tens of thousands of deaths in the Middle East and beyond. Advisors to Bush worried as well that Hussein might have been assembling nuclear weapons. Many in America regarded Hussein as an international outlaw, bound by no rules or sense of decency, and deserving of no respect or mercy.[7]

Yet the argument that Hussein had contributed to the 9/11 attacks was specious. Iraq and Al Qaeda were not natural allies. Hussein was secular and godless. His Baathist Party presided in Iraq over a form of state socialism similar to what the Communist Party had accomplished in the Soviet Union. Restoring the primacy of the Koran, the Caliphate, and the fundamentals of Islam were the furthest things from Hussein's mind. He had played no role in either designing or abetting the attack on the World Trade Center or the Pentagon.

Hussein, like Al Qaeda, did wish America ill. But Hussein had been severely weakened by his war with the United States in the early 1990s and by the harsh sanctions that followed the war and stayed in place for the rest of the decade. These sanctions impoverished Iraq by limiting its ability to sell its oil on world markets. They eroded Hussein's military by inhibiting its capacity to procure new weapons and spare parts. At some point in the 1990s, Hussein had quietly destroyed most stockpiles of his chemical weapons. He did not publicize these acts, preferring to strike a defiant pose and to indulge in blustery rhetoric about annihilating his enemies. Much of his stance was intended to keep his adversaries, internal and external, off balance. In 2001 he was neither preparing for war nor eager to fight. He was not Al Qaeda's ally.[8]

Nevertheless, Bush and his key aides insisted that Hussein and his regime had to be toppled as part of the American retaliation for the September 11 attacks. In his January 2002 State of the Union message, Bush identified Iraq along with Iran and North Korea as members of an "Axis of Evil." Hussein was the alleged linchpin. Defeating him would require the kind of global alliance that had taken out the original Axis of Germany, Italy, and Japan in the 1940s.

In Europe, Bush's claims were greeted with skepticism. The French and the Germans were not convinced that Hussein either possessed WMDs or, if he did, that he would recklessly deploy them. They wanted evidence both of Hussein's stockpiles and of his intent. This required inspections of his WMD sites. Hussein reluctantly agreed to such inspections under the aegis of the United Nations. The Bush administration acceded to the plan, understanding it was the only way to garner broad international support for an attack on Iraq.

The UN inspection team sent to Iraq to scour the countryside for these stockpiles found none. To keep plans for war alive, the Bush administration compelled secretary of state Colin Powell, a man long admired for his integrity, to give misleading testimony to the UN

Security Council in early 2003. Powell claimed to have US intelligence showing that Hussein had outwitted the UN inspectors. Tony Blair of Britain climbed aboard what Bush had begun calling the "Coalition of the Willing." But the French and Germans were unmoved.[9]

Bush wasn't deterred by the failure to find WMDs in Iraq, by the Franco-German challenge to America's leadership, and by credible charges that his administration was not telling the truth. Anti-war rallies erupted across Europe; smaller though significant ones appeared in the United States. Bush insulated himself against these challenges by wrapping his goals in lofty rhetoric. Taking a page from Woodrow Wilson's World War I playbook, Bush claimed that America would go to war not for power or booty but to spread its democratic principles to the world. Arabs wanted freedom and democracy as much as any other people, Bush argued. If America could assist the Iraqi people in deposing Hussein and implanting democracy in Iraq, then similar freedom struggles might ripple out from Baghdad to Syria, Jordan, Egypt, and perhaps even to Turkey and Saudi Arabia. A victory for democracy in Iraq might even prompt Iranians to rise up against their theocratic dictators. Here was an opportunity that the United States and the West more generally could not afford to pass up. This was not, as many Bush critics were charging, an irresponsible war of adventure fought for power, oil, or vengeance. Rather it was a noble cause fought to universalize democracy. Bush assailed his anti-war critics for failing to grasp the magnitude of this opportunity and for condescending to Middle Easterners by writing off their democratic aspirations as secondary to the overriding goal of regional geopolitical stability. The success of Iraqi democracy would "send forth the news, from Damascus to Tehran . . . that freedom can be the future of every nation. The establishment of a free Iraq at the heart of the Middle East," Bush declared, would "be a watershed event in the global democratic revolution."[10]

In Bush's mind, democracy and free markets marched hand in hand. A democratic victory in Iraq would also be a victory for free market capitalism. Bush was encouraged in this thinking by advisors who surrounded him, deputy secretary of defense Paul Wolfowitz foremost among them. Bush and these advisors all believed, as Reagan had, that America's enemies did not stand a chance when the nation flexed its democratic principles, military might, and market capitalism.

They saw little difference between the "experts" who in 2003 opposed a war in Iraq and the naysayers who had long before argued that communism could never be upended and the Soviet Union never defeated. In their eyes, both the Soviet experts and the Middle East naysayers were wrong. If given the chance, Middle Eastern peoples would rise up against their strongmen, embrace freedom, and make their region a center of rather than a graveyard for democracy. All they needed was American support.

Bush harbored an unshakeable belief in the global reach of American ideals and in the beneficence of American power. Oppressed peoples, he reflected nine months after the war in Iraq had begun, "knew of at least one place—a bright and hopeful land—where freedom was valued and secure. And they prayed that America would not forget them, or forget the mission to promote liberty around the world."[11]

Bush had also become a convert to neoliberalism. Free markets released economic energy and political virtue; big government stymied both. Government was necessary to wage war, of course. Accordingly, Bush instructed his secretary of defense, Donald Rumsfeld, to undertake detailed planning for the invasion of Iraq. But Bush ordered no one to develop a serious plan for reconstructing the Iraqi economy and society once the war had ended. There was no need, in Bush's eyes, for the US government to undertake such a reconstruction. The market, once suitably activated, would do that work. In fact, the market, Bush administration officials argued, would be superior to government for executing this plan. In debates with Gore across the 2000 election campaign, Bush had scoffed at his Democratic opponent's suggestion that America should be prepared to undertake nation-building projects in parts of the world beset by war and privation. Government-directed reconstruction of this sort, Bush charged, rarely worked; and it distracted the US Army from its military objectives, thus generating morale problems in its ranks.[12] Reconstruction in Iraq, in Bush's view, would be much better handled by private stakeholders rather than by government bureaucrats.

The assault on Iraq began in late March 2003 with days of massive bombing of Baghdad, military installations, and government nerve centers. Between March 20 and May 2, the United States dropped a mind-boggling 30,000 bombs on Iraq and fired 20,000 cruise missiles at Iraqi targets. The air campaign was accompanied by a lightning-quick advance of a relatively small, motorized, and exceptionally nimble force of 170,000 troops moving overland from bases in nearby nations, especially those in Kuwait. Hussein's army, itself much depleted by years of sanctions, offered only token resistance. US forces reached Baghdad in days; Hussein and top officials in his regime fled. America declared victory, or in the words of a banner hung on an aircraft carrier stationed in San Diego on which Bush landed to mark the triumph, "Mission Accomplished."[13]

But, in truth, the mission had just begun. Someone or some group or institution had to bring a post-Hussein Iraq into being. Suspicious of the State Department because of its alleged "nation-building" proclivities, Bush handed the job of reconstruction to Rumsfeld's Department of Defense. But Rumsfeld had developed no plans, other than to hand the task to a newly created but ill-defined division within Defense, the Office of Reconstruction and Humanitarian Assistance. He sent a junior general, Jay Garner, to Baghdad to take charge. Garner had successfully led small humanitarian missions in the past. He was well meaning and amiable. But nothing prepared him for the scale of the task in Iraq.[14]

With Hussein on the run, the heavily centralized Baathist regime ceased to function. Law and order broke down in cities. Looting of public and private institutions erupted everywhere. American soldiers were mostly told to stand by as the looting raged; Rumsfeld did not want his military to be turned into an occupying police force. He smugly dismissed the disorder as the inevitable corollary of freeing people from a dictatorship. "Freedom's untidy, and people are free to commit crimes and make mistakes and do bad things. . . . Stuff happens."[15] Even if Rumsfeld had given the command to restore order, he did not have nearly enough boots on the ground. An estimated 500,000 troops, nearly three times what America actually had deployed in Iraq, would have been required.

The deeper problem was the overall condition of Iraq. A decade of sanctions had degraded the country's economic base and infrastructure. Electrical and water supply systems worked intermittently if at all. The country's oil extraction and refining industry was near collapse. Numerous buildings and roads had long been deteriorating;

Hussein lacked the funds or the will (or both) to repair them. The US bombing campaign compounded the damaged state of Iraq. It had largely destroyed, for example, the nation's phone system. Years would be needed to put Iraq's economy in order, to rebuild its infrastructure, and to develop political institutions capable of sustaining a democracy.[16]

The magnitude of the task sobered the Department of Defense, which quickly yanked the overmatched Garner from his post and replaced him with Paul Bremer, a lifelong diplomat, onetime executive assistant to Henry Kissinger, former ambassador to the Netherlands, and most recently a dispenser of counter-terrorism advice to corporate clients. Nothing on Bremer's résumé, however, suggested that he was more suited for this job than Garner had been. Rumsfeld and Bush didn't seem to care. They had to give this urgent task to someone. Bush seemed grateful—and more than a bit surprised—that Bremer was willing to take it on.[17]

The Bush administration seemed to want to frame Bremer as their Douglas MacArthur, the general who had presided so effectively over the reconstruction of Japan after World War II. Bremer was given vast, MacArthur-like powers through a new entity, the Coalition Provisional Authority (CPA). But Bremer was no MacArthur. He had little prior experience in the region. He knew nothing about Iraqi society or politics, past or present. He had no skilled staff in place that might have been able to educate him or execute his orders. He received almost no guidance from Bush, Rumsfeld, or anyone else in Washington. The funds allocated to him were woefully inadequate. In July 2003, Bremer estimated he needed $5 billion. By August, he had quadrupled that estimate to $20 billion. This wild escalation simply made clear how little serious planning the Bush administration had done.[18]

Bremer did possess a loathing for the Baathist state that Hussein had built, which he regarded as carrying forward Soviet and Nazi tyranny into the twenty-first century. A deep believer in neoliberal principles himself, Bremer wanted to administer to Iraq the shock therapy implemented in the nations of the former Soviet bloc. "The economic 'system' the Baath Party had adopted," Bremer would later write, "combined the worst of socialism—utopian faith in bureaucratic guidance and state-owned enterprise—with the corruption characteristic of tyrannies. The result was a spectacular misallocation of Iraq's capital resources. The new Iraq needed a modern economy," and it needed one fast.[19]

The only way forward, in Bremer's eyes, was to uproot the Baathist system quickly and comprehensively, as communist systems had been uprooted in the former Soviet Union and its satellites in Eastern Europe in the 1990s. This involved a twofold campaign: first, ban Baathists from economic and political life; and second, privatize all economic activity and institutions immediately. The Baathist command economy would then collapse overnight, and a free market Iraq could be born. Tough medicine, to be sure, but necessary to save a gravely ill patient. Bremer's plans were welcomed by a Bush administration full of Reagan revolution foot soldiers who regarded the triumph over communism as America's greatest victory of the twentieth century. The application of Cold War lessons to Iraq, however, did not go well.

Banning Baathist members from political and economic life meant disbanding the army, whose members had been required to pledge loyalty to the Baath Party. It also meant firing large numbers of professionals and craftsmen, including engineers, teachers, doctors, and electricians, whose skills had given them high status in the Baath Party. They were loyalists to Hussein in name. But what if the loyalty was only skin deep, a pledge made merely because it was the only way for individuals to secure meaningful employment? Bremer didn't bother to ask the question. He saw no need to identify individuals who perhaps should have been exempted from his ban. He also gave little thought to the economic and political effect of dismissing 400,000 young men from the military and another 280,000 who had jobs as policemen via the Ministry of the Interior.[20] Where would they find jobs in Iraq's broken economy? And if they did not, what would these individuals skilled in using firearms do?

Bremer risked alienating as well the professionals dismissed from their jobs, who, like the young ex-soldiers and ex-police, had few prospects for alternative employment. These professionals were disproportionately Sunni Muslims, long a minority but privileged group in Iraq. Hussein was himself Sunni. Shia Muslims, the poorer and more numerous Iraqis, stood to gain from Sunni banishment. But reconfiguring the balance of power between Sunnis and Shiites was also likely to raise tensions between them. It was also likely to enlarge opportunities for neighboring Iran, itself majority Shia, to meddle in Iraqi affairs. Bremer was oblivious to the sectarian split among Iraqi Muslims and thus did not grasp the need to manage it. He and his superiors in Washington had no idea that they were setting the conditions for civil unrest and perhaps civil war inside Iraq.[21]

Equally portentous was Bremer's decision to either shut down or privatize many of the 200 state companies that had formed the core of the Iraqi economy. If these firms clung to their character as state enterprises, they would likely be denied the electricity, the repairs, and resources necessary to make them competitive in the free market economy that Bremer was intent on creating. In Bremer's mind, these state companies were tainted by their history as inefficient, state-run enterprises. The quicker they were sidelined, the better it would be for the reborn Iraqi economy. In their place, Bremer was eager to bring to Iraq big foreign corporations, most of them US-based and owned, that knew what it was like to operate in a capitalist economy. These American multinationals would, in Bremer's eyes, accelerate Iraq's conversion to a market-based system and demonstrate to Iraqis how to make capitalism work.[22]

Giant US firms such as Halliburton and Bechtel scooped up lucrative CPA contracts to rebuild Iraq's infrastructure, its water and electrical systems, its oil industries, its schools, and its hospitals, and so on. These firms were under no obligation to hire Iraqis to work on these projects. They often preferred to hire foreign workers, including tens of thousands from the United States and from neighboring Middle Eastern countries such as Kuwait and Saudi Arabia who were thought to be more reliable and pliable than Iraqis themselves. Once again, Iraqis lost out on jobs and began to feel as though there were no gains to be had from the ousting of Hussein and from the ensuing American occupation.[23]

One of the ironies of Bremer's plan to bring free enterprise to Iraq was that the big American corporations invited in were not being asked to operate in a true free market environment. The CPA reserved many of its big contracts for American firms that, in many cases, were bidding against no one. They were taking few risks, putting little of their own capital into private ventures with uncertain returns. They were privileged players in protected markets, fattening at the US government's Iraq trough.

In the first two years of occupation, these firms often failed to deliver on their promise of getting Iraq's infrastructural systems up and running with speed and efficiency. But they were still handsomely paid for their work. If Hussein had engaged in crony socialism, the Americans were engaging in crony capitalism. None of this was lost on the Iraqis themselves, now reduced to unemployed bystanders in the Iraq rebuilding charade. No wonder many began contemplating using their remaining resources to join an insurgency against the American occupiers and their armies of private contractors.

Naomi Klein, in her book *The Shock Doctrine*, portrays the course of events in Iraq as flowing directly from neoliberal principles cooked up in University of Chicago economics seminars and straightforwardly applied in this unfortunate Arab country. "The 'fiasco' of Iraq," she writes, "is one created by a careful and faithful application of unrestrained Chicago School ideology."[24] But this is too simple a diagnosis. There was nothing careful about the Bush administration's reconstruction work in Iraq. It is the absence of care that is most striking and shocking, apparent in the appointment of two pro-consuls unsuited or unprepared for the task they were handed. It is apparent as well in the skeletal character of the CPA, which Klein herself admits was "far too understaffed and underresourced to pull off its own ambitious plans."[25]

The CPA's typical member was not a skilled administrator and veteran of reconstruction efforts in Bosnia or Somalia—or an expert who had spent years studying successful reconstruction efforts undertaken by the United States sixty years earlier in Germany and Japan—but a young Republican political operative who was encouraged to journey to Baghdad for a tour of duty that sometimes lasted only a few months.[26] These operatives were sequestered in a heavily guarded part of Baghdad known as the Green Zone, formerly a palatial district where Hussein, his family, and elite public servants had resided. There they were entirely cut off from the ebb and flow of life in the real city surrounding them. Almost none of the 7,000 Americans who resided in the Green Zone spoke Arabic or knew anything about Iraqi history or culture. Few attempts were made to compensate for this deficiency. Rather, strenuous efforts were made to render the Zone identical to American areas from which the volunteers in America had come, with shopping areas and entertainments built to resemble home. This effort to create an American suburb on the Euphrates worked up to a point, as long as the electricity flowed.[27]

One Green Zone operative was Andrew Erdmann, a thirty-six-year-old from Rochester, New York, who arrived in Baghdad in summer 2003 to become Iraq's de facto minister of higher education. His qualification: He was a committed Republican and held a PhD in history from Harvard. One of his first tasks was to provide security for Iraq's universities which, like many museums, had been stripped bare by looting. What did he know about higher education in Iraq? Not much. And which places of higher learning should he protect, given that he did not have the resources to protect them all? To answer that question and to educate himself about higher education in Iraq, Erdmann turned to that reliable guide to the educational infrastructure of nations, the *Lonely Planet Guide Book*.[28] Bush appointees like Erdmann, in truth, were little more than tourists, seeing a bit of the world before returning to their "real" work of staffing GOP electoral campaigns in the United States. For them, as for Bush and Rumsfeld, the occupation and reconstruction of Iraq were afterthoughts, not a serious endeavor.[29]

If this was neoliberalism, it was a hastily and poorly conceived version of it. The original architects of neoliberalism understood that markets had to be created through law and sustained by institutions. That the Bush administration could be so nonchalant about deploying neoliberal principles in Iraq and so unprepared for the consequences reveals their carelessness on the one hand and hubris that had come to accompany neoliberal projects on the other. Neoliberals in the Bush administration had forgotten the long and carefully designed path to power their predecessors had undertaken in the United States. To them, market exchange was like breathing air. Both were natural acts. Establishing a neoliberal regime, in their eyes, required little work beyond the removal of government from economic affairs. The release of market forces thought to follow automatically from government's removal—what Adam Smith had called the natural propensity of people to "truck, barter, and exchange"—would do the rest.

Of course, nothing of the sort happened. Hundreds of thousands of Iraqis were turned out of jobs with no prospects for re-employment.

Increasingly they turned their rage on the American occupiers and began conducting a guerilla campaign against them, one marked by the appearance of a simple but terrifying new weapon, the improvised explosive device, or IED—a crude but deadly homemade bomb. These explosives were planted in a road or another location frequented by American soldiers and contractors, and detonated either by pressure placed on the IED by a vehicle's tire (or a soldier's foot) or remotely by a phone signal. IEDs began injuring and killing hundreds and then thousands of Americans.[30]

The insurgents responsible for these acts were also forming militias to provide the security not being supplied by US forces. Increasingly they began taking on other tasks at which America was failing—repairing phone networks, offering generators in emergencies, addressing rudimentary social service needs, and even directing traffic. These militias were not all allied with each other; Sunni-Shia acrimony divided them. The Sunnis, now stripped by the Americans of the privilege they had long enjoyed, feared they would suffer further under a reconstructed Iraq in which Shiites dominated. Their insurgency was meant both to resist the American occupation and to forestall Shia dominance. Shiites were themselves organizing, especially in Baghdad under the leadership of the cleric Moqtada al-Sadr, whose combination of militant anti-Americanism and skill in bringing some order and security to life in parts of Iraq's capital city gave him an ever-increasing following. His Shia faith also brought him closer to the rulers of Iran, who began supporting him with funds and arms, a development that deeply alarmed Iraq's Sunnis. America's thoughtlessly conceived neoliberal reconstruction had sown seeds of sectarian strife that would mar Iraqi life for decades to come.[31]

Poorly planned, the Bush occupation had little chance of achieving its goals. A successful occupation would have required what Bush scorned: a resolute and comprehensive program of US-government superintended social engineering tailored to Iraqi society. America had accomplished this sort of reconstruction in Germany and Japan a little more than a half century before. There were plans of this sort for Iraq. One set had been drawn up by career civil servant Thomas Warrick of the State Department. But it remained locked up in State Department computers and file drawers.[32] The prestige of neoliberalism was such that careful government supervision of that sort was thought to be a thing of the past. Bush believed even more fervently than Clinton that the era of big government was over. Government, in his eyes, did little more than suffocate human talent and drain away innovative market energy. The market, not the state, was the solution to vexing economic problems. The kind of nation-building and democracy-building that Iraq needed never had a chance. The refusal to develop plans squandered immense human and capital resources.

The costs of the Iraq War and occupation were staggering. Nearly 200,000 Iraqis died from armed conflict, and another 650,000 are estimated to have died from war's collateral effects—displacement, disease, malnutrition, and inadequate health care. By 2008, an estimated 4.7 million Iraqis (out of 27 million) had taken flight, becoming refugees abroad or internal exiles in their own land. Nearly 5,000 American servicemen and women died in the conflict and more than 32,000 were injured. Meanwhile, the economic reconstruction of Iraq proceeded much more slowly than expected, even though the US government poured $60 billion into these efforts—with a full $20 billion going to a single division of Halliburton.[33]

The failure to plan for reconstruction or to provide sufficient oversight of the contractors hired to execute projects resulted in work that was often slow to develop and then shoddily done, with vast amounts of money wasted through bribes, pocket-lining, and other forms of corruption. By 2005 and 2006, virtually no one inside or outside the Bush administration was holding up Iraq as an example of free market capitalism at its best. To the contrary, the reconstruction of Iraq had become a debacle. The United States further squandered its prestige by practicing torture at the prison facilities, such as Abu Ghraib, where Iraqi insurgents were held, and by turning over more and more military occupation duties to private contractors whose bands of mercenaries were skilled at fighting but ill-equipped to handle the political challenges of nation-building. The turn toward mercenaries and away from US Army soldiers was meant to demonstrate yet again the superiority of the private to the public sector in the neoliberal world that the Bush administration was so intent on creating.[34]

By 2006–2007, Americans were losing confidence in Bush's assurances that the war was going well. The failure of his reconstruction plan for Iraq raised troubling questions about the viability of neoliberal principles. It began to erode the authority of America's neoliberal order.

Neoliberal Politics at Home

At home, Bush worked hard to persuade Americans that the war in Iraq would not unduly impinge on their way of life. Rumsfeld's plan of attack, based on a small military striking forcefully and winning quickly, was designed to execute a war without taxing American resources. Reconstruction would be done swiftly and on the cheap. Bush was insistent from the war's outset that Americans were to continue living as they always had. He belittled talk of sacrifice. No Americans would be conscripted into the military or asked to forfeit economic opportunity or freedom for the war effort. There would be no reversal of the Bush tax cut, even though the costs of the war were now burdening the US government with large deficits. Bush was emphatic that Americans should continue their free-spending ways. The engine of market capitalism had to be stoked.

Because there was no draft, few American families had to answer the question of whether they would be willing to send a beloved son or daughter to risk death in an ill-conceived war. The anti-Vietnam War New Left had led the struggle to end the draft in the 1960s and 1970s. The replacement of a conscription army with a professional one, however, had boomeranged. It turned out to be easier for Washington decision-makers to deploy professional soldiers who had volunteered for military duty than citizen conscripts who were more likely to raise questions about the merits of a war and whether the sacrifice of their lives was warranted. Had America maintained its tradition of a citizens' army, there almost certainly would have been no war in Iraq in 2003.[35]

Nevertheless, Bush could not really insulate American society from the effects of this "distant" war. The interpenetration of foreign and domestic policies occurred on multiple fronts. Most notably, Bush pushed neoliberal policies at home as hard as he did in Iraq. Neoliberalism was apparent in Bush's deregulatory commitments. His 2001 tax cut was meant to deprive government of a source of funds that it might use for social engineering and redistribution. Bush worked hard (and ultimately unsuccessfully) to replace the reigning form of Social

Security benefits—lifetime government pensions for retirees and their spouses—with Wall Street accounts that workers would, with employer contributions, be instructed to accumulate and manage on their own both before and during retirement. This "investment account for every retiree" plan embodied the neoliberal desire to eliminate lifetime welfare "handouts" that "corroded" an individual's moral integrity. Instead, Bush argued that his plan would enhance the self-sufficient entrepreneurial individual so celebrated in neoliberal thought.

Bush, too, preserved the deregulatory approach to Wall Street that the Clinton administration had advanced. Alan Greenspan, the neoliberal guru who had steered the elder Bush and Clinton administrations in financial matters, was still directing the Federal Reserve. Neither he nor the younger Bush was much troubled by a 2001 bursting of the speculative stock bubble that had brought down dozens of Silicon Valley startups, nor by the ensuing sharp falls in market indexes, especially those like NASDAQ that were heavily weighted toward high-tech stocks. The Greenspan-Bush confidence in the ability of markets to correct themselves seemed to be vindicated by the stock market's recovery in 2003–2004 and a second run of sensational information technology (IT) startups that fueled another steep climb in stock values. Facebook debuted in 2004 and Twitter in 2006. Apple was no longer a startup, but it was still behaving like one, launching its revolutionary iPhone in 2007. This handy computer-in-a-pocket with a stunning digital interface would soon allow hundreds of millions of individuals an easy way to surf the worldwide web at any location and at every moment of the day or night. It also allowed them to explore, simply by tapping their thumbs, hundreds of new apps that were becoming accessible through their phones. The iPhone gave IT innovators and their venture capital supporters everywhere a big boost. Google, meanwhile, was rapidly universalizing internet access and use.[36]

Thomas Friedman, the prominent *New York Times* columnist, caught the hopeful IT spirit of the Bush years in his bestselling book *The World Is Flat*, published in 2005 in the midst of the Iraqi occupation. The book's techno-utopianism echoed that of Clinton-era cyberspace enthusiasts Esther Dyson, George Gilder, and Alvin Toffler. But if the latter group was mostly focused on the cybernetic revolution as an American event, Friedman was struck by its global reverberations.

Friedman was drawn to Bangalore, a city in southern India that had become a high-tech corridor rivaling Silicon Valley in its sophistication and in its embrace of American values and techniques. "Columbus accidentally ran into America but thought he had discovered part of India," Friedman wrote. "I actually found India," but it looked just like America. South Asian Indians "had taken American names," were imitating American accents, and, most important, had embraced "American business techniques at software labs."[37]

If India, in Friedman's view a land of encrusted cultures and reactionary social hierarchies, was being transformed in this way by America's technological revolution, then what part of the world could possibly resist its lures? The rise of IT had played an important if indirect role in undermining communism, and it was propelling the emergence of economic powerhouses that now rivaled Japan in East Asia—South Korea, Taiwan, Singapore, Indonesia, Vietnam, and China among them. The Arab world, Friedman acknowledged, was more resistant. But it, too, he believed, was on the cusp of transformation.

A respect for diversity and difference was foundational to Friedman's high-tech "one-worldism." Friedman's key word was pluralism, which to him connoted a willingness of peoples of different nationalities, races, religions, and ideologies to live together in peace. Pluralism was not simply an ethical creed, though Friedman embraced it as such. It was also, in his eyes, the key to economic innovation and growth. "Where does innovation come from?" Friedman asked in one of his *New York Times* columns. "It comes from mashing up different perspectives, ideas and people. Google began as a mashup between Larry Page and Sergey Brin, a Russian immigrant. The more a society is committed to living by the principles of diversity and pluralism," Friedman asserted, "the more people from different backgrounds will trust each other, and the more they will be able to collaborate, spark new ideas and businesses, to comfortably reach out anywhere in the globe for the best co-creators." Friedman did not explicitly affiliate himself to neoliberalism, but he expressed again and again a commitment to the free mixing of peoples and ideas that was central to the worldview of those who had embraced market freedom. An untrammeled commercial society, in his view, was one in which diversity would flourish.[38] These ideas were very similar to those that Clinton had expressed during his years as president.

Bush shared Friedman's and Clinton's belief in pluralism, a belief that can also be labeled cosmopolitanism. Bush's cosmopolitanism differed from that of Friedman and Clinton in that it was of a "godly" sort: Bush himself had deep faith in the divine and wanted people everywhere to share it. Bush's 1980s religious awakening impelled him to move from Episcopalianism (long his family's religion) to Methodism, but he was not particular about which faith other people espoused. In his eyes, multiple branches of Protestantism were as valid as his own, as were Catholicism, Christian Orthodoxy, Judaism, and Islam. The more pathways to God, in Bush's view, the better. Bush thought this applied not just to Americans but to religious people living beyond America's borders.[39]

Bush's respect for religious pluralism impelled him to hold America's ethnic diversity in high regard. In a 1997 speech to the US Chamber of Commerce, he declared: "We are the United States of America, not the divided states of America. One of our strengths is in our differences." On another occasion he remarked that Texas had become "a diverse state enriched by its many cultures and heritages." And in an address to a group of Latinos in Miami in August 2000, in the midst of his presidential campaign, Bush became effusive in his praise for a new multicultural America:

> America has one national creed, but many accents. We're now one of the largest Spanish-speaking nations in the world. We're a major source of Latin music, journalism, and culture. Just go to Miami, or San Antonio, Los Angeles, Chicago, or West New York, New Jersey . . . and close your eyes and listen. You could just as easily be in Santo Domingo or Santiago or San Miguel de Allende. For years, our nation has debated this change—some have praised it and others have resented it. By nominating me, my party has made a choice to welcome the New America.[40]

Bush is generally given low marks for his treatment of Arab and Muslim immigrants in America after 9/11. That judgment perhaps needs to be rethought in light of the hateful ethnonationalist populism that Donald Trump did so much to promote. While the Bush administration did subject Muslim and Arab communities and immigrants to intensive and intrusive surveillance, it also insisted on distinguishing between the radical Islamic fringe and the Islamic mainstream. In one of his first public speeches after 9/11, Bush called on Americans to respect the legitimacy of Islam and the law-abiding Muslims who practiced it. He never contemplated a mass imprisonment of Muslim Americans of the sort FDR had undertaken with Japanese Americans after December 7, 1941. Bush was keenly aware of the Japanese American precedent, in part because Norman Mineta, a Japanese American who had been "relocated" in 1942, sat in Bush's cabinet as secretary of transportation. At a cabinet meeting on September 12, 2001, Bush declared that his administration would not allow "what happened to Norm in 1942 to happen again" to Arab and Muslim Americans.[41]

Bush's cosmopolitanism and his belief in the value of a diverse society influenced his decision to keep America's immigrant gates open in the years after 9/11. Latinos in particular believed that they had a friend in the White House, and they rewarded him by casting 40 percent of their votes for him in the 2004 election—a doubling of the percentage of Latino votes that Robert Dole had achieved for the Republican Party in 1996 and perhaps the highest ever, before or since, by a Republican presidential candidate. In his second term as president, Bush pushed hard for an immigration reform plan that included a robust path toward citizenship for the millions of undocumented Mexican immigrants living in the United States. Bush had confidence that he could attract sufficient numbers of diverse new Americans to the Republican Party to make the GOP America's majority party for generations to come.[42]

Bush shared Thomas Friedman's faith in the power of pluralism. And he believed, with Friedman, that pluralism and the free movement of people were the keys to innovation, economic growth, and dynamic capitalism. Freedom in all its forms (to move, to mingle, to communicate, to innovate), Bush remarked in 2003, "unleashes human creativity—and creativity determines the strength and wealth of nations."[43] But what to do in situations where dictators or backward-looking elites had shut off their societies from these neoliberal forces? For Bush, as for Friedman, Arab and Muslim societies in the Middle East had posed this challenge in acute form. In such situations, Friedman had argued, pluralism might have to be imposed on a society, perhaps via American bombs and tanks. Friedman had been an early and ardent supporter of

Bush's war in Iraq. Arab societies, he believed, should not be allowed to opt out of one-worldism. The American invasion, he argued, was designed in part to blow apart the institutions and elites that had closed Muslim societies to the open circulation of ideas, to pluralism, and to opportunity and innovation.

Friedman would never reconsider the validity of his twin desires to punish Arabs and Muslims through war and, simultaneously, to liberate them from their closed societies. Not even the failure of the American occupation, its disastrous spillover effects in Syria, or the emergence of brutal ISIS from the wreckage of Iraq and Syria would cause Friedman to admit that the Iraq War may have been a mistake. More than fifteen years after the war began, Friedman remarked: "Wherever I saw a chance to open the door to pluralism in that part of the world, I got behind it." One had to do it, even if there was only the slightest opening, and even if it involved cracking heads. "Because if the Arab world doesn't find its way to engender pluralism, education pluralism, political pluralism," Friedman declared in 2019, "it's going to die." Bush, like Friedman, believed that the Iraq War had given a pluralistic, cosmopolitan world in the Middle East a chance to be born.[44]

This pluralism through war had not worked out so well in the Middle East. But did a commitment to pluralism—and the alleged advances in entrepreneurialism, commerce, and affluence that such a commitment would yield—stand a better chance of succeeding under GOP leadership in the United States? The Bush answer was yes, provided that social policy was reoriented away from a welfare state handout framework and toward a neo-Victorian one prizing self-help and the creation of sturdy, self-reliant individuals able to engage with the market and each other as independent and confident citizens. Many Bush-era policies tilted in this direction. His effort to create a rainbow nation of homeowners was one of the most interesting initiatives in this regard. It is worth a close look.

A Rainbow Nation of Homeowners

Bush's central domestic ambition as president was to make America into an "ownership society," by which he meant a nation in which Americans would control their own retirement accounts, their own health savings accounts (to pay for medical care), and their own homes. Ownership, in Bush's view, was the "path to greater opportunity, more freedom, and more control over . . . life" for all Americans.[45]

Homeownership was central to Bush's vision. As far back as the George H. W. Bush administration, policymakers had been concerned about a poorly performing housing market. Stagnant wages and rising home values had combined to price many working-class and middle-class families out of the housing market. Awareness was growing in policymaking circles, too, that many of these potential homeowners were minorities, mostly black and Latino, who had suffered for decades from discrimination in mortgage issuing practices.[46] Expanding home ownership to minority populations was particularly appealing to neoliberals who saw in it a way to pursue racial equality that sidestepped the policies they despised: federal jobs programs, raising the minimum wage, building public housing, and strengthening labor unions to give workers more leverage in bargaining for higher wages. These programs were thought to involve too much government interference with private markets and private initiative. They were thought to corrode the elements of personhood that Republicans held most dear: independence, self-reliance, enterprising zeal.

Homeownership, on the other hand, would enhance these values, not undermine them. It was a good way for America to deliver on its promise of equality for all citizens, regardless of race. It offered the nation a superior strategy to build a commonality of experience amid its diversity, one that would both deepen a respect for difference and encourage exchange across racial and ethnic lines. It would also bind all Americans to a belief in the virtues of a free market. For Bush, homeownership signified freedom. "It brings pride to people, it's a part of an asset-based society," he remarked in 2002. "It provides an opportunity, if need be, for a mom or a dad to leave something to their child." Bush wanted to put owning a home within the reach of every American, irrespective of color. That meant making a concerted effort to raise minority homeownership rates.[47]

The elder Bush's administration had already led the way in doing so, passing a law to require two government-backed mortgage institutions, the Federal National Mortgage Association (Fannie Mae) and the Federal Home Loan Mortgage Corporation (Freddie Mac), to increase their support of mortgages issued to lower- and middle-income families. These institutions were government sponsored enterprises, or GSEs, authorized to buy up mortgages from commercial banks and, by so doing, to inject both stability and growth into the housing industry. The government, in effect, was putting its imprimatur on millions of private mortgage contracts, ensuring in the process that the market into which Americans had poured so much of their savings would never again collapse as it had in the 1930s. Private banks, in turn, once having sold existing mortgage portfolios to Fannie Mae and Freddie Mac, would have the capital resources to issue another round of home loans.[48]

The Clinton administration instructed Fannie Mae and Freddie Mac to expand the ranks of minority homeowners further by dispensing with the standard 20 percent down payment obligation, a sum usually beyond the reach of poor families. This easing of down payment requirements put mortgages within the grasp of many more people but also made mortgages a riskier proposition. The phrase "subprime mortgage" entered the lexicon of housing industry shoptalk at this time to denote mortgages issued to borrowers deemed to be credit risks. A greater level of risk became a justification, in turn, for imposing high interest rates on subprime mortgages or for offering teasingly low rates at the moment of borrowing, with lenders reserving the right to reset the interest rates at higher levels as the market "demanded." Interest-only mortgages also debuted in the 1990s, with borrowers obligated to make monthly payments on mortgage interest, but not on the mortgage principal.[49]

Lenders sought to secure their money against subprime risk through securitization, a process that began by assembling large numbers of extant mortgages into bundles. These bundles might mix solid and risky mortgages, or keep the safe and risky ones apart, grading them accordingly. All bundles would be sliced into small tranches and dispersed across a vast global base of investors. Even tranches composed exclusively of subprime mortgages were thought to be relatively safe because they would be scattered so widely, dissolved, so to speak, in a vast sea of securities. Big risks would thereby be transmuted into small ones. Or so the theory went.[50]

Private banks eagerly joined in this securitization, competing with Fannie Mae and Freddie Mac to sell subprime tranches to investors everywhere. The part of the banking industry handling the securities (or derivatives as they were increasingly called) into which subprime mortgages had been bundled, was lightly regulated, a hands-off disposition written into law in 2000 as part of the Commodity Futures Modernization Act, another legacy of the Clinton-era neoliberal dispensation. Cumulatively, the various steps taken during the 1990s to ease mortgage access resulted in the rate of homeownership rising across that decade from 64 percent to 67 percent of households, a gain greater than the entire increase of the previous thirty years. The Clinton years opened the door to homeownership to 2.5 million black and Latino families for the first time.[51]

George W. Bush was intent on opening the door wider. Bush outlined a plan for a comprehensive homeownership program in a report he issued in 2002, *A Home of Your Own: Expanding Opportunities for All Americans.* That same year he hosted a Minority Homeownership conference at George Washington University to stress that low-income people of color were to be the main beneficiaries of his housing initiatives. In 2003, he signed into law the American Dream Downpayment Act to help low-income families with the initial home purchase.[52]

As with many of his domestic programs, Bush funded his housing policies at low levels. The costs of the Iraq War along with Bush's refusal to repeal his 2001 tax cut precluded higher expenditures.[53] But the thin funding for homeownership did not trouble Bush and his policymakers. They saw government's role as activating markets rather than substituting government programs for them. In place of providing direct subsidies to weak portions of the housing market, the Bush administration pressured banks and Fannie Mae and Freddie Mac to issue more mortgages to low-income applicants. Fannie Mae and Freddie Mac complied by increasing the proportion of their portfolios holding mortgages issued to underserved populations from 40 to 55 percent. Many of these mortgages were subprime, which doubled across the first Bush administration from 10 to 20 percent of all mortgages issued.[54]

In these circumstances, Bush guided homeownership in America to an all-time peak of 69 percent in 2004. Between 2004 and 2006, black and Latino homeownership also attained its highest rate ever, nearly

50 percent of all households in both groups.[55] From the mid-1990s to mid-2000s, black homeownership had increased by 25 percent, almost twice the rate of the overall homeownership increase (14 percent) and three times as much as the growth in numbers of white owners (7 percent). Latino homeownership shot up by 60 percent over this same stretch. Across the Clinton-Bush years, minorities accounted for a full 40 percent of the increase in numbers of new homeowners.[56] These new owners could look forward to significant increases in their wealth—as long as their homes either held or increased in value.

Bush and his policymakers were proud of this achievement. They had found, they believed, a better route to racial equality than through welfare and affirmative action programs. An interracial nation of homeowners that Bush so ardently desired had begun to emerge. Confident in their economic independence, these homeowners, Bush policymakers believed, would be able to cross racial and ethnic boundaries in ways that allowed the natural diversity of America to flourish. This Bush policy would bring together the two moral codes sustaining the neoliberal order—cosmopolitan diversity and neo-Victorian self-reliance. The neoliberal order could hardly have been stronger, or so Bush administration figures told themselves.

By 2006, however, trouble signs abounded. Making mortgages more available had fueled demand. Increased demand drove home prices upward. The Bush administration and the Federal Reserve responded by encouraging lenders to issue more and more subprime mortgages. Many of these loans went to families whose ability to repay their mortgages was uncertain. Banks, as a result, began attaching all sorts of transaction fees to the mortgage acquisition process, providing their balance sheets with a significant stream of income over the short term and a hedge, of sorts, against the many ill-conceived mortgages that would undoubtedly, at some point, begin to fail.

House-acquiring mania, in the meantime, spread from new buyers to existing ones seeking to profit from the rising value of their homes. Some families bought bigger homes, or second and even third homes, with banks only too eager to facilitate these acquisitions by issuing new mortgages. Some households took out loans—second mortgages, really—on their existing homes, which they then used as their private ATM machines, dispensing cash on demand for all sorts of major purchases: cars and trucks, HD televisions, home additions and remodeling, college tuition for children, and vacations to exotic locales. In a pinch, should these new loans become a burden, borrowers would always be able to sell their homes for a high price, downsize, and pay off their debts. Home loans, in other words, dramatically accelerated levels of consumer spending. In the 1990s, Americans had taken out home equity loans equivalent to 2 to 3 percent of the value of their real estate. Between 2004 and 2006 that percentage had ballooned to approximately 10 percent, injecting an additional trillion dollars into the economy.[57]

The Federal Reserve, under Alan Greenspan's leadership through the entirety of the first George W. Bush administration, stoked this hot housing market by keeping interest rates low. Though aware of the emerging housing bubble, Greenspan did not appear to be troubled by it. He had confidence—too much confidence, it turned out—in the institutions of the newly financialized economy, believing that the fancy toolkit for dispersing risk globally would allow the financial sector to weather whatever storms might be heading its way.

Underlying this confidence lurked a concern, though one that Greenspan was reluctant to verbalize: namely, that the easy money policies he had deployed in response to the 2001 high-tech crash were not producing the expected results. By 2005 or 2006, these policies should have stimulated robust economic growth, jobs, and wage increases. In each of these areas, however, achievements had lagged. Inflation should also have begun to creep up; to forestall this possibility, Greenspan put the Fed on a mild rate-raising course in 2004. Higher interest rates should have dampened consumption and home buying, but they did not. Long-term interest rates remained flat. Inflationary pressures were more or less flat as well. And levels of household and consumer debt continued to soar.

Lawrence Summers, a prominent economist in the Clinton administration soon to play an important role in Barack Obama's first presidential term, gave voice years later to what may have been on Greenspan's mind in 2005 and 2006. In a 2013 speech to the International Monetary Fund, Summers seemed to be suggesting that "even a great [financial] bubble" of the sort that had enveloped America in the new century's first decade had not been enough to stimulate full employment and significant inflation. Why not? Was it possible, Summers wondered, that aggregate global demand, even with easy money, was too weak? Had bubbles become necessary to stimulate demand by making it possible for consumers, now encouraged to deepen the debt side of their household ledger sheets, to increase their purchasing power well beyond what their incomes and savings otherwise would have allowed? Did it follow from Summers's hypothesis that the global economy may have "needed" Americans to spend beyond their means in order to generate sufficient demand to sustain a global production system with enormous capacity?[58]

Greenspan never conceded this point, either in the years up to or following the financial crash of 2008. Yet he was certainly aware of the disproportionate role that American consumers played in the global economy, purchasing an astonishing 16 percent of all global output in 2007.[59] Was it possible that the global economy had indeed become structurally unbalanced, burdened by too much productive capacity on the one hand and too little consumer demand on the other? If that were true, ways would have to be found to augment the latter. Perhaps Greenspan was indeed looking for strategies to allow the world's most important group of consumers to spend beyond their means. This would explain his reluctance to lance the housing bubble at a prudent time and in a prophylactic way.[60]

Like Greenspan, Bush also ignored the warning signs that the economy was in trouble. His conduct of the Iraq War had demonstrated that he could be both overweening in his ambition and careless in devising policies to achieve his outsized goals. The same might be said of his plans for an ownership society. Bush genuinely wanted to expand minority homeownership and was proud of what he had accomplished in this area. But, as in the case of Iraq, Bush was slow to ask how his administration might lock in temporary gains for the long term. There was a whiff of the overprivileged heir in Bush's character, of someone who had never really been held to account. As the scion of a prominent and wealthy political family and with many powerful friends, Bush had long been protected against the worst consequences of his actions. His neoliberal thinking amplified his carelessness on economic matters, for it allowed him to justify his neglect of policy "details" by indulging the neoliberal conceit that government could do little that was right. A president did not have to think carefully about the details of a public policy program because government couldn't really do anything well anyway. When making a choice between empowering government officials to enforce necessary regulations or sidelining these same officials so as to free up the market to do its work, Bush administration officials almost always opted for the latter.[61]

Thus, the Bush team neglected public regulation of the banking industry at a time when careful superintendence of the subprime mortgage market might have made a difference. An investigation undertaken by a team of *New York Times* reporters in December 2008 reported that Bush's first Securities and Exchange Commission (SEC) chair had given investment bankers license by promising them a "kinder, gentler" agency. Bush's second SEC chair lost his job by being "too aggressive" at regulation. Other banking regulators serving Bush took delight in advertising their laissez-faire intentions, as when they "brandished a chain saw over a 9,000-page pile of regulations" to demonstrate their determination "to ease burdens on the industry."

Bush's regulators also undercut efforts by individual states to use "consumer protection laws to crack down on predatory lending."[62] Before his retirement from the Senate in 2002, Senator Phil Gramm of Texas, long a close ally of Bush, had done everything in his power to seal off derivatives from both federal and state oversight. In this permissive environment, it is not surprising that the key securities' ratings agencies—Moody's, Standard and Poor, and Fitch—had compromised themselves. By 2006, an AAA credit rating, long the industry's gold standard, was no longer a reliable guide to the worthiness of a debt instrument. Bush's carelessness in handling the debt implications of his homeownership initiative shared a great deal with Bremer's carelessness in superintending the reconstruction of Iraq.[63]

Fannie Mae and Freddie Mac gave Bush's risk-taking approach additional license. Holders of questionable mortgage securities issued by private banks could take comfort in the knowledge that these two institutions, quasi-public banks in all but name, had issued similar securities. Across the derivatives industry, the belief took hold among investors that the federal government, at the end of the day, would be there to clean up the mess, no matter how large. This belief turned out to be correct. The bill for this developing fiasco would shortly fall due.

Crash

Housing prices peaked in the summer of 2006 and then began to recede. At first it seemed as though this was a rather ordinary contraction that inevitably followed a boom. But by fall 2007 and spring 2008, there were signs of serious trouble. In September 2007 a British bank (Northern Rock) involved in mortgage securitization failed. In March 2008 the American investment house Bear Stearns itself stood at the edge of collapse, saved only by J. P. Morgan Chase's decision to purchase it at a bargain basement price. The Bear Stearns balance sheet was so toxic that J. P. Morgan Chase demanded and received a $13 billion loan from the US Treasury and a commitment from the Fed to take on $30 billion of Bear Stearns's worst assets.[64]

Soon after, word began reaching secretary of the treasury Henry Paulson that Fannie Mae and Freddie Mac might soon be facing a Bear Stearns–like reckoning. Despite opposition from hardline neoliberals in the GOP opposed to any bailout, Paulson secured authorization from Congress in late July to do what was necessary to save these two mammoth lending institutions. By early September 2008, Paulson was staring in disbelief at what the resulting investigations into Fannie Mae and Freddie Mac had revealed: Each of the two agencies was going to need as much as $100 billion to close the gap between debts and assets.

Elements of the GOP rank and file had long despised Fannie Mae and Freddie Mac, regarding them as "mongrel" organizations, public institutions masquerading as instruments of a free market economy. That Fannie Mae and Freddie Mac had been given a mission by Bush to expand their minority outreach through subprime mortgages incensed these Republicans further. They had no use for Bush's cosmopolitanism, his vision of an America strengthened by its diversity. And they were coming to despise Bush and Paulson for their willingness to court the votes of "cosmopolitan" Democrats to get their bailout packages through Congress.[65]

Paulson's more immediate problem, however, was that neither the Bear Stearns bailout nor the emerging Fannie Mae–Freddie Mac package seemed to be righting America's financial ship. By mid-September, two more major US investment houses, Lehman Brothers and Merrill Lynch, stood at the edge of collapse. Wall Street expected that a buyer, likely Bank of America, would save Lehman, the fourth biggest investment bank in the United States. Merrill Lynch, a more recent and upstart house, with a reputation for practices that were sometimes fast and loose, was thought to be a more likely candidate for failure. But at the last moment, Bank of America decided to invest its resources in Merrill rather than Lehman. Merrill was saved, after a fashion, though its shareholders suffered huge losses. Lehman, meanwhile, announced on September 15 that it was out of resources and was shutting its doors for good. World financial markets experienced the failure of Lehman as the equivalent of a small nuclear bomb detonating. Stock market indexes everywhere collapsed.[66]

The Lehman news had barely begun to register when an even more ruinous development threatened: The American International Group (AIG), America's largest insurance company, had massive exposure in the mortgage-backed securities market and was even more integrated into the global financial system than Lehman had been. In mid-September, it announced that it, too, was about to fail. An AIG implosion would be the equivalent of what one Wall Street insider described as an "extinction-level" event.[67] It could not be allowed to happen. On Tuesday, September 16, 2008, the Fed, at the instruction of Ben Bernanke, Greenspan's replacement as Fed chair, rushed in with an $85 billion rescue package similar in size to what it had offered Bear Stearns in March.[68]

This dramatic intervention settled markets momentarily, but both Bernanke and Paulson, as well as their close collaborator, Timothy Geithner, head of the New York branch of the Federal Reserve, knew that more had to be done. Money market funds—a system used globally by millions of consumers as savings accounts and by businesses to park temporarily hundreds of billions in cash—were edging toward default. If they went bust, liquidity would dry up. Like engines operating without oil, the world's financial institutions would then seize up and grind to a halt.

The week that began with Lehman Brothers failing and AIG pushed to the brink thrust the top managers of America's financial system into the most frightening eighteen-day stretch of their lives. Its nearest analogue was the Cuban Missile Crisis, a thirteen-day moment in October 1962. In both crises, a small group of elite US policymakers held the fate of the world in their hands. In 1962, the threat was nuclear annihilation. In 2008, the threat was global financial annihilation. The words later used by these movers and shakers to describe that 2008 moment reflected the existential struggle they felt they were engaged in. Geithner likened his experience to that of Jeremy Renner, who played a bomb-disposal expert in Katherine Bigelow's chilling movie about the Iraq War, *The Hurt Locker*: One misstep, even of the smallest sort, would result in certain death and destruction. Paulson regarded the moment as his private 9/11. Ben Bernanke, a reserved man rarely given to any public display of emotion, simply remarked that he deemed the economic crisis that befell the nation at this time to be the worst America had ever experienced, graver than even the Great Depression itself.[69] Scary words from the scholar who had long regarded the Great Depression as America's gravest challenge.

On September 20, Paulson made an extraordinary request of Congress: that it appropriate the then gargantuan sum of $700 billion to avert financial catastrophe. The language of Paulson's brief memo was startling in terms of the authority it was proposing to invest in the treasury secretary himself: "Decisions by the Secretary pursuant to the authority of this Act," the memo declared, "are non-reviewable and committed to agency discretion, and may not be reviewed by any court of law or any administrative agency." The Treasury, in other words, would have full power to spend the $700 billion as it saw fit. No action by Paulson would be off limits, and none would need congressional approval.[70]

Republicans in Congress exploded in anger at Paulson's attempt to concentrate this level of emergency power in his hands. As they fulminated, another bank, Washington Mutual, went under, unable to survive the $244 billion worth of compromised mortgages in its portfolios. Even this bank's collapse, the largest in American history, was not enough to persuade more than about a third of Republicans in the House of Representatives to vote for Paulson's proposal. The measure, as a result, went down to defeat (228–205) on September 29, 2008. The Dow Jones Industrial Average promptly plummeted 778 points, the largest one-day loss in its history. A trillion dollars of American business wealth had vaporized in a matter of hours.[71] This market loss scared enough Republicans into changing their votes; they then helped to pass a revised Paulson $700 billion package, now known as the Troubled Asset Relief Program (TARP), on Friday, October 3, 2008. TARP's belated approval did not stop the stock exchange from plunging another 800 points when it reopened Monday morning.[72] Nevertheless, it did give Paulson a vital resource. And Bernanke, the world's foremost expert on causes of the Great Depression, was ready to use the Fed aggressively and innovatively to avoid a repeat of that earlier crisis. Because of their leadership and the support of the Democrats in Congress, the United States was able to forestall the annihilation of the world's financial system.[73]

The damage was still huge. When the stock market finally hit its bottom of 6,600 in March 2009, it stood at less than 50 percent of the peak it had achieved a year and a half earlier. By that time as well, housing prices had fallen by a third. Between 2007 and 2009, US households lost somewhere between $11 and $20 trillion in net worth, an aggregate figure encompassing declines in the value of household real estate, stocks, and pensions.[74] By 2011, more than 25 percent of the nation's 45 million mortgages in America were under water—meaning that mortgage debt was greater than a home's market value. The median household lost half of its wealth between 2007 and 2010.

The loss of wealth spread unevenly through the population. The poor suffered more than the rich, the young more than the old, and people of color more than whites. While median white household net worth declined 16 percent between 2005 and 2009, median black household net worth fell by more than half (53 percent), and median Latino household net worth by nearly two-thirds. By 2010, the rate of black homeownership had slumped to 40 percent, wiping out entirely the 25 percent gain the group had enjoyed during the previous twenty years.[75]

Declines in consumption hewed closely to the decline in wealth. The number of cars sold in the United States fell from 16 million in 2007 to 9 million in 2009. In late 2008, General Motors, a corporation with a monthly payroll of almost $500 million, warned that it would be bankrupt by summer 2009. Toyota soon announced that it, too, was in trouble. Oil prices collapsed. The economic slowdown then spread to the electronics giants of East Asia, including Hitachi, Sony, and Panasonic. Unemployment rates shot up, doubling in the United States from 4.7 percent in early 2008 to 9.4 percent in May 2009. Worldwide, an estimated 27 to 40 million jobs disappeared.[76] No previous economic crisis had engulfed the world with this speed and synchronicity.

Obama's Victory and Burden

The financial crisis hit the GOP like a wrecking ball, smashing Bush's dream of making it America's permanent majority party. He ended his presidency as a reviled figure, as Hoover had been in 1932. He had made a mess of the Iraq War. In 2005, public opinion turned even more sharply against him when his administration demonstrated gross incompetence in relieving the suffering in New Orleans caused by the winds and floods of Hurricane Katrina. The financial crisis that erupted under his watch in 2008 was the third strike, convincing nearly all Americans that his administration was no longer fit to govern.[77] In November, Democrats captured both the presidency and majorities in both Houses of Congress (257–178 in the House, 59–41 in the Senate), its first trifecta since 1992.

At the head of this new government was a young and charismatic African American, Barack Hussein Obama, who had seemingly come out of nowhere to defeat Democratic heavyweight Hillary Rodham Clinton in the primaries and then Senate veteran John McCain in the general election. Obama was the first African American to reach the White House, and he got there earlier than anyone thought a black man or woman would.

Obama's triumph over the racial odds generated extraordinary hope and dreams. Many interpreted his victory to mean that America was ready, finally, to break with its racist past and embrace a "post-racial" future. A son of a white mother and black father, Obama presented himself as someone fully able to comprehend both black and white America and to find a way—as his own family had done—to bring those two tribes together. Unbridled joy manifested itself in Washington on the day of his inauguration. People had come from all over the country and braved the bitter cold to make this assembly one of the largest and most festive inaugurations in American history. "Two million people," reported *The Telegraph*, "covered almost every square foot of Washington's two-mile grass runway from the Capitol to the Lincoln

Memorial . . . —a restless sea of red, white, and blue flags that barely stopped waving from freezing dawn to chilly dusk." At this moment, it really did seem that solutions to America's deepest problems might be within reach.[78]

But Obama was also a captive of the moment. He was captive, first of all, to the financial crisis and its effects. The new president, who had inspired millions during his presidential campaign with his message of hope, delivered one of the soberest inaugurals on record. "That we are in the midst of a crisis is now well understood," Obama intoned. "Our economy is badly weakened," he continued. "Homes have been lost, jobs shed, businesses shuttered." There was no sidestepping the reality that "the challenges we face are real. They are serious and they are many. They will not be met easily in a short span of time."[79]

Of course, Obama declared, America would eventually triumph, choosing "hope over fear" as it had always done in the past. For inspiration, Obama reached back to the story of how George Washington's Continental Army had survived the terrible 1777–1778 winter at Valley Forge. Obama underscored for his listeners how close Washington's army and the new nation had come to defeat. "America's leaders had abandoned the capital. The enemy was advancing. The snow was stained with blood. . . . [T]he outcome of our revolution was most in doubt." Only "a small band of patriots huddled by dying campfires on the shores of an icy river" remained to save this would-be republic.[80] Obama felt himself to be one of those isolated patriots in the weeks leading up to his inauguration. He and his comrades had shuddered as they studied the statistics revealing the depth of America's 2008 financial and economic crisis. Getting the country on the path to economic recovery was not going to be easy.

Obama would also prove captive to his own inexperience and resulting caution. He had entered public life as a state senator in Illinois in 1996 and won election to his first national office, the US Senate, in 2004. In 2008, he was still only a one-term senator, a "back-bencher," so to speak, with limited knowledge of the mores of Washington. He had never managed a large agency or enterprise, public or private; nor had he, as senator, moved a major piece of legislation through Congress. He had taken a stand against the Iraq War as early as 2002 while still a state senator in Illinois. It was a principled position and a prescient one, given the disastrous turns the war and subsequent occupation took. It earned him honor and support when he ran in the Democratic primaries against Hillary Clinton, who had voted for war in 2003 when she was a US senator representing New York. In addition to being principled, Obama was a quick study. But he had scant preparation for the numerous and deep challenges that would confront him as he assumed office in January 2009.

Given the severity of the economic crisis, Obama's decisions about whom to appoint to key economics posts in his administration were arguably his most important, at least in the short term. By temperament deliberate, even conservative, Obama opted for an experienced group of advisors, the Clinton Wall Street team, admired for its success in the previous Democratic administration.[81] Robert Rubin had little interest in returning to active administrative duty, but he pushed hard for those who had worked for him at Treasury or at Citigroup (his landing spot after he left the Clinton White House), or both. Geithner, appointed secretary of the treasury, had close links to Rubin, as did Summers, tapped to head the National Economic Council, and Peter Orszag, the new director of the Office of Management and Budget. Michael Froman, Rubin's chief of staff at Treasury for part of the Clinton years, became deputy assistant chief of staff to Obama and the deputy national security advisor for international economic affairs.[82]

The return of the Rubin group to power revealed how strong the bonds forged by Clinton with America's Wall Street elite remained. Obama understood that Rubin's men "were rooted in the centrist, market-friendly economic philosophy of the Clinton Administration."[83] He seems to have pushed to the side the inconvenient knowledge that the Rubin team, through its deregulatory enthusiasms and initiatives, had put the country on the path toward the crisis of 2008. Obama believed that his first duty was to get America's ailing banks—and the global economic system they underwrote—through their financial winter, just as General Washington conceived of his primary goal at Valley Forge as finding a way for his army to survive. "I felt constrained," Obama later explained, "from making any rash moves."[84] An experienced Wall Street team working closely with the banks was the best strategy, Obama believed, to see America through. This is the choice Obama made, thus increasing the likelihood that he would make himself captive, wittingly or not, to a 1990s mode of Democratic Party economic management.[85]

A more radical economic plan would have entailed either nationalizing the banks for a time or breaking them up into small entities, or both. Obama rejected both these policy possibilities, even though a number of his advisors had brought them to his attention. Instead, he adopted Geithner's more limited plan to subject the nineteen largest banks to "stress tests." In this scheme, a team of 200 bank examiners working under Fed management designed a hypothetical economic crisis, and then, with full access to banking records, built models for how every bank was likely to respond to it. The key question was whether banks would have sufficient capital reserves to weather the imagined crisis. If they did not, they were to be told how much they had to raise in private capital markets. If they could not raise these funds, they would be required to take taxpayer capital still residing in Paulson's TARP fund—and thus be subject to that fund's stringent terms.[86]

It was a clever scheme, and it succeeded quickly in restoring confidence in America's giant banks. By the end of June, nine banks had raised the necessary capital and exited from government oversight. By December 2009, the rest had followed. Bank chairmen and government regulators haggled with Fed accountants over the amount of capital that needed to be raised and under what terms, and private bankers groused endlessly about government meddling in their private affairs. But the leaders of the big banks had to be pleased: The government plan set terms that they could meet and put clear limits on the scope and duration of government intervention. Moreover, if the banks got through the stress tests and raised the necessary private capital, they would receive an all-important federal stamp of approval, which would then raise their standing in capital markets and increase dramatically their advantage over the smaller commercial banks that were not subjected to stress tests and thus could not hope to be rewarded with a federal certificate of approval. Through this process, Obama's stress test plan actually ended up increasing the concentration of power and resources in a small number of gigantic financial institutions deemed "too big to fail."[87]

Obama's decision to weight a recovery package so heavily toward financial elites and their institutions did not get good reviews on Main

Street. As millions of Americans were wrestling with the effects of economic calamity on their lives, the bankers responsible for issuing ruinous mortgages seemed to be facing few consequences. The Obama
administration did not send a single banker to jail nor did it compel
any financial institution to pay for its misdeeds by breaking it up. The
administration was not happy with the hundreds of millions of dollars
in bonuses that these banks were paying out to top managers in spring
2009 at the very moment when the economy was sinking to its lowest
point, with near 10 percent unemployment and millions of households
entering foreclosure proceedings. Obama let it be known that he was
"outraged" by AIG's decision in March 2009 to pay out $165 million in
bonuses to the executives of its Financial Products Division, the "brains"
behind the vast derivatives industry whose implosion had been so central to the financial crash. Obama's public rebuke of AIG momentarily
scared Wall Street. But Obama did not follow through with punitive
measures in the form of actual monetary penalties, prosecutions, or the
public shaming that would have occurred had banking executives been
forced to run the gauntlet of congressional hearings.[88]

To be fair, the Obama administration did more than simply attend
to the needs of financial elites. It steered through Congress a $700 bil-
lion stimulus package in February 2009 meant to relieve suffering and
distress by putting government funds in the hands of ordinary workers
and consumers.[89] In a smart and successful move, it compelled a reor-
ganization of the American automobile industry, placing it on a much
sounder economic footing and saving hundreds of thousands of jobs in
the process.[90] But these efforts were not sufficient to imbue a recovery
of the Main Street economy with a robustness that would rival the one
already being felt on Wall Street. Many economists, including some
who had the ear of the president, believed that the stimulus package
ought to have been two to three times larger than it was.[91] The automobile bailout was well designed but limited in its effects. Meanwhile, the
Obama administration did almost nothing to aid the estimated 9 million households facing foreclosure or distressed sales of their homes.[92]
It did have plans to help the poor through a vast national health insurance plan, the centerpiece of Obama's presidential campaign. Part of
Obama's eagerness to wrap up financial recovery efforts with as little
disruption to existing institutions as possible was so he could turn to

health care reform. But his eagerness to move beyond recovery efforts so quickly may have been a strategic error. It might have been wiser for him to have fought for achieving economic fairness and equality for the American people rather than on expanding social welfare.

Though the Obama administration did push through Congress its major health insurance reform act, the Affordable Care Act, in spring 2010, it would take years for its effects to be felt. Meanwhile, economic inequality worsened. By 2012, the Dow Jones Industrial Average had regained the ground it had lost during the Great Recession of 2008–2009. Unemployment, on the other hand, remained far above where it had been in 2007. Job levels would not return to their pre-recession levels for eight long years. During Obama's first term, the income of the top 1 percent of American income earners increased by more than 30 percent; the bottom 99 percent had to settle for a 0.4 percent raise.[93] Young workers experienced years of un- or underemployment, stalling the development of their careers and putting a significant dent in their lifetime earning capacity. The pain experienced in minority communities, home to a disproportionate number of subprime mortgages, went unaddressed. Pain began accumulating, too, in working-class white communities where rates of alcoholism, drug abuse, and suicide soared. In these circumstances, anger at economic inequality began to stir. It would soon escape the periphery of American politics, where decades of neoliberal hegemony had confined it.[94]

Obama's approach to economic recovery damaged that hegemony further by undercutting one of neoliberalism's core propositions: namely, that "freeing markets" from government oversight would lead to opportunity and prosperity for all. Freeing the banks from government regulation had produced first the housing bubble and then financial and economic collapse. In the aftermath of the crash, almost no one believed that the failing financial markets could repair themselves. Markets, it turned out, required government intervention and regulation. But of what sort? Was it right for the Obama administration to have privileged the banks in its recovery plans? Was it appropriate for it to have given private insurance companies a central role in its design of health care reform? Or did these decisions simply demonstrate that government was deepening rather than easing the rigging of American life in favor of large institutions that were already dominant? On the left, socialists began to make themselves heard for the first time in decades, arguing that government had to bring back the robust regulatory apparatus of the New Deal order. On the right, pundits would soon begin to talk about a "deep state" that engineered outcomes for the rich and powerful and that was impervious to popular and democratic control. The political repercussions of the Great Recession of 2008 were about to explode on America, and they would rock the neoliberal order to its core.

By 2009, the setbacks suffered by the American nation during its twenty-first decade were close to overwhelming. Might events have followed a different course? Let us go back for a moment to December 2000. Suppose the Supreme Court had ordered a full recount of Florida ballots in the 2000 election. Suppose that the recount had then elevated Gore rather than Bush to the White House. A Gore administration, in turn, would have been far less likely to respond to the September 11 catastrophe by initiating a war against Saddam Hussein. Iraq, Syria, and the world would then have been spared the calamity of the American occupation and the refugee crisis it spawned.

A Gore administration would also not have made a tax cut its priority. Absent the strains caused by an expensive war and occupation of Iraq, it would have had more resources available for domestic programs. Perhaps, under Gore's leadership, America would have been spared the escalating levels of indebtedness, public and private, that became such a hallmark of the Bush years.

Perhaps. Yet it is important to remember that deregulating finance and deploying risky financial instruments had been as much the work of Democrats as of Republicans. Both sides had used a professed commitment to racial equality and pluralism to gain support for dangerously unsound economic policies. Both thought that Greenspan was a wizard. Both subscribed to the neoliberal shibboleth that market risk was a thing of the past. Technology, it was believed by both parties, had put market perfection within human grasp. Abundance for all would be the result. That was the neoliberal promise. Both Democrats and Republicans had tied their fortunes to delivering on it. Gore, himself, had long been at the center of the Democratic Party's neoliberal campaign, Clinton's trusted techno-utopian lieutenant.

In the aftermath of the Great Recession, globalization and neoliberalism could no longer be promoted as policies that lifted all boats. Techno-utopianism could no longer hide the truth that serious structural imbalances in the global economy threatened not just to collapse economies but to rend the social fabric of nations. The economic hardship and distress caused by the crash would linger for years. Political anger would smolder for a time and then erupt into a series of white-hot insurgencies. The neoliberal order would not be able to withstand the heat.

7

Coming Apart

IN THE YEARS following the Great Crash of 2008–2009, very different groups of Americans began to transmute their economic distress into political anger and protest. Whites who saw themselves standing outside (economically and culturally) the prospering corridors of the neoliberal order launched a Tea Party to reclaim their nation. Young people of different races who discovered that the Great Recession had vaporized the economic opportunities they had thought would be theirs took over a small park in lower Manhattan, announcing they had come to occupy Wall Street; they stayed for months and triggered a national protest against economic inequality. Finally, black anger at the brutal effect of a burst housing bubble and police violence in their communities hardened into the defiant slogan and uprising, Black Lives Matter (BLM).

None of these insurgencies, on its own, was as large or as impactful as either the civil rights or anti-Vietnam War movements of the 1960s (or the labor movement of the 1930s) had been. But the three, in combination, profoundly convulsed American politics, fueling the rise of Donald Trump and Bernie Sanders, leading in 2016 to one of the more remarkable election campaigns in American history. This was the moment when America's neoliberal order began to come apart. We begin this story not with tales of political or ideological rebellion, however, but with an account of the economic and human distress that laid the groundwork for a decade's worth of political explosions.

White Working-Class Distress

The distress and economic dislocation caused by the Great Recession of 2008–2009 came on the heels of decades of deepening economic inequality between those benefiting from the global orientation of the neoliberal order and those who were not. The hemorrhaging of manufacturing employment that had been so manifest a feature of the 1990s and early 2000s continued in the wake of the Great Recession, when 2 million additional jobs disappeared.[1] Workers losing jobs who were fortunate enough to get new ones frequently had to work for lower pay.[2] Their misfortune was not the lot of those further up the income scale. By 2012, the stock market had made up its 2008–2009 losses. There seemed to be no limit to the extravagance of the fortunes piling up in the hands of America's rich. The economic inequality that had become a defining feature of the American economy since the 1980s continued to widen. And the consequences of that chasm were hardening.

Neoliberal social scientist Charles Murray had become increasingly concerned about those consequences for white working-class Americans. Around 2010, he launched a research project to probe the condition of working-class whites during these hard times. For his social laboratory, he chose Fishtown, a long-time white working-class district of North Philadelphia. In 2012, Murray published his sobering findings in his book *Coming Apart*.

Murray homed in on falling marriage rates as the key indicator of social distress. The marriage rate among Fishtown's prime-age whites had fallen precipitously in the fifty years between 1960 and 2010, from 84 percent to 48 percent. Partly this reflected a rising rate of divorce. More alarming to Murray was the proportion of Fishtown inhabitants who had never married. Among those aged thirty to forty-nine, that percentage had increased from 8 percent in 1960 to 25 percent in 2010. A full third of Fishtown's white working-class men had never married. The decline in marriage was not matched by a decline in births, which meant that more and more white Fishtown children were both born out of wedlock and living in single-parent households.[3]

In the nation as a whole, Murray reported, the percentage of children born to unmarried white mothers had increased from 3 percent in 1960 to nearly 30 percent in 2010. Among white mothers with less than a high school education, it had increased from 10 percent to 60 percent. Fewer and fewer children in such circumstances were living in households where an adult man and adult woman were both present. Or, if two adults were present, the chances that the adult man would be the biological father of the resident child decreased over time, as the mother was likely to have had a series of partners and to have had children with multiple men who came and went.[4]

All of Fishtown's other ills, Murray claimed, flowed from the disintegration of marriage and the family as pillars of social life.[5] Like his fellow neoliberal George Gilder, Murray believed that stable marriages were necessary to "domesticate" men, who otherwise would behave irresponsibly at work, at play, and in relationships.[6] Minus such domestication, Murray and Gilder alleged, the male's commitment to work declined. An undomesticated man showed little initiative, was employed episodically (if he was employed at all), and spent too much time "goofing off," drinking, watching television, and sleeping. In Murray's telling, TV watching (and video gaming and internet surfing) had replaced work as the preoccupation of many of Fishtown's men.[7] As industriousness declined, so, Murray rather extravagantly argued, did honesty, integrity, civic involvement, and religious affiliation.

In Fishtown, in other words, the dreaded "underclass" of the 1980s was rising again. Now, however, it was possessing the souls of whites as much as those of blacks. Murray, who had acquired a notorious reputation in some quarters for doubting the adequacy of black culture, reluctantly concluded in 2012 that race made no difference to "the coming apart at the seams," to the "evil effects" of the afflictions he observed in Fishtown and, by extension, the nation.[8] "White America," Murray glumly reported, "is not headed in one direction and nonwhite America in another." Both were heading toward disaster.[9]

Murray's analysis of home life and its dysfunctions rested on an essentialized view of male and female nature: Men were wild and unreliable unless tamed by marriage; women's primary purpose was to bear and raise children. Murray was oblivious to the existence of times and places in which men and women had subscribed to different gender roles and different ways of organizing households and raising children. And Murray's analysis was tainted by racism: The social deterioration in white communities seemed to pain him more than similar processes unfolding in black ones.[10]

Despite his bias, Murray was not wrong about the distress and despair overtaking the lives of many whites. In fact, he may have underestimated their effects. At the very moment during which he was doing his study, rates of self-harm among middle-aged working-class white men aged thirty to forty-nine in America were soaring. The United States had long been exceptional among nations in terms of the levels of mortal violence its people inflicted on each other. But rising rates of self-harm and death among working-class white men were something new. Death due to alcohol and drug poisoning among this group increased fourfold between the years 1999 and 2013; suicides among this group rose nearly 40 percent in the same period. No other group in America—not wealthier whites nor blacks or Latinos of any income or educational group—experienced a parallel rise in rates of self-harm during this time. So pronounced was this rise that the overall mortality rate among working-class middle-aged white men in the United States actually began to increase after decades of decline. A demographic reversal of this sort had never previously been observed to have occurred within any group resident in the advanced industrial nations of North America and Europe, except in moments of war, pandemics, and genocide. The circumstances shaping the life of white working-class men in early twenty-first-century America were, in this respect, unprecedented. Had Murray been aware of this epidemic of self-harm afflicting so many white working-class men, he undoubtedly would have used it to buttress his contention that a portion of white America was indeed coming apart.[11]

Murray was oblivious to the material roots of white despair. *Coming Apart* paid no attention to decades-old patterns of globalization, mounting economic inequality, and the loss of millions of well-paying and secure blue-collar jobs. The Great Recession of 2008–2009 barely makes an appearance in his book. Instead, Murray blamed America's twenty-first-century crisis on the white ruling elite. Members of this elite, Murray charged, had failed to impress on their economic lessers the proper moral and cultural values: industriousness, discipline, self-reliance, and strong families that would inculcate virtue in the young. Echoing Gertrude Himmelfarb, Murray claimed that such inculcation is what the British Victorians had achieved so effectively in the nineteenth century. America's twenty-first-century elite, by contrast, was too imbued with a "live and let live" philosophy—Murray's negative description of an outlook I have elsewhere called (and framed more positively as) the cosmopolitan version of the neoliberal moral code— to assume the reins of national moral leadership. This elite's abdication, in Murray's eyes, resulted in cultural and social calamity for racial kin further down the social scale.[12]

There was condescension (and more than a little crude Marxist analysis) imbedded in Murray's view that America's white working class, once abandoned by their social betters, had settled into a kind of lumpen-proletarian existence. Murray saw little capacity for political assertiveness in this inert mass. There is not a hint in this 2012 book about the political fury that was already smoldering in its ranks, beginning with the Tea Party and culminating in the ethnonationalist populist insurgency that would propel Donald Trump into the White House. But Murray's revealing data about poor whites in Fishtown help us to understand why a political storm was gathering.

Black Suffering

The economic suffering in black communities resulting from the Great Recession was vast, probably greater in the short term than what whites experienced. The homeownership boom of the Clinton-Bush years, which had raised the percentage of minorities owning homes from 40 percent to 50 percent, had promised to narrow the huge wealth gap separating black from white families.[13] But the Great Recession, as we have seen, decimated minority homeowning ranks. Many were unable to make their monthly mortgage payments. Lending institutions were quick to foreclose. Countless families lost their homes and, in the process, whatever wealth they had possessed.[14] Even after the Great Recession had ended in 2009, the percentage of black homeowners with homes under water continued to rise, until it reached 14.2 percent, nearly three times the rate among whites. The disparity between white and black household wealth deepened. In 2010, white households possessed wealth that, on average, was eight times greater than the average among black households. By 2013, white households possessed thirteen times as much wealth as black ones.[15]

Disparities in the economic recovery rates of public versus private sectors of the US economy further widened the black-white economic gulf. About one in five adult African Americans worked in government jobs at the federal, state, and municipal levels, a significantly higher percentage than that of whites. The Great Recession had hit the public sector hard. Plunging house values and forfeited homes stripped many municipalities of the property taxes that had been their principal source of revenue. Most of these municipalities, and the states in whose jurisdictions they resided, were prohibited by law or constitution from operating at a deficit, putting them at a disadvantage in times of recession. The crash of 2008–2009 thus forced these governments to lay off countless employees. The 2009 Obama bailout plan moderated these layoffs for a time by channeling federal funds to city and state governments hobbled by layoffs. But federal assistance ran out before property tax revenues regained their pre-recession levels.[16]

State governments might have raised state income or sales taxes to assist ailing local governments in their midst. But many state legislatures were in the grip of anti-tax coalitions doctrinally opposed to tax increases. This was part of the neoliberal dispensation, which held that government was the problem, not the solution. Society would be best served by stripping governments of power and resources and thus by enlarging the terrain on which free markets could do their work. Among Republicans, governors such as Scott Walker of Wisconsin became the poster boys of the post-recession era, building their reputations by attacking waste and corruption in government and targeting public sector labor unions as the source of these problems. Walker and his allies rolled back the bargaining power of these unions in Wisconsin, shrank the public sector wage bill, and thinned out the ranks of public employees. These initiatives hurt African Americans more than whites for the simple reason that the former were more dependent than whites on public sector jobs.[17]

In these circumstances, the underground economy of drugs, long a source of employment and income in urban black communities, took on additional allure. This illicit economy had always been a dangerous one. Drug dealers and the gangs with which they were associated were armed and did not hesitate to enforce their will through violent means. Rates of homicide among young black males, though falling since the 1970s, were still the highest of any subgroup in the population—76 per 100,000 black men aged twenty-five to thirty-four.[18] Much of this killing was internal to the drug economy, but some of it occurred in confrontations between young black men and urban police forces. The regime of harsh punishment for even minor drug offenses implemented in the 1980s and 1990s remained in force, as did a policing ideology of zero tolerance emanating from Mayor Rudolph Giuliani and his allies in 1990s New York City. Many police forces, meanwhile, had militarized themselves, acquiring levels of armaments and developing rules of engagement that more and more resembled what the US Army and Marines deployed against foreign adversaries than what a domestic constabulary, ideally, should have been doing to maintain the peace among its own citizens.[19] In 2013 and 2014, a spasm of police killings of black men rocked the nation. But years before, a reckoning had begun with the country's mass incarceration regime, a part of America's neoliberal order since the late 1980s.

One trigger had been the publication in 2010 of *The New Jim Crow* by Michelle Alexander, then a little-known law professor at Ohio State University. The figures that Alexander had assembled on the numbers of Americans caught in the criminal justice system were shocking. America, by her calculations, had put more than 7 million people, 1 of every 31 Americans, behind bars, on probation, or on parole. More than 2 million were in prison. Germany imprisoned 93 of every 100,000 people. The United States jailed 750 out of every 100,000. American prisons held more convicts in proportional terms than those of Russia, China, Egypt, Iran, or North Korea. And the American prison population was disproportionately black and Latino. In several American cities, Alexander reported, as many as 80 percent of young African American men had criminal records. The United States was imprisoning a higher percentage of its black population than South Africa did at the height of its apartheid regime.[20]

The New Jim Crow's power derived in part from its ability to marshal these alarming numbers. How could a society that prided itself on its liberal and democratic character—and on its neoliberal freedoms—tolerate the largest mass incarceration regime in the twenty-first-century world? Another part derived from Alexander's sobering analysis of the toll that the absence of fathers was exacting on black families and on children growing up in single-parent households. In sections that resonated powerfully with black readers, Alexander showed how the punishments of those imprisoned never really ended, even years after the imprisoned had served their time. Those released from jail were obligated to report their convictions and jail sentences to potential employers, thereby costing them access to jobs. In many states, ex-prisoners were stripped permanently of the right to vote and other rights associated with citizenship. Few states had mechanisms for restoring men who had served their time to full membership in community life—economic, political, and social. Few legislators who were not themselves part of these minority communities even contemplated the injustice of condemning men who completed their sentences to a lifetime of exclusion, marginality, and impotence. Those within minority communities understood all too well the personal and family suffering accumulating among those unable to escape the stigma of having run afoul of the law.[21] The Great Recession and the economic pain that it caused made the consequences of incarceration and parole all the more severe. Michelle Alexander's book gave those within minority communities as well as those outside them an opportunity to reckon in new ways with a serious social and ethical problem that the nation had ignored for so long. Seeds of protest were being sown.

The Precariat

A very different social group was also experiencing hardship in the wake of the Great Recession. This one came to be dubbed the "precariat," a word first invented as a play on the word "proletariat." Members of this social group had experienced the downside of what was being celebrated as the "gig economy," a world of jobs, opportunities, and affluence that the information technology (IT) revolution had called into being. New digital tools and programs had allegedly made it possible for many individuals to start their own businesses or at least control the circumstances of their work. An enterprising individual could now set him- or herself up in business as an accountant, lawyer, or copyeditor, or as a photographer, potter, or online marketplace seller, without needing to be hired as a salaried employee or as an hourly wage worker. One could do this work part-time or full-time and thus combine it with other activities—going to school, parenting, caring for an elderly parent—far more easily than if one had to report to work from nine to five, five days a week. One could labor from home, or from a nearby café wired for internet. The gig economy was laced with hopes about being one's own boss, enjoying freedom on a daily basis, making money, and living the American dream. Obama's Affordable Care Act facilitated the growth of this economy by making it possible for freelancers and small entrepreneurs to acquire all-important health care insurance at a reasonable cost.

Neoliberalism had provided the conceptual underpinning for the gig economy by theorizing how individuals could transform themselves into entrepreneurs able to monetize material and personal assets in new ways. The novel way of thinking, for example, taught that the assets in which individuals had invested the largest percentage of their income and saving—cars and homes—were being underutilized. Cars sat undriven for many hours every day, generating neither utility nor income. Primary homes or apartments were not underutilized in the same way; but second homes and apartments were. Why not find ways to make these assets income-generating centers for oneself and one's family? The founders of start-ups Airbnb (2008) and Uber (2009) were asking precisely these questions and answering them by persuading armies of homeowners and car owners to monetize their assets through the ingeniously designed computer programs that these new corporations had developed. Rather quickly, legions of cars-for-hire and apartments for short-term rentals inundated and convulsed urban transportation and rental housing industries, with the promise of lower rates for riders and lessees, on the one hand, and robust new sources of income for drivers and lessors, on the other.[22]

There was a downside to this new gig economy, of course. Gig entrepreneurs such as Uber drivers laboring as individuals in a market economy possessed, in reality, little control over critical aspects of their work. They could not easily build costs of pensions or health insurance into the fees they charged for their services. They had no one other than themselves to pay for what an employer's share of Social Security payments would have been. They had no insurance against time lost at work for sickness. These considerations may not have mattered much at a time when markets for gig-worker services were robust and when gig workers were young enough that worries about illness or retirement savings were not a major concern. But what happened when an economic boom ended, when the fees gig workers could command for their services declined as a result, and when corporations shed payroll to get themselves through hard times (as they did massively in the winter of 2008–2009), in the process throwing many more individuals into gig earner ranks? Suddenly many more freelancers were competing to sell their services into smaller, less hospitable markets.

At moments like these, the gig economy began to resemble what economists had long called a casual labor market, casual because the only form of work available was intermittent and inadequate. Casual labor markets worked to the advantage of employers, as these markets were crowded with individuals who had less work than they needed and thus were willing to labor for lower wages and on temporary contracts.[23]

The casual labor market that emerged during and after the Great Recession of 2008–2009 was not equivalent to what leftists conversant with Marx had long called the "proletariat." Its ranks included not just the permanently poor. They included many college graduates, a significant number from solid middle-class and even upper-middle-class families who could not get regular jobs after the crash or who did not want them, having convinced themselves that they could sculpt themselves into masters of the gig economy. They were also a racially diverse group of whites, blacks, Latinos, and others. They trended young. The term "precariat" had been coined by French sociologists in the 1980s, but it remained a marginal term in Anglo-American discourse until the 2010s.[24] Then it took off to describe the rapid expansion of the ranks of those whose circumstances of work were chronically unsettled, subject to market conditions and employer preferences over which they had no control.

Young people from affluent families comprised a significant slice of this precariat, and this mattered politically. Historically, protest movements often swelled when a portion of a society's elite, or would-be elite, lost confidence in the prevailing political order and threw in its lot with the less fortunate.[25] A perception of commonly shared material interests had strengthened such alliances in the past and would soon do so again.

The Tea Party Erupts

The first political turbulence in the post–Great Recession era erupted on the right. A Tea Party for the twenty-first century emerged in response to a seemingly inconsequential rant by CNBC correspondent Rick Santelli reporting from the floor of the Chicago Mercantile Exchange in March 2009.[26]

On learning about another "giveaway" by the Obama administration to Americans whom he regarded as financially irresponsible, Santelli declared (on TV) that he had seen too many bailouts. In a mixture of anger and jest, he called on commodity traders to gather up all the derivatives that had first sustained but were now undermining the financial sector and toss them into the Chicago River, much as the Boston Tea Partiers had dumped unwanted British Tea into the Boston Harbor in 1773. Santelli's call-to-arms went viral, sparking a wave of political organizing by self-fashioning Tea Party groups, some emerging directly from the grassroots, others funded into existence by the Koch brothers, ever eager to rein in what they regarded as the most serious threat to America's future—extravagant government spending.[27]

The Koch brothers controlled one of the country's most powerful industrial conglomerates. Their support for some Tea Party groups revealed how elites were trying to channel this protest. But Tea Party ranks also included a populist current that viewed the spending of the federal government less in terms of simple excess and more in terms of a conspiracy to enrich the ranks of the already wealthy at the expense of ordinary Americans. These Tea Partiers, inspired by the likes of Ron Paul, an eccentric congressman from Texas, focused attention on the high proportion of government bailout money being channeled precisely to those wealthy and powerful financial institutions, such as Bear Stearns and AIG, that had done the most to inflict the Great Recession on America. This coddling of America's rich had to stop, and the only way to do that was to cut the expensive lifelines that the federal government had been throwing out to failing corporations. If upending this process required the end of the federal government in its post-1945 incarnation, so be it. Out of the carnage, Paul and his followers believed, a better America would emerge.[28]

A third Tea Party current combined anger at economic inequality with ethnoracial resentment. Some in the Tea Party ranks began to charge that the worst damage to America was being engineered by an unholy alliance of political-economic elites and the nation's undeserving (and largely nonwhite) poor. Allegations regarding this unholy alliance had been percolating in American society since the days of the Great Society and the civil rights revolution, when Democratic Party liberal elites stood accused of allying themselves with the black poor to win elections and then of using the federal government to aid people of color while either ignoring or actively harming the needs of nation's "best" citizens: God-fearing, law abiding, and Constitution-revering whites. In the aftermath of the Great Recession, a new generation of ethnonationalist populists surged to the fore, feeding on discontent long festering in areas such as Fishtown that Charles Murray had studied. One such agitator, Andrew Breitbart, had in 2005 launched *Breitbart.com*, an irreverent right-wing digital news service that delighted in standing up for the little (white) guy and tilting against liberal establishment elites and their alleged allies in the ranks of the nation's black and Latino poor.[29]

The Tea Party soared to national prominence and influence in August 2009 when its members stormed town hall meetings that had been organized by congressmen and -women to give constituents a chance to air their views on Obama's controversial Affordable Care Act (ACA).[30] Many Tea Party protestors saw "Obamacare" as the latest example of liberal elites aligning themselves with the black and Latino poor to impose a health care delivery system that the country's good (white) citizens did not want. Tea Party activists also began to use their opposition to Obamacare to delegitimate Obama himself.[31]

This delegitimacy campaign rested on a spurious but serious charge: namely, that Obama had not been eligible to run for the presidency, let alone occupy the Oval Office. The Constitution stipulated that a president had to be "a natural born citizen of the United States." It was easy to prove that Obama fit that category. He had been born in Hawaii after it had become a state in 1960. He was therefore a citizen of the United States at birth. Yet, as early as 2008, Obama's opponents began to float the claim that he had been born abroad. The most common claim was that his father, a Kenyan studying economics at the University of Hawaii, had whisked his white American wife (Obama's mother) off to Kenya so that Barack could be born in the paternal parent's homeland.[32]

This preposterous charge came into full, and ugly, view in September 2009 when 75,000 Tea Partiers marched on Washington, ostensibly to protest the ACA. The marchers made their sentiments about Obama known through a plethora of signs, many of them comparing him to Hitler or to hammer-and-sickle socialists. But another theme came up again and again: Obama's alleged identity as an African. The signs were not kind to Obama's paternal African roots. "The Zoo has an African [lion—represented by an image], and The White House has a Lyin' African!" proclaimed several signs held aloft that day. "OBAMA[,] GO BACK HOME TO KENYA AND TAKE YOUR RADICAL LEFT COMMY FRIENDS WITH YA," screamed another. Yet another proclaimed, "Somewhere in Kenya A Village Is Missing An Idiot." As though responding to this declaration, a different poster offered this lost-in-America idiot a "FREE TICKET BACK TO KENYA!!"[33]

This attack on Obama as an African idiot can, of course, be interpreted as simple, anti-black prejudice. But it may be wiser to treat it as complex form of racism, manifesting itself as a revolt against Obama not just because he was black but also because he represented the full flowering of cosmopolitanism as an American creed. Obama had experienced the diversity of the world—and moved easily through its many cultures—more than any previous occupant of the Oval Office. He had been born in America's only majority-minority state—Hawaii. His father was African and Muslim. Barack had spent a good part of his youth in Indonesia, where his mother was doing her anthropological PhD research. His worldliness thrilled the Americans who voted for him and who viewed his election as the dawn of a new America, one that gloried in its diverse, multicultural character. But to millions of whites who were already feeling as though they were being left behind by declining opportunities and by the rising status of people of color both in the United States and abroad, Obama's ascension to the White House—and the adulation bestowed on him throughout the ranks of multicultural America and the multicultural world—felt like another kick to the gut.[34]

The racist opposition to Obama, then, was not just about the alleged idiocy of an "African" president. It was also an attack on America's cosmopolitan turn, its celebration of diversity, and its eagerness to integrate nonwhites into the corridors of American power and privilege. Seen in this way, the hatred of Obama can be interpreted as a protest against the neoliberal regime that was still dominating American life. This regime, in the eyes of Tea Party supporters, stood accused of opening America's gates to the nonwhites of the world and of "swamping" America's white race with "inferior" people of color.

It was but a short step from protesting open borders to revolting against another aspect of the neoliberal regime—the commitment to global free trade that had made America a destination for an unlimited number of "Made in China" goods. China, in this view, was not simply a manufacturing juggernaut that threatened American jobs and economic supremacy; it was also home to the world's largest nonwhite population. In the eyes of certain swaths of Tea Party supporters, the American elite's openness to China was yet another sign that it had become indifferent to the future of America's best citizens—its white population—and that it was willing to relegate these white citizens to the back of the line or abandon them altogether. For many Tea Partiers, Obama's celebration of diversity and pursuit of close economic relations with China signified that he was part of a global multicultural elite that was undermining America's best (white) citizens.[35]

The Rise of Donald Trump

Few grasped the political potential of this ethnonationalist, racially inflected populism better than New York real estate tycoon and reality TV star, Donald Trump. Trump waded into Tea Party politics in 2010 and 2011 partly to take its measure and partly as a hedge against his declining business opportunities and reputation. He had long presented himself as one of the world's wealthiest and most savvy men, claiming to be the consummate real estate dealmaker and to have accumulated piles of money, power, and sexual conquests along the way. By the second decade of the twenty-first century, however, Trump was in economic trouble. Many of his real estate projects, such as his Atlantic City casinos, had failed, making it hard for him to persuade banks to lend him money for new projects. Trump had quietly shifted from real estate development to branding—selling the Trump name to others who would then be allowed to affix it to hotels, golf courses, universities, wine and vodka bottles, and even steaks. His branding career was going reasonably well. But his most successful new vocation turned out to be that of entertainer.[36]

In 2004, Trump began an eleven-year run as host of the NBC reality show *The Apprentice* (and later *The Celebrity Apprentice*), in which two teams of contestants competed ruthlessly against each other to start new businesses, secure deals, deploy new marketing strategies, and sell products. In every episode, the team on the losing side of a week's deal-making gathered with Trump in a TV studio to dissect its failure. Each show would climax with Trump sacking the team member whom he had judged to be the culprit of that week's losses. Audiences delighted in watching Trump jettison a contestant with the words "You're fired!" Trump turned out to be very good at performing the role of chief executive, appearing to weigh the pros and cons of made-for-TV business deals, and at acting decisively. The role brought him hundreds of millions of dollars of income and national fame. But by 2012 and 2013, *The Apprentice* formula was stale and its ratings were slipping.[37] Trump was looking for something new.

Trump had long thought about entering politics, even as he appeared to lack a fixed set of beliefs on many issues of the day.[38] Many who knew Trump were not surprised at his shapeshifting, which they interpreted as manifestations of the shallowness of his political convictions and of his opportunistic nature.

Yet, from the 1980s forward, Trump had been steadfast in holding to several beliefs that converged with Tea Party grievances. First, he had never embraced the neoliberal promise of a world without borders, in which peoples and goods would move easily from country to country. He did not believe in the virtues of free trade. Even the best rules of fair competition, he argued, would fail to restrain power-hungry countries, corporations, or individuals (like himself) from pursuing advantage by whatever means necessary. Only bilateral agreements hammered out by smart dealmakers acting in their self-interest would yield good results both for industries and for countries. Thus, Trump had long attacked the North American Free Trade Agreement (NAFTA) for making North America a free trade zone and the World Trade Organization (WTO) for admitting China into its ranks. In his view, nothing good would result from open borders with Mexico and with China.[39]

Second, Trump had always been an ethnonationalist who believed that America's destiny was to be a white man's country. Like his father, he held that the best people of America were those of European descent. He wanted little to do with African Americans (other than to be seen with a few black celebrities who might improve sales of his brands). He had conspired with his father in the early 1970s to deny blacks opportunities to rent apartments in a Trump housing project in Queens. In 1989, when a white woman jogger was brutally attacked and raped in Central Park and left to die, Trump took out full-page ads in the New York newspapers to condemn the five alleged attackers, all of them teenage blacks and Latinos. Calling for the death penalty to be reinstated in New York so that these teenagers could be executed, Trump went on to declare that "I want to hate these muggers and murderers. They should be forced to suffer."[40] The five accused were convicted (and given long prison sentences) on the basis of evidence so flimsy that the verdicts would later be overturned. But Trump never apologized for his 1989 ads nor did he acknowledge that his purveying false information may have played a role in railroading innocent boys. It had been his mission to guard white America against "dangerous" and "upstart" minority populations, and he would continue to do so.[41]

In Trump's eyes, Barack Hussein Obama was himself a minority upstart—and a particularly dangerous one. Michael Cohen, Trump's long-time consigliere, recalled how Trump, in 2008–2009, "was literally losing his mind watching a handsome and self-evidently brilliant young black man take over [the White House], not only as Commander in Chief, but also as a moral leader and guiding light." In *Disloyal*, his tell-all book of his long association with Trump, Cohen claimed that his one-time boss had actually "hired a Faux-Bama, or fake Obama, to record a video where Trump ritualistically belittled the first black president and then fired him, a kind of fantasy fulfillment that it was hard to imagine any adult would spend serious money living out."[42] By 2011, Trump had put himself at the head of the Tea Party "birther" movement, which was insisting that Obama's "African birth" meant that the latter ought to be removed from the Oval Office. Did Trump believe the canard about Obama having been born in Africa? Probably not. But he did believe that a black man had no business calling the White House home.[43]

If Obama constituted a racial threat from above, the influx of tens of millions of nonwhite immigrants into America constituted a racial threat from below. Trump made an attack on Mexican immigrants the centerpiece of the speech in July 2015 launching his presidential campaign. He charged that rapists filled these immigrants' ranks. "When Mexico sends its people, they're not sending their best. They're not sending you. They're sending people that have lots of problems, and they're bringing those problems. . . .They're bringing drugs. They're bringing crime. They're rapists." He also targeted China, less from an immigration than from a trade point of view. Once again, Trump made race central to his politics: The nonwhites of China were undercutting America with their goods much as the nonwhites of Mexico were undercutting America through their migration. Walls had to be built against both Chinese goods and Mexican migrants. Only then would America's manufacturing prowess and racial integrity be restored.[44]

Trump's third long-standing belief was, in some respects, the most surprising one to find in a New York City billionaire: that America's good, white people had to take the country back from a cosmopolitan elite intent on selling it out. Trump had been raised in Queens, one of New York City's outer boroughs. His father, Fred, a wealthy real estate developer with properties throughout Queens and Brooklyn, had no interest in owning property in Manhattan, nor in becoming part of the Manhattan social elite. Donald, on the other hand, desperately wanted to join Manhattan's upper crust. Donald thought that he could use his father's money and clout to buy Manhattan property and thereby to gain access to this elite. But Donald turned out to be much better at flashing money than at making it. He also proved very good at attracting critical tabloid attention: His failed business ventures, sexual affairs, and marital divorces all seemed to land on the front pages of the *New York Post* and *New York Daily News*.[45] The real estate and cultural lords of Manhattan ridiculed Trump for his boasts, affairs, and affectations. They also knew better than most that Trump's prowess as a real estate dealmaker was a myth, sustained in the public eye only by regular bailouts from pere Trump. They regarded fils Trump as a buffoon and as an individual never to be welcomed into their ranks.[46]

Trump felt this rejection keenly. Gradually but steadily, he made his exclusion from elite Manhattan ranks a point of pride. He populated his corporation not with whiz kids from Ivy League universities but with scrappy Italian and Jewish ethnics, such as Matthew Calamari and Allan Weisselberg, hailing, like himself, from New York's outer boroughs.[47] Trump began to glory in his steak, fries, and ketchup consumption at dinner time—and the lunches from McDonald's that sustained him on many a day—and in his disdain for the fitness and dieting crazes that were increasingly gripping coastal elites. Trump was drawn instead to a radically different aesthetic, namely, the bombastic performance art dominating the World Wrestling Entertainment (WWE) empire assembled by Vince McMahon. Trump relished the crassness, excess, violence, and melodrama of professional wrestling. He sought to cultivate in himself the aggressive, even threatening, masculinity that the stars of this world embodied.[48]

WWE's following was huge. It had no use for the cosmopolitan, "effeminate" pretensions of coastal elites. Wrestling fans regarded the sport's stars as true men of the people, individuals who had been gifted with none of the benefits of America's elites: no high birth, no money, no access to centers of political power. Through the sheer force of their willpower (and steroid injections) and nothing else, idols of the wrestling world had fashioned themselves into rock-hard physical specimens. The seeds of America's greatness lay here, in a professional wrestler's unapologetic will to power. Wrestling audiences delighted in the determination of their heroes to impose their will on opponents and their willingness to use any means, fair and foul, to do so.

Trump's style of populist politics took shape in this aggressive world of staged male combat, a world always teetering—tantalizingly, in the view of many supporters—on the edge of violence. As multicultural America became obsessed with tracking micro-aggressions, those immersed in this parallel universe of professional wrestling delighted in the performance of extravagant macro-aggressions. Trump loved this world. His deep connection to this world, Michael Cohen observed, put him in close touch "with the tastes of baseball-cap wearing, pickup-driving men who otherwise would seem a million miles away from Trump's pampered and gilded gold existence."[49]

In each of Trump's three beliefs—that free trade and open borders were harming America, that America should privilege its people of European descent, and that America's true strength lay in its professional wrestling heartland far more than in the aspirations of America's coastal elites—we can see an incipient attack on America's neoliberal order. Trump's politics challenged neoliberalism's commitment to the free movement of goods and people across national boundaries, its celebration of the diversity of peoples, and its confidence in the wisdom of highly educated and highly cultured globalized elites. To neoliberalism, he increasingly counterposed an ethnonationalist populism that resonated with an aroused Tea Party base eager to refocus America's identity around whiteness, manufacturing, and a plebeian cultural style designed to offend the country's "social betters."

Those who caricatured and dismissed Trump and his politics were slow to grasp his strengths. He had a preternatural feel for how to seize the public's attention in the new media age.[50] He became a master of Twitter, trolling incessantly, understanding from the start that the point of this medium was not to promote truth or gravitas but to provoke and entertain. And the best entertainment, drawing on lessons from his experience with wrestling, was raw: calling Mexicans rapists, poking fun at reporters with physical disabilities, denouncing women correspondents who challenged him as bloody and menstruating hysterics, and stiffing his male competitors with the charge that their penises were small. As Trump's 2015–2016 campaign unfolded, he began rising in the polls, his cause helped by a large number of GOP presidential hopefuls—sixteen at the peak—who did not take him seriously and spent their time attacking each other, confident that the excitement surrounding Trump would soon dissipate of its own accord.

Trump's critics were especially slow to understand the power of the rallies that he began to hold in 2015 and 2016. Most began as tailgating events in parking lots adjacent to rally arenas, modeled on those that football fans had been staging prior to games for decades. Supporters assembled in these lots to share food and drink with each other and to show off their latest Trump paraphernalia—MAGA (Make America Great Again) hats, T-shirts, jerseys, banners, flags mounted on pickup trucks, and so on. All the while soundspeaker systems were blasting out rock and pop music, the content of these songs often utterly incongruous to the purpose of these political gatherings. The song "YMCA," an anthem sung by a gay 1970s disco group known as the Village People, was a favorite at Trump rallies, both outside and inside arenas. The atmosphere at these pre-rally gatherings was invariably upbeat and festive.

Gradually, the crowd moved inside—or at least those in its ranks lucky enough to have secured tickets—to listen to a series of warm-up speakers. Excitement began to build as the moment of Trump's entrance neared. Trump's actual appearance was closely modeled on WWE theatrics: the long buildup, the slow procession down the runway that carried Trump from the wings of the arena to the speaking platform, the blaring of rock music, the feet of fans stomping, their hands clapping, their voices yelling, the champ basking in rapturous applause.

Trump's speeches were always a potpourri of ideas, charges, and attacks. To critics, Trump appeared disorganized, meandering, and often verging on incoherence. But this critique misses the "call and response" character of his oratorical technique. Some of his boasts and tangents fell flat. But others hit home. And when one drew an excited response, Trump doubled down: He would embellish a story, deepen his mockery of an opponent whom he was attacking, frame his intentions and ambitions ever more extravagantly (and belligerently). If he hit on a clever slogan—"Drain the Swamp!"—or devised a devilishly nasty nickname for an adversary—"Crooked Hillary!"—he would repeat it again and again. He would involve the crowd in his performance, encouraging its members to turn clever responses—"Build That Wall" or "Lock Her Up!"—into galvanizing refrains. Trump knew how to excite a crowd. He was brilliantly improvisational. Part of the fun of being in Trump's audience was never knowing what he might say. One could reasonably hope he would utter something completely unexpected, outrageous, or inappropriate. Breaks with decorous, rule-abiding behavior were particularly welcome at his rallies, as they had long been at WWE matches. Trump delighted in playing the "heel," wrestling parlance for the bad guy.

Trump lived for the waves of adulation that washed over him at these rallies. He enjoyed building rapport with the crowd. Maureen Dowd caught this side of Trump in a *New York Times* column she wrote in March 2016, a moment in which his popularity among the GOP rank and file was soaring. "After watching Hillary Clinton, for whom campaigning is a nuisance, and Barack Obama, who disdains politics, it's fun to see someone having fun. Like Bill Clinton, Trump talks and talks to crowds. They feed his narcissism, and in turn, he creates an intimacy even in an arena that leaves both sides awash in pleasure."[51] Everything about these rallies mocked the suave, decorous, and cosmopolitan character of Obama and his chosen successor Hillary Clinton.

The ethos of Trump rallies also took aim at the other moral imperative that had been central to the neoliberal order, and especially to its Republican supporters: the injunction to transform Americans into sturdy, self-reliant, and disciplined selves able to handle the rigors of free market life. Equally important from the perspective of this moral stance had been the injunction to develop strong families and to inculcate moral virtue in the young. Families that adhered to this moral code—so aggressively trumpeted by the likes of Charles Murray, George Gilder, and many other leading neoliberal intellectuals— would then produce citizens with proper integrity and probity. Well-functioning family units would learn to live within their means (and insist that governments do the same) and prepare their members for the rigors of fully engaged free market life.

Trump regarded this GOP moralizing as both boring and out of touch with the real world. Like the audiences who watched WWE, he was more interested in thrills and power than in integrity and discipline. Imposing one's will on one's opponent was more important (and fun) than following the rules.[52] He had little interest in the GOP version of neoliberalism that called for balanced budgets, low debt, cutbacks in entitlements, and a shrinkage in the government payroll. He shared the Koch brothers' antipathy toward government authorities seeking to meddle in rich people's finances and to extract more taxes from private fortunes. For that reason, he supported deregulation. But he never thought that free markets were virtuous institutions capable of instilling ethical behavior in those who participated in commercial exchange. In his eyes, markets were built for manipulation, contracts were made to be broken.

Leading Republicans had seriously underestimated the appeal of Trump's populism, his ethnonationalism, and his amoral "will to power" code. As he began to emerge as the leading vote-getter in the primaries, one Republican luminary after another fell in behind him. Each wagered that he or she would be able to tame Trump before the New York tycoon upended the neoliberal order. In the past, most political insurgents in America had been domesticated in this way. But with Trump, the past proved an unreliable guide to the future. Trump had fired the imaginations of working-class and middle-class whites throughout America. Millions of them who felt left behind, many with education that did not extend beyond high school and whose jobs were particularly vulnerable to globalization, would turn out to vote for Trump in numbers not seen in decades, and perhaps in generations. Trump had unleashed a phenomenal wrecking force on American politics, on the Republican Party, and on the neoliberal order.

Occupy Wall Street

The thunder on the ethnonationalist right was increasingly accompanied by eruptions on the multiracial left. The Santelli-like figure who triggered this uprising was a Canadian of Estonian origins, Kalle Lasn, who for more than two decades had been publishing an anti-capitalist magazine, *Adbusters*, from his base outside Vancouver. Appearing bimonthly, *Adbusters* depicted a world driven to collapse by insatiable consumer appetites generated by the imperatives of capitalist accumulation. The crash of 2008–2009 lent new urgency to the magazine's determination to arouse resistance. In June 2011, Lasn began exchanging thoughts with his chief *Adbusters* collaborator, Micah White of Berkeley, California, about what form this rebellion might take. Almost as a lark, the two of them decided that the best road forward was to occupy Wall Street. On June 9, 2011, Lasn registered the *OccupyWallStreet.org* website.[53]

There was as yet no actual political movement in New York—nor even a plan—to "take over" or even to take on Wall Street. This inconvenient circumstance does not seem to have given Lasn or White pause, nor did the two men seem worried that they lived thousands of miles away from Manhattan. Lasn chose his beloved mother's birthday, September 17, as the date on which to launch the occupation, perhaps as a way of infusing good cheer and good luck into his still fanciful endeavor. *Adbusters'* design team then came up with an arresting poster of a ballerina balancing herself delicately on a raging bull, the animal a reproduction of the massive sculpture sitting outside the entrance to the New York Stock Exchange. The words of the poster were few but direct: "What is our one demand?" a banner across the top read. The answer, written in a banner across the bottom: "#Occupy Wall Street, September 17th. Bring Tent."[54] On July 13, *Adbusters* circulated this call to action to its 70,000 online subscribers. This was the tinder that set off the most important rebellion against concentrated wealth and power in America in seventy years.

Lasn was right to suspect that the time was ripe. Millions of vaporized jobs had yet to re-materialize; wages were stagnant. Many young people, their career aspirations on hold, had fallen into the ranks of the precariat, working only intermittently and for insufficient pay. More and more of them had turned to political organizing, mobilizing to fight municipal budget cuts, to purge excessive money from politics, to relieve millions of young people from the crushing burden of student debt, and to seek ways to reimpose regulation on financial markets. Organizers from among the militants in their ranks met in New York in August to design an action and devise a slogan by which they would be known. "We are the 99 percent" was the phrase they embraced. In making this declaration, they were announcing their readiness to take their stand against the wealthy 1 percent. The widening economic inequality of American life, the architects of this slogan charged, had reached grotesque proportions. It had to be stopped, and then reversed.[55]

Many rallying to the "99 percent" slogan were new to politics. However, their ranks were leavened by anarchists and other veterans of the protests against the WTO that had flared briefly but fiercely in the 1990s. One of the latter was David Graeber, a University of Chicago–trained anthropologist and anarchist thinker then teaching at Goldsmiths, part of the University of London. Graeber had written sweepingly about how debt across the ages had been a key instrument used by elites to ensnare ordinary people in poverty and dependency.

He wanted all debt forgiven immediately, the surest way, he argued, to free people from oppression and bring the world's powerful financial institutions to heel. His book *Debt: The First 5,000 Years*, published in 2011, became a bible of the Occupy movement.[56] He was the closest Occupy came to having an acknowledged leader.

As late as the morning of September 17, the forces that had mobilized to "occupy Wall Street" had (rather incredibly) not yet chosen the site on which they intended to take their stand. But by midday, they were gravitating toward Zuccotti Park, a small public square a few blocks away from Wall Street in one direction and from the site where the World Trade Center towers had once stood in the other. Zuccotti Park had not been cordoned off, the police having deemed it too inconsequential a space to defend. A thousand protesters had gathered there by afternoon, holding the first of many "General Assemblies" to determine how the participants would govern themselves over the coming days and weeks. Three hundred of the protesters had come prepared to spend the night. The occupation was on.

It would last for two months, until the New York City police, under orders from Mayor Michael Bloomberg, evicted the last occupiers on November 15. In the days after September 17, Occupy Wall Street quickly grew into an elaborate encampment of tents and walkways, with a kitchen, wireless, and a library stocked with classic left-wing treatises. The participants were overwhelmingly young—braving the onset of autumn nights in New York City was not advisable for the old—and largely white and middle class, but with a significant nonwhite contingent. Though not formally subscribing to nonviolent principles in the manner of the civil rights movement fifty years before, Occupy had a peaceful, even welcoming, mien. It attracted hundreds and then thousands of spectators, many of them New Yorkers on the way to and from work. Others were out-of-town visitors, keen to gawk at what seemed like the latest of the city's exotic tourist attractions. Onlookers and activists were often seen chatting with each other. Frequently members of the small police detail dispatched to the scene joined in. Impromptu musical jamming and drum sessions were common. The mood was both serious and festive.[57]

In a nation that, during its neoliberal heyday, had decried "class warfare"—pitting one class against another—the slogan "We are the

99 percent" proved surprisingly appealing. Some of that appeal had to do with the slogan's anodyne nature: Virtually every American could claim membership in the 99 percent and thus escape the censure of being part of the despised 1 percent. But part of the slogan's appeal worked in just the opposite way. Finally, a group had dared to say what many had been thinking but had feared to utter: namely, that the magnitude of economic inequality and the resulting gap between the life chances of rich and poor had seriously disfigured American life.[58]

The Zuccotti Park protests drew media attention. Imitation Occupy-style protests and encampments sprang up in innumerable cities across the country. Supporters in foreign cities, including London, Madrid, Tokyo, Sydney, and Buenos Aires, rallied to the cause. Some observers began to wonder whether a global uprising on the scale of 1848, 1917, or 1968 was under way. Occupy Wall Street never achieved that stature. In the short term, organizational chaos and indecision resulted from the movement's anarchist-inflected resistance to having formal leaders. Occupy never issued an effective manifesto (along the lines of the New Left's *Port Huron Statement*), or disseminated an agreed-upon list of concrete demands, or formulated a strategy for achieving them. Nevertheless, this protest, in the longer term, did mark a turning point in American politics and intellectual life. Specifically, it enlarged dramatically the political space for thinking about economic inequality and for challenging the virtues of free market capitalism and other neoliberal beliefs. Across the next five years, left-leaning intellectuals and politicians acquired an influence on American politics that they had not enjoyed since the heyday of the New Deal order in the 1930s and 1940s.[59]

The leftist moment that Occupy inaugurated was marked by the flourishing of the so-called little magazines of the left, old (*Dissent*) and new (*n + 1* and *Jacobin*), full of ideas about how to build radically different futures; by dramatic growth in the membership of the Democratic Socialists of America; by the popularity of books like *Capital in the Twenty-First Century*, an 800-page tome on inequality published by French economist Thomas Piketty in 2013 that sold approximately 3 million hardcover copies in the United States and beyond; by the soaring reputations of left-leaning writer-activists (and anti-neoliberal crusaders) Naomi Klein, Noam Chomsky, and

David Graeber; and by the sudden appearance in electoral politics of individuals who made a critique of free market capitalism—and the concentration of wealth and power that went with it—their signature message. Elizabeth Warren won election as a US senator from Massachusetts in 2012 by making attacks on the dominance and irresponsibility of America's mega-banks the centerpiece of her campaign. Leftist Bill de Blasio had worked with the Sandinistas in Nicaragua in 1990 and honeymooned in Castro's Cuba in 1991. In 2014, he won election as New York mayor, replacing the man, Michael Bloomberg, who had ordered the New York City police to evict the occupiers from Zuccotti Park. And then Bernie Sanders, the US Senate's lone but proud socialist, mounted a surprisingly successful challenge to Hillary Clinton, Obama's heir apparent and neoliberal standard-bearer, in the 2016 Democratic primaries.[60] Sanders's rise on the left, making himself the second most important socialist in American history (after Eugene Victor Debs), was as stunning as Trump's rise on the right. The size and success of Sanders's and Trump's insurgencies signified how much the neoliberal order was unraveling.

"Feeling the Bern"

Sanders, like Trump, had grown up in New York City's outer boroughs—in his case Brooklyn. Like Trump, Sanders would not have stood a chance in national politics in the heyday of the neoliberal order. Neither man possessed Obama's elegance or swag. Neither ever managed to free his speech patterns and accents from their entanglement with New York City twang. Each had a rugged charisma born of the sharp-elbowed life they had experienced growing up in the nation's premier but rough-edged metropolis. Both Sanders and Trump were street scrappers, determined to say what needed to be said rather than what polite company wanted to hear.

In class and ethnic terms, however, Sanders grew up in circumstances a world apart from Trump. He was born in 1941 to a lower-middle-class Jewish family. His mother, always worried that the family would not have enough to make ends meet, died young. Sanders attended James Madison High School in Brooklyn, now justly famous for having produced five Nobel Prize winners (including neoliberal economist

Gary Becker), one Supreme Court justice (Ruth Bader Ginsberg), and three US senators (Sanders, Chuck Schumer, and Norman Coleman). He then went to the University of Chicago, where he did poorly in his formal studies but gained an education in leftist political thought by roaming the stacks in university libraries. Sanders was already engaging with socialists, trade unionists, and civil rights activists in the Chicago area. After graduation, he spent time in Israel, a sojourn that included a significant stint on a kibbutz, Sha'ar HaAmakim, where experiments in actual socialist living were under way. Sanders believed that kibbutzim across Israel had made major strides in collectivizing labor, parenting, and other aspects of life, and in democratizing decision-making. His kibbutz experience deepened Sanders's conviction that socialism offered a superior and humane way of living. Sanders resided in New York only briefly on his return to the United States, decamping for Vermont in 1968, perhaps hoping to re-create in that rural state forms of collectivist and democratic living that he had experienced in Israel. Burlington, Vermont's largest city, was already becoming an outpost of the countercultural and commune-oriented segment of the New Left.[61]

Sanders, however, was not well suited for a career as a hippie or for isolated life on a commune. Politics was his true vocation. He liked argument, electoral contests, and speaking truth to power. He was frank and fearless in promoting his leftist political principles in the several Vermont electoral contests for senator and governor that he entered in the 1970s on a third-party ticket. His views brought him few votes; by the mid-1970s, he was looking for a new career. His passionate supporters asked him not to give up, and several influential backers persuaded him to run as an independent for mayor of Burlington in 1980. He did, winning by the slimmest of margins (twelve votes). His tenure proved popular, as he combined radical political principles with efficient administration and concrete programs to improve daily life for his constituents. Sanders was also surprisingly effective in working with Burlington's business community. He won re-election to the mayoralty three times, and then won election to the House of Representatives in 1990, a post he held until he won election to the US Senate in 2006.[62]

Burlington's concentration of progressive-minded and granola-crunching denizens formed the core of Sanders's base. But he also ran well among Vermont's poor, rural, and Republican-leaning voters. These Vermonters were known for their fierce independence and libertarianism. They were suspicious of all large institutions—private and public—that sought to control their lives. They responded positively to Sanders's argument that the swamping of elections with private corporate money had corrupted America's democratic process, and to his claims that the neoliberal regime of global free trade was the work of a government-corporate elite that was leaving too many ordinary Americans behind. Sanders made concessions to these rural voters, especially apparent in his willingness to respect their right to bear arms. These concessions made it possible for him to make these voters a stable part of his winning Vermont coalition.

Sanders mattered little in national politics across his first thirty years of public service. Vermont was a tiny and sparsely populated state. With the exception of Ben and Jerry's ice cream, trends developing there carried little influence in the nation as a whole. In Congress, Sanders was an independent who called himself a socialist and who usually voted with the Democrats. He had no natural allies and virtually no influence on policy, especially during the years when the neoliberal order was riding high. To Bill Clinton and George W. Bush he was simply a pest, one that could easily be swatted away when he buzzed too close to their ears.

Everything changed, however, after Occupy Wall Street in 2011. As millions suddenly engaged with the issue of economic inequality and what to do about it, they began turning to the man who had been speaking about it directly and passionately for decades. Sanders did not have to change his tune or his stump speech. Rather, the fracture of the neoliberal order had opened up a space in which his words resonated in ways they never had before. Suddenly, in an era when many politicians proved themselves to be fickle, superficial, and easily bought off, the consistency of his politics over the decades came to be seen not as eccentricity but as a mark of integrity and authenticity.

Especially among the young, Sanders acquired the stature of an Old Testament prophet, sent by God from a long exile in the Vermont wilderness to speak the truth and afflict the powerful. With a mop of white hair that was perpetually unkempt, with shambolic dress that was not much of an improvement over a sackcloth, and with an unsmiling and unsparing mien, Sanders looked the part. At his campaign rallies in 2015 and 2016, Sanders thundered on, as one imagines the prophets Isaiah and Jeremiah once did, refusing to soften descriptions of society's evils and the radical work required for redemption. Sanders's supporters could not get enough of him. In 2016, his campaign rallies were the only ones that matched Trump's in terms of size, intensity, and engagement.

When Sanders traveled to New York in January 2016 to confront Wall Street bankers, he was unrelenting in his condemnation of their practices. The "greed, recklessness and illegal behavior on Wall Street," Sanders charged, had "nearly destroyed the U.S. and global economy" in 2008 and 2009. In the eight years since, America's once vaunted middle class had crumbled, its members given little compensation for lost jobs, lost homes, and lost savings. Wall Street, meanwhile, "received the largest taxpayer bailout in the history of the world." Wall Street and corporate America, he declared, were "destroying the fabric of our nation."[63]

To the Wall Streeters listening to his speech, Sanders issued this warning: "If you do not end your greed, we will end it for you."[64] A month later, after emerging victorious in the Iowa caucuses that launched the 2016 presidential contest, Sanders declared that a "political revolution was coming."[65] Were he to win the nomination and then the presidency, he made clear, there would be no more bank bailouts, no more privileges given to finance, no more toleration of a shadow finance sector allowed to operate free of regulation, no more tolerating the existence of banks claiming they had to be bailed out because they were "too big to fail."

Wall Street, of course, was integral to the winning Democratic Party coalition that Bill Clinton assembled in the 1990s. At the time, Robert Rubin from Goldman Sachs was often seen as the most powerful and wisest member of Clinton's cabinet. Obama, meanwhile, had turned over responsibility for handling the 2009 economic recovery to Rubin's Wall Street disciples, including Lawrence Summers, Timothy Geithner, and Peter Orszag. Given this history, the political path advocated by Sanders—effectively calling on the Democrats to break from Wall Street—entailed a radical departure from prevailing Democratic Party politics.

Sanders's attacks in the 2016 campaign on free trade were equally shocking to party leadership. Sanders had opposed NAFTA since its inception. He cast himself against free trade with China as well, believing it was doing more to harm America's working class than to help it. The notion that removing all barriers to trade in the world would lift all boats and spread affluence everywhere was, from Sanders's perspective, nothing more than a neoliberal mirage. Globalization had yielded winners and losers in every country. The winners in America, in Sanders's eyes, were the corporations, the banks, and those deeply invested in the stock market. The losers were America's industrial workers, whose ranks had already been decimated by the flight of jobs to Mexico and China. Those fortunate enough to retain their jobs faced constant pressure from employers to live with reduced wages and benefits. In a debate with Hillary Clinton in early March 2016, Sanders charged that she had undermined the livelihoods of good Americans by "supporting virtually every one of the disastrous trade agreements written by corporate America."[66]

Major differences separated Sanders from Trump. Sanders engaged in none of the slander, personal attacks, and veiled incitement to violence that were part of Trump's campaign arsenal. While Sanders long had harbored qualms about open borders, fearing that the arrival of too many low-skilled migrants would harm the working conditions and wages of America's existing workers, he rejected Trump's ethnonationalism. He had no desire to privilege Americans of European descent over those whose roots lay in Latin America, East and South Asia, and Africa. He engaged in none of the scapegoating of racial minorities and the celebrating of America's "superior" Europeans that Trump was making central to his appeal.

But on questions of free trade and globalization, Sanders's and Trump's positions were virtually indistinguishable. "The legacy of Pennsylvania steelworkers lives in the bridges, railways and skyscrapers that make up our great American landscape," Trump declared to a group of workers near Pittsburgh in 2016. America repaid their loyalty, Trump alleged, "with total betrayal. Our politicians have aggressively pursued a policy of globalization, moving our jobs, our wealth and our factories to Mexico and overseas. Globalization has made the financial elite, who donate to politicians, very, very wealthy." The effects on American workers, meanwhile, had been disastrous. "Many Pennsylvania towns, once thriving and humming"—Trump could have been speaking here of Fishtown—"are now in a state of total disrepair. This wave of globalization has wiped out totally, totally, our middle class. It does not have to be this way. We can turn it around fast."[67]

Many of the words from Trump's Pittsburgh speech could have been lifted directly from a Sanders speech. Neither man was a word-smith. Reading their speeches—as opposed to listening to them—does not inspire. Both men shone in oral argument, however. Both spoke with power and physicality; both liked to issue strongly worded and blunt declarations, sometimes stabbing the air with a pointed finger for emphasis. And the blistering nature of their attacks on free trade and globalization—and on the injury these policies had allegedly done to ordinary working-class Americans while bringing untold riches to America's economic and political elites—hit home.

That these arguments were resonating revealed the extent to which the neoliberal order was fissuring. When neoliberalism was hegemonic, the virtues of free trade and globalization were unassailable. To attack these policies during the neoliberal heyday was to mark oneself as mar-ginal and irrelevant at best and as dangerously delusional at worst. That the two most dynamic contestants for president in 2016, one on the left and the other on the right, were both mounting direct challenges to neoliberal orthodoxies reveals the degree to which the neoliberal order itself was coming under challenge and, perhaps, would soon be knocked from its perch.

Clintonism and Obamaism Lose Their Grip

Caught in the middle of the left-right assault on neoliberalism was Hillary Clinton, the presumptive Democratic Party nominee and the person expected to succeed Obama in the Oval Office. On paper, she was supremely well qualified. She had been a senator from New York and, as secretary of state, a senior and influential figure in the Obama administration. She was brainy, competent, reliable, and experienced. Clinton also had liabilities. She had not done well in her one national election, her fight against Obama to win the 2008 Democratic nomi-nation for president. She did not possess her husband's political skills and suffered additionally for being a woman, and thus thought to be, in some male circles prone to misogyny, a poor fit for the presidency. The resurgent left of the Democratic Party regarded her as a pillar of neoliberal orthodoxy and thus as an obstacle to the political turn they were trying to effect. And the incessant GOP attacks on Hillary and husband, Bill, as corrupt began to diminish support for her across the more conservative sectors of the Democratic Party. It did not help that Hillary's political operation, though well-funded and stuffed with talent, was top heavy and prone to indecision and internal sniping.

Clinton was also out of step with the time. A full participant in her husband's acquiescence to the neoliberal order in the 1990s, she still viewed that political moment as a triumphant one for the Democratic Party. She was thus surprised by the ferocity of Sanders's attack on her for subscribing to free trade and other neoliberal principles. She did not understand why the internationalist credentials she had acquired as a hard-working and world-traveling secretary of state were now seen by many as a liability. She did not seem to comprehend the conflict between the close relations she had developed with world leaders, on the one hand, and the donations these leaders were making to her family's Clinton Foundation, on the other.[68] And why all the fuss about accepting $300,000 fees for giving speeches to Goldman Sachs? Courting Wall Street—and being handsomely compensated for it—had been a staple of Democratic Party politics for more than twenty years. The Democratic Party–Wall Street alliance was necessary, Clinton believed, to raise sufficient funds to win elections. She did not see it detracting from the good work she planned to do for the poor and those suffering from various forms of racial and sex discrimination. The radical and insurgent spirit that had guided so much of Clinton's younger life—and that, she believed, still burned brightly in her convictions—made it hard for her to understand how thoroughly she had come to be seen as encased in the world of a privileged and globe-trotting elite.[69]

Seeking to defuse the Sanders challenge, Clinton moved somewhat left during the 2016 primary season. Still, she was not prepared to rethink the basic principles of her politics. By June 2016 she had assembled sufficient delegates in primary contests to force Sanders from the race and to position her to win the Democratic Party nomination in July. The polls, moreover, were consistently showing Clinton with a commanding lead over Trump. Clinton expected to win the presidency in November by putting together a coalition grounded in the new America, much as Obama had done. Feminists of her generation would stand by her to the last woman. Suburban Republican women, fed up with Trump's misogyny, seemed prepared to defect from the GOP to vote for her. Clinton championed the cause of gay rights far more than either Sanders or Trump. She stood up proudly and forcefully for immigrant rights. And she was sure that she would receive strong support from black voters, who had been loyal to her husband during the eight years of his presidency and to the African American president she had so diligently served for another eight.[70]

Yet, there were danger signals. Support within the black community for Clinton, for example, turned out to be softer than expected. Younger blacks had begun mobilizing against Clinton—and against Obama as well—for being too slow to acknowledge the full scope of black suffering in the aftermath of the Great Recession. As opportunities in America's legal economy shrank, more and more African Americans had turned to the illegal drug economy. This turn brought them into increasing conflict with police forces, whose officers had been given broad discretion and leeway to use force against those deemed to be a threat to public order.[71] The years from 2012 to 2014 saw a sharp rise in incidents of police (and private vigilantes) assaulting young black men. These incidents infuriated African Americans, sparking new forms of protest in their ranks.

Black fury had begun to coalesce in reaction to the February 2012 murder of a black teenager, Trayvon Martin, as he was returning to the Florida home of his father's fiancée after a trip to a convenience store. A white vigilante, George Zimmerman, assaulted and killed him, on the grounds that he (Zimmerman) suspected that Martin was up to no good. An all-white jury in Florida acquitted Zimmerman of wrongdoing in July 2013. A year later, police in Staten Island, New York, had put a small-time street peddler named Eric Garner into a chokehold, forcing him to the ground, cutting off his air supply, thereby killing him. Two weeks later, Michael Brown, an eighteen-year-old in Ferguson, Missouri, got into an altercation with a police officer, Darren Wilson, that resulted in Brown being shot six times. In October 2014, a Chicago police officer emptied round after round into another teen-ager, Laquan MacDonald, after he was down and already dead. In April 2015, Walter Scott of Charleston was chased down on foot by a police officer for a minor motor vehicle infraction (a nonfunctioning brake light) and shot dead. Less than a week later, an injured and tied-up Freddie Gray of Baltimore died after being thrown repeatedly against the hard metal surfaces and edges of a police van in which he had been locked up as officers were transporting him to jail.[72]

These killings led to the eruption of a new protest movement, "Black Lives Matter." Ferguson, Missouri, the site of Michael Brown's death, became ground zero for this movement. The heated protests, confrontations with police, and sit-ins modeled on Occupy Wall Street attracted activists from all over the country and gained national and international attention.

BLM protesters were young, militant, and uncompromising. Across the first half of 2016, black millennials (aged 20 to 35) had shocked Democratic Party pollsters by revealing that they favored Sanders over Clinton by a hefty 44 to 32 percent margin.[73] They supported Sanders's denunciations of the concentration of wealth in the hands of economic elites and endorsed his calls for redistributive justice. They were drawn to his anti-capitalism; many in BLM ranks considered themselves socialists.

BLM activists were also harshly critical of the older generation of black leaders. The latter, BLM alleged, had accommodated themselves to the white power structure that had countenanced the assault on black lives and that had generated so such misery in black communities. BLM targeted their own elders as well for indulging male privilege and het-erosexism. Activists booed the Reverend Jesse Jackson, one-time hero of the civil rights movement, when he addressed them in Ferguson in summer 2014. "The model of the black preacher leading people to the promised land isn't working right now," Alicia Garza, a BLM founder, acidly observed to *New Yorker* writer Jelani Cobb in 2016. Queer and married to a trans male, Garza was particularly critical of the "hyper-bolic masculinity" that had been so intrinsic to, and distorting of, past black freedom struggles. Obama escaped the BLM critique of male privilege, but he still drew fire for being part of a Washington power structure that had done little to improve the lives of the black poor.

Aislinn Pulley, a Chicago community organizer and BLM member, pointedly refused Obama's February 2016 invitation to join a White House discussion about the future of civil rights. Pulley wrote to her followers online that she "could not serve to legitimize the false narrative that the government is working to end police brutality and the institutional racism that fuels it."[74]

Criticism of Obama intensified in BLM ranks across 2016. In a high-profile piece published in the US edition of *The Guardian*, political commentator Keeanga-Yamahtta Taylor charged Obama with abandoning the promises he had made during his two runs for the presidency. "The rise of Black Lives Matter," she wrote, "is, in no small part, a product of his inability or unwillingness to directly and forthrightly address the persistence of racial inequality." Coming to terms with Obama's "paralysis . . . in the face of racism and injustice," Taylor admitted, had been hard. She and many other young blacks had invested much hope in Obama's campaign for the presidency. But Obama, she now bitterly concluded, had done far too little to address the root causes of black suffering and persecution.[75]

If Obama had not done enough, what about his heir apparent, Hillary Clinton? That is precisely the question that two BLM activists put to Clinton at a private fundraiser in South Carolina three days before that state's Democratic primary in February 2016. One of the protesters, Ashley Williams, asked Clinton to apologize for supporting her husband's policy of mass incarceration in the 1990s and for stigmatizing young black men as "super-predators."[76] Williams was booed by the donors who had paid thousands of dollars to hear Clinton speak. A Secret Service detail quickly chased Williams and a protest partner from the meeting. But the BLM disruption of the Clinton fundraiser made national news and inspired others to begin asking Clinton the uncomfortable questions that Williams had put to her. As Taylor would later reflect, "It was an educational moment for a new generation of [black] voters who may have been unaware of the Clintons' complicated history with African Americans."[77]

This "complicated history" continued to trail Hillary through the primaries and then across the general election season. A massive defection by black voters to Trump was never a possibility. The question rather was whether reservations about Clinton and the now fraying

political order that her husband and Obama had done so much to promote might depress black turnout for the 2016 election and thus diminish her chances for beating Donald Trump.

Trump's Triumph

The triumph of Trump on November 8, 2016, was a stunning moment
in the history of American politics. One had to reach all the way back
to Andrew Jackson's victory in 1828 to find a precedent for a candidate
so far removed from the country's reigning political elite winning the
presidency. Even this comparison was a strained one, as Trump was an
outsider to the world of American government and republican inheritance in ways that Jackson never had been.[78]

Trump's margin of victory was slim. A total of 130 million votes had
been cast nationwide. A mere 70,000 votes in the three midwestern
battleground states of Pennsylvania, Michigan, and Wisconsin had decided the victory. Any number of factors could have turned the election in Clinton's direction. Had Clinton been less confident of victory
in these midwestern battleground states, she would have spent more
time (and assembled more votes) in them during the last weeks of
the campaign. A big turnout of blacks in Philadelphia, Detroit, and
Milwaukee on the order of what Obama had mobilized in 2008 and
2012 might also have been sufficient to swing Pennsylvania, Michigan,
and Wisconsin Clinton's way. The airing in early October 2016 of an
Access Hollywood audio tape in which Trump could be heard bragging
in the crudest possible terms about his abusive attitudes toward women
looked for a time as though it might cost him the election, especially as
suburban GOP female voters now seemed poised to cast their ballots
for Clinton in large numbers. But then FBI director James Comey
allowed the electorate to forget about Trump's sexual predations by
announcing, twelve days before the election, that he was reopening an
old investigation into Clinton's use of a private email server for official
business during her tenure as secretary of state. The use of such a private server was technically illegal (even as it was a practice in which
countless public officials, Democrat and Republican, had indulged).
Trump immediately used Comey's announcement as "corroboration"
of all the charges he had been making for months about "Crooked

Hillary." Comey's action had inflicted on Clinton serious reputational damage by the time he announced, only two days before the election, that he was ending his investigation because he had found nothing untoward in Clinton's private emails.[79]

What if Comey had refrained from reopening the email investigation so close to the election? What if Clinton had grasped her peril in the three midwestern battleground states and saturated them with her presence throughout the critical month of October? What if African Americans had turned out for Clinton in Obama-like numbers on election day? Had any of these scenarios unfolded, Clinton might well have won the presidency.

Still, acknowledging the possibility of a Clinton victory should not detract from the magnitude of Trump's achievement. A political novice and iconoclast won far more votes than anyone expected he would. He had bent the Republican Party to his will. The turnout he generated in the bypassed districts of American life far exceeded what virtually every pollster and pundit thought possible. The excitement and energy that Trump unleashed among his supporters far surpassed what Clinton generated among hers. Many who supported Hillary, and even many who worked for her, going door to door to get out the vote, were doing so more to stop Trump than to put another Clinton in the White House.[80]

The enthusiastic support for Trump and the reluctant support for Clinton reveals the deep dissatisfaction with the status quo across broad sectors of the American electorate. Trump supporters understood him to be something of a mad bull. He had hidden nothing from them across the long months of his campaign: not his narcissism, nor his contempt for his opponents, nor his indifference to the conventions of American politics, nor his abusive attitudes toward women and minorities, nor his fascination with violence. Trump supporters understood that they were voting for someone who intended to shake up Washington and break its rules. He was the wrestling "heel" eager to unleash mayhem, and they loved him for it. Only a man of such strength, willfulness, and nastiness, they believed, would be able to drain the Potomac swamp and thereby render the nation's capital uninhabitable to all the vile creatures who allegedly resided within.

The ugly grievance and nihilism of the Trump movement should not distract us from probing the deep and long-brewing frustrations on which they rested. These were frustrations with a political order—and a political elite—thought to have been responsible for too much hardship in America and too few rewards. This elite, and the order it directed, was rooted in both the Republican and Democratic parties. Across the previous thirty years, this elite had supported too many policies now regarded as seriously mistaken: embracing free trade and globalization, deregulating Wall Street, tolerating high—and expanding—levels of economic inequality, locking up a greater percentage of the nation's population than any other country on the planet, and committing the country both to ill-advised wars and to ill-conceived attempts at reconstructing the nations that those wars had destroyed. Clinton was associated with each of these policies, either through her own actions (as senator, she had voted for the war in Iraq in 2003; as secretary of state, she had promoted free trade and globalization) or through those that her husband had put in place during his presidency: deregulating Wall Street, expanding the carceral state, intensifying economic inequality. Seen from this perspective, antipathy to Clinton was rooted not just in personality and misogyny but in anger at a political order—and a political elite perceived to control it—that had failed so manifestly to maintain America's greatness.

The anger and frustration bubbling up not just on the right but on the left, manifest in Sanders's impressive run for the presidency and in BLM's refusal to go along with Obama's preference for soft-pedaling black grievance, provide further evidence that the tectonic plates of American politics were shifting. A new politics was emerging; perhaps a new political order was being born.

A reigning political order does not release its grip easily, however; its decline is marked by contradiction, contestation, and even chaos. And in its chaos, the Trump presidency would have few rivals.

8

The End

FEW WERE AS surprised by the outcome of the 2016 election as Donald Trump himself. He did not really expect to win. He had little familiarity with governance, either in the public or private sector. The Trump Organization, a closely held corporation run by relatively few people, did not prepare him well for leading a sprawling and complex federal state. Moreover, Trump had done little planning for his administration, a critical step for a president-elect with many government appointments to make and numerous policy matters to master. Just three days after the election, Trump fired Chris Christie, former governor of New Jersey turned Trump loyalist, who had been heading up the transition team. Christie's sacking was a sign of things to come.

Trump was impulsive and impatient. His attention span was short. He was suspicious of Washington, DC—not just of the Democratic Party and Obama officeholders, but of the Republican establishment as well. He knew little about the US Constitution and its doctrines: separation of powers, rule of law, independence of the courts. He was annoyed by rules he had to follow, especially when they limited his power. He did not understand how to work with Congress, which explains in part why America's national legislature accomplished so little during his presidency, even during the two-year period (2017–2019) when the GOP controlled both houses.

Indifferent to governing, Trump remained a master at commanding the political stage and thus the attention of the nation. He tweeted constantly to a following larger than 80 million, boasting about his greatness and his accomplishments, on the one hand, and provoking and denouncing his enemies, on the other. A majority of Americans had voted against Trump in 2016; many of them never stopped loathing him. Criticism of him was fierce both inside and outside government. Hopes abounded across the first three years of his presidency that somehow he would be forced to resign or, failing that, be impeached and then removed from office.[1]

Trump had to defend himself multiple times against serious accusations that he had violated election laws. One instance pertained to the 2016 presidential campaign, when he was suspected of conspiring with a foreign government—Russia—to turn voters away from Hillary Clinton and toward him.[2] Another instance occurred in 2019, when he attempted to enlist another foreign government, in this case that of Ukraine, in a scheme to damage the reputation of Joe Biden, the man Trump expected to oppose him in the 2020 presidential race.[3] Trump's alleged conspiracy with Russia triggered a two-year-long investigation by an independent prosecutor, Robert Mueller, that sent several close Trump associates to jail but, in the end, spared Trump himself. Trump's attempt to strong-arm the president of Ukraine sparked another investigation, this time conducted by the Judiciary Committee of the House of Representatives. It resulted in Trump's impeachment by the House for "high crimes and misdemeanors." But Trump survived this ordeal, too, as the Senate, authorized by the Constitution to act as judge and jury in impeachment cases, declined to convict him and remove him from office. Trump declared himself vindicated by the failure of these two investigations to pin him to the mat. His defiant demeanor once again infuriated his critics and thrilled his supporters.[4] His very public trials energized him for a run at a second term.

Among his core supporters, comprising about a third of the electorate, Trump could do no wrong. They hung on his words and took direction from his tweets. They celebrated his willingness to take on any institution or individual, no matter how respected or admired—the CIA, the FBI, federal judges, senators and congressmen, senior members of his own administration—and regardless of the consequences. In their eyes, a gatecrasher like Trump was just what a smug and out-of-touch Washington needed.

Meanwhile, virtually no Americans, irrespective of whether they supported or opposed Trump, could take their eyes off him, or rather off the screens serving up his latest provocations via their social media feeds. No previous president had managed to commandeer so many daily waking hours of so many Americans. Day after day Trump drew both the American media and the American public into his version of "the greatest show on earth"—an unending spectacle of enemies defenestrated, honor defended, accomplishments hailed, and supportive foreign leaders (preferably with an authoritarian bent) lauded. Week after week, and then year after year, Trump's antics gripped, divided, and then exhausted America.

It was often hard to discern a consistent political program amid the heat and smoke that the Trump firestorm generated. But there were, in fact, two such programs issuing from the Trump administration: One pointed in the direction of maintaining the neoliberal order, the other in the direction of dismantling it. The second was the more important of the two, and will likely have the more consequential long-term impact.

The Koch brothers, neoliberals to the core, had despised Trump during the GOP primaries. But Trump's selection of Mike Pence, governor of Indiana, as his running mate, opened up the possibility of a rapprochement between the two camps. The Kochs had been grooming Pence for a position of national leadership. He brought their deregulatory agenda to the White House, along with the hope that he would be able to launch a campaign to strip multiple federal agencies of oversight authority and thus to limit the federal government's ability to regulate the private economy.[5]

Trump had never really believed that markets were perfectible as instruments of exchange, but he signed on to the idea of weakening the federal government anyway. Such an evisceration, he imagined, might expose and then undercut the "deep state" allegedly nestled in the CIA, FBI, and other national security agencies and intent (he believed) on destroying his presidency.[6] Trump also worked closely with Senate majority leader Mitch McConnell to appoint hundreds of judges to the federal bench whom the Federalist Society had identified as reliably deregulatory on economic policy and patriarchal in their approach to family values.[7] Finally, Trump allowed Gary Cohn, whom he had appointed director of the National Economic Council, to proceed with a major revision of the tax code, one that sharply reduced corporate taxes and modestly reduced personal taxes for those in the highest brackets. This package, the principal legislative accomplishment of Trump's presidential tenure, kept neoliberal Republican politicians, including McConnell, in Trump's corner. Cohn was yet another emissary from the Goldman Sachs–Wall Street financial group that had done so much across the previous twenty years to construct and maintain the neoliberal order.

If deregulation, judicial appointments, and tax cuts pointed toward the maintenance of a neoliberal order, however, Trump's assault on free trade and immigration aimed at its destruction. In Trump's eyes, free trade among nations was harming America; so was the free movement of people across national borders. Trump wanted to build walls against both and to allow into America only those goods and individuals that it wanted, and under conditions of its choosing.

Trump seized every opportunity to remove America from the international position it had long held as the leader of a globalizing and free trade world. He criticized Europe both for taking advantage of the United States in trade and for being unwilling to pay a fair share of the costs of maintaining the North Atlantic Treaty Organization (NATO). He became the first president to publicly question the value of NATO, and the close relations between Europe and North America that this multinational defense organization was meant to sustain. He supported Brexit, less out of enthusiasm for a fully independent Britain than out of a desire to hurt the European Union, the sort of globalist and cosmopolitan federation that Trump despised. He mused to the media about withdrawing American troops from South Korea, the Middle East, and elsewhere.[8]

Closer to home, Trump threatened trade wars with Canada and Mexico in order to compel those two countries to renegotiate the North American Free Trade Agreement in ways that made it more favorable to US interests. He altered trade relations in Asia by reversing Obama's decision to have the United States participate in the Trans-Pacific Partnership (TPP), an association joining together twelve Pacific Rim countries in a free trade zone.

One purpose of TPP was to act as a counterweight to China in East Asia. Trump had no intention of going soft on China. To the contrary, he intended to ramp up pressure on the rival whom he regarded as America's principal adversary. But he would not allow American trade policy to be set by an organization in which the US was merely one voice among many. Each trade deal had to be a bilateral agreement with only two signatories. This is how Trump had always done business. The "art of the deal" had worked for him in the private sector and would, he believed, yield equally impressive results in the nation-to-nation negotiations that he intended to promote.

Tariffs were Trump's preferred tool for attacking China. Trump discovered that he could authorize tariffs unilaterally, without the co-operation of Congress, if he claimed that they enhanced national security.[9] Trump understood that imposing tariffs on billions of dollars of Chinese goods might risk retaliation and that such tit-for-tat could easily escalate into a full-scale trade war that might harm the interests of both nations. But Trump was willing to risk such a war, convinced that he would triumph.[10] In September 2019 he imposed $112 billion in taxes on Chinese imports, and threatened to follow that up with another half trillion dollars in tariffs.[11] In October 2019, Trump seemed to wring a concession from China in the form of an agreement on the first installment of a comprehensive trade deal. The two countries signed the agreement in January 2020, with Trump hailing it as a major victory for his administration and for the nation.

Across the first year of the agreement, however, multiple reports suggested that China was doing little to increase its American imports to stipulated goals. As was the case with so many Trump initiatives, there seemed to be little consistency or follow-through. And the outbreak of the Covid-19 pandemic at the very moment when the trade deal was signed upended global trade in ways wholly independent of US-China trade negotiations.[12]

Still, Trump's constant bluster about the evils of free trade, his repeated threats to impose tariffs, and his hostility to the many countries seen by his administration as having gained a trade advantage over the United States pushed a neoliberal world to reassess long-standing beliefs and strategies. Global corporations were finding it increasingly difficult to do long-range planning amid the uncertainties and volatility that Trump had injected into international trade. Their strategy of stretching supply chains around the world had been premised on the notion that goods could cross national boundaries easily and quickly. With this world possibly slipping away, the prudent strategy might now be to produce more goods closer to home either by increasing domestic manufacturing or by developing shorter supply chains with nearby countries with whom relations were secure. This kind of thinking had begun to influence the calculations of corporations even before Covid-19 struck. The arrival of the virus accelerated the turn toward production in one's own nation, in which conditions of manufacturing and transportation were imagined as more stable than in the international arena.[13]

Economists studying international trade were not surprised by these developments. Their data showed that total international merchandise trade—"the sum of exports and imports of commodities and manufactured goods"—had actually peaked in 2008, when it accounted for 51 percent of the world's output. It plummeted during the Great Recession of 2008–2009, then began to recover. Yet even in 2020, it did not match 2008 levels.[14] Twenty-first-century globalization, in other words, may have crested and begun to recede before Trump took office; his protectionist policies may have been pushing on an open door. The belief in a world with no national borders, in which goods could be produced everywhere and sold anywhere with a minimum of friction, had been a cardinal principle of the neoliberal order. As this belief lost influence, so did the order that it had done so much to bring into being. "Protectionism" had been a dirty word of political economy for thirty years. It no longer was, not for Republicans and not for Democrats. Producers and consumers in various countries had begun to question the pursuit of a borderless world. Trump was one of many politicians around the globe who were rising to power by amplifying these doubts and by promising a protectionist future.

Part of Trump's pitch was that free trade had benefited only the "globalists." In an ad released in the final days of the 2016 presidential campaign, Trump had proclaimed that "a global power structure" had "robbed our working class, stripped our country of its wealth, and put that money into the pockets of a handful of large corporations and political entities."[15] Trump promised that his presidency would upend that power structure and substitute for it one that benefited ordinary Americans. During the first two years of his presidency, Trump made a symbolic show of siding with workers—posing alongside Harley motorcycles, climbing into cabs of long-distance trucks, browbeating a few employers into postponing plans to move jobs abroad—but he did little substantively to improve their economic condition. His tax code reform stimulated job creation and some rise in wages, at least in the short term. But overall, it increased rather than cut economic inequality in America.[16]

Trump preferred to make his appeal to "the people" on ethnonationalist rather than economic grounds. He identified immigrants rather than "robber barons" as the chief threat to the average American's well-being. America would become great again, Trump repeatedly insisted, if it took back control of its borders, built a southern wall, and denied entrance to immigrants deemed unworthy of membership in the American nation. Thus, after becoming president, Trump did not stop hurling vitriol at Mexican immigrants. He made known his wish to slow to a trickle migration from "shithole" nations in Central America, the Caribbean, and Africa.[17] He issued multiple executive orders barring migrants from majority Muslim countries such as Iran, Iraq, Libya, Somalia, Sudan, Syria, and Yemen. These last measures became known as the "Muslim ban."[18] And, at the southern border, Trump implemented a "zero tolerance" policy toward Mexicans and Central Americans crossing into the United States without permission. Any undocumented immigrant was to be charged with a misdemeanor and imprisoned while awaiting a hearing, a trial, or deportation. The Trump administration decided to subject asylum seekers to this harsh treatment as well, reversing a previous policy, one consonant with American refugee law, that had allowed such individuals to stay in the United States—and out of jail—until their cases could be heard in a US immigration court. Sweeping across the Southwest with its dragnet, the Trump administration not only imprisoned the undocumented. It also increasingly separated minors from their parents, sending these children to detention facilities often hundreds of miles away from where the parents themselves were being held.

This last policy quickly caused administrative chaos, as parents and children became the responsibility of different US agencies that often made no effort to work with each other or to keep records on which children belonged to which parents. Parents were frequently deported having no knowledge of where their children were being held and having no way of getting in touch with them—and thus of getting them back. The Trump administration effectively orphaned thousands of children, many of them arriving as part of refugee families fleeing persecution in their Central American countries of origin.

Separated children were kept for weeks in detention cages without adequate food, water, sanitation, or adult supervision. The Trump administration seemed indifferent to the cruelty inflicted upon those caught in its sweeps along the southern border. It was no accident that the migrants treated in this way were people of color from Central America, individuals not fit, in Trump's eyes, to be part of the American nation.[19]

Porous borders had been part of the neoliberal dispensation. More than 30 million migrants had come to America between the 1970s and 2010s.[20] Both Republican and Democratic presidents had supported immigration. Ronald Reagan had created a path toward citizenship for millions of undocumented migrants. George W. Bush imagined a North American Union, similar to the European Union, that would have allowed the free movement of goods and people throughout the northern half of the Western Hemisphere.[21] The *Wall Street Journal* had long regarded the free movement of people and a free market economy as essential components of a free society. Trump broke with these Republican traditions and, in the process, repudiated principles central to neoliberalism.

America, in Trump's eyes, ought to be populated by people of European descent. The nation was meant to be white, and mostly Christian. Walls needed to be built to protect America's racial character. Internally, white privilege had to be restored. White nationalist groups saw in Trump an ally. He rarely criticized them, even when he was brought under extreme pressure to do so, as he was in the aftermath of a white nationalist, neo-Nazi protest in Charlottesville, Virginia, in August 2017 that turned violent and then deadly.[22]

Trump's ethnonationalism always had a class dimension to it. Trump imagined that he was standing up for the little (white) guy who lived in America's heartland and whose life had been undercut by globalizing elites. In Trump's eyes, these elites' pursuit of free trade had stripped America of manufacturing jobs and undercut the wages for the blue-collar work that remained. Elite support for the movement of migrants across national borders, Trump believed, had brought many more people of color to America, rendering the nation less and less recognizable in the process. A diverse America, in the eyes of Trump and his supporters, signaled the nation's decline.

For a time, Trump's commitment to deregulation and tax cuts coexisted with his desire to "protect" America from foreign goods and foreign peoples. But somewhere between summer 2017 and spring 2018, his administration reached a tipping point, symbolized by the growing discomfort and then departure of its chief neoliberal policymaker, Gary Cohn. Cohn had been upset by Trump's refusal in 2017 to condemn the violent acts and hateful speech of white nationalist protesters in Charlottesville, which had been directed not just at blacks but at Jews (Cohn was himself Jewish). Cohn stayed on to secure tax code reform in December 2017. But when Trump moved in March 2018 to impose heavy tariffs on imported steel, Cohn had had enough. This neoliberal could no longer justify working for the ethnonationalist and protectionist Trump.

As was the case with his protectionism, Trump's ethnonationalism was part of a global trend. Victor Orbán in Hungary, Vladimir Putin in Russia, Narendra Modi in India, and Xi Jinping in China wanted their nations to privilege certain ethnocultural groups defined by race or religion or both: Catholics and Protestants in Hungary, Christian Orthodox in Russia, Hindus in India, and the Han in China. These ethnonationalist leaders were united—and connected to Trump—in their loathing of Islam and their desire to keep Muslims out of their countries or in subservient, second-class positions. These heads of state had their counterparts in Muslim countries, too, notably Recep Erdoğan in Turkey and the royal family ruling Saudi Arabia. All these leaders, non-Muslim and Muslim, were deeply hostile to the pluralism and cosmopolitanism that had been so integral to the neoliberal order. Presidents Bush and Obama, in different but complementary ways, had both worked to spread cosmopolitan values across America (and beyond). Trump wanted to purge these values from the land.[23]

The ethnonationalist leaders, Trump included, also possessed authoritarian tendencies. They were impatient with parliaments, independent judiciaries, and other aspects of liberal democracy often associated with systems of neoliberal rule. They saw themselves and each other as strongmen determined to take care of the right people and able to make the tough decisions necessary to do so. They wanted the planet to be governed by force rather than by international law and multinational nongovernmental organizations. They sought a world divided into blocs—East Asia, North America, northern Eurasia, the Middle East, and South Asia among them—each controlled by a regional hegemon. This world would be far from flat; rather, tall, jagged, and hard-to-scale walls would separate blocs (and often the nations within them) from each other.[24] In this imagined future, the United States would withdraw from its seventy-five-year role as the world's policeman and from its responsibility as the enforcer of liberal and neoliberal rules of global order. In words and deeds, Trump was taking steps to make this vision a reality.

Some of Trump's fellow strongmen had also begun to obstruct the free flow not just of trade and migrants but of information. The internet had been integral to the triumph of the neoliberal order, its provision of instantaneous and global flows of unlimited data promising to turn markets into perfect instruments of economic exchange, development, and prosperity. But the free flow of information also permitted a free flow of ideas that might threaten, at some point, to upend authoritarian rule. Thus, the Xi regime decided to create a separate information technology system for its nation, one controlled not by Google, Facebook, and Twitter but by Chinese authorities, the Chinese Communist Party in particular. Putin was determined to do the same in Russia. Trump lagged behind Xi and Putin, and for good reason: The free publicity that US social media platforms had given him had facilitated his political rise. But by the end of his presidency, he, too, along with populist elements of the GOP, was becoming hostile to the private power of America's social media companies and beginning to issue calls to break them up or put them under stiffer regulation.[25]

Left Revival

Trump wanted the breakup of the neoliberal order to benefit the authoritarian right. But the breakup was also benefiting a social democratic left that Bernie Sanders, Elizabeth Warren, and others had been infusing with new life. Trump's constant talk of putting tariffs on imports, stopping the free movement of people across borders, and challenging media companies had the effect of widening the space in which those engaged in politics could think more freely—and ambitiously—about the proper role of government in economic life. If the government could shape markets via tariffs and immigration restriction, might there be other ways in which the state could exercise authority over the economy? If social media companies could be regulated or broken up, what about other corporations that had accumulated too much power?

More and more, the 2010s were coming to resemble the 1930s and the 1970s, earlier moments when the decline of a dominant political order had allowed ideas long consigned to the periphery of American politics to move into the mainstream. If the ability to control the ideological mainstream was a sign of a political order's triumph, the loss of that ability signaled a political order's demise. Trump's work, along with that of Bernie Sanders, in undermining neoliberal hegemony created additional opportunities for once peripheral political ideas and initiatives to flourish.

Across the 2010s, progressives built an institutional infrastructure to broadcast their ideas and initiatives. New think tanks, such as the Washington Center for Equitable Growth (2013) and New Consensus (2018), appeared; so did new activist groups, including Justice Democrats (2017), the Sunrise Movement (2017, focused on climate issues), and Momentum (2014), determined to pull American politics to the left.[26] A new sense of political possibility also reinvigorated older left/liberal groups and publications, such as the Center for American Progress, *Daily Kos* (a blog), the *Nation*, the *Atlantic*, and the *American Prospect*, a liberal/progressive journal that counted Robert Reich, now a professor at Berkeley, as one of its editors. Meanwhile, in 2017, the left-leaning *Rachel Maddow Show* achieved the top ranking among non-sports cable TV shows. Left-leaning donors with ample reserves, such as

George Soros and his Open Society Foundations, began to encourage and coordinate the kind of fundraising efforts that every movement in America aspiring to become a political order requires. And the William and Flora Hewlett Foundation, the Omidyar Network (established in 2004 by eBay founder Pierre Omidyar), and the Berggruen Institute began contemplating more and more how they might deploy their resources to reshape the ideological mainstream, following the model set by neoliberal think tanks in the 1970s.[27]

In the 2018 elections, the left turned its newly-acquired institutional capacity and ideological ferment into a measure of political power. Four left/progressive Democrats won congressional seats: Alexandra Ocasio-Cortez (New York), Ilhan Omar (Minnesota), Ayanna Pressley (Massachusetts), and Rashida Tlaib (Michigan). Their success, in turn, vaulted two leftists, Bernie Sanders (again), and Elizabeth Warren, into frontrunner status for the 2020 Democratic nomination for president. Warren built a national reputation in the aftermath of the financial crash of 2008–2009 by exposing the predatory lending practices used by banks to exploit ordinary borrowers. Later, and especially in her 2020 campaign, Warren began targeting as well the nation's social media and e-commerce companies—Google, Amazon, Facebook, Twitter, Apple, and Microsoft—for having accumulated too much wealth and power. Her staff worked to revive America's anti-monopoly protest tradition, which a hundred years earlier had energized a progressive political movement that had checked private economic power both by breaking up large corporations and subjecting the ones that remained intact to effective public regulation. Sanders shared Warren's antagonism to corporate power. If anything, his plans were more ambitious than hers, as he sought to make his social democratic vision a reality in American life.[28]

Pandemic

The 2020 presidential campaign coincided with the onset of the Covid-19 pandemic, which lent new urgency to the issues that critics of neoliberalism had been raising. In political economic terms, the pandemic worked to intensify a development that the decline in the neoliberal order had already set in motion: namely, a conviction that government was the only institution with the wherewithal to address severe economic and social hardship. The central state in America had always been allowed to grow beyond its customary bounds in times of emergency—war, natural disasters, public health crises. In a rare display of unity—and reflecting the magnitude of the challenge posed by the virus—Republicans and Democrats agreed in March 2020 to pass a $2.4 trillion relief package, encompassing measures intended to help individuals and families, on the one hand, and small businesses and corporations, on the other.[29] This package was more than twice the size of the one passed under Obama in response to the Great Recession of 2009. Despite its size, it generated almost no dissent on either side of the partisan divide. It also distributed as many benefits (measured in terms of dollars) to individuals and small businesses as it did to large corporations—a principle of equity that the Obama rescue plan of 2008–2009 had so strikingly failed to achieve. Jerome Powell, the Trump-appointed chairman of the Federal Reserve, supported this aggressive intervention of government into the markets in stark departure from Fed practice during the Alan Greenspan era.[30]

The Trump administration, meanwhile, shifted $10 billion from a portion of this mega-bill allocated for hospitals and health care providers to pharmaceutical companies, hoping thereby to incentivize the latter to invest in rapid vaccine development. This initiative, known as Operation Warp Speed, turned out to be the Trump administration's most important contribution to the fight against the virus, but one for which Trump himself was reluctant to take credit. He feared offending the large numbers in GOP ranks who were opposed to taking new vaccines.[31]

Trump did not take full advantage of his powers during the pandemic. The Defense Production Act of 1950 gave him the authority to direct any sector of the private economy to shift production to materials required for national security. To fight the coronavirus, he could have ordered manufacturing companies to produce ventilators, masks, and other personal protective equipment (PPE) that hospital staffs so urgently needed. He could have commandeered private transportation networks to rush these materials to the cities, towns, and rural areas where they were needed. Trump may also have had the authority, under the Public Health Act of 1944, to impose quarantines on parts of the country struck hard by the virus and even to impose bans on travel within the United States.[32]

Trump was reluctant to exercise this authority—a strange stance on his part, given his desire to be seen as a king who respected no limits on his power. His reluctance arose in part from his desire to play down the threat of the disease, hoping to convey through his words and deeds its failure to dominate either him or the country. Trump refused to wear a mask. He made little effort to conduct social distancing at meetings, to take public health precautions at his rallies, or to encourage his millions of evangelical supporters to protect themselves when they went to church to worship. Instead, Trump pretended that the disease was not really dangerous, largely ignored the sick and dying, and told Americans repeatedly that the economy and the nation would soon rebound to full operation and health. In the process, he compromised the work of the Centers for Disease Control (CDC), the agency of the federal government long admired for its skill and efficiency at identifying and devising treatment plans for new diseases. This agency, as with so many others in the federal government during the Trump years, had seen appropriations cut, key directors appointed for reasons of political loyalty rather than merit or scientific expertise, and doctors and other professionals demoralized (and then exiting the agency in large numbers).

Rather than empower the CDC to do its work, Trump seemed to prefer promoting quack cures that he had learned about on social media or from friends or followers. Trump actually seemed to think he could bluff his way past the virus, as he had with so many human adversaries in the past. Half a million Americans died on Trump's callous watch.

The manifest incompetence of Trump's administration in the face of the coronavirus damaged him politically, especially among suburban middle-class Republican and independent voters who in 2016 had given him their votes. His loss of voters in each of these groups probably cost Trump the 2020 election.

A New Political Order?

In 2019 and the first quarter of 2020, few people thought much of Joe Biden, the former senator and vice-president. Across a forty-seven-year career of public service, most of them spent as a senator from Delaware, he had done little to suggest that he might be someone who could lead America out of a crisis. He was experienced, loyal, and garrulous but not particularly distinguished or eloquent. Few could point to a significant piece of legislation that bore his name or recall a memorable speech he had given. He was old, and he looked it. His performances in several of the early presidential primary debates were poor, and he never seemed able to match his younger and more vigorous rivals on stage. Trump mocked him as "Sleepy Joe." Significant numbers of pundits and voters interpreted a speech impediment he had had since childhood as indicating the onset of dementia. A lackluster showing in the January 2020 Iowa caucuses—the first test faced by Democratic hopefuls contending for the 2020 nomination—confirmed many in their belief that he was not the man for the job.

Biden, however, resurrected his candidacy in an impressive showing in the South Carolina primary in February 2020, largely because African American voters supported him. That victory in turn propelled Biden to wins in a string of Super Tuesday primaries in southern states in early March. The nomination was now his to lose. Still, many were drawn to him not because of his charisma, talent, or policy chops but because he seemed to be the only Democratic candidate capable of stopping Trump, given that Biden was a moderate and would appeal to voters who might not cast a ballot for a socialist, a candidate of color, or a woman.

Given these low expectations, Biden's performance between March 2020 and March 2021 was something of a revelation. He defeated Trump on November 3, 2020, beating him in both the popular vote and in the electoral college. He showed an impressive grasp of the political moment. He demonstrated that, unlike Trump, he could speak directly to the suffering that so many Americans were experiencing because of the pandemic. Across his life, Biden had suffered personal tragedy.[33] He had learned to speak publicly of his grief and loss, and about the ability to overcome such loss through love and connection, and through faith and poetry. The Bible and the Irish poets of his ancestors' homeland became his touchstones. He liked to share Biblical and Irish verses with those who entered his life. As he recovered repeatedly from his grief, Biden accumulated a reservoir of empathy that he was able to draw on to console others who had, like him, suffered loss.[34] Biden, then, turned out to be a man emotionally well suited to help others struggling to carry on in the time of Covid-19.[35]

Biden also understood that America was at an inflection point.[36] He had concluded that the Democratic politics that he had inherited from Clinton and Obama no longer sufficed. The shocks that America had experienced in the twelve years or so since Obama's first victory in 2008 had been too great. These had included the Great Recession and the long-term economic suffering in both black and white America that issued from it; the rise of right-wing populism in the Republican Party; the damage that Trump had done to American government and American democracy; and now, the toll exacted by the pandemic. Biden did not say in so many words that the neoliberal order was crumbling. But he had concluded that one era of American politics was ending and that a new era was emerging. The moment demanded, he believed, that he think big and act boldly.

On taking office in January 2021, Biden had his staff propose multiple major initiatives that in number and ambition rivaled what Franklin Roosevelt proposed and passed into law during his first hundred days in office in 1933. Biden's initiatives included a campaign to vaccinate a large majority of adult Americans; a massive $1.9 trillion rescue plan to assist individuals and businesses in surviving the ongoing economic collapse that the pandemic had caused; even more massive plans to improve America's physical and social infrastructure, at a combined cost of $4 to $5 trillion; strong voting rights legislation to prevent states from interfering with the ability of people of color to cast their ballots; comprehensive immigration reform that would put millions of undocumented people on the road to citizenship and establish humanitarianism as a core principle of the nation's immigration policy; and a variety of major efforts to root out structural racism from American life.

Biden did not come close to matching Roosevelt's record of passing fifteen major pieces of legislation in 100 days; no president has or likely ever will. But Biden did launch a vigorous vaccination campaign and he did steer the nearly $2 trillion American Rescue Plan through Congress. Over the summer and into the fall of 2021, Biden secured passage of a bipartisan $1 trillion plan to improve the nation's physical infrastructure. And in November 2021, the Democratic-controlled House passed his $1.75 trillion plan to improve "social infrastructure," an omnibus package that included child tax credits to allow working parents to provide adequate care for their offspring, subsidies to support workers looking after America's large elderly population, and investments in green technology to push America into a carbon-free future.[37]

Federal expenditures approved during the first year of his presidency constituted a greater percentage of GDP than those of the New Deal itself; they almost reached World War II levels.[38] Biden's proposals, in combination, represented a bold departure from the Obama administration, which had always been concerned about balancing expenditures against revenues and with demonstrating fiscal responsibility.

This expansive and aggressive program reflected, in part, the integration of a revived left into the Biden administration. In summer 2020, Biden had agreed to set up six joint Biden-Sanders "unity task forces" to bring the center and left of the Democratic Party closer together.[39] The plans they developed for the economy, the climate crisis, racial justice, and the like shaped the platform adopted at the Democratic Party convention in August 2020 and informed, in turn, the legislative proposals that Biden began unveiling soon after taking office in January 2021. These task forces allowed maverick economists like Darrick Hamilton of The New School and Stephanie Kelton of Stonybrook University, who were promoting fresh approaches to race and economics on the one hand and to monetary theory on the other, to influence the incoming administration.

The rapprochement between center and left also informed Biden's decisions to bring individuals with progressive politics into his brain trust. He appointed Heather Boushey (former president of the Center for Equitable Growth) and Jared Bernstein (a veteran of the progressive Economic Policy Institute) to the Council of Economic Advisers, and big tech critic Lina Khan (Columbia Law School) to the chairpersonship of the Federal Trade Commission. Khan's anti-trust ally, Timothy Wu (also of Columbia Law School), became White House advisor on technology and competition policy. In September 2021, Biden nominated Saule Omarova, a radical Cornell Law School professor, for comptrollership of the currency. A similar dialogue between the Democratic Party left and center had characterized the heyday of the New Deal. The existence of such dialogue did not indicate that the left was gaining the upper hand or even that its influence on Biden would endure. Voices on the left could be ignored, even purged, as had happened in the 1930s; indeed, Omarova fell victim to such a campaign when Republicans and moderate Democrats joined hands to make sure that her nomination would not get through the Senate. Still, despite the Omarova setback, Sanders's and Warren's supporters had gained seats at the table. The distinguished and formerly influential neoliberal economist Lawrence Summers had not.[40]

The proliferation of new policy ideas and think tanks, the rise of tightly networked groups of political activists, and the emergence of a left-liberal bloc of newspapers, magazines, cable TV anchors, bloggers, podcasters, and social media influencers suggest that a new progressive political order was taking shape. But it was still in its formative—and thus vulnerable—stages. It was not yet clear that there would be enough deep-pocketed donors to support the continued ascent of such a political order if its leaders went through with their threats to target Wall Street and Silicon Valley wealth and power. Nor was it clear whether Biden would be strong and charismatic enough to hold together his center-left coalition when internal divisions arose or when domestic and international developments extraneous to his core ambitions intruded. Biden believed he possessed the mettle. But his poor handling of the withdrawal of US forces from Afghanistan in August 2021 suggested to many Americans that he did not.[41]

Biden, moreover, needed to surmount at least three other challenges if he was going to turn his 2020 victory into something more enduring. The first challenge concerned the climate crisis bringing droughts and fires, hurricanes and floods, and rapidly swelling streams of refugees fleeing lands no longer habitable. Biden made the achievement of a Green New Deal central to his agenda. It is not yet clear, however, whether any democratically elected leader will be able to marshal levels of popular support sufficient to uproot industries and ways of living that must be ended if global warming is to be stopped. The New Deal never faced an existential question of this sort. To the contrary, it constructed a political order on the assumption that fossil-fuel energy reserves would sustain a full-employment, high-wage economy forever.[42]

Biden's second challenge centered on race. African American voters had saved Biden's presidential run by turning out for him in large numbers in the February 2020 South Carolina Democratic primary. In the general election, Stacey Abrams, voting rights activist in Georgia and former minority leader in the Georgia House of Representatives, played an indispensable role in winning her state for Biden and in sending two Democrats to the US Senate. Without those two Georgia Democrats, Biden would have fallen short of a Democratic majority in Congress's upper house and likely would have seen his ambitious legislative agenda thwarted by Republican opposition.

Biden had paid off part of his debt to African American voters by making Kamala Harris his running mate, thus giving her the opportunity to become the first African American vice-president in American history. But that was hardly sufficient, especially given the magnitude of the racial justice uprising triggered by the police murder of George Floyd in Minneapolis on May 25, 2020. Floyd, an African American man, had been arrested that day for allegedly passing a counterfeit $20 bill at a convenience store. When four officers arrived on the scene, they subdued Floyd, and forced him to the ground. One of the four, Derek Chauvin (a white officer), then used deadly force by placing his knee hard into the back of Floyd's neck for an interminable nine minutes, ignoring Floyd's repeated cries that he could not breathe. At some point in that nine-minute span, Floyd lost consciousness and died. Bystanders recorded visual images of Chauvin's knee on Floyd's neck along with Floyd's desperate pleas for help.[43]

The Chauvin-Floyd clip went viral on social media, triggering an explosion of protest involving hundreds of thousands and then millions in cities, large and small, North and South, East and West. The ranks of the protesters included whites and Latinos in addition to blacks, making the protests among the most diverse demonstrations in American history against racial terror and injustice. "Black Lives Matter" signs sprouted everywhere on the lawns of homeowners and the windows of apartment dwellers and were chalked into or painted on the streets of numerous cities. The protests carried on for weeks. Most were peaceful, though the anger of protesters was palpable throughout, as was their conviction that uprooting racism from American life required more than mild reform; it required drastic action such as "defunding the police."[44] In some locales, such as Portland, Oregon, protest turned violent.

Biden never signed off on "defunding the police," a solution he regarded as dangerous and unworkable.[45] But he understood from the start that he could not do what his Democratic predecessors in the Oval Office had repeatedly done: subordinate racial justice to other, more "pressing" or "important" matters. Franklin Roosevelt had refused to support civil rights legislation for fear of offending the white South, a critical part of his New Deal coalition. Obama, in his own way and for different reasons, was himself reluctant to throw his support behind legislation meant specifically to address discrimination against black people.

Biden was determined to chart a different course. He became the first president in American history to use the phrase "structural racism" in his inaugural address and to pledge that his administration would do everything within its power to eliminate it. He included within the first piece of legislation he signed as president a program to assist black farmers whose families had lost property across the generations on account of predatory practices by banks and speculators. This was an early effort to put into practice calls for America to make "reparations" to blacks for the dispossession they had endured during slavery and beyond.[46]

It remained to be seen, however, whether Biden would succeed in passing both race-specific legislation and laws meant to improve the circumstances of all Americans—including working-class whites (and Trump supporters) who had suffered poverty and exploitation and whom Biden hoped to bring back into the Democratic Party. Progressing on both fronts simultaneously had always been a difficult challenge for Democrats. Biden was old enough to remember the backlash against Lyndon Johnson's Great Society programs for allegedly prioritizing the needs of the country's black citizens over those of its white ones. The left-leaning think tanks and journals that had sprouted in the 2010s were full of ideas and hope for addressing simultaneously issues of class and race.[47] But white backlash still loomed as a threat to Biden's incipient political order.

Biden's third challenge was to govern boldly and successfully with a divided Congress—and when democracy itself in America was increasingly under siege. In the 2020 elections, the Democratic Party had not matched Biden's performance. It lost seats in the House relative to 2018, shrinking its majority to single digits. And despite winning two seats in Georgia, the Democrats still had the barest of majorities in the Senate—50, or 51, if Kamala Harris, authorized as vice-president to cast the deciding vote in the event of a tie, was counted. Thus, to enact any piece of legislation that all Republicans opposed, Biden needed every Democratic senator to support him. Franklin Roosevelt, by contrast, had enjoyed gigantic majorities of 313 to 122 in the House and of 58 to 37 in the Senate during his first two years in office (1933–1935). His congressional majorities actually increased in the 1934 elections. FDR was operating in a political universe radically different from the one that Biden inhabited. Roosevelt could ignore a recalcitrant senator or two, or more. Biden could not, and he faced two: Joe Manchin (West Virginia) and Kyrsten Sinema (Arizona), who emerged as nemeses to him and his political program.

Donald Trump's refusal to accept that he had lost the election only deepened the political challenge that Biden faced. Trump did not concede in the days, weeks, or even months after the election. He thus broke a tradition extending back to the second half of the nineteenth century, one that had long helped to make the United States a model for executing peaceful transfers of power from one elected leader to another.

Trump had convinced himself that he had in fact not lost the election, that millions of fake ballots had been added to Biden's totals and millions of "real" ballots had been subtracted from his totals. Exposing the perfidy that allegedly underlay the election results reported on November 3 became Trump's obsession. For the remainder of his presidency, he filed spurious lawsuits in state after state, challenging vote totals and demanding recounts and audits.[48] As virtually every one of his challenges failed, Trump encouraged his supporters to descend on Washington, DC, on January 6, 2021, when Congress was convening to certify the electoral college results from the fifty states. This January 6 session was purely procedural and ceremonial, an opportunity for Congress to do what it had done after every presidential election for more than two centuries: put its formal seal of approval on the presidential contender who had won the electoral college. But Trump had convinced his supporters, and a sizable group of Republican senators and congressmen, that Congress still could intervene to alter the results of the election and give him the second term he believed he deserved.

Tens of thousands of Trump supporters traveled to Washington for the January 6 rally; several thousand, at Trump's urging, then stormed the Capitol. The Capitol Police were unprepared and quickly overwhelmed by the Trump mob determined to force its way into the Capitol by any means necessary. Trump seemed mesmerized by the scenes of Capitol Hill bedlam and violence appearing on the TV screens he was watching from the safety of the White House. As with most of his initiatives as president, his coup was poorly planned. It failed, order was restored, Congress certified the election results that evening, and Trump left the White House on the morning of January 20, flying to Florida. Biden was inaugurated several hours later.[49]

A majority of senators and congressmen and congresswomen showed courage and resolve in completing the transition between presidencies in such trying circumstances. But the personal and political trauma unleashed by the events of January 6 were not so easily overcome. The desecration of the Capitol by the supporters of a sitting president was an event without precedent in American history. The Trump mob had gone berserk, smashing the heads of policemen with fire-extinguishers, breaking many windows and doors, and ransacking offices. One group of rioters, including an individual dressed in Viking garb, took over the Senate chamber. Other assailants were hunting congressmen, congresswomen, senators, and a vice president whom they had been told to despise and, if captured, to harm. Trump showed no remorse for the fury and violence he had unleashed. To the contrary, he seemed emboldened by the events of January 6, forming what looked like a government-in-exile at Mar-a-Lago as a first step on his path back to power.

These events underscored how dangerous the break-up of a political order can be. In the coup's aftermath, millions of Americans found themselves thinking the unthinkable: namely, that American democracy itself might not survive Trump. The January 6 coup had failed; the next one, many Americans feared, might succeed. A new political order, if one were to arise, might come from the right and be authoritarian to the core.[50] It might be deeply illiberal; and its democratic character might be nothing more than a veneer—not unlike what was passing for democracy in Russia and Turkey.

At least one man looked at the debacle overtaking America with considerable satisfaction. Americans may have forgotten about the Cold War, but Vladimir Putin had not. Putin understood that the neoliberal order Trump had done so much to undermine was the one whose ascent in the 1980s and early 1990s had triggered the Soviet Union's disintegration. What could be better for Putin than to witness, thirty years later, the coming apart of a political order that had been the source of Russia's greatest humiliation? That Putin had played a role in burdening America with what looked like a bleak future—he had meddled in the 2016 election campaign in an attempt to help Trump win—surely only increased his satisfaction.

Of course, Putin had not manufactured Trump or his Make America Great Again movement. Trump was the homegrown product of a political order that, in the eyes of majorities of Americans, on the left and right, had failed. A neoliberal order prizing global free markets and free movement of people had left too many people behind. It had favored Wall Street over Main Street; tolerated extreme levels of inequality; ignored the problem of mass incarceration and the massive loss of wealth experienced by minority homeowners in the wake of the Great Recession; legitimated a war on Iraq that America had no business fighting and then a reckless stab at reconstruction that failed in Iraq and that spread additional misery to much of the Middle East. Distress in America had been palpable years before Trump seized America's political stage. That a master manipulator of grievance and resentment would arise in this moment hardly seems surprising.

Trump's work in taking apart the neoliberal order had given others—including a revivified left—belief that the political future they desired for America might now be within reach. Biden had great hopes for America. He understood that America and the world stood at a crucial point of transition. Across much of his first year, Biden thought that he could deliver the bold and dynamic leadership that the moment required. But he stumbled in fall and winter 2021–2022, failing to get Senate approval for his landmark social infrastructure bill, now labeled "Build Back Better." Manchin of West Virginia, the crucial fiftieth vote, repeatedly backed out of deals that Biden thought were clinched, humiliating the president and infuriating the Democratic left, which had agreed, for the sake of getting Manchin on board, to shrink drastically the size of Build Back Better from $5 trillion to less than $2 trillion.

Biden then got assistance from an unexpected source. On February 24, 2022, an overconfident Putin invaded Ukraine, intending to take back a territory that had become independent of Russia in 1991. In the 2010s, Ukraine had drawn increasingly close to the West, to the

European Union, and to NATO. These developments had alarmed Putin, both for security reasons and because he regarded Ukraine and its culture as intrinsic parts of historic Russia. Putin had already seized Crimea from Ukraine in 2014, encountering only token Western resistance. Now, sensing weakness in Biden, arising both from the botched US withdrawal from Afghanistan and from the president's domestic political troubles, Putin struck at Ukraine from the East with a large and mechanized land force. He expected a quick and easy victory, with tanks entering Kyiv (Ukraine's capital) in a matter of days, the Ukrainian president Volodymyr Zelenskyy deposed, and Ukrainians rushing into the streets to celebrate Putin for reunifying the Ukrainian and Russian peoples.

Nothing of the sort happened. Zelenskyy donned the mantle of Winston Churchill and framed the war as a fight to the death for Western freedoms and civilization. This diminutive actor, heretofore much more adept at comedy than statecraft, rallied both his people and the West to a display of unity and resistance that shocked Russia and exposed the Russian military as decrepit and Putin's regime as incompetent, cruel, and delusional. Biden seized the moment as an opportunity to rehabilitate America's traditional post–World War II role as leader of the free world, persuading European nations to form a united front and sending vital intelligence and military equipment to Zelenskyy's government and armed forces.

Some believed that Ukraine's and the West's impressive mobilization against autocratic aggression would reinvigorate a neoliberal order committed to peace, liberal democracy, and the free movement of capital, people, goods, and information. But the war has done much to distance the world from key neoliberal principles. Multiple European nations resolved to end their dependence on Russian oil and gas. Russia, meanwhile, in its effort to conquer Ukraine, blockaded the Black Sea ports from where Ukraine had long shipped millions of tons of grain to the Global South. Suddenly, many nations of the world were without essential supplies of energy and food. The war intensified concerns within the United States that China might invade its own "Ukraine"—the island of Taiwan sitting just off China's southeastern coast—and thus deprive the West of Taiwanese semi-conductor chips on which so many of its computers, cars, phones, electrical grids, air traffic control systems, and industrial machinery depended.

What were governments in the United States and other nations confronting shortages of critical materials to do? The answer to many was clear: National security required that governments now take steps to shorten supply chains, reshore manufacturing of essential goods, and advance new technologies to the point where they might power a country's machinery when war interrupted the flow of oil and gas across national borders. National security, in other words, demanded that states intervene in markets; decisions about how and where to procure essential goods could no longer be left entirely to individual corporations, and especially not to multinational ones indifferent to a single country's welfare. Every state needed an industrial policy that took its people's well-being into account and that prioritized public welfare over private gain.

Globalization would not be abandoned in the new world taking shape, but it would become more strategic. Borders mattered. A key principle that had propelled the neoliberal order's ascent in the 1980s and 1990s—that capital would be free to travel to any spot on the globe in search of cheap labor, efficient production, and ample profits—was now being challenged. The sanctions imposed by the West on Russia for its aggression—the seizure of the assets that the country held in Western banks, the ban on investment by private companies in Russia—drove home the point that capital was no longer free to roam. The world was no longer flat.[51]

This kind of thinking—elevating national security above capitalist freedom—impelled a bipartisan majority in Congress to pass the Chips and Science Act in August 2022. The act appropriated nearly $300 billion in federal subsidies to spur research into and production of semi-conductor computer chips in the United States, and thus lessen the country's dependence for this critical good on Taiwan and China. This new interest in bending the private economy to national security imperatives may also have persuaded Manchin, no friend of the green energy revolution, to support in summer 2022 the largest investment—nearly $400 billion—in green energy incentives and subsidies that the US government had ever made. The Biden Administration called this piece of legislation the Inflation Reduction Act in part to give Manchin cover in his coal-producing state of West Virginia for his green energy conversion. Why did Manchin, at this eleventh-hour, decide to support the cause of green energy? Hard-to-decipher tactical considerations having to do with his own political future may have been foremost in Machin's mind. But it is also possible that Manchin's conversion was influenced in part by his own growing appreciation that America's long-term well-being would be guaranteed not just by free enterprise but also by a state-managed program of energy diversification, now imagined as a tool not just for combating climate change but also for assisting the country in its quest for energy independence and, thus, for national security.[52]

The Russia–Ukraine war, then, seemed to be strengthening forces that were spurring movement away from a neoliberal political economy, to widen spaces in which a progressive politics might flourish, and to allow Biden to pursue a robust industrial policy, meant to be the linchpin of a new political order.[53] Yet, paradoxically, the war, in the short-term, also imperiled Biden's and the Democrats' hold on political power, by triggering a sharp rise in inflation in the United States and other countries in the six months after the conflict broke out.

Inflationary pressures had been building across 2021–2022, the year of the $1.9 trillion American Rescue Plan's implementation. The act was meant to spur consumer spending and economic growth. It did both. However, foreign manufacturing centers and globe-spanning supply chains, still hobbled by the pandemic, could not provision the US marketplace with goods quickly enough to meet rising demand. Inflationary pressures intensified when the Russia–Ukraine War then obstructed the flow of Russian oil and gas and Ukrainian grain to their customary international destinations. Energy and food costs shot up, creating by late summer 2022 the worst inflationary bubble in fifty years. Central banks responded by sharply raising interest rates, hoping that the consequent increases in borrowing costs (and the likely slide in real estate and equity values that would ensue) would soften consumer demand, without throwing national economies into a full-blown recession.

Inflation peaked in September–October 2022, just as the midterm contests in the United States were climaxing. It was assumed that American voters who faced surging gasoline and supermarket prices would blame the Democrats for economic misfires occurring on the latter's watch. Predictions abounded that Republicans would rout Democrats in November. But in a surprising outcome that bucked the longstanding trend of a midterm for the president's party, the Democrats kept a slim majority in the Senate while only narrowly losing the House. They benefited from women voters turning out for Democrats in large number to express their outrage at the decision (in June 2022) by a Republican-dominated Supreme Court's to reverse *Roe v. Wade*, the 1973 ruling that had made abortion a constitutionally protected right. The Democrats did well enough in the November 2022 elections to believe that they would have a shot in 2024 at retaking both houses of Congress and winning the presidency once again.[54]

Political developments across the next two years could break the Democrats' way. Inflation could be tamed by 2024, and economic growth invigorated. By then, too, many more of the Biden administration's projects to improve US infrastructure, reshore manufacturing, and advance the green revolution may have yielded early results, making the benefits of a government-directed industrial policy more visible to a broad cross section of American voters.

Yet establishing a new political order is never a simple or easy task. Even a victory in the 2024 elections would be but a second step in a process that will require several more. The Democrats have yet to find a formula for building the kind of large and durable electoral majorities that would allow a progressive political order to achieve levels of dominance once enjoyed by the New Deal.[55] The volatility that American politics acquired in the decade after the 2008–2009 financial crash has yet to ebb. And the grip of Trumpism on portions of the US electorate remains strong, and the threats to American democracy real. Marjorie Taylor Greene, a prominent Republican Congresswoman from Georgia, has been pushing her colleagues not just to oppose the Biden administration at every turn but also to wreak havoc on the ability of the House of Representatives—and thus of Congress more generally—to govern. Generating chaos and paralysis on Capitol Hill, in turn, may swell popular support yet again for a strongman (or strongwoman) to sweep into Washington in 2024 and set things right. Overseas, strongman Putin may yet recover from early missteps and win his war of aggression against Ukraine—or even radically expand the conflict across Europe, with devastating consequences. The specter of authoritarianism, both at home and abroad, has yet to be extinguished. Americans thus must reckon with the possibility that they will be living amid the ruins of a once vaunted neoliberal order for some time to come.[56]

As with all fallen political orders, there will be structures—ideological and institutional—that survive and prolong the life of neoliberalism in some form. Various Republican governors are determined to keep aloft the banner of deregulation, promoting it as the best path toward a future that enshrines personal freedom. But a presidential victory by someone like Governor Ron DeSantis of Florida in 2024 would be unlikely to trigger a straightforward restoration of a neoliberal order. More likely would be a deepening of the political configuration that merges elements of neoliberalism with aspects of Trump-style GOP populism.

The entrenched financialization of the American economy likewise offers no guarantee that a neoliberal order will soon be restored. Central banks in the United States and elsewhere grew larger and accumulated more power in the aftermath of the Great Recession; they continue to play a key role in shaping the economy. Jerome Powell, the chairman appointed by Trump to succeed Janet Yellen to head the Federal Reserve, wielded Fed power boldly in response to the pandemic-induced economic collapse of 2020. The speed and amplitude of his actions matched those of Ben Bernanke when the latter was responding to the Great Recession. Both broke decisively with Greenspan-style reluctance to interfere with the "natural" operation of markets.

Central banks such as the Federal Reserve are often regarded as a form of elite rule, far more inclined to protect the interests of capital and shareholders than of ordinary citizens. But Powell's 2020 interventions in the economy also marked a departure for the Federal Reserve, manifest in its support of vast government aid for small business, for the unemployed, for families in need of child support, and for the relief of individuals unable to pay their rent.

The Fed did not devise such policies, of course; Congress did. But Powell signaled that these sorts of actions were essential to the nation's economic welfare. He urged Congress to move quickly on them. With his encouragement, the federal government did much more to assist ordinary Americans in the wake of the pandemic than it had in the aftermath of the Great Recession. The scale of assistance not only provided relief to tens of millions. It also began to alter somewhat the balance of power between the poor and rich in American society. Many in the ranks of the poor quit their jobs across the pandemic's first eighteen months; significant numbers among those who remained employed felt emboldened to demand wage increases and other improvements in the conditions of their work. The American labor movement, in turn, began to show signs of vigor after decades of futility. By the end of 2021, wages for low-income earners had begun to rise more rapidly than those for high-income earners. That had not happened in forty years.[57]

Is it possible, then, to read into the Fed's 2020–2021 actions the emergence of a newly democratized politics of public finance? If so, it is happening by increasing rather than reducing the powers of the Fed and by deploying them to benefit a far-larger cross-section of Americans. The repurposing of the Fed may turn out to be a moment of exception that ended once fears of pandemic illness and death receded. The 2022 inflation spike saw the Fed focus, perhaps inevitably, on its more traditional role of calming financial markets. Nevertheless, the Fed's 2020–2021 moment of populist experimentation will not be forgotten, and will likely inspire future efforts to substantively change a key government agency's political character.[58] If future experiments of this sort do occur, we may need to move away from understanding "financialization" simply as a code word for neoliberal triumph and as indicating instead the opening of a new terrain on which elite and popular forces vie for influence and control.

The survival of cultural elements of neoliberalism likewise offers no guarantee that the neoliberal order itself is alive and well. Cultivating "entrepreneurs" of the self has long been a cardinal feature of the neoliberal order, and it shows no sign of waning. This principle has manifested itself in Silicon Valley entrepreneurs and Wall Street hedge fund managers fashioning themselves into "masters of the universe"; in hundreds of thousands of automobile owners responding to Uber's and Lyft's invitation to become "entrepreneurs" in their own right by gaining the "freedom to choose" when and for how long they would drive their private cars as taxis; in "analytics" movements in baseball and other sports seeking to sculpt athletes' performance through a far more systematic study of human inputs and outputs than had ever been attempted before; and in the obsession of millions of individuals with constantly measuring steps walked, miles run, calories consumed, and energy expended. Tens of millions are engaged daily in parallel kinds of endless calculations to determine their popularity (or lack thereof) on Twitter, Facebook, and Instagram. Never have so many people been preoccupied by such constant self-scrutiny.

The information technology revolution, another key feature of the neoliberal order, made possible this phenomenon of perpetual counting and measuring. In the utopian 1990s, the self-knowledge resulting from this revolution was held up as liberating, as delivering on the neoliberal promise of personal freedom and emancipation. Now that the technological utopianism of the 1990s and 2000s is gone, the measurement imperative that remains has become as much a mechanism for tyrannizing the self—with the relentless injunction to do or be better—as for realizing the full possibilities of one's person-hood. No political movement to release individuals from this tyranny of self-scrutiny has yet gained traction; but perhaps a visionary with a Stewart Brand-like imagination will arise to call for freeing human consciousness from tech-imposed fetters.[59]

The mere survival of elements of an order, therefore, should not be mistaken for the order itself surviving. Social Security is still a popular welfare policy in the United States, nearly ninety years after the New Deal brought it into existence. But the New Deal order of which it was so essential a part is long gone. Vestiges of the neoliberal order will be with us for years and perhaps decades to come. But the neoliberal order itself is broken.

A political order must have the ability to shape the core ideas of political life. It must be able to do so not just for one political party's most ardent supporters but for people located across the political spectrum. The New Deal order sold a large majority of Americans on the proposition that a strong central state could manage a dynamic but dangerous capitalist economy in the public interest. The neoliberal order persuaded a large majority of Americans that free markets would unleash capitalism from unnecessary state controls and spread prosperity and personal freedom throughout the ranks of Americans and then throughout the world. Neither of these propositions today commands the support or authority that they once possessed. Political disorder and uncertainty reign. What comes next is the most important question the United States, and the world, now face.

NOTES

⸺◈⸺

Introduction

1. Steve Fraser and Gary Gerstle, eds., *The Rise and Fall of the New Deal Order, 1930–1980* (Princeton, NJ: Princeton University Press, 1989). See also Gary Gerstle, Nelson Lichtenstein, and Alice O'Connor, "Introduction," to Gary Gerstle, Nelson Lichtenstein, and Alice O'Connor, eds., *Beyond the New Deal Order: U.S. Politics and Society from the Great Depression to the Great Recession* (Philadelphia: University of Pennsylvania Press, 2019), 1–16; Gary Gerstle, "America's Neoliberal Order," in Gerstle, Lichtenstein, and O'Connor, eds., *Beyond the New Deal Order*, 257–278; Gary Gerstle, "The Rise and Fall (?) of the Neoliberal Order," *Transactions of the Royal Historical Society* 28 (2018), https://www.cambridge.org/core/journals/trans actions-of-the-royal-historical-society/article/abs/rise-and-fall-of-ameri cas-neoliberal-order/8A1A9D4E2E1ABBB04D39055D35F9AA51, accessed September 26, 2021. For a parallel effort to broaden the ways in which we think about political time in the United States, see Stephen Skowronek, *Presidential Leadership in Political Time: Reprise and Reappraisal*, 3rd ed. (2008; Lawrence: University of Kansas Press, 2020).

2. For an introduction to conservative thought, see Jerry Z. Muller, ed., *Conservatism: An Anthology of Social and Political Thought from David Hume to the Present* (Princeton, NJ: Princeton University Press, 1997); Andrew Bacevich, ed., *American Conservatism: Reclaiming an Intellectual Tradition* (New York: Library of America, 2020); and Corey Robin, *The Reactionary Mind: Conservatism from Edmund Burke to Donald Trump*, 2nd ed. (New York: Oxford University Press, 2017.

3.   The process of bringing the economic transformation of the late
     twentieth century more to the fore is already under way. See Adam
     Tooze, *Crashed: How a Decade of Financial Crises Changed the World*
     (New York: Penguin Books, 2018); Adam Tooze, *Shutdown: How Covid
     Shook the World's Economy* (New York: Viking, 2021); Binyamin Appelbaum,
     *The Economists' Hour: False Prophets, Free Markets, and the Fracture of
     Society* (New York: Little, Brown and Company, 2019); Zachary D. Carter,
     The Price of Peace: Money, Democracy, and the Life of John Maynard Keynes
     (New York: Random House, 2020); Lawrence R. Jacobs and Desmond
     King, *Fed Power: How Finance Wins* (2016; New York: Oxford University
     Press, 2021); Jonathan Levy, *Ages of American Capitalism: A History of the
     United States* (New York: Random House, 2021); Margaret O'Mara, *The
     Code: Silicon Valley and the Remaking of America* (New York: Penguin
     Books, 2019). Romain Huret, Nelson Lichtenstein, and Jean-Christian Vinel,
     eds., *Capitalism Contested: The New Deal and Its Legacies* (Philadelphia:
     University of Pennsylvania Press, 2020)

4.   This argument appears in many works on neoliberalism. See, for example,
     articles by William Davies: "What Is 'Neo' About Neoliberalism?" *New
     Republic*, July 13, 2017, https://newrepublic.com/article/143849/neo-neolib
     eralism, accessed June 10, 2021; "The New Neoliberalism," *New Left
     Review* 101 (September–October 2016), https://newleftreview.org/issues/
     ii101/articles/william-davies-the-new-neoliberalism, accessed June 10,
     2021. See also William Davies, *The Limits of Neoliberalism: Authority,
     Sovereignty, and the Logic of Competition* (2015; London: SAGE, 2017).

5.   See William J. Novak, "The Myth of the Weak American State," *American
     Historical Review* 113 (June 2008), 752–772. See also the roundtable
     responses to Novak: John Fabian Witt, "Law and War in American
     History," *American History Review* 115 (June 2010), 768–778; Gary Gerstle,
     "A State Both Strong and Weak," *American Historical Review* 115 (June
     2010), 779–785; Julia Adams, "The Puzzle of the American State . . . and
     Its Historians," *American Historical Review* 115 (June 2010), 786–791; and
     Novak's response, William J. Novak, "Long Live the Myth of the Weak
     State? A Response to Adams, Gerstle and Witt," *American Historical Review*
     115 (June 2010), 792–800; William J. Novak, *The People's Welfare: Law
     and Regulation in Nineteenth-Century America* (Chapel Hill: University of
     North Carolina Press, 1996); R. M. Bates, "Government by Improvisation?
     Towards a New History of the Nineteenth-Century American State,"
     Journal of Policy History 33 (2021), https://www.cambridge.org/core/journals/
     journal-of-policy-history/article/abs/government-by-improvisation-towards-
     a-new-history-of-the-nineteenthcentury-american-state/80DAFA991E456
     F52C82B224E5D2B5B40, accessed September 6, 2021; Gary Gerstle, *Liberty
     and Coercion: The Paradox of American Government from the Founding
     to the Present* (Princeton, NJ: Princeton University Press, 2015); Stephen
     Skowronek, *Building a New American State: The Expansion of National
     Administrative Capacity, 1877–1920* (New York: Cambridge University Press,

1982); Brian Balogh, *A Government Out of Sight: The Mystery of National Authority in Nineteenth-Century America* (New York: Cambridge University Press, 2009); James T. Sparrow, Stephen W. Sawyer, and William J. Novak, eds., *Boundaries of the State in US History* (Chicago, IL: University of Chicago Press, 2015).

6. See, for example, F. A. Hayek, *The Constitution of Liberty: The Definitive Edition*, edited by Ronald Hamowy, vol. 17 of *The Collected Works of F. A. Hayek* (1960; Chicago, IL: University of Chicago Press, 2011), 529–530; and Milton Friedman, *Capitalism and Freedom*, 40th anniversary ed. (1962; Chicago, IL: University of Chicago Press, 2002), 5–6.

7. Until recently, many historians have been reluctant to deploy the term "neoliberal" in their writing about the second half of the twentieth century. That reluctance is now on the wane. For an example of this earlier skepticism, and debates about it, see Daniel Rodgers, "The Uses and Abuses of 'Neoliberalism,'" *Dissent* (Winter 2018), https://www.dissentmagazine.org/article/uses-and-abuses-neoliberalism-debate; and "Debating the Uses and Abuses of 'Neoliberalism': A Forum," with comments by Julia Ott, Nathan Connolly, Mike Konczal, and Timothy Shenk, and a reply by Daniel Rodgers, *Dissent*, January 22, 2018, https://www.dissentmagazine.org/online_articles/debating-uses-abuses-neoliberalism-forum, accessed September 28, 2021. See also Kim Phillips-Fein, "The History of Neoliberalism," in Brent Cebul, Lily Geismer, and Mason B. Williams, eds., *Shaped by the State: Toward a New Political History of the Twentieth Century* (Chicago, IL: University of Chicago Press, 2019), 347–362; Rajesh Venugopal, "Neoliberalism as Concept," *Economy and Society* 44 (May 2015), 165–187; and Angus Burgin, "The Neoliberal Turn," unpublished essay in author's possession.

   For some of the best work on neoliberalism written by historians, see Angus Burgin, *The Great Persuasion: Reinventing Free Markets Since the Depression* (Cambridge, MA: Harvard, 2012); Quinn Slobodian, *Globalists: The End of Empire and the Birth of Neoliberalism* (Cambridge, MA: Harvard University Press, 2018); and Amy C. Offner, *Sorting Out the Mixed Economy: The Rise and Fall of Welfare and Developmental States in the Americas* (Princeton, NJ: Princeton University Press, 2019).

   The literature on neoliberalism written by political theorists and social scientists is rich. Important works include Michel Foucault, *The Birth of Biopolitics: Lectures at the Collège de France, 1978–1979*, trans. Graham Burchell (2004; New York: Picador, 2008); David Harvey, *A Brief History of Neoliberalism* (New York: Oxford University Press, 2005); Jamie Peck, *Constructions of Neoliberal Reason* (New York: Oxford University Press, 2010); Wendy Brown, *Undoing the Demos: Neoliberalism's Stealth Revolution* (New York: Zone Books, 2015); Melinda Cooper, *Family Values: Between Neoliberalism and the New Social Conservatism* (New York: Zone Books, 2017); Monica Prasad, *The Politics of Free Markets: The Rise of Neoliberal Economic Policies in Britain, France, Germany, and the United States* (Chicago, IL: University of Chicago Press, 2006); Monica Prasad, *Starving the Beast: Ronald Reagan and the Tax*

Cut Revolution (New York: Russell Sage Foundation, 2018); Greta R. Krippner, *Capitalizing on Crisis: The Political Origins of the Rise of Finance* (Cambridge, MA: Harvard University Press, 2012); Mark Blyth, *Austerity: The History of a Dangerous Idea* (New York: Oxford University Press, 2013); Philip Mirowski and Dieter Plehwe, eds., *The Road from Mont Pèlerin: The Making of the Neoliberal Thought Collective* (Cambridge, MA: Harvard University Press, 2009); Loïc Wacquant: *Punishing the Poor: The Neoliberal Government of Social Insecurity* (Durham, NC: Duke University Press, 2009); Davies, *The Limits of Neoliberalism*; Pierre Dardot and Christian Laval, *The New Way of the World: On Neo-Liberal Society*, trans. Gregory Elliott (2009; New York: Verso, 2013); Jonathan Hopkin, *Anti-System Politics: The Crisis of Market Liberalism in Rich Democracies* (New York: Oxford University Press, 2020). Valuable recent anthologies on neoliberalism include Damien Cahill, Melinda Cooper, Martijn Konings, and David Primrose, eds., *The SAGE Handbook of Neoliberalism* (London: SAGE, 2018); and Jamie Peck and Nik Theodore, eds., *Neoliberalism's Authoritarian (Re)Turns,* an issue of *South Atlantic Quarterly* 118 (April 2019), 240 pp.

8.   Nancy MacLean, *Democracy in Chains: The Deep History of the Radical Right's Stealth Plan for America* (New York: Penguin Books, 2017); Slobodian, *Globalists;* Wacquant, *Punishing the Poor;* Jane Mayer, *Dark Money: The Hidden History of the Billionaires Behind the Rise of the Radical Right* (New York: Anchor Books, 2016); Mirowski and Plehwe, eds., *The Road from Mont Pèlerin*; Wolfgang Streek, *How Will Capitalism End?* (New York: Verso, 2016).

9.   Goodman, *Growing Up Absurd: Problems of Youth in the Organized Society* (1960; New York: New York Review of Books Classics, 2012); "Port Huron Statement," 1962, Sixties Project, http://www2.iath.virgi nia.edu/sixties/HTML_docs/Resources/Primary/Manifestos/SDS_Por t_Huron.html, accessed September 9, 2021. The contributions of the New Left to neoliberalism (discussed in Chapter 3) have gone largely unappreciated. For recent work that points in this direction, see Paul Sabin, "Environmental Law and the End of the New Deal Order," in Gerstle, Lichtenstein, and O'Connor, eds., *Beyond the New Deal Order* and Reuel Schiller, "Regulation and the Collapse of the New Deal Order, or How I Learned to Stop Worrying and Love the Market," in Gerstle, Lichtenstein, and O'Connor, eds., *Beyond the New Deal Order,* 186–203 and 168–185; Paul Sabin, *Public Citizens: The Attack on Big Government and the Remaking of American Liberalism* (New York: W. W. Norton, 2021); Lily Geismer, "Agents of Change: Microenterprise, Welfare Reform, the Clintons, and Liberal Forms of Neoliberalism," *Journal of American History* 107 (June 2020), 107–131; Lily Geismer, "Change Their Heads: The National Homeownership Strategy, Asset Building and Democratic Neoliberalism," 2019 Organization of American Historians (OAH) paper, in author's possession. I have

also found the writings of Michel Foucault, Jamie Peck, and Daniel T. Rodgers extremely helpful in understanding how neoliberal ideas ranged widely across the political landscape. See Foucault, *The Birth of Biopolitics*, 215–289; Peck, *Constructions of Neoliberal Reason*; Daniel T. Rodgers, *Age of Fracture* (Cambridge, MA: Belknap Press of Harvard University Press, 2011).

10. Burgin, *The Great Persuasion;* Slobodian, *Globalists;* Harvey, *A Brief History of Neoliberalism;* Offner, *Sorting Out the Mixed Economy.* See also Noam Chomsky, *Profit Over People: Neoliberalism and the Global Order* (New York: Seven Stories Press, 1999); Naomi Klein, *The Shock Doctrine: The Rise of Disaster Capitalism* (New York: Picador, 2008); Daniel Stedman Jones, *Masters of the Universe: Hayek, Friedman, and the Birth of Neoliberal Politics* (Princeton, NJ: Princeton University Press, 2012).

11. This view is one that Eric Hobsbawm long advanced. See Hobsbawm, *The Age of Extremes: A History of the World, 1914–1991* (New York: Vintage Books, 1994). In more recent years, it has become a major theme in the writing of Odd Arne Westad. See, for example, Westad, *The Cold War: A World History* (New York: Basic Books, 2017). See also Stephen A. Smith, ed., *The Oxford Handbook of the History of Communism* (New York: Oxford University Press, 2014).

12. The theory of totalitarianism as elaborated by Hannah Arendt and others is now regarded as flawed. But this critique should not be allowed to obscure the conviction of many during the middle decades of the twentieth century that the theory provided the truest insight available into the nature of communist regimes. Hannah Arendt, *Origins of Totalitarianism* (New York: Schocken Books, 1951).

13. This point is so common in the literature that it verges on the axiomatic. See, for example, Ellen Schrecker, *Many Are the Crimes: McCarthyism in America* (Boston: Little, Brown, 1998), and my own earlier work, including Gary Gerstle, *Working-Class Americanism: The Politics of Labor in a Textile City, 1914–1960* (New York: Cambridge University Press, 1989). For a fuller list of citations, see the relevant notes in Chapter 1.

14. I made this point for the first time in *Liberty and Coercion: The Paradox of American Government from the Founding to the Present* (Princeton, NJ: Princeton University Press, 2015), Chapter 8.

15. On the stakes of this global struggle, see Hobsbawm, *The Age of Extremes*, and Westad, *The Cold War.*

16. In thinking through this moral perspective and its connection to neoliberalism, Melinda Cooper's work has been indispensable. See her *Family Values;* see also Nancy Fraser, *Fortunes of Feminism: From State-Managed Capitalism to Neoliberal Crisis* (New York: Verso, 2013), and Nancy Fraser, *The Old Is Dying and the New Cannot Be Born: From Progressive Neoliberalism to Trump and Beyond* (New York: Verso, 2019).

17.   See, for example, Andrew Hartman, *The War for the Soul of America: A History of the Culture Wars* (Chicago, IL: University of Chicago Press, 2015), and Kevin M. Kruse and Julian E. Zelizer, *Fault Lines: A History of the United States Since 1974* (New York: W. W. Norton, 2019).

18.   Alan I. Abramowitz, *The Polarized Public: Why American Politics Is So Dysfunctional* (New York: Pearson, 2013); Abramowitz, *The Disappearing Center: Engaged Citizens, Polarization, and American Democracy* (New Haven, CT: Yale University Press, 2010); Sam Rosenfeld, *The Polarizers: Postwar Architects of Our Partisan Era* (Chicago, IL: University of Chicago Press, 2017); Daniel Schlozman and Sam Rosenfeld, "The Hollow Parties," in F. Lee and N. McCarty, eds., *Can America Govern Itself?* (New York: Social Science Research Council, 2019), 120–152.

19.   On these signal moments, see also Skowronek, *Presidential Leadership in Political Time*.

Chapter 1

1.   David E. Hamilton, "Herbert Hoover: Life in Brief," Miller Center, University of Virginia, https://millercenter.org/president/hoover/life-in-brief, accessed September 9, 2021. For more on Hoover, see Joan Hoff Wilson, *Forgotten Progressive* (1975; Long Grove, IL: Waveland Press, 1992); William E. Leuchtenburg, *Herbert Hoover: The American Presidents Series: The 31st President, 1929–1933* (New York: Times Books, Henry Holt, 2009); Glen Jeansonne and David Luhrssen, *Herbert Hoover: A Life* (New York: New American Library, 2016); Kenneth Whyte, *Hoover: An Extraordinary Life in Extraordinary Times* (New York: Knopf Doubleday, 2017).

2.   On the impact of the Great Depression, see William E. Leuchtenburg, *Franklin D. Roosevelt and the New Deal, 1932–40* (1963; New York: Harper Perennial, 2013); David M. Kennedy, *Freedom from Fear: The American People in Depression and War, 1929–1945* (New York: Oxford University Press, 1999); Arthur M. Schlesinger Jr., *The Crisis of the Old Order: 1919–1933, The Age of Roosevelt*, vol. 1 (1957; New York: First Mariner Books, 2003); Robert S. McElvaine, *The Great Depression: America, 1929–1941* (1984; New York: Three Rivers Press, 2009).

3.   The phrase is drawn from FDR's acceptance speech in 1932. Franklin D. Roosevelt, "Address Accepting the Presidential Nomination, 1932," https://www.presidency.ucsb.edu/documents/address-accepting-the-presidential-nomination-the-democratic-national-convention-chicago-1, accessed July 6, 2021.

4.   Kristi Anderson, *The Creation of a Democratic Majority, 1928–1936* (Chicago, IL: University of Chicago Press, 1979); Paul Kleppner, *Who Voted? The Dynamics of Electoral Turnout, 1870–1980* (New York: Praeger, 1982); Nancy J. Weiss, *Farewell to the Party of Lincoln: Black Politics in the Age of FDR* (Princeton, NJ: Princeton University Press, 1983); Steve Fraser,

"The 'Labor Question,'" in Steve Fraser and Gary Gerstle, eds., *The Rise and Fall of the New Deal Order, 1930–1980* (Princeton, NJ: Princeton University Press, 1989), 55–84; Thomas Ferguson, "Industrial Conflict and the Coming of the New Deal: The Triumph of Multinational Liberalism in America," in Fraser and Gerstle, eds., *The Rise and Fall of the New Deal Order*, 3–31; Michael Bernstein, "Why the Great Depression Was Great: Toward a New Understanding of the Interwar Economic Crisis in the United States," in Fraser and Gerstle, eds., *The Rise and Fall of the New Deal Order*, 33–54; Bert Cochran, *Labor and Communism: The Conflict That Shaped American Unions* (Princeton, NJ: Princeton University Press, 1977); Walter Dean Burnham, *Critical Elections and the Mainsprings of American Politics* (New York: W. W. Norton, 1970).

5. Jordan A. Schwarz, *The New Dealers: Power Politics in the Age of Roosevelt* (New York: Knopf, 1993); McElvaine, *The Great Depression*; Arthur Schlesinger Jr., *The Coming of the New Deal, 1933–1935*, vol. 2 of *The Age of Roosevelt* (1958; New York: First Mariner Books, 2003); Richard H. Pells, *Radical Visions and American Dreams: Culture and Social Thought in the Depression Years* (1973; Champaign: University of Illinois Press, 1998); Michael Denning, *The Cultural Front: The Laboring of American Culture in the Twentieth Century* (New York: Verso, 1996); Barbara Melosh, *Engendering Culture: Manhood and Womanhood in New Deal Public Art and Theater* (Washington, DC: Smithsonian Institution Press, 1991); Lauren Sklaroff, *Black Culture and the New Deal: The Quest for Civil Rights in the Roosevelt Era* (Chapel Hill: University of North Carolina Press, 2009); Eric Rauchway, *Why the New Deal Matters* (New Haven, CT: Yale University Press, 2021).

6. Schlesinger, *The Coming of the New Deal*; Leuchtenburg, *Franklin D. Roosevelt and the New Deal*; Ira Katznelson, *Fear Itself: The New Deal and the Origins of Our Time* (New York: Liveright, 2013).

7. Zachary D. Carter, *The Price of Peace: Money, Democracy, and the Life of John Maynard Keynes* (New York: Random House, 2020); Timothy Shenk, "Inventing the American Economy" (PhD dissertation, Columbia University, 2016); Jonathan Levy, *Ages of American Capitalism: A History of the United States* (New York: Random House, 2021), 391–435.

8. Angus Burgin, *The Great Persuasion: Reinventing Free Markets Since the Depression* (Cambridge, MA: Harvard University Press, 2015).

9. Irving Bernstein, *The Turbulent Years: A History of the American Worker, 1933–1941* (Chicago, IL: Haymarket Books, 2010); Jerold S. Auerbach, *Labor and Liberty: The La Follette Committee and the New Deal* (Indianapolis, IN: Bobbs-Merrill, 1966); Fraser, "The 'Labor Question'"; Nelson Lichtenstein, *State of the Union: A Century of American Labor* (Princeton, NJ: Princeton University Press, 2002); Jefferson Cowie, *The Great Exception: The New Deal and the Limits of American Politics* (Princeton, NJ: Princeton University Press, 2016); Bruce Nelson, *Workers*

on the Waterfront: Seamen, Longshoremen, and Unionism in the 1930s
(Chicago: University of Illinois Press, 1990).

10. Lichtenstein, *State of the Union*, 20–97; Gary Gerstle, *Liberty and Coercion: The Paradox of American Government from the Founding to the Present* (Princeton, NJ: Princeton University Press, 2015), chapter 7; Nelson Lichtenstein, *The Most Dangerous Man in Detroit: Walter Reuther and the Fate of American Labor* (New York: Basic Books, 1995); Lizabeth Cohen, *Making a New Deal: Industrial Workers in Chicago, 1919–1939* (New York: Cambridge University Press, 1990); Christopher L. Tomlins, *The State and the Unions: Labor Relations, Law, and the Organized Labor Movement in America, 1880–1960* (New York: Cambridge University Press, 1985); Steve Fraser, *Labor Will Rule: Sidney Hillman and the Rise of American Labor* (New York: Free Press, 1993); James A. Gross, *The Making of the National Labor Relations Board: A Study in Economics, Politics and Law, 1933–1937* (Albany: State University of New York Press, 1974); Nelson Lichtenstein and Howell Harris, eds., *Industrial Democracy in America: The Ambiguous Promise* (Washington, DC: Woodrow Wilson Center Press, 1993).

11. Sidney Fine, *Sit-Down: The General Motors Strike of 1936–1937* (Ann Arbor: University of Michigan Press, 1969); Lichtenstein, *The Most Dangerous Man in Detroit*; Eric J. Hobsbawm, *The Age of Extremes: A History of the World, 1914–1991* (New York: Pantheon Books, 1994), 9.

12. Lichtenstein, *The Most Dangerous Man in Detroit*, 288; Lichtenstein, *State of the Union*.

13. Gerstle, *Liberty and Coercion*, chapters 7 and 8; Thomas Piketty, *Capital in the Twenty-First Century* (Cambridge, MA: Belknap Press of Harvard University Press, 2014).

14. Paul Krugman, *The Conscience of a Liberal* (New York: W. W. Norton, 2007), 46–47.

15. The turn toward government as a key facilitator of personal freedom was an instance of what the political philosopher Isaiah Berlin would later the label the shift from "negative liberty" to "positive liberty." See Isaiah Berlin, "Two Concepts of Liberty," in *Liberty*, ed. Henry Hardy (New York: Oxford University Press, 2002).

16. *The Communications Act of 1934*, 47 U.S.C. § 151 et se, https://transit ion.fcc.gov/Reports/1934new.pdf, accessed July 6, 2021. The 1934 Communications Act adhered to principles worked out in the Radio Act of 1927. On these two acts, and the "public interest" principles on which they were founded, see Willard D. Rowland Jr., "The Meaning of the 'Public Interest' in Communications Policy, Part I: Its Origins in State and Federal Regulation," *Communications Law and Policy* 2 (1997), 309–328; Willard D. Rowland Jr., "The Meaning of the 'Public Interest' in Communications Policy, Part II: Its Implementation in Early Broadcast Law and Regulation," *Communications Law and Policy* 2

(1997), 363–396; Erwin G. Krasnow, Lawrence D. Longley, and Herbert A. Terry, *The Politics of Broadcast Regulation*, 3rd ed. (New York: St. Martin's Press, 1982); Susan J. Douglas, *Inventing American Broadcasting, 1899–1922* (Baltimore, MD: Johns Hopkins University Press, 1987); and Patricia Auhferheide, *Communications Policy and the Public Interest: The Telecommunications Act of 1996* (New York: Guildford Press, 1999), 5–18.

17. On the consumption ideal and the New Deal, see Fraser, "The 'Labor Question' "; Cohen, *Making a New Deal*; Lizabeth Cohen, *A Consumers' Republic: The Politics of Mass Consumption in Postwar America* (New York: Knopf, 2003); Meg Jacobs, *Pocketbook Politics: Economic Citizenship in Twentieth-Century America* (Princeton, NJ: Princeton University Press, 2004); Robert M. Collins, *More: The Politics of Economic Growth in Postwar America* (New York: Oxford University Press, 2000).

18. In 1956, Arthur M. Schlesinger Jr. coined the term "qualitative liberalism" to denote the cultivation of personhood that he hoped modern liberalism would nourish. He contrasted this liberalism with the "quantitative liberalism" oriented to providing individuals with good jobs, sound incomes, employment security, and full access to the American marketplace. The phrases "qualitative" and "quantitative" liberalism themselves were not quite right and were never widely adopted either in or beyond the academy. But they did signal modern liberalism's aspiration to cultivate personhood in ways that purely economic measures of well-being could not grasp. See Arthur M. Schlesinger Jr., "The Future of Liberalism: The Challenge of Abundance," *Reporter* 14, May 3, 1956. John Kenneth Galbraith was thinking along similar lines in his influential book, *The Affluent Society* (Boston, MA: Houghton Mifflin, 1958). On the New Deal's reliance on the social sciences, see Richard S. Kirkendall, *Social Scientists and Farm Politics in the Age of Roosevelt* (Columbia: University of Missouri Press, 1966); Gene M. Lyons, *The Uneasy Partnership: Social Science and the Federal Government in the Twentieth Century* (New York: Russell Sage Foundation, 1969); Alice O'Connor, *Poverty Knowledge: Social Science, Social Policy, and the Poor in Twentieth-Century U.S. History* (Princeton, NJ: Princeton University Press, 2002); Romain D. Huret and John Angell, *The Experts' War on Poverty: Social Research and the Welfare Agenda in Postwar America* (Ithaca, NY: Cornell University Press, 2018); Michael A. Bernstein, *A Perilous Progress: Economists and the Public Purpose in Twentieth-Century America* (Princeton, NJ: Princeton University Press, 2001); Carter, *The Price of Peace*; Andrew Jewett, *Science, Democracy, and the American University: From the Civil War to the Cold War* (New York: Cambridge University Press, 2012); Wendy L. Wall, *Inventing the "American Way": The Politics of Consensus from the New Deal to the Civil Rights Movement* (New York: Oxford University Press, 2008); David Paul Haney, *The Americanization of Social Science: Intellectuals and Public Responsibility*

in the Postwar United States (Philadelphia, PA: Temple University Press, 2008).

19. My interpretation dissents from the argument that a number of historians studying the origins of the religious right have made in the last few years: namely, that evangelical religion was much more central to American political life in the 1930s, 1940s, and 1950s than we had once thought. Evangelicals were certainly laying the foundation for a political offensive that would become powerful and influential in the 1970s and 1980s. But their political influence was secondary during the years when the New Deal order was riding high. The re-introduction of Protestant-Catholic antagonisms to Democratic Party politics during these years would have re-ignited the cultural wars that had torn apart the party in the 1920s and quite possibly would have stalled the New Deal order's quest for hegemony. Indeed, it was only when Protestants and Catholics buried their antagonisms in the 1960s and 1970s that religious influence on American politics began to soar again. For works that examine religion and politics during these years, see Kevin M. Kruse, *One Nation Under God: How Corporate America Invented Christian America* (New York: Basic Books, 2015); Darren Dochuk, *From Bible Belt to Sunbelt: Plain-Folk Religion, Grassroots Politics, and the Rise of Evangelical Conservatism* (New York: W. W. Norton, 2011); Darren Dochuk, *Anointed with Oil: How Christianity and Crude Made Modern America* (New York: Basic Books, 2019); Kevin Schultz, *Tri-Faith America: How Postwar Catholics and Jews Held America to Its Protestant Promise* (New York: Oxford University Press, 2011); David A. Hollinger, *After Cloven Tongues of Fire: Protestant Liberalism in Modern American History* (Princeton, NJ: Princeton University Press, 2013); John T. McGreevy, *Catholicism and American Freedom: A History* (New York: W. W. Norton, 2004); Frances FitzGerald, *The Evangelicals: The Struggle to Shape America* (New York: Simon and Schuster, 2017); Matthew Avery Sutton, *American Apocalypse: A History of Modern Evangelicalism* (Cambridge, MA: Belknap Press of Harvard University Press, 2014). The book on the post-1960s rapprochement between American Catholics and Protestants and its consequences for American politics has yet to be written.

20. Katznelson, *Fear Itself*; Ira Katznelson, *When Affirmative Action Was White: An Untold History of Racial Inequality in Twentieth-Century America* (New York: W. W. Norton, 2005).

21. Jean-Christian Vinel, *The Employee: A Political History* (Philadelphia: University of Pennsylvania Press, 2013); Lichtenstein, *State of the Union.*

22. Fraser and Gerstle, *The Rise and Fall of the New Deal Order*, introduction, ix–xxv.

23. I once heard Theodore Draper call the twentieth century the communist century. He was right to do so.

24. On the impact of communism, see Hobsbawm, *The Age of Extremes*; Tony Judt, *Postwar: A History of Europe Since 1945* (New York: Penguin, 2006); Ian Kershaw, *Europe: The Global Age, 1950–2017* (New York: Penguin, 2019); Odd Arne Westad, *The Cold War: A World History* (New York: Basic Books, 2017). For anticommunism's impact on American life, see Ellen Schrecker, *Many Are the Crimes: McCarthyism in America* (Boston, MA: Little, Brown, 1998); M. J. Heale, *American Anti-Communism: Combating the Enemy Within, 1830–1970* (Baltimore, MD: Johns Hopkins University Press, 1990).

25. See, for example, Ellen Schrecker, *Many Are the Crimes*; Richard H. Pells, *The Liberal Mind in a Conservative Age: American Intellectuals in the 1940s and 1950s*, 2nd rev. ed. (Middletown, CT: Wesleyan University Press, 1989).

26. Westad, *The Cold War*; Hobsbawm, *The Age of Extremes*; Silvio Pons, *The Global Revolution: A History of International Communism, 1917–1991*, trans. Allan Cameron (2012; New York: Oxford University Press, 2014); Arno J. Mayer, *Wilson vs. Lenin: Political Origins of the New Diplomacy 1917–1918* (New York: Meridian Books, 1969); Thomas J. Knock, *To End All Wars: Woodrow Wilson and the Quest for a New World Order* (New York: Oxford University Press, 1992); Erez Manela, *The Wilsonian Moment: Self-Determination and the International Origins of Anticolonial Nationalism* (New York: Oxford University Press, 2007); Adom Getachew, *Worldmaking After Empire: The Rise and Fall of Self-Determination* (Princeton, NJ: Princeton University Press, 2019).

27. Westad, *The Cold War*.

28. Stephen Kotkin, *Stalin: Paradoxes of Power, 1878–1928*, vol. 1 (London: Penguin, 2014).

29. Adam Tooze, *The Deluge: The Great War and the Remaking of the Global Order, 1916–1931* (New York: Penguin, 2014).

30. From 5 to 18 percent. Hobsbawm, *The Age of Extremes*, 96.

31. David C. Engerman, *Know Your Enemy: The Rise and Fall of America's Soviet Experts* (New York: Oxford University Press, 2009); Michael David Fox, *Showcasing the Great Experiment: Cultural Diplomacy and Western Visitors to the Soviet Union, 1921–1941* (New York: Oxford University Press 2012).

32. Joshua B. Freeman, *Behemoth: A History of the Factory and the Making of the Modern World* (New York: W. W. Norton, 2018), 199–200, 205.

33. Lichtenstein, *The Most Dangerous Man in Detroit*, 36–46.

34. Kotkin, *Stalin*; Stephen Kotkin, *Magnetic Mountain: Stalinism as a Civilization* (Berkeley: University of California Press, 1995); Timothy Snyder, *Bloodlands: Europe Between Hitler and Stalin* (London: Vintage, 2010); Mark Mazower, *Dark Continent: Europe's Twentieth Century* (London: Allen Lane, 1998); Robert Conquest, *The Harvest of Sorrow: Soviet Collectivization and the Terror-Famine* (New York: Oxford

University Press, 1986); Robert Conquest, *The Great Terror: A Reassessment* (London: Hutchinson, 1990).

35.   Schrecker, *Many Are the Crimes*; Denning, *The Cultural Front*; Harvey Klehr, *The Heyday of American Communism: The Depression Decade* (New York: Basic Books, 1984); Irving Howe and Lewis Coser, *The American Communist Party: A Critical History, 1919–1957* (Boston, MA: Beacon Press, 1957); Irving Howe, *Socialism and America* (San Diego, CA: Harcourt Brace Jovanovich, 1985), chapter 10; Maurice Isserman, *Which Side Were You On?: The American Communist Party During the Second World War* (Middletown, CT: Wesleyan University Press, 1982); Gerstle, *Liberty and Coercion*, chapters 6–8.

36.   Stephen Kotkin, *Armageddon Averted: The Soviet Collapse, 1970–2000* (New York: Oxford University Press, 2001), 32; Isserman, *Which Side Were You On?*; Pons, *The Global Revolution*, chapters 2–3; Hobsbawm, *The Age of Extremes*, chapter 5; Richard J. Evans, *The Third Reich at War* (New York: Penguin, 2009), chapters 1–2. Phillips Payson O'Brien has recently argued that the Germans were also hobbled in their attack on the Soviet Union by the need to divert airplanes and other resources to the western front to defend their homeland against the Allied air assault that began in 1943. See his *How the War Was Won: Air-Sea Power and Allied Victory in World War II* (New York: Cambridge University Press, 2019).

37.   Westad, *The Cold War*, 74.

38.   Gerald Horne, *Race War! White Supremacy and the Japanese Attack on the British Empire* (New York: New York University Press, 2004).

39.   Roosevelt, Wallace, and several other advisors did not regard a possible Soviet takeover of Eastern Europe as the first step toward the domination of all of Europe and then of the world. They were more inclined to view Soviet designs on Eastern Europe as a defensive maneuver to protect the Russian homeland from yet another German invasion. On this view of the Soviet Union, see Daniel Yergin, *Shattered Peace: The Origins of the Cold War and the National Security State* (Boston, MA: Houghton Mifflin, 1977).

40.   George Orwell, *Animal Farm: A Fairy Story* (London: Secker and Warburg, 1945), and *Nineteen Eighty-Four* (London: Secker and Warburg, 1949); Arthur Koestler, *Darkness at Noon* (London: Macmillan, 1940); Hannah Arendt, *The Origins of Totalitarianism* (New York: Schocken Books, 1951); Benjamin L. Alpers, *Dictators, Democracy, and American Public Culture: Envisioning the Totalitarian Enemy, 1920s–1950s* (Chapel Hill: University of North Carolina, 2003); Louis Menand, *The Free World: Art and Thought in the Cold War* (New York: Farrar, Strauss and Giroux, 2021), chapter 4.

41.   Quote drawn from Wilfried Loth, *The Division of the World, 1941–1955* (London: Routledge, 1988), 137–138. See, also, Joseph Marion Jones, *The Fifteen Weeks: An Inside Account of the Genesis of the Marshall Plan* (1955;

Boston, MA: Mariner Books, 1965), 140 and passim; Dean Acheson, *Present at the Creation: My Years in the State Department* (New York: W.W. Norton, 1969), 226–235. See also Yergin, *Shattered Peace.*

42. Quoted in Loth, *The Division of the World*, 137. William L. Clayton, under secretary of the department of commerce, reported to members of the Truman administration that western Europe was full of "hunger, economic misery and frustration." The majority of European countries, he continued, were standing "on the very brink and may be pushed over at any time; others are gravely threatened." Economic collapse would be followed by a communist takeover of power. Without American aid of enormous proportions "such affairs will become so hopeless that the seeds of World War III will inevitably be sown." See William L. Clayton, "Memorandum on the Creation of a National Council of Defense," March 5, 1947, https://www.marshallfoundation.org/library/documents/memorandum-creation-national-council-defense/, accessed July 22, 2021; and William L. Clayton, "The European Crisis Memorandum," May 27, 1947, https://www.marshallfoundation.org/library/documents/european-crisis-memorandum-secretary-economic-affairs-clayton/, accessed July 22, 2021.

43. Michael J. Hogan, *The Marshall Plan: America, Britain and the Reconstruction of Western Europe, 1947–1952* (Cambridge: Cambridge University Press, 1987); Thomas J. Schwartz, *America's Germany: John J. McCloy and the Federal Republic of Germany* (Cambridge, MA: Harvard University Press, 1991).

44. National Security Council, "NSC 68: United States Objectives and Programs for National Security," April 14, 1950, https://www.mtholy oke.edu/acad/intrel/nsc-68/nsc68-1.htm, accessed July 2, 2021; Michael J. Hogan, *Cross of Iron: Harry S. Truman and the Origins of the National Security State, 1945–1954* (Cambridge: Cambridge University Press, 1998); John Lewis Gaddis, *Strategies of Containment: A Critical Appraisal of American National Security Policy During the Cold War* (1982; New York: Oxford University Press, 2005); Melvyn P. Leffler, *A Preponderance of Power: National Security, the Truman Administration, and the Cold War* (Stanford, CA: Stanford University Press, 1992); John Lewis Gaddis, *The United States and the Origins of the Cold War, 1941–1947* (New York: Columbia University Press, 1972); Katznelson, *Fear Itself,* Part IV; Schrecker, *Many Are the Crimes*; David Caute, *The Great Fear: The Anti-Communist Purge Under Truman and Eisenhower* (New York: Simon and Schuster, 1978); David Oshinsky, *A Conspiracy So Immense: The World of Joe McCarthy* (New York: Free Press, 1983); Heale, *American Anti-Communism*; Landon R. Y. Storrs, *The Second Red Scare and the Unmaking of the New Deal Left* (Princeton, NJ: Princeton University Press, 2013); Neal Gabler, *An Empire of Their Own: How the Jews Invented Hollywood* (New York: Crown, 1988), 351–386;

Ellen Schrecker, *No Ivory Tower: McCarthyism and the Universities* (New York: Oxford University Press, 1986); Cochran, *Labor and Communism*; Harvey A. Levenstein, *Communism, Anticommunism, and the CIO* (Westport, CT: Greenwood Press, 1981); Stephen J. Whitfield, *The Culture of the Cold War*, 2nd ed. (Baltimore, MD: Johns Hopkins University Press, 1996); Menand, *The Free World*.

45. See Arthur M. Schlesinger Jr., *The Vital Center: The Politics of Freedom* (Boston, MA: Houghton Mifflin, 1949).

46. Alonzo Hamby, "The Vital Center, the Square Deal, and the Quest for a Liberal Political Economy," *American Historical Review* 77 (June 1972), 653–678; Godfrey Hodgson, *America in Our Time: From World War II to Nixon* (New York: Doubleday, 1976); Pells, *The Liberal Mind in a Conservative Age*; Schrecker, *Many Are the Crimes*; Jonathan Bell, *The Liberal State on Trial: The Cold War and American Politics in the Truman Years* (New York: Columbia University Press, 2004); Iwan Morgan and Robert Mason, eds., *The Liberal Consensus Reconsidered: American Politics and Society in the Postwar Era* (Gainesville: University Press of Florida, 2019); Storrs, *The Second Red Scare and the Unmaking of the New Deal Left*; Vinel, *The Employee*.

47. This is a somewhat different argument from the one offered by E. J. Dionne, in *Why Americans Hate Politics*, where he stressed the important role of William F. Buckley in disciplining the right wing of his movement in order to fashion a conservatism that might enable it at some point to bid for mainstream support. Here I argue that the bulk of the Republican Party capitulated to the core political economic principles for the sake of waging a successful Cold War against communism. In the short term, this capitulation had the effect of deepening the marginalization of Buckley and his supporters. E. J. Dionne Jr., *Why Americans Hate Politics* (New York: Simon and Schuster, 1991).

48. For more on Robert A. Taft, see James T. Patterson, *Mr. Republican: A Biography of Robert A. Taft* (Boston, MA: Houghton Mifflin, 1972).

49. Quoted in Patterson, *Mr. Republican*, 151–152.

50. Quoted in Patterson, *Mr. Republican*, 157.

51. Geoffrey Matthews, "Robert A. Taft, the Constitution, and American Foreign Policy, 1939–53," *Journal of Contemporary History* 17 (July 1982), 508–509.

52. Patterson, *Mr. Republican*, 216–217. By 1941, Taft had to concede that a Nazi-dominated world would not be ideal, but he insisted that it was still better than war and that it would not cause America's demise as a "great and prosperous democracy." Vernon Van Dyke and Edward Lane Davis, "Senator Taft and American Security," *Journal of Politics* 14 (May 1952), 182.

53. Robert A. Taft, *The Papers of Robert A. Taft*, vol. 3, *1945–1948*, ed.
     Clarence E. Wunderlin (Kent, OH: Kent State University Press, 2003),
     passim.

54. As late as September 1941 Taft was adamant that "the threat of attack by
     Hitler is, and always has been, a bugaboo to scare the American people
     into war." Van Dyke and Lane Davis, "Senator Taft and American
     Security," 179–180; Robert A. Taft, "Washington Report," August 3, 1949,
     quoted in John E. Moser, "Principles Without a Program: Senator Robert
     A. Taft and American Foreign Policy," *Ohio History* 108 (1999), 177–92.
     For more on Taft's foreign policy positions during the Cold War, see his *A
     Foreign Policy for Americans* (New York: Doubleday, 1951).

55. Harold Lasswell, "The Garrison State," *American Journal of Sociology* 46
     (1941), 455–468. See also Aaron L. Friedberg, *In the Shadow of the Garrison
     State: America's Anti-Statism and Its Cold War Grand Strategy* (Princeton,
     NJ: Princeton University Press, 2000).

56. Dwight D. Eisenhower, Inaugural Address, January 20, 1953, https://
     www.presidency.ucsb.edu/documents/inaugural-address-3, accessed
     September 10, 2019.

57. Quoted in Stephen E. Ambrose, *Eisenhower: Soldier and President*
     (New York: Simon and Schuster, 1990), 298.

58. From 1947 to 1960, real wages in the auto industry nearly doubled.
     Lichtenstein, *The Most Dangerous Man in Detroit*, 288; Lichtenstein, *The
     State of the Union*, 56.

59. Gerstle, *Liberty and Coercion*, 273.

60. Dwight D. Eisenhower, "Radio and Television Address to the
     American People on the Tax Program," March 15, 1954, *Public Papers
     of the Presidents of the United States: Dwight D. Eisenhower, 1954*
     (Washington, DC: Government Printing Office, 1960), 313–318. See also
     John F. Witte, *The Politics and Development of the Federal Income Tax*
     (Madison: University of Wisconsin Press, 1985), 146–150; and Iwan W.
     Morgan, *Eisenhower Versus "the Spenders": The Eisenhower Administration,
     the Democrats, and the Budget, 1953–60* (New York: St. Martin's
     Press, 1990).

61. Ambrose, *Eisenhower*, 545.

62. Federal-Aid Highway Act of 1956, Public Law 627, June 29, 1956; Tom
     Lewis, *Divided Highways: Building the Interstate Highways, Transforming
     American Life* (Ithaca, NY: Cornell University Press, 2013); Earl Swift, *The
     Big Roads: The Untold Story of the Engineers, Visionaries, and Trailblazers
     Who Created the American Superhighways* (Boston, MA: Houghton
     Mifflin, 2011); Owen D. Gutfreund, *Twentieth-Century Sprawl: Highways
     and the Reshaping of the American Landscape* (New York: Oxford
     University Press, 2004); David James St. Clair, *The Motorization of
     American Cities* (New York: Praeger, 1986); Dianne Perrier, *Onramps and*

Overpasses: A Cultural History of Interstate Travel (Gainesville: University Press of Florida, 2009).

63.   Elaine Tyler May, *Homeward Bound: American Families in the Cold War Era* (New York: Basic Books, 1988), 16–20.

64.   Eisenhower to Edgar Newton Eisenhower, November 8, 1954, *The Papers of Dwight D. Eisenhower*, vol. 15, *The Presidency: The Middle Way* (Baltimore, MD: Johns Hopkins University Press, 1996), 1386.

65.   On Buckley's beginnings, see Dionne, *Why Americans Hate Politics*, and Carl T. Bogus, *Buckley: William F. Buckley Jr. and The Rise of American Conservatism* (New York: Bloomsbury Press, 2011).

66.   On Reagan, see Chapters 3 and 4 of this book.

67.   Henry Hazlitt, "Ike's Semi New Deal," *Newsweek*, February 15, 1954, in Henry Hazlitt, *Business Tides: The Newsweek Era of Henry Hazlitt*, (Auburn, AL: Ludwig von Mises Institute, 2011), 343–344.

68.   Henry Hazlitt, "Still More Inflation?," *Newsweek*, March 8, 1954, in Hazlitt, *Business Tides*, 346.

69.   Henry Hazlitt, "The Policy Is Inflation," *Newsweek*, July 5, 1954, in Hazlitt, *Business Tides*, 352–353.

70.   On Milton Friedman's use of the term, see his "The Economy: We Are All Keynesians Now," *Time*, December 31, 1965, http://content.time.com/time/subscriber/article/0,33009,842353,00.html, accessed July 10, 2019. Nixon would himself run with this phrase in 1968 and beyond. See Daniel Stedman Jones, *Masters of the Universe: Hayek, Friedman, and the Birth of a Neoliberal Politics* (Princeton, NJ: Princeton University Press, 2014), 221.

Chapter 2

1.   Ira Katznelson, *Fear Itself: The New Deal and the Origins of Our Time* (New York: Liveright, 2013); Ira Katznelson, *When Affirmative Action Was White: An Untold History of Racial Inequality in Twentieth-Century America* (New York: W. W. Norton, 2005); David A. Bateman, Ira Katznelson, and John S. Lapinski, *Southern Nation: Congress and White Supremacy After Reconstruction* (New York: Russell Sage Foundation and Princeton, NJ: Princeton University Press, 2020).

2.   Gary Gerstle, *American Crucible: Race and Nation in the Twentieth Century* (Princeton, NJ: Princeton University Press, 2017), chapters 4–5.

3.   Gerald Horne, *Race War! White Supremacy and the Japanese Attack on the British Empire* (New York: New York University Press, 2004); Odd Arne Westad, *The Cold War: A World History* (New York: Basic Books, 2019); Nico Slate, *Colored Cosmopolitanism: The Shared Struggle for Freedom in the United States and India* (Cambridge, MA: Harvard University Press, 2012); Penny M. von Eschen, *Race Against Empire: Black Americans and Anticolonialism, 1937–1957* (Ithaca, NY: Cornell University Press, 1997); Penny M. von Eschen, *Satchmo Blows Up the World: Jazz Ambassadors*

Play the Cold War (Cambridge, MA: Harvard University Press, 2004); Merve Fejzula, "Negritude and Black Cultural Citizenship Across Senegal, Nigeria, and the United States, 1945–66" (PhD dissertation, University of Cambridge, 2019); Sarah C. Dunstan, *Black Activism in the French Empire and the United States from World War I to the Cold War* (Cambridge: Cambridge University Press, 2021); Adom Getachew, *Worldmaking after Empire: The Rise and Fall of Self-Determination* (Princeton, NJ: Princeton University Press, 2019).

4.   Mary L. Dudziak, *Cold War Civil Rights: Race and the Image of American Democracy* (Princeton, NJ: Princeton University Press, 2000), chapters 2–5.

5.   Dudziak, *Cold War Civil Rights*, chapters 2–5. Brief for the United States as amicus curiae, 7–8, *Brown v. Board of Education*, 347 U.S. 483 (1954). See also John David Skrentny, "The Effect of the Cold War on African-American Civil Rights: America and the World Audience," *Theory and Society* 27 (1998), 237–285; Brenda Gayle Plummer, *Rising Wind: Black Americans and U.S. Foreign Affairs, 1935–1960* (Chapel Hill: University of North Carolina Press, 1996); Jonathan Rosenberg, *How Far the Promised Land? World Affairs and the American Civil Rights Movement from the First World War to Vietnam* (Princeton, NJ: Princeton University Press, 2006). See also Gerstle, *American Crucible*, 249–250 and passim.

6.   That the American foreign policy establishment was driven more by Cold War considerations than a conviction that African Americans deserved full equality and justice also explains their vacillation on civil rights and their disinclination to advance the cause unless pushed to do so by black protesters who sought and gained international media attention.

7.   For the Kennedy speech, see John F. Kennedy, "Radio and Television Report to the American People on Civil Rights," in *Public Papers of the Presidents of the United States, John F. Kennedy*, January 1 to November 22, 1963 (Washington, DC: Government Printing Office, 1964), 468–469. The literature on the civil rights movement is vast. For a sampling, see Harvard Sitkoff, *The Struggle for Black Equality, 1954–1980* (New York: Hill and Wang, 1981); Robert Weisbrot, *Freedom Bound: A History of America's Civil Rights Movement* (New York: W. W. Norton, 1990); David J. Garrow, *Bearing the Cross: Martin Luther King, Jr., and the Southern Christian Leadership Conference* (New York: W. Morrow, 1986); Taylor Branch, *Parting the Waters: America in the King Years, 1954–63* (New York: Simon and Schuster, 1988), and Taylor Branch, *Pillar of Fire: America in the King Years, 1963–1965* (New York: Simon and Schuster, 1998); Clayborne Carson, *In Struggle: SNCC and the Black Awakening of the 1960s* (Cambridge, MA: Harvard University Press, 1981); George M. Fredrickson, *Black Liberation: A Comparative History of Black Ideologies in the United States and South Africa* (New York: Oxford University Press, 1995); William H. Chafe, *Civilities and Civil Rights: Greensboro, North Carolina, and the Black Struggle for Freedom* (New York: Oxford University Press, 1980);

Aldon Morris, *The Origins of the Civil Rights Movement: Black Communities Organizing for Change* (New York: Free Press, 1984); Robert Korstad and Nelson Lichtenstein, "Opportunities Found and Lost: Labor, Radicals, and the Early Civil Rights Movement," *Journal of American History* 75 (December 1988), 786–811; Jacquelyn Dowd Hall, "The Long Civil Rights Movement and the Political Uses of the Past," *Journal of American History* 91 (March 2005), 1233–1263; Charles Payne, *I've Got the Light of Freedom: The Organizing Tradition and the Mississippi Freedom Struggle* (Berkeley: University of California Press, 1995); Carl M. Brauer, *John F. Kennedy and the Second Reconstruction* (New York: Columbia University Press, 1977); Arthur M. Schlesinger Jr., *A Thousand Days: John F. Kennedy in the White House* (Boston, MA: Houghton Mifflin, 1965).

8. Julian E. Zelizer, *The Fierce Urgency of Now: Lyndon Johnson, Congress, and the Battle for the Great Society* (New York: Penguin, 2015); Robert Dallek, *Flawed Giant: Lyndon Johnson and His Times, 1961–1973* (New York: Oxford University Press, 1998); Robert A. Caro, *The Years of Lyndon Johnson: The Passage of Power* (New York: Knopf, 2012); Bruce J. Schulman, *Lyndon B. Johnson and American Liberalism: A Brief Biography with Documents* (Boston, MA: Bedford Books of St. Martin's Press, 1995).

9. Zelizer, *The Fierce Urgency of Now*; Clay Risen, *The Bill of the Century: The Epic Battle for the Civil Rights Act* (New York: Bloomsbury, 2014); Nancy MacLean, *Freedom Is Not Enough: The Opening of the American Workplace* (New York: Russell Sage Foundation and Cambridge, MA: Harvard University Press, 2006), part I. A fight at the 1964 Democratic Party Convention over who would be seated as the Mississippi delegation—the "lily-white" delegates elected by the Mississippi Democratic Party or the delegates from the Mississippi Freedom Democratic Party, a newly formed multiracial group born of the civil rights movement in the state—illuminates how Johnson struggled (unsuccessfully) to commit the nation to racial equality while keeping the white South in the Democratic Party. See Godfrey Hodgson, *America in Our Time: From World War II to Nixon – What Happened and Why* (New York: Doubleday, 1976), 213–218; Theodore H. White, *The Making of the President, 1964* (New York: Atheneum, 1965), 243–293; James Forman, *The Making of Black Revolutionaries: A Personal Account* (Washington, DC: Open Hand, 1985), 386–395; Len Holt, *The Summer That Didn't End: The Story of the Mississippi Civil Rights Project of 1964* (New York: Morrow, 1965), 149–183; John Lewis with Michael D'Orso, *Walking with the Wind: A Memoir of the Movement* (New York: Simon and Schuster, 1998), 283–299; Nelson Lichtenstein, *The Most Dangerous Man in Detroit: Walter Reuther and the Fate of American Labor* (New York: Basic Books, 1995), 392–395; Kevin Boyle, *The UAW and the Heyday of American Liberalism, 1945–1968* (Ithaca, NY: Cornell University Press, 1995), 193–196; Todd Gitlin, *The*

Sixties: Years of Hope, Days of Rage (New York: Bantam Books, 1987), 151–162; Branch, *Pillar of Fire*, 456–476.

10. Fredrik Logevall, *Embers of War: The Fall of an Empire and the Making of America's Vietnam* (New York: Random House, 2012); William Appleman Williams, Thomas McCormick, Lloyd Gardner, and Walter LaFeber, eds., *America in Vietnam: A Documentary History* (New York: Anchor Books and Doubleday, 1985); Marilyn Young, *The Vietnam Wars, 1945–1990* (New York: HarperCollins, 1991); George C. Herring, *America's Longest War: The United States and Vietnam, 1950–1975* (New York: Knopf, 1979); Max Hastings, *Vietnam: An Epic History of a Divisive War, 1945–1975* (New York: HarperCollins, 2018); Mark Atwood Lawrence, *Assuming the Burden: Europe and the American Commitment to War in Vietnam* (Berkeley: University of California Press, 2005); Mark Atwood Lawrence, *The Vietnam War: A Concise International History* (New York: Oxford University Press, 2008).

11. Fredrik Logevall, *Choosing War: The Lost Chance for Peace and the Escalation of War in Vietnam* (Berkeley: University of California Press, 1999); Andrew Preston, *The War Council: McGeorge Bundy, the NSC, and Vietnam* (Cambridge, MA: Harvard University Press, 2010); David E. Kaiser, *American Tragedy: Kennedy, Johnson, and the Origins of the Vietnam War* (Cambridge, MA: Belknap Press of Harvard University Press, 2000).

12. Gitlin, *The Sixties*; Maurice Isserman and Michael Kazin, *America Divided: The Civil War of the 1960s* (New York: Oxford University Press, 2000); Maurice Isserman and Michael Kazin, "The Failure and Success of the New Radicalism," in Steve Fraser and Gary Gerstle, eds., *The Rise and Fall of the New Deal Order, 1930–1980* (Princeton, NJ: Princeton University Press, 1989), 212–242; Simon Hall, *Peace and Freedom: The Civil Rights and Antiwar Movements in the 1960s* (Philadelphia: University of Pennsylvania Press, 2004); Elizabeth Hinton, *America on Fire: The Untold History of Police Violence and Black Rebellion Since the 1960s* (New York: Liveright, 2021). On the South's turn toward the GOP, see Kevin P. Phillips, *The Emerging Republican Majority* (New York: Anchor Books, 1970). On the erosion of support for the Democrats, South and North, see Jonathan Rieder, "The Rise of the Silent Majority," in Fraser and Gerstle, eds., *The Rise and Fall of the New Deal Order, 1930–1980*, 243–268.

13. Daniel Sargent, "The United States and the Third Globalization," paper presented at the Annual Meeting of the American Historical Association, January 2020, Washington, DC, pp. 1–2, in author's possession. See also Daniel J. Sargent, *A Superpower Transformed: The Remaking of American Foreign Policy in the 1970s* (New York: Oxford University Press, 2015).

14. Colin Gordon, *Dead on Arrival: The Politics of Health Care in Twentieth-Century America* (Princeton, NJ: Princeton University Press, 2003),

210–260; Jennifer Klein, *For All These Rights: Business, Labor, and the Shaping of America's Public-Private Welfare State* (Princeton, NJ: Princeton University Press, 2003), 204–254; Jacob S. Hacker, *The Divided Welfare State: The Battle over Public and Private Social Benefits in the United States* (New York: Cambridge University Press, 2002). On the Treaty of Detroit, see Nelson Lichtenstein, *State of the Union: A Century of American Labor* (Princeton, NJ: Princeton University Press, 2002), 123–128.

15. Michael J. Hogan, *The Marshall Plan: America, Britain and the Reconstruction of Western Europe, 1947–1952* (Cambridge: Cambridge University Press, 1987); Judith Stein, *Pivotal Decade: How the United States Traded Factories for Finance in the 1970s* (New Haven, CT: Yale University Press, 2010), 6; Quinn Slobodian, *Globalists: The End of Empire and the Birth of Neoliberalism* (Cambridge, MA: Harvard University Press, 2018); Barry J. Eichengreen, *Globalizing Capital: A History of the International Monetary System* (Princeton, NJ: Princeton University Press, 1998).

16. Throughout this period imports and exports comprised less than 10 percent of the country's GDP. Two decades of rapid European and Japanese growth (1945–1965) barely dented the United States' share of the world's capital stock and economic output. Stein, *Pivotal Decade*, 7.

17. Quoted in Stein, *Pivotal Decade*, 7.

18. Imports from Japan grew a remarkable 96 percent between 1967 and 1970. The United States was hurt during these years by the need to divert a huge portion of its resources to its military, much of it, in the era of Vietnam, being spent abroad, worsening America's balance of payments ledger sheet. Stein, *Pivotal Decade*, 7.

19. Daniel Rowe, "Beyond Reaganomics: The Long Economic Crisis and the Rebuilding of America, 1974–1988" (DPhil dissertation, University of Oxford, 2019), 136.

20. For an early evaluation of these trends, see Richard J. Barnet and Ronald E. Müller, *Global Reach: The Power of the Multinational Corporations* (New York: Simon and Schuster, 1974). See also Robert B. Reich, *The Work of Nations: Preparing Ourselves for Twenty-First-Century Capitalism* (New York: Vintage, 1991).

21. Stein, *Pivotal Decade*, 35, 37 (quote from 37).

22. This gap emerged even as the United States began extracting oil from vast, newly discovered oil fields in Texas. Even with this Texas surge, demand in the country outstripped supply. Meg Jacobs, *Panic at the Pump: The Energy Crisis and the Transformation of American Politics in the 1970s* (New York: Hill and Wang, 2016); Darren Dochuk, *Anointed by Oil: How Christianity and Crude Made Modern America* (New York: Basic Books, 2019).

23. Stein, *Pivotal Decade*, 74–100.

24. Stein, *Pivotal Decade*, 74–81 and passim.

25. Steven A. Schneider, *The Oil Price Revolution* (Baltimore, MD: Johns Hopkins University Press, 1983), 103.

26. Keynesian doctrine taught that unemployment and inflation were not supposed to rise at the same time. When unemployment rose and fewer workers were being paid, consumers had less money in their pockets. They therefore spent less, rendering prices soft and vulnerable to decline, a decline that would, in turn stimulate new purchasing, more hiring, and then a return to an expanding economy. Administrations adhering to Keynesian doctrine could manage and sometimes accelerate recovery through monetary policy (lowering interest rates in a recession) and fiscal policy (cutting taxes during a recession to put more money in the hands of consumers). They could also impose wage and price controls temporarily as a mid-course correction to the business cycle.

27. Jacobs, *Panic at the Pump*; David Farber, *Taken Hostage: The Iran Hostage Crisis and America's First Encounter with Radical Islam* (Princeton, NJ: Princeton University Press, 2005); Stuart E. Eizenstat, *President Carter: The White House Years* (New York: St. Martin's Publishing Group, 2018); Julian E. Zelizer, *Jimmy Carter: The American Presidents Series: The 39th President, 1977–1981* (New York: Henry Holt, 2010). For a global perspective on the effects of the energy crisis on the West, see Helen Thompson, *Disorder: Hard Times in the Twenty-First Century* (Oxford: Oxford University Press, 2022).

28. Stein, *Pivotal Decade*, 244.

29. General Motors lost $763 million in 1980, Ford $1.5 billion (second worst in corporate history), and Chrysler $1.7 billion (largest corporate loss in American history); Rowe, "Beyond Reaganomics," 107–108, 115–116.

30. Stein, *Pivotal Decade*, 252–253; Brock W. Yates, *The Decline and Fall of the American Automobile Industry* (New York: Vintage, 1984).

31. Stein, *Pivotal Decade*, 206.

32. *New York Daily News*, October 29, 1975, cover; https://www.google.com/url?sa=t&rct=j&q=&esrc=s&source=web&cd=&ved=2ahUKEwiw-PD8vfTxAhUHxBQKHZOTBikQFjADegQIEBAD&url=https%3A%2F%2Fwww.nydailynews.com%2Fnew-york%2Fpresident-ford-announces-won-bailout-nyc-1975-article-1.2405985&usg=AOvVawoJpIWziHveHa3CJbYej1PB, accessed July 20, 2021; Kim Phillips-Fein, *Fear City: New York's Fiscal Crisis and the Rise of Austerity Politics* (New York: Henry Holt, 2017).

33. Barry Bluestone and Bennett Harrison, *The Deindustrialization of America: Plant Closings, Community Abandonment, and the Dismantling of Basic Industry* (New York: Basic Books, 1982).

34. Spike Lee brilliantly captured the raw tensions between blacks and Italians in his series of New York–based films, including *Do the Right Thing* (1989) and *Jungle Fever* (1991). On tensions unleashed on blacks and whites by the declining urban economy, see J. Anthony

Lukas, *Common Ground: A Turbulent Decade in the Lives of Three American Families* (New York: Knopf, 1985); Ronald P. Formisano, *Boston Against Busing: Race, Class, and Ethnicity in the 1960s and 1970s* (Chapel Hill: University of North Carolina Press, 1991); Jonathan Rieder, *Canarsie: The Jews and Italians of Brooklyn Against Liberalism* (Cambridge, MA: Harvard University Press, 1985); Jim Sleeper, *The Closest of Strangers: Liberalism and the Politics of Race in New York* (New York: W. W. Norton, 1990); Jerald E. Podair, *The Strike That Changed New York: Blacks, Whites, and the Ocean Hill–Brownsville Crisis* (New Haven, CT: Yale University Press, 2002); Thomas J. Sugrue, *The Origins of the Urban Crisis: Race and Inequality in Postwar Detroit* (1996; Princeton, NJ: Princeton University Press, 2005); Heather Ann Thompson, *Whose Detroit? Politics, Labor, and Race in a Modern City* (Ithaca, NY: Cornell University Press, 2001).

35.   Stein, *Pivotal Decade*, 231.

36.   On Watergate and Nixon's resignation, see Rick Perlstein, *Nixonland: The Rise of a President and the Fracturing of America* (New York: Simon and Schuster, 2008).

37.   Zelizer, *Jimmy Carter*; Eizenstat, *President Carter*; Kai Bird, *The Outlier: The Unfinished Presidency of Jimmy Carter* (New York: Crown, 2021); Lawrence Wright, *Thirteen Days in September: Carter, Begin, and Sadat at Camp David* (New York: Knopf, 2014).

38.   Charles Mohr, "Carter, with a Long List of Campaign Promises, Now Faces the Problem of Making Good on Them," *New York Times*, November 15, 1976.

39.   Bird, *The Outlier*, 185.

40.   Eizenstat, *President Carter*, 384–387. For insights into the ways in which Nader-like progressive politics began to erode the regulatory regime of the New Deal order, see Reuel Schiller, "Regulation and Collapse of the New Deal Order, or How I Learned to Stop Worrying and Love the Market," and Paul Sabin, "Environmental Law and the End of the New Deal Order," both in Gary Gerstle, Alice O'Connor, and Nelson Lichtenstein, *Beyond the New Deal Order: U.S. Politics from the Great Depression to the Great Recession* (Philadelphia: University of Pennsylvania Press, 2019), 168–185, and 186–212. See also Paul Sabin, *Public Citizens: The Attack on Big Government and the Remaking of American Liberalism* (New York: W. W. Norton, 2021); Thomas K. McCraw, *Prophets of Regulation: Charles Francis Adams, Louis D. Brandeis, James M. Landis, Alfred E. Kahn* (Cambridge, MA: Belknap Press of Harvard University Press, 1984); and Stein, *Pivotal Decade*, 250–252.

41.   James Carter, "State of the Union Address," January 19, 1978, https://mille rcenter.org/the-presidency/presidential-speeches/january-19-1978-state-union-address, accessed February 9, 2020.

42. Alfred E. Kahn, *Lessons from Deregulation: Telecommunications and Airlines After the Crunch* (Washington, DC: Brookings Institution Press, 2003).

43. Jimmy Carter, "Economic Renewal Program Remarks," August 28, 1980, *Public Papers of the Presidents of the United States: Jimmy Carter 1980–81*, vol. 2, 1587 (Washington, DC: Government Printing Office, 1982). In his 1980 primary campaign against Carter, Kennedy called for a "Marshall Plan for America" and a "public-private 'American reindustrialization corporation.'" Rowe, "Beyond Reaganomics," 152; Bill Stahl, "Sen. Kennedy Calls for a New Partnership," *Los Angeles Times*, May 21, 1980; Sidney Blumenthal, "Drafting a Democratic Industrial Plan," *New York Times*, August 28, 1983, https://www.nytimes.com/1983/08/28/magaz ine/drafting-a-democratic-industrial-plan.html, accessed July 22, 2021; Jefferson Cowie, *Stayin' Alive: The 1970s and the Last Days of the Working Class* (New York: New Press, 2010).

44. Volcker wanted to shrink the money supply to break the back of inflation and create a stable environment for American business. Volcker was not going to use the power of the Federal Reserve to pursue full employment. He did not regard job creation as part of the Fed's mandate. Jonathan Levy, *Ages of American Capitalism: A History of the United States* (New York: Random House, 2021), 597–608.

45. Carl W. Biven, *Jimmy Carter's Economy: Policy in an Age of Limits* (Chapel Hill: University of North Carolina Press, 2002); Bruce J. Schulman, *The Seventies: The Great Shift in Culture, Society, and Politics* (New York: Da Capo Press, 2002); Stephen Skowronek, *The Politics Presidents Make: Leadership from John Adams to Bill Clinton*, 2nd ed. (1993; Cambridge, MA: Belknap Press of Harvard University Press, 1998), 361–406.

   Carter also appeared indecisive in foreign affairs, especially in regard to the Islamic Republic of Iran, which held fifty-two American hostages seized at the US embassy for more than a year. In his effort to make human rights a cardinal principle of American foreign policy, Carter displayed far more conviction and consistency. On the Iran crisis, see David Farber, *Taken Hostage*. On Jimmy Carter and human rights, see David F. Schmitz and Vanessa Walker, "Jimmy Carter and the Foreign Policy of Human Rights: The Development of a Post–Cold War Foreign Policy," *Diplomatic History* 28 (January 2004), 113–143; Mary E. Stuckey, *Jimmy Carter, Human Rights, and the National Agenda* (College Station: Texas A & M University Press, 2009); Zelizer, *Jimmy Carter*; Samuel Moyn, *The Last Utopia: Human Rights in History* (Cambridge, MA: Harvard University Press, 2010); Eizenstat, *President Carter: The White House Years*.

46. Robert C. Allen, "The Rise and Decline of the Soviet Economy," *Canadian Journal of Economics / Revue canadienne d'économique* 34

(2001), 859–881; William Easterly and Stanley Fischer, "The Soviet Economic Decline," *World Bank Economic Review* 9 (September 1995), 341–371; Johanna Bockman, *Markets in the Name of Socialism: The Left-Wing Origins of Neoliberalism* (Stanford, CA: Stanford University Press, 2011); Maurice Meisner, *Mao's China and After: A History of the People's Republic*, 3rd ed. (New York: Simon and Schuster, 1999), 449–454; Ezra F. Vogel, *Deng Xiaoping and the Transformation of China* (Cambridge, MA: Harvard University Press, 2011); Perry Anderson, "Two Revolutions," *New Left Review* 61 (January–February 2010), https://newlef treview.org/issues/ii61/articles/perry-anderson-two-revolutions, accessed July 10, 2021.

47. On the idea of free enterprise and its place in American political and popular thought, see Lawrence Glickman, *Free Enterprise: An American History* (New Haven, CT: Yale University Press, 2019).

Chapter 3

1. The phrase "thought collective" to describe the aspirations of the Mont Pèlerin Society appears in Philip Mirowski and Dieter Plehwe, eds., *The Road from Mont Pèlerin: The Making of the Neoliberal Thought Collective* (Cambridge, MA: Harvard University Press, 2009). On the origins of the term itself, see Ludwick Fleck, *Genesis and Development of a Scientific Fact*, Thaddeus J. Trenn and Robert K. Merton, eds., trans. Fred Bradley and Thaddeus J. Trenn (1935; Chicago, IL: University of Chicago Press, 1979), 38-51.

2. Michel Foucault, *The Birth of Biopolitics: Lectures at the Collège de France, 1978–1979*, trans. Graham Burchell (2004; New York: Picador, 2008), 218.

3. Stephen W. Sawyer and Daniel Steinmetz-Jenkins, eds., *Foucault, Neoliberalism, and Beyond* (London: Rowman and Littlefield, 2019), is indispensable on Foucault's thinking about neoliberalism. See, in particular, Sawyer's and Steinmetz-Jenkins's "Introduction"; Michael Behrent, "A Liberal Despite Himself: Reflections on a Debate, Reappraisals of a Question"; and Daniel Zamora, "Finding a 'Left Governmentality': Foucault's Last Decade," vii–xxi, 1–32, and 33–52, all in *Foucault, Neoliberalism, and Beyond*. See also Daniel Zamora and Michael C. Behrent, eds., *Foucault and Neoliberalism* (Cambridge: Polity Press, 2016).

4. Jamie Peck, *Constructions of Neoliberal Reason* (New York: Oxford University Press, 2010), xiii. On the varied meanings of neoliberalism across time and (international) space, see also Angus Burgin's superb essay, "The Neoliberal Turn." Paper in author's possession.

5. Gary Gerstle, "The Protean Character of American Liberalism," *American Historical Review* 99 (October 1994), 1043–1073.

6. *Declaration of Independence*, July 4, 1776, https://www.archives.gov/found ing-docs/declaration-transcript, accessed September 13, 2021; Bernard

Bailyn, *The Ideological Origins of the American Revolution* (Cambridge, MA: Belknap Press of Harvard University Press, 1967); Gordon S. Wood, *The Creation of the American Republic, 1776–1787* (Chapel Hill: University of North Carolina Press, 1969); Eric Foner, *Tom Paine and Revolutionary America* (New York: Oxford University Press, 1976); Gordon S. Wood, *The Radicalism of the American Revolution* (New York: Vintage Books, 1993); Thomas Bender, *A Nation Among Nations: America's Place in World History* (New York: Hill and Wang, 2006), chapter 2; David Armitage, *The Declaration of Independence: A Global History* (Cambridge, MA: Harvard University Press, 2007); Joanna Innes and Mark Philp, eds., *Re-Imagining Democracy in the Age of Revolutions: America, France, Britain, and Ireland* (New York: Oxford University Press, 2013); Eric Hobsbawm, *The Age of Revolution: Europe, 1789–1848* (New York: New American Library, 1962).

7. Gary Gerstle, *Liberty and Coercion: The Paradox of American Government from the Founding to the Present* (Princeton, NJ: Princeton University Press, 2015), chapter 1.

8. Adam Smith, *An Inquiry into the Nature and Causes of the Wealth of Nations*, ed. Edwin Cannan (1776; reprint, New York: Modern Library, 1965), 13 and passim; Gerstle, *Liberty and Coercion*, chapter 1. The emancipatory character of liberal thought, in its eighteenth-century guise, is often underestimated. See Istvan Hont and Michael Ignatieff, "Needs and Justice in the Wealth of Nations: An Introductory Essay," in Istvan Hont and Michael Ignatieff, eds., *Wealth and Virtue: The Shaping of Political Economy in the Scottish Enlightenment* (New York: Cambridge University Press, 1983), 1–44; Gerstle, "The Protean Character of American Liberalism."

9. Helena Rosenblatt, *The Lost History of Liberalism: From Ancient Rome to the Twenty-First Century* (Princeton, NJ: Princeton University Press, 2018); the following four books by David Brion Davis: *The Problem of Slavery in Western Culture* (Ithaca, NY: Cornell University Press, 1966); *The Problem of Slavery in the Age of Revolution, 1770–1823* (Ithaca, NY: Cornell University Press, 1975); *The Problem of Slavery in the Age of Emancipation* (New York: Knopf, 2014); and *Inhuman Bondage: The Rise and Fall of Slavery in the New World* (New York: Oxford University Press, 2006); Thomas L. Haskell, "Capitalism and the Origins of the Humanitarian Sensibility, Part I," *American Historical Review* 90 (April 1985), 339–361, and "Capitalism and the Origins of the Humanitarian Sensibility, Part II," *American Historical Review* 90 (June 1985), 547–566; Christopher Leslie Brown, *Moral Capital: Foundations of British Abolitionism* (Chapel Hill: University of North Carolina, 2006); Sally G. McMillen, *Seneca Falls and the Origins of the Women's Rights Movement* (New York: Oxford University Press, 2008); Sean Wilentz, *Chants Democratic: New York City and the Rise of the American Working Class, 1788–1850* (New York: Oxford University Press, 1984); Leslie Butler,

Critical Americans: Victorian Intellectuals and Transatlantic Liberal Reform (Chapel Hill: University of North Carolina Press, 2007).

10.   Walter Lippmann, *The Good Society* (1937; London: Billing and Sons, 1944), 192–193.

11.   Adam Gopnik, *A Thousand Small Sanities: The Moral Adventure of Liberalism* (New York: Basic Books, 2019); Eric Foner, *Free Soil, Free Labor, Free Men: The Ideology of the Republican Party Before the Civil War* (New York: Oxford University Press, 1970); Eric Foner, *The Fiery Trial: Abraham Lincoln and American Slavery* (New York: W. W. Norton, 2010); John Vincent, *The Formation of the British Liberal Party, 1857–1868* (New York: Scribners, 1967); Jonathan Parry, *The Rise and Fall of Liberal Government in Victorian Britain* (New Haven, CT: Yale University Press, 1993); Eugenio F. Biagini, *Liberty, Retrenchment and Reform: Popular Liberalism in the Age of Gladstone, 1860–1880* (Cambridge: Cambridge University Press, 1992); John Stuart Mill, *On Liberty* (London: J. W. Parker and Son, 1859). On mid-century French liberalism, see Aurelian Craiutu, *Liberalism Under Siege: The Political Thought of the French Doctrinaires* (Lanham, MD: Lexington Books, 2003); Stephen W. Sawyer, *Demos Assembled: Democracy and the International Origins of the Modern State, 1840–1880* (Chicago, IL: University of Chicago Press, 2018); Walter Dennis Gray, *Interpreting American Democracy in France: The Career of Édouard Laboulaye, 1811–1883* (Newark: University of Delaware Press, 1994); Stephen W. Sawyer, "Édouard Laboulaye and the Statue of Liberty: Forging the Democratic Experience," *La lettre du Collège de France* 4 (2008–2009), 55–57, https://journals.openedition.org/lettre-cdf/782, accessed September 8, 2021; Yasmin Sabina Khan, *Enlightening the World: The Creation of the Statue of Liberty* (Ithaca, NY: Cornell University Press, 2010); W. Caleb McDaniel, *The Problem of Democracy in the Age of Slavery: Garrisonian Abolitionists and Transatlantic Reform* (Baton Rouge: Louisiana State University Press, 2013).

12.   Eric Foner, *Reconstruction: America's Unfinished Revolution, 1863–1877* (New York: HarperCollins, 1988); David W. Blight, *Race and Reunion: Civil War in American Memory* (Cambridge, MA: Harvard University Press, 2001); Steven Hahn, *A Nation Under Their Feet: Black Political Struggles in the Rural South from Slavery to the Great Migration* (Cambridge, MA: Harvard University Press, 2005); Gregory P. Downs, *After Appomattox: Military Occupation and the Ends of War* (Cambridge, MA: Harvard University Press, 2015); Gerstle, *Liberty and Coercion*, chapters 2–3; C. Vann Woodward, *The Strange Career of Jim Crow* (New York: Oxford University Press, 1955).

13.   Christopher Tomlins uses the phrase "counterfeit liberty" in his book *The State and the Unions: Labor Relations, Law, and the Organized Labor Movement in America, 1880–1960* (New York: Cambridge University Press, 1985). On the fear that unrest in the South might spread to the

North, see Heather Cox Richardson, *The Death of Reconstruction: Race, Labor, and Politics in the Post–Civil War North, 1865–1901* (Cambridge, MA: Harvard University Press, 2001). For more on industrial unrest in the late nineteenth century, see Richard White, *The Republic for Which It Stands: The United States During Reconstruction and the Gilded Age, 1865–1896* (New York: Oxford University Press, 2017); William E. Forbath, *Law and the Shaping of the American Labor Movement* (Cambridge, MA: Harvard University Press, 1991); Gerstle, *Liberty and Coercion*, chapter 7. On the fear inspired in the United States by the Paris Commune, see Stephan Thernstrom, *Poverty and Progress: Social Mobility in a Nineteenth-Century City* (Cambridge, MA: Harvard University Press, 1964). On the building of armories in northern cities triggered by the Paris Commune and domestic labor insurrection, see Robert M. Fogelson, *America's Armories: Architecture, Society, and Public Order* (Cambridge, MA: Harvard University Press, 1989). On the appeal of radicalism, see Nick Salvatore, *Eugene V Debs: Citizen and Socialist* (Urbana: University of Illinois Press, 1982, and James Green, *Death in the Haymarket: A Story of Chicago, the First Labor Movement and the Bombing That Divided Gilded Age America* (New York: Pantheon, 2006).

14. The preoccupation with order, or "ordered liberty," threads its way through the writing of Woodrow Wilson and Theodore Roosevelt, two prominent figures in American politics who would come to be associated with American progressivism, the forerunner of modern American liberalism. On Roosevelt, see Gary Gerstle, *American Crucible: Race and Nation in the Twentieth Century* (2001; Princeton, NJ: Princeton University Press, 2017), chapters 1–2. On Wilson, see Gary Gerstle, "Race and Nation in the Thought and Politics of Woodrow Wilson," in John Milton Cooper Jr., ed., *Reconsidering Woodrow Wilson: Progressivism, Internationalism, War, and Peace* (Baltimore, MD: Johns Hopkins University Press, 2008), 93-124. On Social Darwinism, see Richard Hofstadter, *Social Darwinism in American Thought, 1860–1915* (Philadelphia: University of Pennsylvania Press, 1944). On the international implications of these views, see Marilyn Lake and Henry Reynolds, *Drawing the Global Colour Line: White Men's Countries and the Question of Racial Equality* (Melbourne, Australia: Melbourne University Publishing, 2008); Paul A. Kramer, *The Blood of Government: Race, Empire, the United States, and the Philippines* (Chapel Hill: University of North Carolina Press, 2006); Duncan Bell, *Reordering the World: Essays on Liberalism and Empire* (Princeton, NJ: Princeton University Press, 2016); Duncan Bell, *Dreamworlds of Race: Empire and the Utopian Destiny of Anglo-America* (Princeton, NJ: Princeton University Press, 2020); Jennifer Pitts, *A Turn to Empire: The Rise of Imperial Liberalism in Britain and France* (Princeton, NJ: Princeton University Press, 2005); Peter James Hudson, *Bankers and Empire: How Wall Street Colonized the Caribbean*

(Chicago, IL: University of Chicago Press, 2017); Mae Ngai, *The Chinese Question: The Gold Rushes and Global Politics* (New York: W. W. Norton, 2021); Saul Dubow and Gary Gerstle, "Race, Ethnicity, and Nation," in Eugenio F. Biagini and Gary Gerstle, eds., *A Cultural History of Democracy in the Modern Age* (London: Bloomsbury, 2021), 149–170; Jane Burbank and Frederick Cooper, *Empires in World History: Power and the Politics of Difference* (Princeton, NJ: Princeton University Press, 2008).

15. Lippmann, *The Good Society*, 182. On Lippmann's turn to socialism, see Ronald Steel, *Walter Lippmann and the American Century* (New York: Little, Brown, 1980), and Tom Arnold-Forster, *Walter Lippmann: An Intellectual Biography* (Princeton, NJ: Princeton University Press, forthcoming).

16. L. T. Hobhouse, *Liberalism* (New York: Henry Holt, 1911); J. A. Hobson, *Crisis of Liberalism: New Issues for Democracy* (London: P. S. King and Son, 1909); Taylor C. Boas and Jordan Gans-Morse, "Neoliberalism: From New Deal Philosophy to Anti-Liberal Slogan," *Studies in Comparative International Development* 44 (June 2009), 137–161; Herbert Croly, *The Promise of American Life* (1909; Boston: Northeastern University Press, 1989); Theodore Roosevelt, "The New Nationalism," in Roosevelt, *The New Nationalism* (New York: Outlook, 1910), 3–33; Gerstle, *American Crucible*, chapter 2; Gerstle, "The Protean Character of American Liberalism"; George E. Mowry, *Theodore Roosevelt and the Progressive Movement* (Madison: University of Wisconsin Press, 1946); Charles Forcey, *The Crossroads of Liberalism: Croly, Weyl, Lippmann, and the Progressive Era, 1900–1925* (New York: Oxford University Press, 1961); Louise W. Knight, *Jane Addams: Spirit in Action* (New York: W. W. Norton, 2010); Arthur S. Link, *Woodrow Wilson and the Progressive Era, 1910–1917* (New York: Harper, 1954); Thomas J. Knock, *To End All Wars: Woodrow Wilson and the Quest for a New World Order* (New York: Oxford University Press, 1992). See also Pierre Dardot and Christian Laval, *The New Way of the World: On Neoliberal Society*, trans. Gregory Elliott (2009; New York: Verso, 2013), chapter 1.

17. Roosevelt, "The New Nationalism," 23–24. On Progressivism more generally, see Michael McGerr, *A Fierce Discontent: The Rise and Fall of the Progressive Movement in America, 1870-1920* (New York: Oxford University Press, 2003); James T. Kloppenberg, *Uncertain Victory: Social Democracy and Progressivism in European and American Thought, 1870–1920* (New York: Oxford University Press, 1986); Daniel T. Rodgers, *Atlantic Crossings: Social Politics in a Progressive Age* (Cambridge, MA: Harvard University Press, 1998).

18. Quoted in David Green, *Shaping Political Consciousness: The Language of Politics in America from McKinley to Reagan* (Ithaca, NY: Cornell University Press, 1987), 119; see also *The Public Papers and Addresses of Franklin D. Roosevelt, 1938* (New York: Macmillan, 1941), xxix–xxx. On

Roosevelt and liberalism, see the following three books of Arthur M. Schlesinger Jr.: *The Crisis of the Old Order: 1919–1933, The Age of Roosevelt*, vol. 1 (1957; New York: First Mariner Books, 2003); *The Coming of the New Deal, 1933–1935, The Age of Roosevelt*, vol. 2 (1958: New York: First Mariner Books, 2003); *The Politics of Upheaval, 1935–1936, The Age of Roosevelt*, vol. 3 (1960; New York: First Mariner Books, 2003). See, also, David M. Kennedy, *Freedom from Fear: The American People in Depression and War, 1929–1945* (New York: Oxford University Press, 1999); Ira Katznelson, *Fear Itself: The New Deal and the Origins of Our Time* (New York: Liveright, 2013); Steve Fraser and Gary Gerstle, eds., *The Rise and Fall of the New Deal Order, 1930–1980* (Princeton, NJ: Princeton University Press, 1989); Gerstle, *American Crucible*, chapter 4; Eric Rauchway, *Why the New Deal Matters* (New Haven, CT: Yale University Press, 2021).

19. Irving Howe, *Socialism and America* (San Diego, CA: Harcourt Brace Jovanovich, 1985); Steve Fraser, "The 'Labor Question,'" in Fraser and Gerstle, eds., *The Rise and Fall of the New Deal Order*; Gerstle, *Liberty and Coercion*, chapter 7.

20. See Gerstle, *American Crucible*, chapter 2; Gerstle, "Race and Nation in the Thought and Politics of Woodrow Wilson;" and Adom Getachew, *Worldmaking After Empire: The Rise and Fall of Self-Determination* (Princeton, NJ: Princeton University Press, 2019).

21. Herbert Hoover, "The Road to Freedom," *Speech to the Republican National Convention, Cleveland, Ohio* (June 10, 1936), in Hoover, *Addresses upon the American Road, 1933–1938* (New York: Scribner's Sons, 1938), 181.

22. Lippmann, *The Good Society*, 190.

23. Lippmann, *The Good Society*, 134.

24. Lippmann, *The Good Society*, 135–136.

25. Lippmann, *The Good Society*, 210–233; see also Arnold-Forster, *Walter Lippmann*.

26. Lippmann, *The Good Society*, 330.

27. At about the same time (and from a more left perspective), Karl Polanyi was developing similar arguments about how states structure and aid markets. These arguments would cohere into his influential 1944 book, *The Great Transformation*. Polanyi did not participate in the Colloque Lippmann, although his brother, Michael Polanyi (scientist, economist, philosopher), did. Karl Polanyi, *The Great Transformation: The Political and Economic Origins of Our Time* (New York: Farrar and Rinehart, 1944).

28. A record of the discussions at Colloque Lippmann can be found in Jurgen Reinhoudt and Serge Audier, eds., *The Walter Lippmann Colloquium: The Birth of Neo-Liberalism* (London: Palgrave Macmillan, 2018). Lippmann himself showed little interest in the proceedings, his time in Paris far more focused on pursuing an affair than on charting a new course for liberalism. Angus Burgin, *The Great Persuasion: Reinventing Free Markets*

Since the Depression (Cambridge, MA: Harvard, 2012) and Quinn Slobodian, *Globalists: The End of Empire and the Birth of Neoliberalism* (Cambridge, MA: Harvard University Press, 2018) both offer excellent accounts of these convocations. On Lippmann in the 1930s, see Steel, *Walter Lippmann and the American Century*, 285-366, and Arnold-Forster, *Walter Lippmann.*

29. Mirowski and Plehwe, eds., *The Road from Mont Pèlerin.*

30. Burgin, *The Great Persuasion*; Slobodian, *Globalists.*

31. Foucault, *Birth of Biopolitics*, 215.

32. F. A. Hayek, *The Constitution of Liberty: The Definitive Edition*, ed. Ronald Hamowy (1960; Chicago, IL: University of Chicago Press, 2011), vol. 17 of *The Collected Works of F. A. Hayek.*

33. Nancy MacLean stresses the importance of order to liberalism, though this was a much broader phenomenon (and less conspiratorial) than her historical account stretching from John C. Calhoun to James Buchanan suggests. See Nancy MacLean, *Democracy in Chains: The Deep History of the Radical Right's Stealth Plan for America* (New York: Penguin Books, 2017).

34. Foucault, *Birth of Biopolitics*, 226.

35. Burgin, *The Great Persuasion*, and Slobodian, *Globalists*; both are illuminating on the German ordo-liberals.

36. See Gary S. Becker, *Human Capital: A Theoretical and Empirical Analysis, with Special Reference to Education* (Chicago, IL: University of Chicago Press, 1964); and Gary S. Becker, *A Treatise on the Family*, enlarged ed. (Cambridge, MA: Harvard University Press, 1991). See also Foucault, *Birth of Biopolitics*, 215–265; and Henri Lepage, *Tomorrow, Capitalism: The Economics of Economic Freedom* (La Salle, IL: Open Court, 1982; originally published as *Demaine le capitalism*, trans. Sheilagh C. Ogilvie [Paris: Librairie générale française, 1978]), 161–183.

37. Jean-Luc Migué, "Méthodologie économique et économie non-marchande," paper presented to the conference of French-language economists (Quebec, May 1976), and reproduced in *Revue d'économie politique* (1977), 44f. The quoted material appears in Henri Lepage, *Tomorrow, Capitalism*, 171.

38. Wendy Brown, *Undoing the Demos: Neoliberalism's Stealth Revolution* (New York: Zone Books, 2015), 10.

39. On Bentham, see Jeremy Bentham, *An Introduction to the Principles of Morals and Legislation* (1789; London: Andesite Press, 2015); Leslie Stephen, *The English Utilitarians* (Cambridge: Cambridge University Press, 2011); Charles Warren Everett, *Jeremy Bentham* (London: Weidenfeld & Nicolson, 1969); Frederick Rosen, "The Origins of Liberal Utilitarianism: Jeremy Bentham and Liberty," in Richard Paul Bellamy, ed., *Victorian Liberalism: Nineteenth-Century Political Thought and Practice* (London: Routledge, 1990), 58–70; Philip Schofield, *Utility*

and Democracy: The Political Thought of Jeremy Bentham (Oxford: Oxford University Press, 2006); Michel Foucault, *Discipline and Punish: The Birth of the Prison* (New York: Pantheon, 1977).

40. Quoted by Foucault, *Birth of Biopolitics*, 243; from Wilhelm Röpke, *The Social Crisis of Our Time* (1946; Chicago, IL: University of Chicago Press, 1950), part two, chapter 3, 238.

41. Slobodian, *Globalists*, 149–172, is particularly good on Röpke's turn toward South Africa and racism.

42. Useful perspectives on the intersections of moral corrosion, race, and neoliberalism in the United States can be found in Brown, *Undoing the Demos*; Peck, *Constructions of Neoliberal Reason*; MacLean, *Democracy in Chains*; Loïc Wacquant: *Punishing the Poor: The Neoliberal Government of Social Insecurity* (Durham, NC: Duke University Press, 2009); Melinda Cooper, *Family Values: Between Neoliberalism and the New Social Conservatism* (New York: Zone Books, 2017); and Kim Phillips-Fein, *Fear City: New York's Fiscal Crisis and the Rise of Austerity Politics* (New York: Metropolitan Books, 2017).

43. For the complete collection of Henry Hazlitt's *Newsweek* columns, see *Business Tides: The Newsweek Era of Henry Hazlitt*, Kindle ed. (Auburn, AL: Ludwig von Mises Institute, 2011).

44. Milton Friedman, *Capitalism and Freedom*, 40th anniversary ed. (1962; Chicago, IL: University of Chicago Press, 2002).

45. On Reagan's 1950s work for General Electric, see Jacob Weisberg, *Ronald Reagan: The American Presidents Series: The Fortieth President, 1981–1989* (New York: Henry Holt, 2016), and Thomas W. Evans, "The GE Years: What Made Reagan Reagan," *History News Network*, January 8, 2007, https://historynewsnetwork.org/article/32681, accessed December 2, 2019. On Goldwater's early career, see Elizabeth Tandy Shermer, *Sunbelt Capitalism: Phoenix and the Transformation of American Politics* (Philadelphia: University of Pennsylvania Press, 2013); Elizabeth Tandy Shermer, ed., *Barry Goldwater and the Remaking of the American Political Landscape* (Tucson: University of Arizona Press, 2013); Rick Perlstein, *Before the Storm: Barry Goldwater and the Unmaking of the American Consensus* (New York: Hill and Wang, 2001). See also Barry M. Goldwater, *The Conscience of a Conservative* (Shepherdsville, KY: Victor, 1960).

46. Barry Goldwater, "Acceptance Speech," the Republican Nomination for President, Cow Palace, San Francisco, July 16, 1964, www.washingtonpost.com/wp-srv/politics/daily/may98/goldwaterspeech.htm, accessed November 29, 2019.

47. William H. Whyte, *The Organization Man* (New York: Simon and Schuster, 1956); David Riesman, *The Lonely Crowd: A Study of the Changing American Character* (New Haven, CT: Yale University Press, 1950); C. Wright Mills, *White Collar: The American Middle Classes* (New York: Oxford University

Press, 1951); Richard Hofstadter, *The American Political Tradition and the Men Who Made It* (New York: Knopf, 1948); Paul Goodman, *Growing Up Absurd: Problems of Youth in the Organized Society* (1960; New York: New York Review of Books Classics, 2012).

48.   Ronald Reagan, "Commencement Address," Eureka College, June 7, 1957, http://www.shoppbs.org/wgbh/amex/reagan/filmmore/reference/prim ary/eureka.html, accessed September 9, 2021.

49.   Richard White, *"It's Your Misfortune and None of My Own": A New History of the American West* (Norman: University of Oklahoma Press, 1991), tells this story of the West well.

50.   Benedict Anderson, *Imagined Communities: Reflections on the Origin and Spread of Nationalism* (New York: Verso, 1983).

51.   John F. Kennedy, "Acceptance Speech," Democratic Nomination for President, Memorial Coliseum, Los Angeles, July 15, 1960, The American Presidency Project, University of California, Santa Barbara, https://www.presidency.ucsb.edu/documents/address-accepting-the-democratic-nom ination-for-president-the-memorial-coliseum-los, accessed September 9, 2021

52.   Hayek, *The Constitution of Liberty*, 286 and passim.

53.   Hayek, *The Constitution of Liberty*. See, for example, 88–89, 111–12, 526–27.

54.   Hayek, *The Constitution of Liberty*, 531.

55.   Allen Ginsberg, "Howl," *Poetry Foundation*, https://www.poetryfoundat ion.org/poems/49303/howl, accessed September 9, 2021.

56.   Goodman, *Growing Up Absurd*, 22–23.

57.   Goodman, *Growing Up Absurd*, 41.

58.   "Port Huron Statement," 1962, Sixties Project, http://www2.iath.virgi nia.edu/sixties/HTML_docs/Resources/Primary/Manifestos/SDS_Por t_Huron.html, accessed September 9, 2021; Richard Flacks and Nelson Lichtenstein, ed., *The Port Huron Statement: Sources and Legacies of the New Left's Founding Manifesto* (Philadelphia: University of Pennsylvania Press, 2015); Todd Gitlin: *The Sixties: Years of Hope, Days of Rage* (New York: Bantam Books, 1987).

59.   On the early New Left, see Maurice Isserman, *If I Had a Hammer: The Death of the Old Left and the Birth of the New Left* (New York: Basic Books, 1989); Rebecca Klatch, *A Generation Divided: The New Left, the New Right, and the 1960s* (Berkeley: University of California Press, 1999). On the Free Speech Movement specifically, see W. J. Rorabaugh, *Berkeley at War: The 1960s* (New York: Oxford University Press, 1989); Robert Cohen and Reginald E. Zelnik, eds., *The Free Speech Movement: Reflections on Berkeley in the 1960s* (Berkeley: University of California Press, 2002); Neil J. Smelser, *Reflections on the University of California from the Free Speech Movement to the Global University* (Berkeley: University of California Press, 2010). A key figure of the Free

Speech Movement in Berkley was Mario Savio, whose impassioned speech from the steps outside Sproul Hall, Berkeley, crystallized the sentiments of the New Left: "There's a time when the operation of the machine becomes so odious, makes you so sick at heart that you can't take part! You can't even passively take part! And you've got to put your bodies upon the gears and upon the wheels, upon the levers, upon all the apparatus—and you've got to make it stop! And you've got to indicate to the people who run it, to the people who own it—that unless you're free the machine will be prevented from working at all!" Mario Savio, "Sit-in Address on the Steps of Sproul Hall," University of California, Berkeley, December 2, 1964, https://americanrhetoric.com/speeches/mariosaviosproulhallsitin.html, accessed September 9, 2021. Robert Cohen, *Freedom's Orator: Mario Savio and the Radical Legacy of the 1960s* (New York: Oxford University Press, 2009); Robert Cohen, ed., *The Essential Mario Savio: Speeches and Writings That Changed America* (Berkeley: University of California Press, 2014).

60. Gitlin, *The Sixties*; Godfrey Hodgson, *America in Our Time: From World War II to Nixon—What Happened and Why* (New York: Doubleday, 1976), 288–305. Nancy Fraser has also identified leftist influences on neoliberalism, or what she calls, "progressive neoliberalism." See, for example, Nancy Fraser, *The Old Is Dying and the New Cannot Be Born: From Progressive Neoliberalism to Trump and Beyond* (London: Verso, 2019).

61. Ayn Rand, *The Fountainhead* (1943; New York: Signet, 1993); Ayn Rand, *Atlas Shrugged* (1957; New York: Signet, 1992). On Rand, see Jennifer Burns, *Goddess of the Market: Ayn Rand and the American Right* (New York: Oxford University Press, 2009); Anne C. Heller, *Ayn Rand and the World She Made* (New York: Doubleday, 2009); and Lisa Duggan, *Mean Girl: Ayn Rand and the Culture of Greed* (Oakland: University of California Press, 2019).

62. Burns, *Goddess of the Market*, 68, 114.

63. Duggan, *Mean Girl*, 10–11; Cass R. Sunstein, "The Siren of Selfishness," *New York Review of Books*, April 9, 2020, https://www.nybooks.com/articles/2020/04/09/ayn-rand-siren-selfishness/, accessed September 14, 2021. The 1960s and 1970s moment of Rand encounter was very different from later ones experienced by Paul Ryan, Peter Theil, Mike Pompeo, and others at a time when neoliberalism was already riding high. For Rand's influence on these subsequent neoliberals, see Jonathan Freedland, "The New Age of Ayn Rand: How She Won Over Trump and Silicon Valley," *The Guardian*, April 10, 2017, https://www.theguardian.com/books/2017/apr/10/new-age-ayn-rand-conquered-trump-white-house-silicon-valley, accessed December 17, 2021, and Corey Robin, "Metaphysics and Chewing Gum," in Robin, *The Reactionary Mind: Conservatism from*

Edmund Burke to Donald Trump (New York: Oxford University Press, 2018), 167–187.

64. John Ganz, "The Forgotten Man," *The Baffler*, December 15, 2017, https://thebaffler.com/latest/the-forgotten-man-ganz, accessed July 21, 2021; Murray N. Rothbard, ed., *Left & Right: A Journal of Libertarian Thought (Complete, 1965–1968)* (Auburn, AL: Ludwig von Mises Institute, 2007).

65. Ronald Radosh and Murray N. Rothbard, eds., *A New History of Leviathan: Essays on the Rise of the American Corporate State* (New York: E. P. Dutton, 1972).

66. Some of the key works of the corporate liberal school include Gabriel Kolko, *The Triumph of Conservatism: A Re-Interpretation of American History, 1900–1916* (Glencoe, IL: Free Press of Glencoe, 1963); Gabriel Kolko, *Main Trends in Modern American History* (1976; New York: Pantheon, 1984); James Weinstein, *The Corporate Ideal in the Liberal State, 1900–1918* (Boston, MA: Beacon Press, 1968); Ronald Radosh, "The Myth of the New Deal," in Radosh and Rothbard, eds., *A New History of Leviathan*, 146–187; Barton J. Bernstein, "The Conservative Achievements of Liberal Reform," in Barton J. Bernstein, ed., *Towards a New Past: Dissenting Essays in American History* (New York: Pantheon, 1968), 263–288; Martin Sklar, *The Corporate Reconstruction of American Capitalism, 1890–1916: The Market, the Law, and Politics* (New York: Cambridge University Press, 1988).

67. On Kesey and the Merry Pranksters, see Tom Wolfe, *The Electric Kool-Aid Acid Test* (1968; New York: Bantam Books, 1969).

68. Stewart Brand, *Whole Earth Catalog*, 1st ed. (Menlo Park, CA: Portola Institute, 1968).

69. Anna Wiener, "The Complicated Legacy of Stewart Brand's 'Whole Earth Catalog,'" *New Yorker*, November 16, 2018, https://www.newyorker.com/news/letter-from-silicon-valley/the-complicated-legacy-of-stewart-brands-whole-earth-catalog, accessed April 10, 2021; Fred Turner, *From Counterculture to Cyberculture: Stewart Brand, the Whole Earth Catalogue, and the Rise of Digital Utopianism* (Chicago, IL: University of Chicago Press, 2006), 61–62; Margaret O'Mara, *The Code: Silicon Valley and the Remaking of America* (New York: Penguin Press, 2019). Recent essays by Reuel Schiller and Paul Sabin are also illuminating about the New Left's contribution to neoliberalism. See Reuel Schiller, "Regulation and the Collapse of the New Deal Order, or How I Learned to Stop Worrying and Love the Market," and Paul Sabin, "Environmental Law and the End of the New Deal Order," both in Gary Gerstle, Nelson Lichtenstein, and Alice O'Connor, eds., *Beyond the New Deal Order: U.S. Politics from the Great Depression to the Great Recession* (Philadelphia: University of Pennsylvania Press, 2019), 168–185 and 186–203, respectively. See also Paul Sabin, *Public Citizen: The Attack on Big Government and the Remaking of American Liberalism* (New York: W. W. Norton, 2021). On Steve Jobs,

see Walter Isaacson, *Steve Jobs* (New York: Simon and Schuster, 2011). See also Lily Geismer, "Change Their Heads: The National Homeownership Strategy, Asset Building and Democratic Neoliberalism," 2019 Organization of American Historians paper, in author's possession; and Lily Geismer, "Agents of Change: Microenterprise, Welfare Reform, the Clintons, and Liberal Forms of Neoliberalism," *Journal of American History* 107 (June 2020), 107–131.

70. A full genealogy of that heist remains to be written. But see Lawrence Glickman's suggestive essay, "Everyone Was a Liberal," *Aeon*, July 5, 2016, https://aeon.co/essays/everyone-was-a-liberal-now-no-one-wants-to-be, accessed September 28, 2021. See also Lawrence B. Glickman, *Free Enterprise: An American History* (New Haven, CT: Yale University Press, 2019).

71. Friedman, *Capitalism and Freedom*, 5–6.

72. Hayek, *The Constitution of Liberty*, 529–530.

Chapter 4

1. Lewis F. Powell Jr., "Confidential Memo [to Eugene B. Sydnor Jr., US Chamber of Commerce]: Attack on American Free Enterprise System," August 23, 1971, https://law2.wlu.edu/deptimages/Powell%20Archives/PowellMemorandumTypescript.pdf, accessed September 14, 2021; Kim Phillips-Fein, *Invisible Hands: The Making of the Conservative Movement from the New Deal to Reagan* (New York: W. W. Norton, 2009).

2. Quoted in Phillips-Fein, *Invisible Hands*, 162.

3. Phillips-Fein, *Invisible Hands*, 169

4. Phillips-Fein, *Invisible Hands*, 169–173.

5. Jane Mayer, *Dark Money: The Hidden History of the Billionaires Behind the Rise of the Radical Right* (New York: Anchor Books, 2016)

6. Sidney Blumenthal, *The Rise of the Counter-Establishment: The Conservative Ascent to Political Power* (New York: Times Books, 1986).

7. Jefferson Cowie, *Stayin' Alive: The 1970s and the Last Days of the Working Class* (New York: New Press, 2010), 261–312; Benjamin C. Waterhouse, *Lobbying America: The Politics of Business from Nixon to NAFTA* (Princeton, NJ: Princeton University Press, 2014), 76–139.

8. From 89 to 821, to be exact. Phillips-Fein, *Invisible Hands*, 185–188. On the history of PACs, see Emily J. Charnock, *The Rise of Political Action Committees: Interest Group Electioneering and the Transformation of American Politics* (New York: Oxford University Press, 2020).

9. Phillips-Fein, *Invisible Hands*, 185–188; see also Alice O'Connor, "Financing the Counter-Revolution," in Bruce Schulman and Julian E. Zelizer, eds., *Rightward Bound: Making America Conservative in the 1970s* (Cambridge, MA: Harvard University Press, 2008), 148–168.

10. Phillips-Fein, *Invisible Hands*, 245–246; William E. Simon, *A Time for Truth* (New York: Reader's Digest Press, 1978), xi, xv.

11. Phillips-Fein, *Invisible Hands*, 245–246. For another neoliberal manifesto from the era, see George Gilder, *Wealth and Poverty* (New York: Basic Books, 1981). See also Mayer, *Dark Money*; Nancy MacLean, *Democracy in Chains: The Deep History of the Radical Right's Stealth Plan for America* (New York: Penguin Books, 2017); Blumenthal, *The Rise of the Counter-Establishment*.

12. On the decline of productivity, see Robert J. Gordon, *The Rise and Fall of American Growth: The U.S. Standard of Living Since the Civil War* (Princeton, NJ: Princeton University Press, 2017).

13. On the shock of labor law reform defeat, see Cowie, *Stayin' Alive*, 288–296.

14. David Hamilton Golland, *Constructing Affirmative Action: The Struggle for Equal Employment Opportunity* (Lexington: University of Kentucky Press, 2011); Nancy MacLean, *Freedom Is Not Enough: The Opening of the American Workplace* (Cambridge, MA: Harvard University Press, 2006), Part I.

15. David A. Hollinger, *Post-Ethnic America: Beyond Multiculturalism* (New York: Basic Books, 1995), 19–50.

16. On the history of human relations, see Frank Dobbin and Frank R. Sutton, "The Strength of a Weak State: The Rights Revolution and the Rise of Human Resources Management Divisions," *American Journal of Sociology* 104 (September 1998), 441–476; MacLean, *Freedom Is Not Enough*, 302–314; Anne B. Fisher, "Businessmen Like to Hire by the Numbers," *Fortune*, September 16, 1985, 26–30.

17. Mayer, *Dark Money*; Phillips-Fein, *Invisible Hands*, passim; Elizabeth Tandy Shermer, *Sunbelt Capitalism: Phoenix and the Transformation of American Politics* (Philadelphia: University of Pennsylvania Press, 2013).

18. The Pews, owner of a major oil company, were another family that regarded its enterprise in these sorts of proprietary terms and who established the Pew Foundation to shape political debate. See Michael Lind, "Conservative Elites and the Counterrevolution Against the New Deal," in Steve Fraser and Gary Gerstle, eds., *Ruling America: A History of Wealth and Power in a Democracy* (Cambridge, MA: Harvard University Press, 2005), 250–285. See also Darren Dochuk, *Anointed with Oil: How Christianity and Crude Made Modern America* (New York: Basic Books, 2019).

19. Steve Fraser, "'The Labor Question,'" in Steve Fraser and Gary Gerstle, eds., *The Rise and Fall of the New Deal Order, 1930–1980* (Princeton, NJ: Princeton University Press, 1989), 55–84.

20. On Reagan's pre-presidential career, see Lou Cannon, *President Reagan: The Role of a Lifetime* (New York: Simon and Schuster, 1991); Lou Cannon, *Governor Reagan: His Rise to Power* (New York: PublicAffairs, 2003); Rick Perlstein, *The Invisible Bridge: The Fall of Nixon and the Rise of Reagan* (New York: Simon and Schuster, 2014); Iwan Morgan,

Reagan: American Icon (New York: Bloomsbury, 2016); Leo Sands, "Governor Ronald Reagan and the Assault on Welfare" (undergraduate dissertation, University of Cambridge, 2016).

21. Ronald Reagan, "Address Accepting the Presidential Nomination at the Republican National Convention in Detroit," July 17, 1980, https://www.youtube.com/watch?v=e8IWm8m2F8M, accessed September 2, 2020. Reagan spoke these words: "I believe this generation of Americans today also has a rendezvous with destiny." See also Gil Troy, *Morning in America: How Ronald Reagan Invented the 1980s* (Princeton, NJ: Princeton University Press, 2013).

22. Garry Wills, *Reagan's America: Innocents at Home* (1987; New York: Penguin Press, 2000); Debora Silverman, *Selling Culture: Bloomingdale's, Diana Vreeland, and the New Aristocracy of Taste in Reagan's America* (New York: Pantheon Books, 1989); Michael Rogin, *Ronald Reagan the Movie and Other Episodes in Political Demonology* (Los Angeles: University of California Press, 1988).

23. Gerald Ford, a Republican, succeeded Nixon in 1974, but he was never elected, losing his only race for the presidency in 1976.

24. Michael Kazin, *What It Took to Win: A History of the Democratic Party* (New York: Farrar, Straus and Giroux, 2022); Michael Kazin, *The Populist Persuasion: An American History* (New York: Basic Books, 1995), chapters 9–10; Dan T. Carter, *The Politics of Rage: George Wallace, the Origins of the New Conservatism, and the Transformation of American Politics* (New York: Simon and Schuster, 1995); Kevin P. Phillips, *The Emerging Republican Majority* (New York: Anchor Books, 1970); Dan T. Carter, *From George Wallace to Newt Gingrich: Race in the Conservative Counterrevolution, 1963–1994* (Baton Rouge: Louisiana State University Press, 1996); Elizabeth Hinton, *America on Fire: The Untold History of Police Violence and Black Rebellion Since the 1960s* (New York: Liveright, 2021); Gary Gerstle, *Liberty and Coercion: The Paradox of American Government from the Founding to the Present* (Princeton, NJ: Princeton University Press, 2016), chapter 9; Kevin M. Kruse, *White Flight: Atlanta and the Making of Modern Conservatism* (Princeton, NJ: Princeton University Press, 2005); Matthew D. Lassiter, *The Silent Majority: Suburban Politics in the Sunbelt South* (Princeton, NJ: Princeton University Press, 2006).

25. In 1952, Eisenhower called on all Americans to have faith in God though he didn't "care what it [the faith] is." Patrick Henry, "'And I Don't Care What It Is': The Tradition-History of a Civil Religion Proof-Text," *Journal of the American Academy of Religion* 49 (March 1981), 41. My interpretation of Eisenhower dissents somewhat from the argument offered by Kevin M. Kruse in *One Nation Under God: How Corporate America Invented Christian America* (New York: Basic Books, 2015), and is closer to that of Kevin Schultz, *Tri-Faith America: How Postwar Catholics and Jews*

Held America to Its Protestant Promise (New York: Oxford University Press, 2011). For more on the secular character of the New Deal order, see Chapter 1 of this book.

26. *Engel v. Vitale*, 370 U.S. 421 (1962). On the precedent for *Engel*, see *Everson v. Board of Education*, 330 U.S. 1 (1947).

27. "The Inaugural Address of Governor George C. Wallace," January 14, 1963, Montgomery, Alabama, typescript, 6–7, Alabama Department of Archives and History, http://digital.archives.alabama.gov/cdm/ref/collect ion/voices/id/2952, accessed March 24, 2020.

28. Quoted in Darren Dochuk, *From Bible Belt to Sun Belt: Plain-Folk Religion, Grassroots Politics, and the Rise of Evangelical Conservatism* (New York: W. W. Norton, 2011), 240. See also William Curtis Martin, *With God on Our Side: The Rise of the Religious Right in America* (New York: Broadway Books, 1996); Frances Fitzgerald, *The Evangelicals: The Struggle to Shape America* (New York: Simon and Schuster, 2017); Eric R. Crouse, *The Cross and Reaganomics: Conservative Christians Defending Ronald Reagan* (Lanham, MD: Lexington Books, 2013); and Kristin Kobes Du Mez, *Jesus and John Wayne: How White Evangelicals Corrupted a Faith and Fractured a Nation* (New York: Liveright, 2020).

29. Later Reagan would take up the cause of Christian schools and universities that were being threatened with the loss of their tax-exempt status on account of their refusal to prioritize civil rights law over religious beliefs. Joseph Crespino, *In Search of Another America: Mississippi and the Conservative Counterrevolution* (Princeton, NJ: Princeton University Press, 2007).

30. Jerry Falwell, *Listen, America!* (Garden City, NY: Doubleday, 1980), 13. Falwell refers to Friedman and to William Simon on multiple occasions in this book. See, also, Jerry Falwell, *Strength for the Journey: An Autobiography* (New York: Simon and Schuster, 1987); Frances Fitzgerald, *The Evangelicals: The Struggle to Shape America* (New York: Simon and Schuster, 2017), 291–318; Beatrice Wong, "Jerry Falwell and American Politics, c. 1970–2000" (undergraduate dissertation, University of Cambridge, 2021); Susan Friend Harding, *The Book of Jerry Falwell: Fundamentalist Language and Politics* (Princeton, NJ: Princeton University Press, 2000).

31. Because of third-party candidate John B. Anderson, Reagan's share of the popular vote did not reach the 60 percent levels characteristic of lopsided victories in two-way presidential races, but the 10 percent differential between Reagan and Carter (50.7 to 41 percent) was nevertheless huge. For a breakdown of the results of the 1980 presidential election, see https://www.presidency.ucsb.edu/statistics/elections/1980, accessed September 14, 2021.

32. On the shift of northern white ethnics to Reagan, see Jonathan Rieder, *Canarsie: The Jews and Italians of Brooklyn Against Liberalism* (Cambridge, MA: Harvard University Press, 1985); Samuel G. Freedman, *The Inheritance: How Three Families and the American Political Majority Moved from Left to Right* (New York: Simon and Schuster, 1996); J. Anthony Lukas, *Common Ground: A Turbulent Decade in the Lives of Three American Families* (New York: Knopf, 1985); Ronald P. Formisano, *Boston Against Busing: Race, Class, and Ethnicity in the 1960s and 1970s* (Chapel Hill: University of North Carolina Press, 1991); Jim Sleeper, *The Closest of Strangers: Liberalism and the Politics of Race in New York* (New York: W. W. Norton, 1990).

33. On the air-traffic controllers' strike and its consequences, see Joseph A. McCartin, *Collision Course: Ronald Reagan, the Air Traffic Controllers, and the Strike That Changed America* (New York: Oxford University Press, 2011). The percentage of non-agricultural workers belonging to unions declined across the decade from about 20 percent to 15 percent. The continuing robustness of unions in the public sector obscured the steeper percentage decline in union membership in the private sector. Gerald Mayer, "Union Membership Trends in the United States," *Congressional Research Service* (Washington, DC: Congressional Research Service, 2004), https://hdl.handle.net/1813/77776, accessed March 27, 2020; Eric Morath, "U.S. Union Membership Hits Another Record Low," *Wall Street Journal*, January 22, 2020, https://www.wsj.com/articles/u-s-union-membership-hits-another-record-low-11579715320, accessed March 27, 2020.

34. W. Elliot Brownlee, *Federal Taxation in America: A Short History*, 2nd ed. (Washington, DC: Woodrow Wilson International Center for Scholars, 2004), 147–177; Cathie Jo Martin, "American Business and the Taxing State: Alliances for Growth in the Postwar Period," in *Funding the Modern American State, 1941–1995: The Rise and Fall of the Era of Easy Finance*, ed. W. Elliot Brownlee (Washington, DC: Woodrow Wilson Center Press, 1996), 353–406; Herbert Stein, *Presidential Economics: The Making of Economic Policy from Roosevelt to Clinton*, 3rd rev. ed. (Washington, DC: American Enterprise Institute for Public Policy Research, 1994), 235–411; John F. Witte, *The Politics and Development of the Federal Income Tax* (Madison: University of Wisconsin Press, 1985), 220–243; Sheldon D. Pollack, *The Failure of U.S. Tax Policy: Revenue and Politics* (University Park: Pennsylvania State University Press, 1996), 87–115; McCartin, *Collision Course*; Nelson Lichtenstein, *State of the Union: A Century of American Labor* (Princeton, NJ: Princeton University Press, 2013); Gerstle, *Liberty and Coercion*, chapter 10; Monica Prasad, *Starving the Beast: Ronald Reagan and the Tax Cut Revolution* (New York: Russell Sage Foundation, 2018); Sidney Blumenthal, "Defining 'Reaganomics,'" *Boston Globe*, November 2, 1980, H10.

35. Sean Wilentz, *The Age of Reagan: A History, 1974–2008* (New York: HarperCollins, 2008), 196–200.

36. Daniel Rowe, "Beyond Reaganomics: The Long Economic Crisis and the Rebuilding of America, 1974–1988" (DPhil dissertation, University of Oxford, 2019), 162.

37. Lee Edwards, *To Preserve and Protect: The Life of Edwin Meese III* (Washington, DC: Heritage Foundation, 2005); Charles Connor, "Rethinking the Robert Bork Affair" (undergraduate dissertation, University of Cambridge, 2018).

38. Laura Kalman, *The Strange Career of Legal Liberalism* (New Haven, CT: Yale University Press, 1996), 132.

39. Robert J. Bork, "Neutral Principles and Some First Amendment Problems," *Indiana Law Journal* 47 (1971), 1–35; Robert J. Bork, "We Suddenly Feel That the Law Is Vulnerable," *Fortune*, December 1971, 115–117, 136–138, 143; Robert J. Bork, *The Tempting of America: The Political Seduction of the Law* (New York: Free Press, 1990). See also Keith Whittington, "The New Originalism," *Georgetown Journal of Law and Public Policy* 2 (2004), 599–613; Jonathan O'Neill, "Shaping Modern Constitutional Theory: Bickel and Bork Confront the Warren Court," *Review of Politics* 65 (2003), 325–354; Daniel T. Rodgers, *Age of Fracture* (Cambridge, MA: Harvard University Press, 2011), 232–342; Steven M. Teles, *The Rise of the Conservative Legal Movement: The Battle for Control of the Law* (Princeton, NJ: Princeton University Press, 2008), chapter 5; Jeffrey Toobin, *The Nine: Inside the Secret World of the Supreme Court* (New York: Doubleday, 2007), 12–13. See also Charles Connor, "The Judges' Wars: Explaining the Battles over Judicial Nominations in Reagan's Second Term" (MPhil dissertation, University of Cambridge, 2019).

40. Richard A. Epstein, "The Proper Scope of the Commerce Power," *Virginia Law Review* 73 (November 1987), 1454, 1451. Others who shared this restrictive view of the powers granted to Congress by the commerce clause include Albert Abel, "The Commerce Clause in the Constitutional Convention and in Contemporary Comment," *Minnesota Law Review* 25 (1941), 432–494; Raoul Berger, "Judicial Manipulation of the Commerce Clause," *Texas Law Review* 74 (1995–96), 695–717; Grant Nelson and Robert Pushaw, "Rethinking the Commerce Clause: Applying First Principles to Uphold Federal Commercial Regulations but Preserve State Control over Social Issues," *Iowa Law Review* 85 (1999–2000), 1–173; Randy Barnett, "The Original Meaning of the Commerce Clause," *University of Chicago Law Review* 68 (2001), 101–147; Randy Barnett, "New Evidence on the Original Meaning of the Commerce Clause," *Arkansas Law Review* 55 (2003), 847–900; Bork, "We Suddenly Feel That the Law Is Vulnerable," 115–117, 136–138, 143; Grover Norquist, *Leave Us Alone: Getting the Government's Hands Off Our Money, Our Guns, Our*

Lives (New York: William Morrow, 2008). See, also, William Grieder, "The Right's Grand Ambition: Rolling Back the Twentieth Century," *Nation*, May 12, 2003, 2.

41. Teles, *The Rise of the Conservative Legal Movement.*

42. Quoted in Julian E. Zelizer, "How Washington Helped Create the Contemporary Media: Ending the Fairness Doctrine in 1987," in Bruce J. Schulman and Julian E. Zelizer, eds., *Media Nation: The Political History of News in Modern America* (Philadelphia: University of Pennsylvania Press, 2017), 178. See also Anna Cardoso, "The Rise of the Right-Wing Media and the Repeal of the Fairness Doctrine in the USA" (undergraduate dissertation, University of Cambridge, 2019).

43. Cardoso, "Rise of the Right-Wing Media," 34–35, 43.

44. Ronald Reagan, "Veto—S. 742 Message from the President of the United States Returning Without My Approval S. 742, The Fairness in Broadcasting Act of 1987, Which Would Codify the So-Called Fairness Doctrine," June 19, 1987 (Washington, DC: Government Printing Office, 1987).

45. "Kucinich Revives 'Hush Rush' Movement," *Rush Limbaugh Show*, May 19, 2011, https://www.rushlimbaugh.com/daily/2011/05/19/kucinich_rev ives_hush_rush_movement/, accessed March 26, 2020.

46. Fox dropped this slogan only in 2017. Michael M. Grynbaum, "Fox Drops Its 'Fair and Balanced' Motto," *New York Times*, June 14, 2017, https://www.nytimes.com/2017/06/14/business/media/fox-news-fair-and-balanced.html, accessed March 26, 2020.

47. Gabriel Sherman, *The Loudest Voice in the Room: How the Brilliant, Bombastic Roger Ailes Built Fox News—and Divided a Country* (New York: Random House, 2014).

48. Ronald Reagan, "Address to the Members of the British Parliament," June 8, 1982, *Public Papers of the Reagan Presidency* (Washington, DC: Government Printing Office, 1983), 742–748, https://www.reagan library.gov/archives/speech/address-members-british-parliament, accessed 14 December 2021; Wilentz, *Age of Reagan*, 154, 206; Rachel Maddow, *Drift: The Unmooring of American Military Power* (New York: Crown, 2012), 64; Julian E. Zelizer, *Arsenal of Democracy: The Politics of National Security—from World War II to the War on Terrorism* (New York: Basic Books, 2010), 300–354; Michael Sherry, *In the Shadow of War: The United States Since the 1930s* (New Haven, CT: Yale University Press, 1995), chapter 8; John Lewis Gaddis, *Strategies of Containment: A Critical Appraisal of American National Security Policy During the Cold War*, rev. ed. (New York: Oxford University Press, 2005), 342–379.

49. On the rise of the carceral state, see Ruth Wilson Gilmore, *Golden Gulag: Prisons, Surplus, Crisis, and Opposition in Globalizing California* (Berkeley: University of California Press, 2007); Heather Ann Thompson, "Why Mass Incarceration Matters: Rethinking Crisis, Decline, and

Transformation in Postwar American History," *Journal of American History* 97 (December 2010), 703–734; Heather Ann Thompson, *Blood in the Water: The Attica Prison Uprising of 1971 and Its Legacy* (New York: Pantheon Books, 2016); Michelle Alexander, *The New Jim Crow: Mass Incarceration in the Age of Colorblindness* (New York: New Press, 2010); Robert Perkinson, *Texas Tough: The Rise of America's Prison Empire* (New York: Henry Holt, 2010); Marie Gottschalk, *The Prison and the Gallows: The Politics of Mass Incarceration in America* (New York: Cambridge University Press, 2006); Marie Gottschalk, *Caught: The Prison State and the Lockdown of American Politics* (Princeton, NJ: Princeton University Press, 2015); Elizabeth Hinton, *From the War on Poverty to the War on Crime: The Making of Mass Incarceration in America* (Cambridge, MA: Harvard University Press, 2016); Hinton, *America on Fire*; Julilly Kohler-Hausmann, *Getting Tough: Welfare and Imprisonment in 1970s America* (Princeton, NJ: Princeton University Press, 2017); Robert T. Chase, *We Are Not Slaves: State Violence, Coerced Labor, and Prisoners' Rights in Postwar America* (Chapel Hill: University of North Carolina Press, 2019); Loïc Wacquant, *Punishing the Poor: The Neoliberal Government of Social Insecurity* (Durham, NC: Duke University Press, 2009); Loïc Wacquant, *Prisons of Poverty* (1999; Minneapolis: University of Minnesota, 2009).

50.   "The American Underclass," *Time*, August 29, 1977, 14–15.

51.   Ken Auletta, *The Underclass* (New York: Random House, 1982). On alternative ways of understanding urban poverty and crime in 1980s America, see Michael B. Katz, *The Undeserving Poor: From the War on Poverty to the War on Welfare* (New York: Pantheon Books, 1989); Michael B. Katz, ed., *The "Underclass" Debate: Views from History* (Princeton, NJ: Princeton University Press, 1993); William Julius Wilson, *The Truly Disadvantaged: The Inner City, the Underclass, and Public Policy* (Chicago, IL: University of Chicago Press, 1987); Thomas J. Sugrue, *The Origins of the Urban Crisis: Race and Inequality in Postwar Detroit* (1996; Princeton, NJ: Princeton University Press, 2014); Carl Nightingale, *On the Edge: A History of Poor American Children and Their American Dreams* (New York: Basic Books, 1993); and Walter Johnson, *The Broken Heart of America: St. Louis and the Violent History of the United States* (New York: Basic Books, 2020).

52.   Others in this group included the literary critic Allan Bloom; William J. Bennett, Reagan's secretary of education; editor of *Commentary* magazine Norman Podhoretz; senator from New York Daniel Patrick Moynihan; and social theorist Francis Fukuyama. Social scientists Daniel Bell and Nathan Glazer hovered around its fringes, as did the historian and social critic Christopher Lasch. They were often grouped under the label "neoconservative." For a sampling of their writing, see Daniel Bell, *The Cultural Contradictions of Capitalism* (New York: Basic

Books, 1976); Christopher Lasch, *The Culture of Narcissism: American Life in an Age of Diminishing Expectations* (New York: W. W. Norton, 1979); Allan Bloom, *The Closing of the American Mind: How Higher Education Has Failed Democracy and Impoverished the Souls of Today's Students* (New York: Simon and Schuster, 1987); William J. Bennett, *The Book of Virtues: A Treasury of Great Moral Stories* (New York: Simon and Schuster, 1993); Irving Kristol, *Neoconservatism: The Autobiography of an Idea* (New York: Free Press, 1995). See also Peter Steinfels, *The Neoconservatives: The Origins of a Movement: From Dissent to Political Power* (New York: Simon and Schuster, 1979); Murray Friedman, *The Neoconservative Revolution: Jewish Intellectuals and the Shaping of Public Policy* (Cambridge, MA: Harvard University Press, 2005); Christopher Demuth and William Kristol, eds., *The Neoconservative Imagination: Essays in Honor of Irving Kristol* (Washington, DC: American Enterprise Institute for Public Policy Research, 1995); and Alexander Jacobs, *American Counter-Enlightenment: Social Critics and the Uses of Conservatism* (Cambridge, MA: Harvard University Press, forthcoming).

53. Gertrude Himmelfarb, *The De-Moralization of Society: From Victorian Virtues to Modern Values* (New York: Knopf, 1995), 256.

54. Thomas Sowell, *Ethnic America: A History* (New York: Basic Books, 1981); Thomas Sowell, *The Thomas Sowell Reader* (New York: Basic Books, 2011); Gilder, *Wealth and Poverty*.

55. Charles Murray, *Losing Ground: American Social Policy, 1950–1980* (New York: Basic Books, 1984); Richard J. Herrnstein and Charles Murray, *The Bell Curve: Intelligence and Class Structure in American Life* (New York: Free Press, 1994). See also Steve Fraser, ed., *The Bell Curve Wars: Race, Intelligence, and the Future of America* (New York: Basic Books, 1995); Quinn Slobodian and Stuart Schrader, "The White Man Unburdened: How Charles Murray Stopped Worrying and Learned to Love Racism," *The Baffler 40* (July 2018), https://thebaffler.com/salvos/the-white-man-unburdened-slobodian-schrader, accessed March 28, 2020.

Buchanan's anti-Latin American immigrant views came into focus during his 1992 and 1996 campaigns for the GOP presidential nomination, most strikingly in his "culture war speech" at the 1992 GOP convention. See Patrick Buchanan, "1992 Republican National Convention Speech," August 17, 1992; http://buchanan.org./blog/1992-rep ublican-national-convention-speech-148, accessed September 14, 2021. Buchanan later elaborated on this theme in books such as *The Death of the West: How Dying Populations and Immigrant Invasions Imperil Our Country and Civilization* (New York: St. Martin's, 2001), and *State of Emergency: The Third World Invasion and the Conquest of America* (New York: Thomas Dunne Books, St. Martin's Press, 2006).

56. For an interesting exploration of how this message of self-improvement flowed across class lines and with a strong self-help religious inflection,

see Jessica Burch, " 'Soap and Hope': Direct Sales and the Culture of
Work and Capitalism in Postwar America" (PhD dissertation, Vanderbilt
University, 2015) .

57.   Melinda Cooper, *Family Values: Between Neoliberalism and the New Social
Conservatism* (New York: Zone Books, 2019).

58.   John A. Lawrence, *The Class of '74: Congress After Watergate and the Roots
of Partisanship* (Baltimore, MD: Johns Hopkins University, 2018); John
A. Lawrence, "How the 'Watergate Babies' Broke American Politics,"
Politico, May 26, 2018, https://www.politico.com/magazine/story/2018/
05/26/congress-broke-american-politics-218544, accessed August 4, 2021;
Kevin M. Kruse and Julian E. Zelizer, *Fault Lines: A History of the United
States Since 1974* (New York: W. W. Norton, 2019), 128–129; Kenneth S.
Baer, *Reinventing Democrats: The Politics of Liberalism from Reagan to
Clinton* (Lawrence: University of Kansas Press, 2000); Al From, *The New
Democrats and the Return to Power* (New York: Palgrave Macmillan, 2013);
Kazin, *What It Took to Win*; Iwan Morgan, "Jimmy Carter, Bill Clinton,
and the New Democratic Economics," *Historical Journal* 47 (2004),
1015–1039; and Nelson Lichtenstein, *A Fabulous Failure: Bill Clinton and
American Capitalism* (forthcoming).

59.   Charles Peters, "A Neo-Liberal's Manifesto," *Washington Post*, September
5, 1982, https://www.washingtonpost.com/archive/opinions/1982/09/05/
a-neo-liberals-manifesto/21cf41ca-e60e-404e-9a66-124592c9f70d/, accessed
July 26, 2021; Charles Peters and Philip Keisling, eds., *A New Road for
America: The Neoliberal Movement* (Lanham, MD: Madison Books, 1985).
See also Randall Rothenberg, *The Neoliberals: Creating the New American
Politics* (New York: Simon and Schuster, 1984); Corey Robin, "The First
Neoliberals," *Jacobin*, April 28, 2016, https://www.jacobinmag.com/2016/
04/chait-neoliberal-new-inquiry-democrats-socialism/, accessed August
1, 2021; and Brent Cebul, "Supply-Side Liberalism: Fiscal Crisis, Post-
Industrial Policy, and the Rise of the New Democrats," *Modern American
History* 2 (July 2019), 139–164.

60.   They ought "not to be confused," Lekachman added, "with traditional,
highly honorable liberal aspirations for full employment, universal health
coverage, tax equity, adequate housing, urban rehabilitation, integration
of minorities into the labor force, and the mild redistribution of income,
wealth and power." Robert Lekachman, "Atari Democrats," *New York
Times*, October 10, 1982, https://www.nytimes.com/1982/10/10/opinion/
atari-democrats.html, accessed July 26, 2021.

61.   Paul E. Tsongas, "Atarizing Reagan," *New York Times*, March 1, 1983,
https://www.nytimes.com/1983/03/01/opinion/atarizing-reagan.html,
accessed July 26, 2021.

62.   Leslie Wayne, "Designing a New Economics for the 'Atari Democrats,' "
New York Times, September 26, 1982, https://www.nytimes.com/1982/09/

26/business/designing-a-new-economics-for-the-atari-democrats.html, accessed March 20, 2019.

63. For a transcript of the "New Orleans Declaration," see "Repost: The Manifesto of the Third Way Democrats—the New Orleans Declaration," *abiasedperspective, Luke Phillips Blog*, https://abiasedperspective.wordpr ess.com/2015/04/07/repost-the-manifesto-of-the-third-way-democrats-the-new-orleans-declaration/, accessed April 2, 2020. See also Robin Toner, "Eyes to Left, Democrats Edge Toward the Center," *New York Times*, March 25, 1990, https://www.nytimes.com/1990/03/25/us/eyes-to-left-democrats-edge-toward-the-center.html, accessed August 4, 2021; Baer, *Reinventing Democrats*; From, *The New Democrats and the Return to Power*; Kazin, *What It Took to Win*; Morgan, "Jimmy Carter, Bill Clinton, and the New Democratic Economics"; Jon F. Hale, "The Making of the New Democrats," *Political Science Quarterly* 110 (Summer 1995), 207–232.

64. "Repost: The Manifesto of the Third Way Democrats—the New Orleans Declaration," *abiasedperspective, Luke Phillips Blog*.

65. From, *The New Democrats and the Return to Power*.

66. Democrats held power in at least one of the houses of Congress across the 1980s. On the persistence of Democratic Party power and politics through the 1980s, see the essays in Julian E. Zelizer, *Governing America: The Revival of Political History* (Princeton, NJ: Princeton University Press, 2012), and Julian E. Zelizer, "The Unexpected Endurance of the New Deal Order: Liberalism in the Age of Reagan," in Gary Gerstle, Nelson Lichtenstein, and Alice O'Connor, *Beyond the New Deal Order: U.S. Politics from the Great Depression to the Great Recession* (Philadelphia: University of Pennsylvania Press, 2019), 71–92.

67. On Rohatyn, see Rowe, "Beyond Reaganomics," 166. On the appeal of Japan and its state-directed industrial policy to some American reformers, see Ezra F. Vogel, *Japan as Number One: Lessons for America* (Cambridge, MA: Harvard University Press, 1979); Chalmers Johnson, *MITI and the Japanese Miracle: The Growth of Industrial Policy, 1925–1975* (Stanford, CA: Stanford University Press, 1982); Otis L. Graham Jr., *Losing Time: The Industrial Policy Debate* (Cambridge, MA: Harvard University Press, 1992); Waterhouse, *Lobbying America*; Jennifer A. Delton, *The Industrialists: How the National Association of Manufacturers Shaped American Capitalism* (Princeton, NJ: Princeton University Press, 2020), 237–290. For a cultural perspective on these developments, see Andrew C. McKevitt, *Consuming Japan: Popular Culture and the Globalizing of 1980s America* (Chapel Hill: University of North Carolina Press, 2017).

Chapter 5

1. Ian Kershaw, *The Global Age: Europe, 1950–2017* (New York: Viking, 2018), 391.

2. Vladimir Putin, *First Person: An Astonishingly Frank Self-Portrait by Russia's President Vladimir Putin* (New York: PublicAffairs, 2000), 78; Masha Gessen, *The Man Without a Face: The Unlikely Rise of Vladimir Putin* (New York: Riverhead 2012), 66–70.

3. Stephen Kotkin, *Armageddon Averted: The Soviet Collapse, 1970–2000* (New York: Oxford University Press, 2001), 63; Robert C. Allen, "The Rise and Decline of the Soviet Economy," *Canadian Journal of Economics / Revue canadienne d'économique* 34 (2001), 859–881; William Easterly and Stanley Fischer, "The Soviet Economic Decline," *World Bank Economic Review* 9 (September 1995), 341–371.

4. Kotkin, *Armageddon Averted*; Robert Service, *The End of the Cold War: 1985–1991* (London: Macmillan, 2015).

5. William Taubman, *Gorbachev: His Life and Times* (New York: W.W. Norton, 2017); Vladislav M. Zubok, *A Failed Empire: The Soviet Union from Stalin to Gorbachev* (Chapel Hill: University of North Carolina Press, 2009).

6. Ezra F. Vogel, *Deng Xiaoping and the Transformation of China* (Cambridge, MA: Belknap Press of Harvard University Press, 2013). For a fascinating exploration of the divergent paths of the two communist empires, Soviet and Chinese, see Perry Anderson, "Two Revolutions," *New Left Review* 61 (January/February 2010), https://newleftreview.org/iss ues/ii61/articles/perry-anderson-two-revolutions, accessed July 28, 2021.

7. Jeffrey A. Engel, *When the World Seemed New: George H. W. Bush and the End of the Cold War* (Boston: Houghton Mifflin, 2017), chapter 16.

8. Taubman, *Gorbachev*, chapters 14–19. On the end of the Soviet experiment, see also Odd Arne Westad, *The Cold War: A World History* (New York: Basic Books, 2019); Eric J. Hobsbawm, *The Age of Extremes: A History of the World, 1914–1991* (New York: Pantheon Books, 1994); and Tony Judt, *Postwar: A History of Europe Since 1945* (London: Penguin, 2005).

9. Don Oberdorfer, "Leaders Come to Grips with Post–Cold War Era," *Washington Post*, November 30, 1989, https://www.washingtonpost.com/ archive/politics/1989/11/30/leaders-come-to-grips-with-post-cold-war-era/ dc5c8ec3-1648-4afc-9bdd-9e580a53c866/, accessed July 28, 2021.

10. John Lewis Gaddis, *We Now Know: Rethinking Cold War History* (New York: Oxford University Press, 1997); John Lewis Gaddis, *The United States and the End of the Cold War: Implications, Reconsiderations, Provocations* (New York: Oxford University Press, 1992).

11. Marc Levinson, *Outside the Box: How Globalization Changed from Moving Stuff to Spreading Ideas* (Princeton, NJ: Princeton University Press, 2020), 121, 94; Joshua B. Freeman, *Behemoth: A History of the Factory and the Making of the Modern World* (New York: W. W. Norton, 2018), 270–313.

12. Nelson Lichtenstein, *State of the Union: A Century of American Labor* (Princeton, NJ: Princeton University Press, 2002), 213.

13. Leon Fink and Brian Greenberg, *Upheaval in the Quiet Zone: 1199/SEIU and the Politics of Health Care Unionism*, 2nd ed. (Champaign: University of Illinois Press, 2009).

14. One study estimated that in the 1990s, unions lost two thirds of the elections in which employers deployed the threat of plant closure. Kate Bronfenbrenner, "We'll Close! Plant Closings, Plant-Closing Threats, Union Organizing and NAFTA," *Multinational Monitor* 18 (March 1997), 8–14; Kate Bronfenbrenner, "Raw Power: Plant-Closing Threats and the Threat to Union Organizing," *Multinational Monitor* 21 (December 2000), 24–30; Joshua B. Freeman, *American Empire: The Rise of a Global Power, the Democratic Revolution at Home, 1945–2000* (New York: Viking, 2012), Part III; Lichtenstein, *State of the Union*; chapter 6; Levinson, *Outside the Box*; Godfrey Hodgson, *More Equal Than Others: America from Nixon to the New Century* (Princeton, NJ: Princeton University Press, 2004), 45; Century Foundation, *What's Next for Organized Labor* (New York: Century, 1999).

15. Lawrence Mishel and Julia Wolfe, "CEO Compensation Has Grown 940% Since 1978," Economic Policy Institute, August 14, 2019, https://www.epi.org/publication/ceo-compensation-2018/, accessed September 8, 2020. See also Kevin M. Kruse and Julian E. Zelizer, *Fault Lines: A History of the United States Since 1974* (New York: W. W. Norton, 2019), 234.

16. Nancy MacLean, *Freedom Is Not Enough: The Opening of the American Workplace* (Cambridge, MA: Harvard University Press, 2006); Kruse and Zelizer, *Fault Lines*, 235; Robert D. Putnam, *Bowling Alone: The Collapse and Revival of the American Community* (New York: Simon and Schuster, 2000), 196–197; Jacob S. Hacker, *The Great Risk Shift: The New Economic Insecurity and the Decline of the American Dream* (New York: Oxford University Press, 2006); Godfrey Hodgson, *More Equal than Others*; Steve Fraser, *The Age of Acquiescence: The Life and Death of American Resistance to Organized Wealth and Power* (New York: Little, Brown, 2015), chapter 12.

17. Francis Fukuyama, *The End of History and the Last Man* (New York: Free Press, 1992). This was an outgrowth of Fukuyama's essay "The End of History?" published in *National Interest* 16 (Summer 1989), 3–18.

18. On decline of social democracy in Europe, see Tony Judt, *Ill Fares the Land* (New York: Penguin Books, 2010) and Judt, *Postwar*; Sheri Berman, *The Primacy of Politics: Social Democracy and the Making of Europe's Twentieth Century* (New York: Cambridge University Press, 2006); James T. Kloppenberg and John Gee, "Social and Economic Democracy," in Eugenio F. Biagini and Gary Gerstle, eds., *A Cultural History of Democracy: The Modern Age* (London: Bloomsbury, 2021), 81–106.

19. Howard Brick and Christopher Phelps, *Radicals in America: The U.S. Left Since the Second World War* (New York: Cambridge University

Press, 2015); Robert O. Self, *All in the Family: The Realignment of American Democracy Since the 1960s* (New York: Hill and Wang, 2013); Michael Kazin, *American Dreamers: How the Left Changed a Nation* (New York: Random House, 2011), 252–278; Richard Rorty, *Achieving Our Country: Leftist Thought in Twentieth-Century America* (Cambridge, MA: Harvard University Press, 1998); Nancy Fraser and Axel Honneth, *Redistribution or Recognition: A Political-Philosophical Exchange* (New York: Verso, 2003); Nancy Fraser, *Fortunes of Feminism: From State-Managed Capitalism to Neoliberal Crisis* (New York: Verso, 2013).

20. Engel, *When the World Seemed New*, passim.

21. Jon Meacham, *Destiny and Power: The American Odyssey of George Herbert Walker Bush* (New York: Random House, 2015); Timothy Naftali, *George H. W. Bush: The American Presidents' Series: The 41st President, 1989–1993* (New York: Times Books and Henry Holt, 2007).

22. On the Bush family's move to Texas and its consequences, see Gary Gerstle, "Minorities, Multiculturalism and the Presidency of George W. Bush," in Julian E. Zelizer, ed., *The Presidency of George W. Bush: A First Historical Assessment* (Princeton, NJ: Princeton University Press, 2010), 252–281.

23. Kruse and Zelizer, *Fault Lines*, 189.

24. Maureen Dowd reported this quip in her column, "The 1992 Campaign: Campaign Memo; Voters Want Candidates to Take a Reality Check," *New York Times*, February 17, 1992, https://www.nytimes.com/1992/02/17/us/the-1992-campaign-campaign-memo-voters-want-candidates-to-take-a-reality-check.html, accessed July 29, 2021.

25. On NAFTA, see Engel, *When the World Seemed New*; Benjamin C. Waterhouse, *Lobbying America: The Politics of Business from Nixon to NAFTA* (Princeton, NJ: Princeton University Press, 2014), 243–247; Maxwell A. Cameron and Brian W. Tomlin, *The Making of NAFTA: How the Deal Was Done* (Ithaca, NY: Cornell University Press, 2000); Gwen Ifill, "The 1992 Campaign: The Democrats: With Reservations, Clinton Endorses Free-Trade Pact," *New York Times*, October 5, 1992, https://www.nytimes.com/1992/10/05/us/1992-campaign-democrats-with-reservations-clinton-endorses-free-trade-pact.html, accessed August 9, 2021; Bill Clinton, "Remarks at the Signing Ceremony for the Supplemental Agreements to the North American Free Trade Agreement," September 14, 1993, https://www.presidency.ucsb.edu/documents/remarks-the-signing-ceremony-for-the-supplemental-agreements-the-north-american-free-trade, accessed May 21, 2018; Bill Clinton, "Remarks on Signing the North American Free Trade Agreement Implementation Act," December 8, 1993, https://www.presidency.ucsb.edu/documents/remarks-signing-the-north-american-free-trade-agreement-implementation-act, accessed May 21, 2018.

26. Patrick Joseph Buchanan, "Culture War Speech: Address to the Republican National Convention, August 17, 1992," *Voices of Democracy: The U.S. Oratory Project*, https://voicesofdemocracy.umd.edu/buchanan-culture-war-speech-speech-text/, accessed May 19, 2020.

27. See, also, Patrick Buchanan, *The Death of the West: How Dying Populations and Immigrant Invasions Imperil Our Country and Civilization* (New York: St. Martin's, 2001), and *State of Emergency: The Third World Invasion and the Conquest of America* (New York: Thomas Dunne Books, St. Martin's Press, 2006).

28. Gerald Posner, *Ross Perot: His Life and Times* (New York: Random House, 1996); Ken Gross, *Perot: The Man Behind the Myth* (New York: Random House, 2012).

29. Dave Maraniss, *First in His Class: A Biography of Bill Clinton* (New York: Simon and Schuster, 1996); Bill Clinton, *My Life* (New York: Knopf, 2004); William Chafe, *Bill and Hillary: The Politics of the Personal* (New York: Farrar, Straus and Giroux, 2012); Michael Tomasky, *Bill Clinton: The American Presidents' Series, The 42nd President, 1993–2001* (New York: Times Books, 2017).

30. On his late-night bull sessions and other glimpses into Clinton's complicated, private world, see Taylor Branch, *The Clinton Tapes: Wrestling History with the President* (New York: Simon and Schuster, 2009).

31. Maraniss, *First in His Class.*

32. Lawrence R. Jacobs and Theda Skocpol, *Health Care Reform and American Politics: What Everyone Needs to Know* (New York: Oxford University Press, 2010).

33. Steve Gillon, *The Pact: Bill Clinton, Newt Gingrich, and the Rivalry That Defined a Generation* (New York: Oxford University Press, 2008); Julian E. Zelizer, *Burning Down the House: Newt Gingrich and the Rise of the New Republican Party* (New York: Penguin Books, 2020); Sean Wilentz, *The Age of Reagan: A History, 1974–2008* (New York: HarperCollins, 2008).

34. Dick Morris and Eileen McGann, *Because He Could* (New York: HarperCollins, 2004).

35. Wilentz, *The Age of Reagan*, and Joseph E. Stiglitz, *The Roaring Nineties: A New History of the World's Most Prosperous Decade* (New York: W. W. Norton, 2003).

36. Clinton, "Remarks on Signing the North American Free Trade Agreement Implementation Act."

37. David E. Rosenbaum, "The Budget Struggle; Clinton Wins Approval of His Budget Plan as Gore Votes to Break Senate Deadlock," *New York Times*, August 7, 1993, https://www.nytimes.com/1993/08/07/us/budget-struggle-clinton-wins-approval-his-budget-plan-gore-votes-break-senate.html, accessed August 9, 2021; Eric Pianin and David S. Hilzenrath, "Senate Passes Clinton Budget Bill, 51–50, After Kerrey Reluctantly Casts

'Yes' Vote," *Washington Post*, August 7, 1993, https://www.washingtonpost.
com/archive/politics/1993/08/07/senate-passes-clinton-budget-bill-51-50-
after-kerrey-reluctantly-casts-yes-vote/e9c37591-86f5-4ca8-ad84-f6e836899
9cb/, accessed August 9, 2021; Steven Greenhouse, "When Robert Rubin
Talks . . . ," *New York Times*, July 25, 1993, https://www.nytimes.com/
1993/07/25/business/when-robert-rubin-talks.html, accessed August 8,
2021; David E. Sanger, "Robert E. Rubin—Treasury Secretary," *New York
Times*, December 14, 1996, https://www.nytimes.com/1996/12/14/us/rob
ert-e-rubin-treasury-secretary.html, accessed August 8, 2021.

38.   Kruse and Zelizer, *Fault Lines*, 210.

39.   Lawrence H. Summers, "The Great Liberator," *New York Times*,
November 19, 2006.

40.   For the attacks on big-city machines that sprang from the Great Society's
Community Action Programs, see Allen J. Matusow, *The Unraveling of
America: A History of Liberalism in the 1960s* (New York: Harper and Row,
1984). On the New Left's contribution to neoliberalism's emergence, see
Reuel Schiller, "Regulation and the Collapse of the New Deal Order or
How I Learned to Stop Worrying and Love the Market," and Paul Sabin,
"Environmental Law and the End of the New Deal Order," both in Gary
Gerstle, Nelson Lichtenstein, and Alice O'Connor, eds., *Beyond the New
Deal Order* (Philadelphia: University of Pennsylvania Press, 2019), 186-
203 and 168-185. See also Paul Sabin, *Public Citizen: The Attack on Big
Government and the Remaking of American Liberalism* (New York: W.
W. Norton, 2021).

41.   See Chapter 3 for more on Nader and the New Left origins of
neoliberalism.

42.   See Chapter 4, and Kenneth S. Baer, *Reinventing Democrats: The Politics
of Liberalism from Reagan to Clinton* (Lawrence: University of Kansas
Press, 2000; Al From, *The New Democrats and the Return to Power*
(New York: Palgrave Macmillan, 2013); Michael Kazin, *What It Took to
Win: A History of the Democratic Party* (New York: Farrar, Straus and
Giroux, 2022); Iwan Morgan, "Jimmy Carter, Bill Clinton, and the New
Democratic Economics," *Historical Journal* 47 (2004), 1015–1039; Lily
Geismer, *Don't Blame Us: Suburban Liberals and the Transformation of the
Democratic Party* (Princeton, NJ: Princeton University Press, 2015).

43.   Kruse and Zelizer, *Fault Lines*, 232; Margaret O'Mara, *The Code: Silicon
Valley and the Remaking of America* (New York: Penguin Press, 2019).

44.   President William Jefferson Clinton, "2000 State of the Union Address,"
January 27, 2000, reprinted in the *New York Times*, January 28, 2000,
https://www.nytimes.com/2000/01/28/us/state-union-president-clinton-
state-union-strongest-it-has-ever-been.html, accessed July 14, 2020.

45.   O'Mara, *The Code*; Fred Turner, *From Counterculture to
Cyberculture: Stewart Brand, the Whole Earth Network, and the Rise of
Digital Utopianism* (Chicago, IL: University of Chicago Press, 2008).

46. Alvin and Heidi Toffler had outlined their theory of the three waves in their bestselling 1980 book, *Third Wave* (New York: Bantam Books, 1980). Alvin Toffler had risen to prominence with his previous book *Future Shock* (New York: Random House, 1970).

47. Esther Dyson, George Gilder, George Keyworth, and Alvin Toffler, "Cyberspace and the American Dream: A Magna Carta for the Knowledge Age," http://www.pff.org/issues-pubs/futureinsights/fi1.2mag nacarta.html, accessed July 29, 2021.

48. Dyson et al., "Cyberspace and the American Dream."

49. Dyson et al., "Cyberspace and the American Dream." Alvin Toffler had been born to Jewish immigrants in New York in 1928 and was exposed across his childhood and adolescence to leftist ideas circulating in his extended family milieu. He met his future wife, Heidi (Adelaide Elizabeth Farrell), while both were civil rights and labor activists in the 1940s. See Jill Leovy, "Alvin Toffler, Author of 1970 Bestseller 'Future Shock,' Dies at 87," *Los Angeles Times*, June 29, 2016, https://www.lati mes.com/local/obituaries/la-me-alvin-toffler-20160629-snap-story.html, accessed July 29, 2021; Kenneth Schneider, "Alvin Toffler, Author of 'Future Shock,' Dies at 87," *New York Times*, June 29, 2021, https://www. nytimes.com/2016/06/30/books/alvin-toffler-author-of-future-shock-dies-at-87.html, accessed July 29, 2021; David Henry, "Alvin Toffler, Author of Best-Selling 'Future Shock' and 'The Third Wave,' Dies at 87," *Washington Post*, June 29, 2016, https://www.washingtonpost.com/busin ess/alvin-toffler-author-of-best-selling-future-shock-and-the-third-wave-dies-at-87/2016/06/29/0d63748c-3e09-11e6-80bc-d06711fd2125_story.html, accessed August 10, 2021. See also Toffler's interview with Kevin Kelly, "Anticipatory Democracy," *Wired*, July 1, 1996, https://kk.org/wp-content/ uploads/2010/06/Alvin-Toffler.pdf, accessed August 10, 2021.

50. Dyson et al., "Cyberspace and the American Dream." See also Jill Lepore, *These Truths: A History of the United States* (New York: W. W. Norton, 2019), Part IV.

51. Dyson et al., "Cyberspace and the American Dream."

52. George Gilder, *Wealth and Poverty* (New York: Basic Books, 1981). On Dyson, see Paulina Borsook, "Release," *Wired*, May 1, 1993, https://www. wired.com/1993/05/dyson-3/, accessed August 12, 2021; Claudia Dreifus, "The Cyber-Maxims of Esther Dyson," *New York Times*, July 7, 1996, https://www.nytimes.com/1996/07/07/magazine/the-cyber-maxims-of-est her-dyson.html?searchResultPosition=2, accessed August 10, 2021.

53. O'Mara, *The Code*, 325.

54. Esther Dyson, "Friend and Foe," *Wired*, August 1, 1995, https://www. wired.com/1995/08/newt/, accessed August 10, 2021.

55. Steve Gillon has grasped the ways in which the thinking of adversaries Clinton and Gingrich converged. See Gillon, *The Pact*.

56. On Silicon Valley and visions of personal freedom, see O'Mara, *The Code*, and Turner, *From Counterculture to Cyberculture*.

57. Vice President Al Gore, *The Gore Report on Reinventing Government: Creating a Government That Works Better and Costs Less* (New York: Times Books, 1993); Stephen Barr, "Reinventing Government Is an Idea Whose Time Has Come—Again," *Washington Post*, October 22, 2000, https://www.washingtonpost.com/archive/local/2000/10/22/reinventing-government-is-an-idea-whose-time-has-come-again/b52a1e17-d18a-438e-ab48-a9e5eabad6c8/, accessed August 9, 2021; Ronald C. Moe, "The 'Reinventing Government' Exercise: Misinterpreting the Problem, Misjudging the Consequences," *Public Administration Review* 54 (March–April 1994), 111–122; William A. Galston and Geoffrey L. Tibbetts, "Reinventing Federalism: The Clinton/Gore Program for a New Partnership Among the Federal, State, Local and Tribal Governments," *Publius: The Journal of Federalism* 24 (Summer 1994), 23–48; Jonathan D. Breul and John M. Kamensky, "Federal Government Reform: Lessons from Clinton's 'Reinventing Government' and Bush's 'Management Agenda' Initiatives," *Public Administration Review* 68 (November–December 2008), 1009–1026; Charles C. Clark, "Reinventing Government—Two Decades Later," *Government Executive*, April 26, 2013, https://www.govexec.com/management/2013/04/what-reinvention-wrought/62836/, accessed August 9, 2021; Nelson Lichtenstein, *A Fabulous Failure: Bill Clinton and American Capitalism* (forthcoming). On the Clinton presidency more generally, see William C. Berman, *From the Center to the Edge: The Politics and Policies of the Clinton Presidency* (Lanham, MD: Rowman and Littlefield, 2001); Haynes Johnson, *The Best of Times: America in the Clinton Years* (New York: Harcourt, 2001); Joe Klein, *The Natural: The Misunderstood Presidency of Bill Clinton* (New York: Doubleday, 2002); Alex Waddan, *Clinton's Legacy? A New Democrat in Governance* (New York: Palgrave, 2002); Nigel Hamilton, *Bill Clinton: An American Journey—Great Expectations* (New York: Random House, 2003); John F. Harris, *The Survivor: Bill Clinton in the White House* (New York: Random House, 2005); Nigel Hamilton, *Bill Clinton: Mastering the Presidency* (New York: Public Affairs, 2007); Jack Godwin, *Clintonomics: How Bill Clinton Reengineered the Reagan Revolution* (New York: American Management Association, 2009).

58. On the regulatory apparatus for the communication industry established in the 1930s and how it evolved over the twentieth century, see Patricia Aufderheide, *Communications Policy and the Public Interest: The Telecommunications Act of 1996* (New York: Guildford Press, 1999); Erik Barnouw, *A Tower in Babel: A History of Broadcasting in the United States to 1933* (New York: Oxford University Press, 1966); Erik Barnouw, *The Golden Web: A History of American Broadcasting, 1933–1953* (New York: Oxford University Press, 1968); Erik Barnouw,

The Image Empire: A History of American Broadcasting from 1953 (New York: Oxford University Press, 1970); Susan Douglas, *Inventing American Broadcasting, 1899–1922* (Baltimore, MD: Johns Hopkins University Press, 1989); Robert McChesney, *Telecommunications, Mass Media, and Democracy: The Battle for Control of U.S. Media, 1928–1935* (New York: Oxford University Press, 1995); James A. Baughman, *Same Time, Same Station: Creating American Television, 1948–1961* (Baltimore, MD: Johns Hopkins University Press, 2007); Julian E. Zelizer, "How Washington Helped Create the Contemporary Media: Ending the Fairness Doctrine in 1987," in Bruce J. Schulman and Julian E. Zelizer, eds., *Media Nation: The Political History of News in Modern America* (Philadelphia: University of Pennsylvania Press, 2017), 176-189; Anna Cardoso, "The Rise of the Right-Wing Media and the Repeal of the Fairness Doctrine in the USA" (undergraduate dissertation, University of Cambridge, 2019).

59. See, in particular, Walter Lippmann, *Public Opinion* (New York: Harcourt Brace, 1922) and *The Phantom Public* (New York: Harcourt Brace, 1925).

60. On the Fairness doctrine, see Zelizer, "How Washington Helped Create the Contemporary Media," and Cardoso, "The Rise of the Right-Wing Media and the Repeal of the Fairness Doctrine in the USA."

61. One of the key promoters of this vision was cyber-utopian (and longtime lyricist for the Grateful Dead) John Perry Barlow. See his "A Declaration of the Independence of Cyberspace," issued by Electronic Frontier Foundation, February 8, 1996, https://www.eff.org/cyberspace-independe nce, accessed July 29, 2021. Barlow also wrote frequently for *Wired* at this time: "Jack In?" *Wired*, February 1, 1993, https://www.wired.com/1993/02/ jack-in/, accessed August 9, 2021; "The Economy of Ideas," *Wired*, March 1, 1994, https://www.wired.com/1994/03/economy-ideas/, accessed August 9, 2021; "Jackboots on the Infobahn," *Wired*, April 1, 1994, https://www. wired.com/1994/04/privacy-barlow/, accessed August 9, 2021; "Declaring Independence," *Wired*, June 1, 1996, https://www.wired.com/1996/06/ independence/, accessed August 9, 2021; "The Powers That Were," *Wired*, September 1, 1996, https://www.wired.com/1996/09/netizen-10/, accessed August 9, 2021; "The Next Economy of Ideas," *Wired*, October 1, 2000, https://www.wired.com/2000/10/download/, accessed August 9, 2021.

62. Aufderheide, *Communications Policy and the Public Interest.*

63. On the development of the legislation itself and its ambition, see Stiglitz, *The Roaring Nineties,* 87–114; author's phone interview with Stiglitz, May 19, 2020.

64. In one column, Kitman wrote, "I felt like the muckraker Ida Tarbell researching her history of the Standard Oil Company in the mid-1890s as I watched the progress of the new Telecommunications Act sailing through the Give-Them-Everything Congress of 1995." Marvin Kitman,

"The New Robber Barons Telecommunications Act Plays Monopoly with Our Money," *Newsday*, combined editions [Long Island, NY], August 10, 1995, B65.

65. Kitman, "The New Robber Barons." This point of view informs Fraser, *Age of Acquiescence* and Richard White, *The Republic for Which It Stands: The United States During Reconstruction and the Gilded Age 1865–1896* (New York: Oxford University Press, 2017).

66. Marvin Kitman, "Telecom 'Competition'?" *Newsday*, February 18, 1996, 19.

67. Additional Marvin Kitman *Newsday* articles on this subject include: "How to Block This Highway?" *Newsday*, October 18, 1993; "Telecom Act: No Contest Law's Passage May End Competition for Phone, Cable Firms," *Newsday*, August 14, 1995; "The Great Cable Caper," *Newsday*, August 20, 1995; "The Big Get Bigger," *Newsday*, September 3, 1995; "A Cable-Merger Monster," *Newsday*, October 1, 1995; "Octopus Inc. 'NewsHour,'" *Newsday*, October 15, 1995; "Dole's Tilting at TV Titans," *Newsday*, January 21, 1996; "Telecom 'Competition,'" *Newsday*, February 18, 1996; "Ratings Schmatings: It's a Hoax," *Newsday*, January 12, 1997; "Hold the Phone, Mr. Gore / Ever Hear of the Vice President in Hollywood?," *Newsday* October 27, 1997; "Phone and Cable Sharks Merge in a Feeding Frenzy," *Newsday*, June 29, 1998. On the evolution of this legislation, see "Telecommunication Talks," *New York Times*, January 6, 1994, D9; Mary Lu Carnevale, "Commerce Secretary Proposes Changes for Telecommunications Bill in Senate," *Wall Street Journal*, February 23, 1994, A2; "Toward a Free Market in Telecommunications," *Wall Street Journal*, April 19, 1994, A20; Edmund L. Andrews, "House Set to Pass Changes in Telecommunications Rules," *New York Times*, June 27, 1994, D1; Jube Shiver Jr., "Telecommunications Bill Faces Extinction in Senate," *Los Angeles Times*, August 5, 1994, D1; Mike Mills, "Meeting of the Media Giants: Executives and Republicans Trade Views on Telecommunications Law," *Washington Post*, January 21, 1995, C1; Daniel Pearl, "Telecom Deregulation Spawns Rival Bills," *Wall Street Journal*, May 3, 1995, B6; Daniel Pearl, "House Is Expected to Push for Radical Deregulation of Telecommunications," *Wall Street Journal*, June 19, 1995, B1; Jon Van, "'Devil in Details' Visits Deregulation," *Chicago Tribune*, August 8, 1995, C1; Edmund L. Andrews, "For Telecommunications Bill, Time for Some Horse Trading," *New York Times*, December 4, 1995, D1; Mike Mills, "From the Hill's Telecom Tales, a Few Holiday Honors," *Washington Post*, December 24, 1995, 81.

68. Quoted in O'Mara, *The Code*, 332–333.

69. On the effort to insert pornography controls into the legislation, see Pearl, "House Is Expected to Push for Radical Deregulation of Telecommunications"; Andrews, "For Telecommunications Bill, Time for Some Horse Trading"; Mike Godwin, *Cyber Rights: Defending Free*

Speech in the Digital Age (Cambridge, MA: MIT Press, 2003), chapter 10. On efforts to strengthen the FCC and enable it to create an effective regulatory framework for the new bill, see Leslie Cauley, "Telecom Law Faces Challenge in Court," *Wall Street Journal*, August 29, 1996, A3; Mike Mills and Paul Fahri, "This Is a Free Market?" *Washington Post*, January 19, 1997, H1; Mark Rockwell, "Gore, Hundt: Telecom Competition Will Take Time," *CommunicationsWeek*, Manhasset 652, March 3, 1997, T21; John Rendleman and Salvatore Salamone, "Hundt Leaves Office—FCC Chairman Feels Satisfied with Telecom Rulings," *Communications Week*, Manhasset 666, June 2, 1997, 8; Bill Frezza, "Reed Hundt Leaves Mixed Legacy at FCC," *Network Computing*, August 1, 1997, 35.

70. *The Communications Act of 1934*, 47 U.S.C. § 151, Pub. L. 73-416, 48 Stat. 1064, https://transition.fcc.gov/Reports/1934new.pdf, accessed August 10, 2021; Jeff Kosseff, *The Twenty-Six Words That Created the Internet* (Ithaca, NY: Cornell University Press, 2019).

71. Stiglitz, *The Roaring Nineties*, 91; author's interview with Stiglitz.

72. O'Mara, *The Code*, 329–338.

73. Quoted in O'Mara, *The Code*, 336.

74. Lepore, *These Truths*, 729–738.

75. Lepore, *These Truths*, 737.

76. Nicholas Lemann, *Transaction Man: The Rise of the Deal and the Decline of the American Dream* (New York: Farrar, Straus and Giroux, 2019).

77. Ron Suskind, *Confidence Men: Wall Street, Washington, and the Education of a President* (New York: HarperCollins, 2011), 60.

78. Adam Tooze, *Crashed: How a Decade of Financial Crises Changed the World* (New York: Penguin Books, 2018); Dylan Gottlieb, "Yuppies: Young Urban Professionals and the Making of Postindustrial New York" (PhD dissertation, Princeton University, 2020).

79. See, for example, Greta R. Krippner, *Capitalizing on Crisis: The Political Origins of the Rise of Finance* (Cambridge, MA: Harvard University Press, 2011).

80. Stiglitz, *Roaring Nineties*, 158–167; Lemann, *Transaction Man*; Binyamin Appelbaum, *The Economists' Hour: False Prophets, Free Markets, and the Fracture of Society* (New York: Little, Brown, 2019), chapter 10; Zachary D. Carter, *The Price of Peace: Money, Democracy, and the Life of John Maynard Keynes* (New York: Random House, 2020), chapter 17.

81. Shortly after Margaret Thatcher's death, Conor Burns, a Conservative MP, recounted this exchange between Thatcher and a guest at a campaign dinner in his honor: "Asked by a guest at the pre-dinner reception what her greatest achievement was, she replied robustly: 'Tony Blair and New Labour—we forced our opponents to change.'" Conor Burns, "Conor Burns MP: My Fondest Farewell to Margaret Thatcher," *The Telegraph*, April 14, 2013, https://www.telegraph.co.uk/news/polit ics/margaret-thatcher/9991815/Conor-Burns-MP-My-fondest-farew

ell-to-Margaret-Thatcher.html, accessed August 10, 2021. Blair himself almost admitted as much in comments after Thatcher's death: "I always thought my job was to build on some of the things she had done rather than reverse them." "Tony Blair: 'My Job Was to Build on Some Thatcher Policies,'" *BBC News*, April 8, 2013, https://www.bbc.co.uk/news/av/uk-politics-22073434, accessed August 11, 2021. In a 2002 (London) *Times* article, key New Labour advisor Peter Mandelson proclaimed, "We are all Thatcherites now." Reported in Matthew Tempest, "Mandelson: We Are All Thatcherites Now," *The Guardian*, June 10, 2002, https://www.theg uardian.com/politics/2002/jun/10/labour.uk1, accessed August 10, 2021.

82.   Joseph Stiglitz, *The Euro: How a Common Currency Threatens the Future of Europe* (New York: W. W. Norton, 2016).

83.   Tooze, *Crashed*, 81–82.

84.   Tooze, *Crashed*, 80–84.

85.   Robert B. Reich, *Locked in the Cabinet* (New York: Knopf, 1997), 282.

86.   Reich, *Locked in the Cabinet*, 80–83.

87.   See, for example, Robert B. Reich, *The Work of Nations: Preparing Ourselves for 21st-century Capitalism* (New York: Knopf, 1991).

88.   Reich, *Locked in the Cabinet*, 95.

89.   Lichtenstein, *State of the Union*, 212–276.

90.   On the history of welfare reform, see Michael D. Katz, *The Price of Citizenship: Redefining the American Welfare State* (Philadelphia: University of Pennsylvania Press, 2001).

91.   Reich, *Locked in the Cabinet*, 211–212.

92.   Reich, *Locked in the Cabinet*, 211–218.

93.   Reich, *Locked in the Cabinet*, 303–306.

94.   Before his departure, Reich asked the president to do more in his second term to help America's poor. All Clinton could say was: "I've got to deal with these Republicans." Clinton had to deal as well with a neoliberal order that the Republicans had established and that Clinton, across his two terms, felt obligated to secure. Reich, *Locked in the Cabinet*, 347.

95.   "Testimony of Ralph Nader Before the Committee on the Budget, U.S. House of Representatives," June 30, 1999, https://web.archive.org/web/20120204172344/http://www.nader.org/releases/63099.html, accessed April 27, 2020. Nader's protest in Congress took popular form in massive protests against global capital in Seattle in 1999. On Seattle, see Richard Saich, "Social Movements and Resistance to Neoliberalism in America, 1979–2000" (PhD dissertation, University of Cambridge, 2022).

96.   On Clinton's embrace of multiculturalism more generally, see Gary Gerstle, *American Crucible: Race and Nation in the Twentieth Century* (2001; Princeton, NJ: Princeton University Press, 2017), chapter 9.

97.   Clinton regarded the 1993 Oslo Accords between the Israeli government and the Palestine Liberation Organization and the 1998 Good Friday Accords between Protestants and Catholics in Northern Ireland as two

of his greatest achievements. He regarded the last-minute collapse of the ambitious 2000 peace negotiations he had been undertaking with Israel and the PLO as one of his greatest disappointments. See Clinton, *My Life*, 882–945.

98. Clinton, "Address Before a Joint Session of the Congress on the State of the Union," January 27, 2000, https://www.presidency.ucsb.edu/docume nts/address-before-joint-session-the-congress-the-state-the-union-7, accessed August 12, 2021; see also Gerstle, *American Crucible*, chapter 9.

99. These spatial patterns and their political ramifications will be discussed further in Chapter 7.

100. James Q. Wilson, *Thinking About Crime* (1975; New York: Basic Books, 2013). On the hiring of more police and their militarization in the 1990s, see Michelle Alexander, *The New Jim Crow: Mass Incarceration in the Age of Colorblindness* (New York: New Press, 2010), 71–83; "Cops or Soldiers?," *The Economist*, March 20, 2014, https://www.economist.com/united-states/2014/03/20/cops-or-soldiers, accessed September 14, 2021; "How America's Police Became So Heavily Armed," *The Economist*, May 18, 2015, http://www.economist.com/blogs/economist-explains/2015/05/economist-explains-22, accessed September 14, 2021; Joshua Holland, "Cops, Gun Culture and Anti-Government Extremism," *Bill Moyers & Company*, August 26, 2014, http://billmoyers.com/2014/08/26/cops-gun-culture-and-anti-government-extremism/, accessed September 14, 2021.

101. Alexander, *The New Jim Crow*. For a fuller discussion of mass incarceration and its consequences, see Chapters 4 and 7.

102. Gottlieb, "Yuppies."

103. For a sympathetic treatment of Giuliani's mayoralty and rise to power, see Fred Siegel, *The Prince of the City: Giuliani, New York, and the Genius of American Life* (New York: Encounter Books, 2006). On the deployment of the broken windows theory by then New York City police commissioner William Bratton, see William Bratton and Peter Knobler, *Turnaround: How America's Top Cop Reversed the Crime Epidemic* (New York: Random House, 1998).

104. For an early and influential (and mocking) portrait of Yuppies, see David Brooks, *Bobos in Paradise: The New Upper Class and How They Got There* (New York: Simon and Schuster, 2000).

105. For a sampling of these attacks on Bill and Hillary Clinton, see David Brock, *The Seduction of Hillary Rodham* (New York: Free Press, 1996). Brock later recanted his own attacks and turned his partisan fury on his former GOP allies. See David Brock, *Blinded by the Right: The Conscience of an Ex-Conservative* (New York: Crown, 2002). In the 1990s, however, he helped to deepen the cultural fissures between the two parties.

106. On the culture wars, see Andrew Hartman, *A War for the Soul of America: A History of the Culture Wars* (Chicago, IL: University of

Chicago Press, 2015); Robert Hughes, *Culture of Complaint: A Passionate Look at the Ailing Heart of America* (New York: Oxford University Press, 1993). On the political divisions arising from those wars, see Zelizer and Kruse, *Fault Lines*, and Alan I. Abramowitz, *The Polarized Public: Why American Government Is So Dysfunctional* (1994; New York: Pearson, 2012). Abramowitz's "polarization thesis" has become a major area of study for students of American politics.

Chapter 6

1. "Watching for the Y2K Bug," *New York Times*, December 30, 1999, 26; Andy Beckett, "The Bug That Didn't Bite," *The Guardian*, April 24, 2000, https://www.theguardian.com/technology/2000/apr/24/y2k.g2, accessed August 12, 2021; Francine Uenuma, "20 Years Later, the Y2K Bug Seems Like a Joke—Because Those Behind the Scenes Took It Seriously," *Time*, December 30, 2019, https://time.com/5752129/y2k-bug-history/, accessed August 12, 2021. For a cache of the contemporary reporting of the *New York Times* on the millennium bug, see https://archive.nytimes.com/www.nytimes.com/library/tech/reference/millennium-index.html, accessed August 12, 2021.

2. Jeffrey Toobin, *Too Close to Call: The Thirty-Six-Day Battle to Decode the 2000 Election* (New York: Random House, 2001); Peter Baker and Susan Glasser, *The Man Who Ran Washington: The Life and Times of James A. Baker III* (New York: Doubleday, 2020); *Bush v. Gore*, 531 U.S. 98 (2000); Howard Gillman, *The Votes That Counted: How the Court Decided the 2000 Presidential Election* (Chicago, IL: University of Chicago Press, 2001).

3. Lawrence Wright, *The Looming Tower: Al-Qaeda's Road to 9/11* (New York: Knopf, 2006).

4. On the Bush administration's preoccupation with future terrorist attacks, see Robert Draper, *Dead Certain: The Presidency of George W. Bush* (New York: Free Press, 2007); and Robert Draper, *To Start a War: How the Bush Administration Took America into Iraq* (New York: Penguin Press, 2020).

5. U.S. House, 107th Congress, 1st Sess., H.R. 3162, *USA Patriot Act*, Version 1, October 23, 2001. This was also the moment when Guantanamo was established as a place to hold suspected terrorists indefinitely without charging them and without giving them a trial. Jonathan M. Hansen, *Guantánamo: An American History* (New York: Hill and Wang, 2011).

    See also Michael J. Strauss, *The Leasing of Guantanamo Bay* (Westport, CT: Praeger Security International, 2009), and Gary Gerstle and Desmond King, "Spaces of Exception in American History," in Gary Gerstle and Joel Isaac, eds., *States of Exception in American History* (Chicago, IL: University of Chicago Press, 2020).

6. Carter Malkasian, *The American War in Afghanistan: A History* (New York: Oxford University Press, 2021).

7. Draper, *To Start a War*.

8. For a time in the 1980s, when he was warring against Iran, Hussein had actually allied himself with the United States, Draper, *To Start a War*; James Mann, *The Rise of the Vulcans: The History of Bush's War Cabinet* (New York: Penguin Press, 2004).

9. Draper, *To Start a War*.

10. George W. Bush, "President Bush Discusses Freedom in Iraq and Middle East: Remarks by the President at the 20th Anniversary of the National Endowment for Democracy," address to the United States Chamber of Commerce, November 6, 2003, https://georgewbush-whitehouse.archi ves.gov/news/releases/2003/11/20031106-2.html, accessed September 2, 2021; George W. Bush, "President Addresses Nation, Discusses Iraq, War on Terror," June 28, 2005, https://georgewbush-whitehouse.archives.gov/ news/releases/2005/06/20050628-7.html, accessed September 2, 2021. On America's longer and broader struggle in the Middle East, see Andrew J. Bacevich, *America's War in the Greater Middle East: A Military History* (New York: Random House, 2016).

11. Bush, "President Bush Discusses Freedom in Iraq and Middle East." On Wolfowitz and others in the administration urging the Iraq War on Bush, see Draper, *To Start a War*.

12. The Commission on Presidential Debates, "Transcript of 3 October 2000 debate between George W. Bush and Albert Gore," https://www.deba tes.org/voter-education/debate-transcripts/october-3-2000-transcript/, accessed September 2, 2021.

13. George Packer, *The Assassins' Gate: America in Iraq* (New York: Farrar, Straus and Giroux, 2005); Thomas E. Ricks, *Fiasco: The American Military Adventure in Iraq* (New York: Penguin Press, 2006); Naomi Klein, *The Shock Doctrine: The Rise of Disaster Capitalism* (New York: Penguin Press, 2008), 419; Bob Woodward, *Bush at War* (New York: Simon and Schuster, 2002); Bob Woodward, *State of Denial: Bush at War, Part II* (New York: Simon and Schuster, 2006); Bush gave his carrier speech on May 1, 2003. Ricks, *Fiasco*, 145.

14. Packer, *Assassins' Gate*.

15. Sean Laughlin, "Rumsfeld on Looting in Iraq: 'Stuff Happens,'" CNN, April 12, 2003, https://edition.cnn.com/2003/US/04/11/sprj.irq.pentagon/, accessed September 26, 2021.

16. Klein, *Shock Doctrine*, Part 6; Lionel Beehner, "Iraq's Faltering Infrastructure," Council on Foreign Relations, June 22, 2006, https:// www.cfr.org/backgrounder/iraqs-faltering-infrastructure, accessed February 18, 2021.

17. Draper, *To Start a War*.

18. L. Paul Bremer III, *My Year in Iraq: The Struggle to Build a Future of Hope* (New York: Simon and Schuster, 2006), 125.

19. Bremer, *My Year in Iraq*, 63.

20. Ricks, *Fiasco*, 158 and passim.

21. Ricks, *Fiasco*.

22. Klein, *Shock Doctrine*, 441–442 and passim.

23. Many of Halliburton's contracts were funneled through its subsidiary, Kellogg, Brown, and Root (KBR). Klein, *Shock Doctrine*, Part 6, passim; Packer, *Assassins' Gate*.

24. Klein, *Shock Doctrine*, 444.

25. Klein, *Shock Doctrine*, 447.

26. Ricks, *Fiasco*, 202.

27. Rajiv Chandrasekaran, *Imperial Life in the Emerald City: Inside Iraq's Green Zone* (London: Bloomsbury, 2006).

28. Packer, *Assassins' Gate*, 127.

29. Other similarly unqualified young Republicans were thrust into equally consequential posts. A twenty-four-year-old political science major from Yale was asked to restart Baghdad's stock exchange. See Yochi J. Dreazen, "How a 24-Year-Old Got a Job Rebuilding Iraq's Stock Market," *Wall Street Journal*, January 28, 2004, https://www.wsj.com/articles/SB1075244 35490013389, accessed September 16, 2021.

30. Ricks, *Fiasco*.

31. Ricks, *Fiasco*.

32. Packer, *Assassins' Gate*, 124.

33. On the costs of war, see Michael B. Kelley and Geoffrey Ingersoll, "By the Numbers: The Staggering Cost of the Iraq War," *Business Insider*, March 20, 2013, https://www.businessinsider.com/iraq-war-facts-numb ers-stats-total-2013-3?r=US&IR=T, accessed September 2, 2021; Roberta Cohen, "Iraq's Displaced: Where to Turn?," *Brookings Institute Report* (2008), https://www.brookings.edu/articles/iraqs-displaced-where-to-turn/, accessed September 2, 2021; Klein, *Shock Doctrine*, Part 6, passim; Beehner, "Iraq's Faltering Infrastructure"; Mohammed Hayder Sadeq and Sabah al-Anbaki, "Cell Phone Service Spotty, but Reception's Been Great," *USA Today*, March 3, 2005, https://usatoday30.usatoday.com/ news/world/iraq/2005-03-03-cell-phones_x.htm, accessed September 6, 2021; "Lacking Water and Power, Iraqis Run Out of Patience in the Searing Summer Heat," *The Guardian*, August 16, 2003, https://www.theg uardian.com/world/2003/aug/16/iraq, accessed September 6, 2021.

34. On Abu Ghraib, see Mark Danner, *Torture and Truth: America, Abu Ghraib, and the War on Terror* (New York: New York Review of Books, 2004); Seymour M. Hersh, *Chain of Command: The Road from 9/11 to Abu Ghraib* (New York: HarperCollins, 2004); Philip Gourevitch and Errol Morris, *The Ballad of Abu Ghraib* (London: Picador, 2008); Karen J. Greenberg and Joshua L. Dratel, eds., *The Torture Papers: The Road to*

Abu Ghraib (New York: Cambridge University Press, 2005). On the turn to private soldiers and contractors, see Jeremy Scahill, *Blackwater: The Rise of the World's Most Powerful Mercenary Army* (New York: PublicAffairs, 2007); and Jeremy Scahill, *Dirty Wars: The World Is a Battlefield* (New York: PublicAffairs, 2013).

35. On the turn to an all-volunteer army, see Beth Bailey, *America's Army: Making the All-Volunteer Force* (Cambridge, MA: Harvard University Press, 2009).

36. On Bush's neoliberal policies, see John Robert Greene, *The Presidency of George W. Bush* (Lawrence: University Press of Kansas, 2021); Peter Baker, *Days of Fire: Bush and Cheney in the White House* (New York: Doubleday, 2013).

37. Thomas L. Friedman, *The World Is Flat: A Brief History of the Twenty-First Century* (New York: Farrar, Straus and Giroux, 2005), 5; see also Thomas L. Friedman, *The Lexus and the Olive Tree: Understanding Globalization* (New York: Random House, 1999).

38. Thomas L. Friedman, "Three Cheers for Pluralism over Separatism," *New York Times*, September 20, 2014, https://www.nytimes.com/2014/09/21/opinion/sunday/thomas-l-friedman-three-cheers-for-pluralism-over-sep aratism.html, accessed August 31, 2021.

39. Gary Gerstle, "Minorities, Multiculturalism, and the Presidency of George W. Bush," in Julian Zelizer, ed., *The Presidency of George W. Bush: A First Historical Assessment* (Princeton, NJ: Princeton University Press, 2010), 252–281; Jacob Weisberg, *The Bush Tragedy* (New York: Random House, 2008), 51–54. Bush remained committed to pluralism as a virtue, as his public address marking the twentieth anniversary of 9/11 reveals. See Amy B. Wang and Caroline Anders, "George W. Bush Compares 'Violent Extremists at Home' to 9/11 Terrorists in 20th Anniversary Speech," *Washington Post*, September 11, 2021, https://www.washingtonpost.com/politics/2021/09/11/george-w-bush-compares-violent-extremists-home-911-terrorists-20th-anniversary-speech/, accessed September 13, 2021.

40. John O'Sullivan, "Bush's Latin Beat: A Vision, but a Faulty One," *National Review*, July 23, 2001, 35–36.

41. Draper, *Dead Certain*, 147.

42. In Bush's view, the free movement of people into the United States—and the opening of borders between the United States and Mexico and the United States and Canada—would strengthen US capitalists throughout the hemisphere by encouraging free trade, specialization, and an unending supply of low-wage labor. On Bush's vision of a hemispheric economy led by American business, see Gerstle, "Minorities, Multiculturalism, and the Presidency of George W. Bush." Estimates of the percentage of the Hispanic vote won by Bush in 2004 vary from 35 to 45 percent, but the "standard statistic," writes a leading group of political

scientists, "has become 40%." See David L. Leal, Stephen A. Nuno, Johngo Lee, and Rudolfo O. de la Garza, "Latinos, Immigration, and the 2006 Midterm Election," *PS: Political Science and Politics* 41 (April 2008), 309. See also David L. Leal, Matt A. Barreto, Jongho Lee, and Rodolfo O. de la Garza, "The Latino Vote in the 2004 Election," *PS: Political Science and Politics* 38 (January 2005), 41–49; Ruy Teixeira, "44 Percent of Hispanics Voted for Bush?" *AlterNet.org*, November 24, 2004, https://www.alternet.org/2004/11/44_percent_of_hispanics_voted_for_bush/, accessed September 2, 2021; and Roberto Suro, Richard Fry, and Jeffrey Passel, "Hispanics and the 2004 Election: Population, Electorate and Voters," *Pew Hispanic Center, a Pew Research Center Project*, June 27, 2005, https://www.pewresearch.org/hispanic/2005/06/27/hispanics-and-the-2004-election/, accessed September 6, 2021.

43. Bush, "President Bush Discusses Freedom in Iraq and Middle East"; Bush, "President Addresses Nation, Discusses Iraq, War on Terror."

44. Philip Weiss, "'I Would Do It Again'—Tom Friedman Stands by Support for Iraq War in 'Personal Crusade' to Change Arab World," *Mondoweiss*, November 22, 2019, https://mondoweiss.net/2019/11/i-would-do-it-again-tom-friedman-stands-by-support-for-iraq-war-in-personal-crusade-to-change-arab-world/, accessed March 5, 2021.

In 2003, shortly after America declared victory in Iraq, Friedman made this admission to his *New York Times* readers. It had been important for America, Friedman wrote, "to hit someone in the Arab-Muslim world." It didn't have to be Iraq. It could have been Saudi Arabia or Pakistan. But "Afghanistan wasn't enough." The hit had to be bigger. It was the only way, he argued, to break the "Arab-Muslim" world's attachment to terror and to its twin, a closed society, and to convey to inhabitants of that world that the West was serious about protecting its open, pluralistic society. Friedman believed he was ventriloquizing Bush, saying what Bush would not, because "the Bush team never dared to spell out the real reason for the war." Thomas L. Friedman, "Because We Could," *New York Times*, June 4, 2003, https://www.nytimes.com/2003/06/04/opinion/because-we-could.html, accessed July 28, 2021.

45. George W. Bush, "President's Remarks at the 2004 Republican National Convention," September 2, 2004, https://georgewbush-whitehouse.archives.gov/news/releases/2004/09/20040902-2.html, accessed September 1, 2021.

46. Thomas J. Sugrue, *Origins of the Urban Crisis: Race and Inequality in Postwar Detroit* (Princeton, NJ: Princeton University Press, 2014); David M. P. Freund, *Colored Property: State Policy and White Racial Politics in Suburban America* (Chicago, IL: University of Chicago Press, 2007); Ira Katznelson, *When Affirmative Action Was White: An Untold History of Racial Inequality in Twentieth-Century America* (New York: W. W. Norton, 2005); Richard Rothstein, *The Color of*

Law: A Forgotten History of How Our Government Segregated America (New York: Liveright, 2017); Mechele Dickerson, *Homeownership and America's Financial Underclass: Flawed Premises, Broken Promises, New Prescriptions* (New York: Cambridge University Press, 2014); Keeanga-Yamahtta Taylor, *Race for Profit: How Banks and the Real Estate Industry Undermined Black Homeownership* (Chapel Hill: University of North Carolina Press, 2019).

47. George W. Bush, "President Hosts Conference on Minority Homeownership," George Washington University, Washington, DC, October 15, 2002, https://georgewbush-whitehouse.archives.gov/news/releases/2002/10/20021015-7.html, accessed September 10, 2021.

48. George H. W. Bush signed the Federal Housing Enterprises Financial Safety and Soundness Act into law in 1992. He had also launched the HOPE (Homeownership and Opportunity for People Everywhere) Initiative in 1989, which offered $2.1 billion in grants to encourage an expansion of home ownership among low-income families. "White House Fact Sheet on the HOPE Initiative: Homeownership and Opportunity for People Everywhere," November 10, 1989, https://www.presidency.ucsb.edu/documents/white-house-fact-sheet-the-hope-initiative-homeownership-and-opportunity-for-people, accessed September 8, 2021. See also Dickerson, *Homeownership and America's Financial Underclass*, 72, and passim. On GSEs, see also Adam Tooze, *Crashed: How a Decade of Financial Crises Changed the World* (New York: Penguin Books, 2018), 46–49.

49. Nearly 10 percent of mortgages issued during the Clinton administration were judged to be risky, or subprime. They were popular with investors because they carried higher interest rates. Many were backed by GSEs Fannie Mae and Freddie Mac, giving investors confidence that the government was backstopping their investment. Dickerson, *Homeownership and America's Financial Underclass*, 78, and passim.

50. Tooze, *Crashed*, chapter 2, passim.

51. Dickerson, *Homeownership and America's Financial Underclass*, 184; Tooze, *Crashed*, chapter 2; Nicholas Lemann, *Transaction Man: The Rise of the Deal and the Decline of the American Dream* (New York: Farrar, Straus and Giroux, 2019), chapter 4.

52. *American Dream Downpayment Act*, 2003, Pub.L. 108–186, https://www.congress.gov/congressional-report/108th-congress/house-report/164, accessed September 10, 2021; Brian Sullivan, "Bush Signs American Dream Downpayment Act," HUD News Release, December 16, 2003, https://archives.hud.gov/news/2003/pr03-140.cfm, accessed September 10, 2021. For a collection of Bush administration documents on homeownership, see the archived George W. Bush White House website's "Policies in Focus: Homeownership," webpage: https://georgewbush-whitehouse.archives.gov/infocus/homeownership/, accessed September 9,

2021. See also George W. Bush, "Radio Address by the President to the Nation," June 9, 2001, https://georgewbush-whitehouse.archives.gov/news/releases/2001/06/20010608-7.html, accessed September 10, 2021; Bush, "National Homeownership Month, 2002," June 4, 2002, https://georgewbush-whitehouse.archives.gov/news/releases/2002/06/20020604-23.html, accessed September 10, 2021; Bush, "President Focuses on Home-Ownership in Radio Address," June 15, 2002, https://georgewbush-whitehouse.archives.gov/news/releases/2002/06/20020615.html, accessed September 10, 2021; "Fact Sheet: President Bush Calls for Expanding Opportunities to Homeownership," https://georgewbush-whitehouse.archives.gov/news/releases/2002/06/20020617.html, accessed September 10, 2021; Bush, "President Calls for Expanding Opportunities to Home Ownership," St. Paul AME Church, Atlanta, Georgia, June 17, 2002, https://georgewbush-whitehouse.archives.gov/news/releases/2002/06/20020617-2.html, accessed September 10, 2021; Bush, "President Reiterates Goal on Homeownership," Department of Housing and Development, Washington, DC, June 18, 2002, https://georgewbush-whitehouse.archives.gov/news/releases/2002/06/20020618-1.html, accessed September 10, 2021; Bush, "National Homeownership Month, 2003," June 13, 2003, https://georgewbush-whitehouse.archives.gov/news/releases/2003/06/20030613.html, accessed September 10, 2021; Bush, "President's Remarks to the National Association of Home Builders," Greater Columbus Convention Center, Columbus, OH, October 2, 2004, https://georgewbush-whitehouse.archives.gov/news/releases/2004/10/20041002-7.html, accessed September 10, 2021; Bush, "National Homeownership Month, 2005," May 25, 2005, https://georgewbush-whitehouse.archives.gov/news/releases/2005/05/20050525-14.html, accessed September 10, 2021; Bush, "President Discusses Education, Entrepreneurship & Home Ownership at Indiana Black Expo," RCA Dome, Indianapolis, IN, July 14, 2005, https://georgewbush-whitehouse.archives.gov/news/releases/2005/07/20050714-4.html, accessed September 10, 2021; Bush, "National Homeownership Month, 2006," May 24, 2006, https://georgewbush-whitehouse.archives.gov/news/releases/2006/05/20060524-6.html, accessed September 10, 2021; Bush, "President Pleased by House Passage of the 'Expanding American Homeownership Act of 2006,'" July 26, 2006, https://georgewbush-whitehouse.archives.gov/news/releases/2006/07/20060726.html, accessed September 10, 2021.

53. Bush's No Child Left Behind program suffered from insufficient funding, as did his pledge to shift welfare work from the government to churches. See Gerstle, "Minorities, Multiculturalism, and the Presidency of George W. Bush."

54. Dickerson, *Homeownership and America's Financial Underclass*, 78, 108.

55. Dickerson, *Homeownership and America's Financial Underclass*, 184-185.

56. The rate of white homeownership remained larger still (76 percent), but the gap between white and nonwhite rates had narrowed considerably. Dickerson, *Homeownership and America's Financial Underclass*, 184.

57. Matthew C. Klein and Michael Pettis, *Trade Wars Are Class Wars: How Rising Inequality Distorts the Global Economy and Threatens International Peace* (New Haven, CT: Yale University Press, 2020), 207.

58. Laurence H. Summers, "Speech at IMF Fourteenth Annual Research Conference in Honor of Stanley Fischer," *Larrysummers.com*, November 8, 2013, http://larrysummers.com/imf-fourteenth-annual-research-confere nce-in-honor-of-stanley-fischer/, accessed September 2, 2021. For insight into Greenspan, see Binyamin Appelbaum, *The Economists' Hour: How the False Prophets of Free Markets Fractured Our Society* (New York: Little, Brown, 2019), 298–308.

59. American homeowners, Adam Tooze has noted, "were the greatest source of demand for the world economy." Tooze, *Crashed*, 43.

60. Sebastian Mallaby, *The Man Who Knew: The Life and Times of Alan Greenspan* (New York: Penguin Press, 2016); Robert D. Auerbach, *Deception and Abuse at the Fed: Henry B. Gonzalez Battles Alan Greenspan's Bank* (Austin: University of Texas Press, 2008).

61. Gerstle, "Minorities, Multiculturalism, and the Presidency of George W. Bush"; Weisberg, *The Bush Tragedy*; Draper, *Dead Certain*; Ron Suskind, *The Price of Loyalty: George W. Bush, the White House, and the Education of Paul O'Neil* (New York: Simon and Schuster, 2004).

62. Jo Becker, Sheryl Gay Stolberg, and Stephen Labaton, "Bush Drive for Home Ownership Fueled Housing Bubble," *New York Times*, December 21, 2008, https://www.nytimes.com/2008/12/21/business/worldbusiness/ 21iht-admin.4.18853088.htm, accessed September 2, 2021.

63. Kevin M. Kruse and Julian E. Zelizer, *Fault Lines: A History of the United States Since 1974* (New York: W. W. Norton, 2019), 292.

64. Tooze, *Crashed*, 171.

65. Representative Ron Paul from Texas was one of their leaders. The bailout of Bear Stearns had created a fissure in the GOP between the true believers in deregulation and the party's business elite. The latter argued that neoliberal principles had to be compromised on occasion for the sake of a financial system's overall health. The Fannie Mae and Freddie Mac bailout widened that fissure into a chasm. Tooze, *Crashed*, 172–174.

66. To this day, we do not know why the Bush administration did not step up to save Lehman. Had top economic officials been intimidated from saving yet another private bank by an outraged GOP rank and file? Did they think that the Lehman collapse was bearable, and even useful in setting limits on their willingness to bail out financial institutions? Or had the Bush advisors simply miscalculated? Whatever the motivation, the refusal to step in backfired. On the crisis days of September and October 2008, see Andrew Ross Sorkin, *Too Big to Fail: Inside the Battle to Save Wall*

Street (London: Allen Lane, 2009); David Wessel, *In FED We Trust: Ben Bernanke's War on the Great Panic* (London: Scribe, 2009); Ron Suskind, *Confidence Men: Wall Street, Washington, and the Education of a President* (New York: HarperCollins, 2011); Jonathan Levy, *Ages of American Capitalism: A History of the United States* (New York: Random House, 2021), 702–732; Lawrence Jacobs and Desmond King, *Fed Power: How Finance Wins* (2016; New York: Oxford University Press, 2021); Ben S. Bernanke, *The Federal Reserve and the Financial Crisis* (Princeton, NJ: Princeton University Press, 2013); Ben S. Bernanke, Timothy F. Geithner, and Henry M. Paulson Jr., *Firefighting: The Financial Crisis and Its Lessons* (New York: Penguin Press, 2019).

67.   Tooze, *Crashed*, 178; Congressional Oversight Panel, "The AIG Rescue, Its Impact on Markets, and the Government's Exit Strategy," *June Oversight Report*, June 10, 2010, https://fraser.stlouisfed.org/files/docs/his torical/fct/cop_report_20100610.pdf, accessed September 2, 2021.

68.   To secure those credits, AIG had to hand over to the Fed tens of billions of dollars in share certificates, accept an 80 percent federal government equity share (tantamount to a temporary nationalization), and compel its shareholders to receive pennies on every dollar of AIG shares they held. Tooze, *Crashed*, 178.

69.   Henry M. Paulson Jr., *On the Brink: Inside the Race to Stop the Collapse of the Global Financial System* (New York: Grand Central, 2010); Ben S. Bernanke, *The Courage to Act: A Memoir of a Crisis and Its Aftermath* (New York: W. W. Norton, 2015); Timothy F. Geithner, *Stress Test: Reflections on Financial Crises* (New York: Crown, 2014).

70.   David M. Herszenhorn, "Administration Is Seeking $700 Billion for Wall Street," *New York Times*, September 20, 2008, https://www.nytimes.com/ 2008/09/21/business/21cong.html, accessed September 6, 2021.

71.   By the end of November, the Dow would stand at 7,552.29, almost a third below where it had been in September.

72.   By this point, the stock market had lost nearly 20 percent of its value in one week.

73.   Bernanke, *The Courage to Act*; Bernanke, *Federal Reserve and the Financial Crisis*.

74.   "Great Recession," *Encyclopedia Britannica*, https://www.britannica.com/ topic/great-recession, accessed September 8, 2021; Tooze, *Crashed*, 156.

75.   Dickerson, *Home Ownership and America's Financial Underclass*, 15, 184, passim.

76.   Tooze, *Crashed*, 157–160.

77.   Bush's approval rating stood at 20 percent in his last month in office. Suskind, *Confidence Men*, 124.

78.   Tom Leonard, "Barack Obama Inauguration: Two Million Turn Out to Greet Their New President," *The Telegraph*, January 21, 2009. http://www.telegraph.co.uk/news/worldnews/barackobama/4300880/

Barack-Obama-inauguration-Two-million-turn-out-to-greet-their-new-president.html, accessed June 10, 2021. On the rise of Obama, see Barack Obama, *Dreams from My Father: A Story of Race and Inheritance* (New York: Crown, 2004); Barack Obama, *The Audacity of Hope: Thoughts on Reclaiming the American Dream* (New York: Crown, 2006); David Remnick, *The Bridge: The Life and Rise of Barack Obama* (London: Pan Macmillan, 2010); James T. Kloppenberg, *Reading Obama: Dreams, Hope, and the American Political Tradition* (Princeton, NJ: Princeton University Press, 2011); Michael Tesler and David O. Sears, *Obama's Race: The 2008 Election and the Dream of a Post-Racial America* (Chicago, IL: University of Chicago Press, 2010); Fredrick Harris, *The Price of the Ticket: Barack Obama and the Rise and Decline of Black Politics* (New York: Oxford University Press, 2012); Gary Gerstle, "The Age of Obama, 2000–2016," in *American Crucible: Race and Nation in the Twentieth Century* (2001; Princeton, NJ: Princeton University Press, 2017), 375–426.

79. Barack Obama, "President Barack Obama's Inaugural Address," January 21, 2009, https://obamawhitehouse.archives.gov/blog/2009/01/21/president-Barack- obamas-inaugural-address, accessed June 10, 2021.

80. Obama, "Inaugural Address."

81. In his memoir, Obama refers to his "conservative temperament" and its influence on his decision making. Barack Obama, *A Promised Land* (New York: Crown, 2020), 211. "With the world economy in free fall," Obama remarked, "my number-one task was not remaking the economic order. It was preventing further disaster. For this I needed people who had managed crises before."

82. Suskind, *Confidence Men.*

83. Obama, *A Promised Land,* 214.

84. Obama, *A Promised Land,* 297.

85. Suskind, *Confidence Men,* 124–196.

86. Tooze, *Crashed,* 291–307.

87. By 2013, J. P. Morgan, Goldman Sachs, Bank of America, Citigroup, Wells Fargo, and Morgan Stanley were 37 percent larger than they had been in 2008. Tooze, *Crashed,* 316; Sorkin, *Too Big to Fail.*

88. Tooze, *Crashed,* 306, 292–293.

89. Tooze, *Crashed,* 277–290.

90. Steven Rattner, *Overhaul: An Insider's Account of the Obama Administration's Emergency Rescue of the Auto Industry* (Boston, MA: Houghton Mifflin Harcourt, 2010).

91. Joseph E. Stiglitz, *Freefall: Free Markets and the Sinking of the Global Economy* (New York: W. W. Norton, 2010). Obama might have built an economic advisory team around Paul Volcker, who had broken with neoliberal orthodoxy and was prepared to restructure America's financial sector, even to the point of dismantling Wall Street's debt machine.

Others who might have held important roles were Austin Goolsbee of the University of Chicago, Robert Reich and Laura Tyson of Berkeley, and Gary Gensler, a onetime Rubin protégé now breaking with the Goldman Sachs model of economic management.

92. Tooze, *Crashed*, 280; Dickerson, *Homeownership and America's Financial Underclass*, passim.

93. Tooze, *Crashed*, 463.

94. Martin Wolf, "The Rescue of Bear Stearns Marks Liberalisation's Limit," *The Financial Times*, March 25, 2008, https://www.ft.com/content/8ced5 202-fa94-11dc-aa46-000077b07658, accessed August 31, 2021.

Chapter 7

1. Anne Case and Angus Deaton, *Deaths of Despair and the Future of Capitalism* (Princeton, NJ: Princeton University Press, 2020), 160–161. America lost one of four manufacturing jobs to China in the years between 1990 and 2015. Marc Levinson, *Outside the Box: How Globalization Changed from Moving Stuff to Spreading Ideas* (Princeton, NJ: Princeton University Press, 2020), 173.

2. On wage trends and stagnation, see "Real Wage Trends 1979–2019," *Congressional Research Service*, December 28, 2020, https://fas.org/sgp/crs/misc/R45090.pdf, accessed June 28, 2021; Drew Desilva, "For Most U.S. Workers, Real Wages Have Barely Budged in Decades," *Pew Research Center Report*, August 7, 2018, https://www.pewresearch.org/fact-tank/2018/08/07/for-most-us-workers-real-wages-have-barely-budged-for-deca des/, accessed June 28, 2021.

3. Charles Murray, *Coming Apart: The State of White America, 1960–2010* (New York: Crown Forum, 2012), 153–171.

4. Murray, *Coming Apart*, 153–171.

5. Murray, *Coming Apart*, 172–229.

6. This view, of course, rests on an essentialized view of the male character and is easy to dispute. I refer to it here to narrate Murray's view of the social disintegration that followed in Fishtown upon the collapse of the institution of marriage. For George Gilder's view of these matters, see his *Sexual Suicide* (New York: Bantam Books, 1975), and *Wealth and Poverty* (New York: Basic Books, 1981).

7. In 1960, more than 80 percent of Fishtown households had someone working more than forty hours a week; by 2010, barely half did. Murray, *Coming Apart*, 184–185.

8. Murray, *Coming Apart*, 273, 281.

9. Murray, *Coming Apart*, 281. Some background on Murray: In the 1980s, Murray had published *Losing Ground*, a searing indictment of the welfare state for allegedly promoting all the wrong behaviors among the poor. Written from a neoliberal perspective (Murray became a member of the Mont Pèlerin Society in 2000), *Losing Ground* purported to demonstrate

that welfare programs encouraged the poor to stay on welfare rather than to look for work; to deepen their dependence on government rather than to incentivize them to become self-reliant; and to keep them mired in poverty rather than motivating them to build stable, working-class lives. Murray had presented himself as indifferent to race. The disagreeable behaviors he observed, Murray claimed, resulted from the structure of incentives built into the American welfare state and not from the impoverished character of—or other deficiencies in—minority cultures. *Losing Ground*, nevertheless, focused most of its attention on the problems of the black poor. Among the many 1980s readers who had already come to believe in the rise of a dangerous and racialized "underclass," it deepened skepticism about the adequacy of black culture. In 1994, Murray reinforced that skepticism and revealed his own racial biases when he, along with Richard J. Hernnstein, published *The Bell Curve: Intelligence and Class Structure in American Life* (New York: Free Press), which claimed to offer "scientific" proof of black inferiority. Throughout this period, Murray had maintained a largely unspoken belief in the strength of white culture and its ability to sustain the white poor. Thus, having to report in 2010 that the white poor were suffering from the same "failures" of culture as were the black poor was a bitter pill for Murray to swallow. Charles Murray, *Losing Ground: American Social Policy, 1950–1980* (1984; New York: Basic Books, 2015); Steven Fraser, ed., *The Bell Curve Wars: Race, Intelligence, and the Future of America* (New York: Basic Books, 1995); Quinn Slobodian and Stuart Schrader, "The White Man Unburdened: How Charles Murray Stopped Worrying and Learned to Love Racism," *The Baffler* 40 (July 2018), https://thebaffler.com/salvos/the-white-man-unburdened-slobod ian-schrader, accessed September 8, 2021; and Quinn Slobodian, "Racial Science Against the Welfare State: Richard Lynn, Charles Murray, Thilo Sarrazin," unpublished paper presented to Modern Europe Colloquium, Yale University, April 2018, in author's possession.

10.   The mournful tone coursing its way through *Coming Apart* for a lost world of white America anticipated that of *Hillbilly Elegy: A Memoir of a Family and Culture in Crisis*, the bestselling book published by J. D. Vance in 2016. Readers would find in both books plausible explanations for why legions of white "dispossessed" Americans were turning to Donald Trump to restore a way of life that had been stripped from them. J. D. Vance, *Hillbilly Elegy: A Memoir of a Family and Culture in Crisis* (New York: Harper, 2016). A large social science literature on this subject has appeared in the last few years. See, for example, Arlie Hochschild, *Strangers in Their Own Land: Anger and Mourning on the American Right* (New York: New Press, 2016); Katherine Cramer, *The Politics of Resentment: Rural Consciousness in Wisconsin and the Rise of Scott Walker* (Chicago, IL: University of Chicago Press, 2016); Jonathan M. Metzl, *Dying of Whiteness: How the Politics of Racial Resentment Is Killing*

America's Heartland (New York: Basic Books, 2019); Joan C. Williams, *White Working Class: Overcoming Class Cluelessness in America* (Boston, MA: Harvard Business Review Press, 2017); Nancy Isenberg, *White Trash: The 400-Year Untold History of Class in America* (New York: Viking, 2016); Jefferson Cowie, *Stayin' Alive: The 1970s and the Last Days of the Working Class* (New York: New Press, 2010).

11. The increases were most pronounced among those with the least education and thus stuck at the lower end of the income scale. Anne Case and Angus Deaton, "Rising Morbidity and Mortality in Midlife Among White Non-Hispanic Americans in the 21st Century," *Proceedings of the National Academy of Sciences* 112 (December 2015), https://www.pnas.org/content/pnas/112/49/15078.full.pdf?source=post_page, accessed April 12, 2021. See also Case and Deaton, *Deaths of Despair and the Future of Capitalism*; Metzl, *Dying of Whiteness*; Patrick Radden Keefe, *Empire of Pain: The Secret History of the Sackler Dynasty* (New York: Doubleday, 2021). For more on declining fortunes of those in America with only a high school education, see Raj Chetty, David Grusky, Maximilian Hell, Nathaniel Hendren, Robert Manduca, and Jimmy Narang, "The Fading American Dream: Trends in Absolute Income Mobility Since 1940," *Science* 356 (April 28, 2017), 398–406. On wage trends and stagnation, see "Real Wage Trends 1979–2019," *Congressional Research Service*; Desilva, "For Most U.S. Workers, Real Wages Have Barely Budged in Decades"; Thomas Piketty and Emmanuel Saez, "Inequality in the Long Run," *Science* 344 (May 2014), 838–843.

12. Murray, *Coming Apart*, 289–299.

13. This gap in wealth was significantly greater than the gap in income, in part because many black families had been denied access to real estate for generations. During the second half of the twentieth century, homes became the largest and most profitable investment for many American families. The wealth gap between white and black families widened as the former began to lock in the trans-generational benefits of homeownership denied the latter. A growing awareness of this disparity had informed the Clinton-Bush drive to increase dramatically the numbers of minority homeowners. See Chapter 6.

14. As noted in Chapter 6, the median black household net worth fell by a staggering 53 percent between 2005 and 2009 while the white median fell by only 16 percent. In the wake of the Great Recession, disparities in household earnings also widened, as black households lost 11.1 percent of their income stream while white households lost 5.2 percent. Some of this divergence stemmed from stark differences in unemployment rates, which, in 2012, stood at 13.4 percent for blacks, nearly three quarters higher than the overall rate of 7.8 percent. "Wealth Gap Rises to Record Highs Between Whites, Blacks, Hispanics," *Pew Research Center Report*, July 26, 2011, accessed June 28, 2021, https://www.pewresearch.org/soc

ial-trends/2011/07/26/wealth-gaps-rise-to-record-highs-between-whi
tes-blacks-hispanics/; Mechele Dickerson, *Homeownership and America's
Financial Underclass: Flawed Premises, Broken Promises, New Prescriptions*
(New York: Cambridge University Press, 2014). The US Bureau of
Labor Statistics reported slightly different figures on black versus white
unemployment rates. See "Labor Force Characteristics by Race and
Ethnicity, 2012," *US Bureau of Statistics Reports*, Report 1044, October
2013, https://www.bls.gov/opub/reports/race-and-ethnicity/archive/race
_ethnicity_2012.pdf, accessed June 28, 2021. For more on the racial
wealth gap, see Dawn Turner Trice, "Black Middle Class Economically
Vulnerable," *Chicago Tribune*, October 7, 2012, https://www.chicago
tribune.com/news/ct-xpm-2012-10-07-ct-met-black-middle-class-auster
ity-20121007-story.html, accessed June 28, 2021; "King's Dream Remains
an Elusive Goal; Many Americans See Racial Disparities," *Pew Research
Center Report*, August 22, 2013, accessed June 28, 2021; Edward Luce,
"The Riddle of Black America's Rising Woes Under Obama," *Financial
Times*, October 12, 2014, http://www.ft.com/cms/s/2/5455efbe-4fa4-11e4-
a0a4-00144feab7de.html, accessed September 8, 2021; Rakesh Kochhar
and Richard Fry, "Wealth Inequality Has Widened Along Racial,
Ethnic Lines Since End of Great Recession," *Pew Research Center Report*,
December 12, 2014, https://www.pewresearch.org/fact-tank/2014/12/12/
racial-wealth-gaps-great-recession/, accessed September 8, 2021; Gillian
B. White, "The Recession's Racial Slant," *The Atlantic*, June 24, 2015,
https://www.theatlantic.com/business/archive/2015/06/black-recession-
housing-race/396725/, accessed July 28, 2021; Neil Irwin, Claire Cain
Miller, and Margot Sanger-Katz, "America's Racial Divide, Charted,"
New York Times, August 19, 2014, http://www.nytimes.com/2014/08/
20/upshot/americas-racial-divide-charted.html, accessed September 8,
2021; Annie Lowrey, "Wealth Gap Among Races Has Widened Since
Recession," *New York Times*, April 28, 2013, https://www.nytimes.com/
2013/04/29/business/racial-wealth-gap-widened-during-recession.html,
accessed September 8, 2013; Michael Fletcher, "A Shattered Foundation,"
Washington Post, January 24, 2015, https://www.washingtonpost.com/sf/
investigative/2015/01/24/the-american-dream-shatters-in-prince-georges-
county/, accessed September 8, 2021; Kimbriell Kelly, John Sullivan, and
Steven Rich, "Broken by the Bubble," *Washington Post*, January 25, 2015,
http://www.washingtonpost.com/sf/investigative/2015/01/25/in-fairwood-
dreams-of-black-wealth-foundered-amid-the-mortgage-meltdown/,
accessed September 8, 2021; Patricia Cohen, "Public-Sector Jobs Vanish,
Hitting Blacks Hard," *New York Times*, May 24, 2015, https://www.nyti
mes.com/2015/05/25/business/public-sector-jobs-vanish-and-blacks-take-
blow.html, accessed September 8, 2021.

15.   Kochhar and Fry, "Wealth Inequality Has Widened Along Racial, Ethnic
      Lines Since End of Great Recession."

16. Cohen, "Public-Sector Jobs Vanish, Hitting Blacks Hard."
17. On Scott Walker and Wisconsin politics, see Cramer, *The Politics of Resentment*; Dan Kaufman, *The Fall of Wisconsin: The Conservative Conquest of a Progressive Bastion and the Future of American Politics* (New York: W. W. Norton, 2018); Jason Stein and Patrick Marley, *More Than They Bargained For: Scott Walker, Unions, and the Fight for Wisconsin* (Madison: University of Wisconsin Press, 2013); Steven Greenhouse, "Scott Walker Woos CPAC Boasting About Crusade Against Wisconsin Unions," *The Guardian*, February 27, 2015, accessed September 8, 2021; Dan Kaufman, "Scott Walker and the Fate of the Union," *New York Times Magazine*, June 12, 2015, https://www.nytimes. com/2015/06/14/magazine/scott-walker-and-the-fate-of-the-union.html, accessed September 8, 2021; Nicky Woolf, "Scott Walker's 'Draconian' Labor Plan to Call for Ending Federal Workers' Unions," *The Guardian*, September 14, 2015, https://www.theguardian.com/us-news/2015/sep/ 14/scott-walker-union-plan-labor-laws, accessed September 8, 2021. For Walker's own perspective on his governorship, see Scott Walker and Marc Thiessen, *Unintimidated: A Governor's Story and a Nation's Challenge* (New York: Penguin Press, 2013).
18. Neil Irwin, Claire Cain Miller, and Margot Sanger-Katz, "America's Racial Divide: Charted," *New York Times*, April 19, 2014, https://www. nytimes.com/2014/08/20/upshot/americas-racial-divide-charted.html, accessed April 19, 2021 ; see, also, Centers for Disease Control and Prevention, "Table 29: Death Rates for Homicide, by Sex, Race, Hispanic Origin, and Age: United States, Selected Years, 1950, 2016" (Washington, DC: US Department of Health & Human Services, 2017), https://www. cdc.gov/nchs/data/hus/2017/029.pdf, accessed December 19, 2021.
19. "Cops or Soldiers?" *The Economist*, March 20, 2014, https://www.econom ist.com/united-states/2014/03/20/cops-or-soldiers, accessed September 8, 2021; "How America's Police Became So Heavily Armed," *The Economist*, May 18, 2015, http://www.economist.com/blogs/economist-explains/2015/ 05/economist-explains-22, accessed September 8, 2021; Joshua Holland, "Cops, Gun Culture and Anti-Government Extremism," *Bill Moyers & Company*, August 26, 2014, http://billmoyers.com/2014/08/26/cops-gun-culture-and-anti-government-extremism/, accessed September 8, 2021.
20. Michelle Alexander, *The New Jim Crow: Mass Incarceration in the Age of Colorblindness* (New York: New Press, 2010), 6-7.
21. Alexander, *The New Jim Crow*. For more on race, neoliberalism, and prisons, see Marie Gottschalk, *Caught: The Prison State and the Lockdown of America's Politics* (Princeton, NJ: Princeton University Press, 2015); Ruth Gilmore Wilson, *Golden Gulag: Prisons, Surplus, Crisis, and Opposition in Globalizing California* (Berkeley: University of California Press, 2007); Heather Ann Thompson, *Blood in the Water: The Attica Prison Uprising of 1971 and Its Legacy* (New York: Pantheon, 2016);

Elizabeth Hinton, *From the War on Poverty to the War on Crime: The Making of Mass Incarceration in America* (Cambridge, MA: Harvard University Press, 2016); Julilly Kohler-Hausmann, *Getting Tough: Welfare and Imprisonment in 1970s America* (Princeton, NJ: Princeton University Press, 2017). Irwin, Miller, and Sanger-Katz, *America's Racial Divide: Charted.*

22.   On the new gig economy, see Sarah Kessler, *Gigged: The Economy, the End of the Job and the Future of Work* (London: Random House Business, 2019); Jia Tolentino, "The Gig Economy Celebrates Working Yourself to Death," *New Yorker*, March 22, 2017, https://www.newyorker.com/cult ure/jia-tolentino/the-gig-economy-celebrates-working-yourself-to-death, accessed June 28, 2021; Nathan Heller, "Is the Gig Economy Working?" *New Yorker*, May 8, 2017, https://www.newyorker.com/magazine/2017/ 05/15/is-the-gig-economy-working, accessed June 28, 2021; Nicole Kobie, "What Is the Gig Economy and Why Is It So Controversial?" *Wired*, September 14, 2018, https://www.wired.co.uk/article/what-is-the-gig-economy-meaning-definition-why-is-it-called-gig-economy, accessed September 8, 2021; Jill Lepore, "What's Wrong with the Way We Work," *New Yorker*, January 11, 2021, https://www.newyorker.com/magazine/ 2021/01/18/whats-wrong-with-the-way-we-work, accessed June 28, 2021; E. Tammy Kim, "The Gig Economy Is Coming for Your Job," *New York Times*, January 10, 2020, https://www.nytimes.com/2020/01/10/opin ion/sunday/gig-economy-unemployment-automation.html, accessed September 8, 2021; Aarian Marshall, "With $200 Million, Uber and Lyft Write Their Own Labor Law," *Wired*, April 11, 2020, https://www. wired.com/story/200-million-uber-lyft-write-own-labor-law/, accessed September 8, 2021. For the origins of Uber and Airbnb specifically, see Brad Stone, *The Upstarts: Uber, Airbnb and the Battle for the New Silicon Valley* (London: Corgi, 2018); Leigh Gallagher, *The Airbnb Story: How to Disrupt an Industry, Make Billions of Dollars . . . and Plenty of Enemies* (London: Virgin Books, 2018); Mike Isaac, *Super Pumped: The Battle for Uber* (New York: W. W. Norton, 2019).

23.   The classic historical work on casual labor markets is Gareth Stedman Jones, *Outcast London: A Study in the Relationship Between Classes in Victorian Society* (1971; London: Verso, 2013). For more recent works on the subject, see Guy Standing, *The Precariat: The New Dangerous Class* (London: Bloomsbury, 2011); Alexandrea J. Ravenelle, *Hustle and Gig: Struggling and Surviving in the Sharing Economy* (Oakland: University of California Press, 2019); Ruth Milkman and Ed Ott, eds., *New Labor in New York: Precarious Workers and the Future of the Labor Movement* (Ithaca, NY: Cornell University Press, 2014).

24.   For the origin of the term "precariat," see https://www.macmillandiction ary.com/buzzword/entries/precariat.html, accessed December 15, 2021, and Standing, *The Precariat.*

25. See Steve Fraser and Gary Gerstle, "Introduction," in Steve Fraser and Gary Gerstle, eds., *Ruling America: A History of Wealth and Power in a Democracy* (Cambridge, MA: Harvard University Press, 2005), 1–26.

26. For Rick Santelli's rant, see https://www.cnbc.com/video/2015/02/06/ santellis-tea-party-rant-february-19-2009.html, accessed June 22, 2021; Phil Rosenthal, "Rant Goes Viral, Raising Profile of CNBC's Rick Santelli," *Chicago Tribune*, February 23, 2009, https://www.chicagotrib une.com/news/ct-xpm-2009-02-23-0902220319-story.html, accessed June 22, 2021.

27. On the origins of the Tea Party, see Theda Skocpol and Vanessa Williamson, *The Tea Party and the Remaking of Republican Conservatism* (New York: Oxford University Press, 2012); Jill Lepore, *The Whites of Their Eyes: The Tea Party's Revolution and the Battle over American History* (Princeton, NJ: Princeton University Press, 2011); Michael Leahy, *Covenant of Liberty: The Ideological Origins of the Tea Party Movement* (New York: HarperCollins, 2012). On the Koch brothers and their involvement with the Tea Party, see Jane Mayer, *Dark Money: The Hidden History of the Billionaires Behind the Rise of the Radical Right* (New York: Anchor Books, 2016).

28. On the populist character of the Tea Party, see Dick Armey and Matt Kibbe, *Give Us Liberty: A Tea Party Manifesto* (New York: HarperCollins, 2010); Elizabeth Price Foley, *The Tea Party: Three Principles* (Cambridge: Cambridge University Press, 2012); Rachel M. Blum, *How the Tea Party Captured the GOP: Insurgent Factions in American Politics* (Chicago, IL: University of Chicago Press, 2020); Andrew J. Perrin, Steven J. Tepper, Neal Caren, and Sally Morris, "Political and Cultural Dimensions of Tea Party Support, 2009–2012," *Sociological Quarterly* 55 (Fall 2014), 625–652; Rand Paul, *The Tea Party Goes to Washington* (Nashville, TN: Center Street, 2011); Liz Halloran, "What's Behind the New Populism?" *NPR.org*, February 5, 2010, https://www. npr.org/templates/story/story.php?storyId=123137382, accessed June 28, 2021; Walter Russell Mead, "The Tea Party and American Foreign Policy: What Populism Means for Globalism," *Foreign Policy*, March / April, 2011, https://www.foreignaffairs.com/articles/united-states/2011- 03-01/tea-party-and-american-foreign-policy, accessed September 8, 2021. On Ron Paul, see Kelefa Sanneh, "Party Crasher: Ron Paul's Unique Brand of Libertarianism," *New Yorker*, February 19, 2012, https://www. newyorker.com/magazine/2012/02/27/party-crasher, accessed September 8, 2021; David Kirby and Emily Ekins, "Ron Paul and the Tea Party Playbook," August 10, 2012, *Cato.org*, https://www.cato.org/comment ary/ron-paul-tea-party-playbook, accessed June 28, 2021. Ron Paul has published several short books outlining his political beliefs including *The Revolution: A Manifesto* (New York: Grand Central, 2008) and *Liberty*

Defined: 50 Essential Issues That Affect Our Freedom (New York: Grand
Central, 2011).

29. Donald Trump would become a follower of *Breitbart* soon after it
launched, and he was an amplifier in his speeches and tweets of its
"reporting." After Andrew Breitbart's sudden and premature death in 2012,
Steve Bannon became *Breitbart*'s guiding force. See Breitbart.com, passim;
Joshua Green, *Devil's Bargain: Steve Bannon, Donald Trump, and the
Storming of the Presidency* (New York: Penguin Press, 2017); David Carr,
"The Provocateur," *New York Times*, April 13, 2012, accessed December
15, 2021; Rebecca Mead, "Rage Machine: Andrew Breitbart's Empire of
Bluster," *New Yorker*, May 17, 2010, https://www.newyorker.com/magaz
ine/2010/05/24/rage-machine, accessed September 8, 2021; James Rainey,
"Breitbart.com Sets Sights on Ruling the Conservative Conversation," *Los
Angeles Times*, August 1, 2012, https://www.latimes.com/entertainment/
la-xpm-2012-aug-01-la-et-breitbart-20120801-story.html, accessed June 28,
2021. For examples of Breitbart reporting, see James M. Simpson, "Agenda
21 Part I: A Global Economic Disaster in the Making," Breitbart.com,
January 17, 2011, https://www.breitbart.com/politics/2011/01/17/age
nda-21-part-i-a-global-economic-disaster-in-the-making/, accessed June
28, 2021; James M. Simpson, "Agenda 21 Part II: Globalist Totalitarian
Dictatorship Invading a Town Near You—With Your Permission,"
Breitbart.com, January 23, 2011, https://www.breitbart.com/politics/2011/
01/23/agenda-21-part-ii-globalist-totalitarian-dictatorship-invading-a-town-
near-you-with-your-permission/, accessed June 28, 2021.

30. Skocpol and Williamson, *The Tea Party and the Remaking of American
Conservatism*. On the fury of Tea Partiers at Obama, see the following
accounts of town hall meetings sponsored by the Tea Party in August
2009: Jessica Rinaldi, "Protesters Disrupt Town Hall Healthcare Talks,"
Reuters, August 11, 2009, accessed December 15, 2021; Kevin Hechtkopf,
"Rally Interrupts Dem Rep.'s Health Care Town Hall," CBSNews.com,
August 3, 2009, http://www.cbsnews.com/news/rally-interrupts-dem-reps-
health-care-town-hall/, accessed December 15, 2021; Ian Urbina, "Beyond
Beltway, Health Debate Turns Hostile," *New York Times*, August 7, 2009,
http://www.nytimes.com/2009/08/08/us/politics/08townhall.html?_r=
0&mtrref=www.google.co.uk&gwh=78FBE4E211C423033E3096984
A6D2F17&gwt=pay, accessed December 15, 2021.

31. On the battle over health care, see Lawrence R. Jacobs and Theda
Skocpol, *Health Care Reform and American Politics: What Everyone Needs
to Know* (New York: Oxford University Press, 2010); Paul Starr, *Remedy
and Reaction: The Peculiar American Struggle over Health Care Reform*
(New Haven, CT: Yale University Press, 2013); Steven Brill, *America's
Bitter Pill: Money, Politics, Backroom Deals, and the Fight to Fix Our
Broken Healthcare System* (New York: Random House, 2015).

32. Amy Hollyfield, "Obama's Birth Certificate: Final Chapter," *PolitiFact*, June 27, 2008, http://www.politifact.com/truth-o-meter/article/2008/jun/27/obamas-birth-certificate-part-ii/, accessed June 28, 2021; Jess Henig, "Born in the U.S.A.," *FactCheck.org*, August 21, 2008, http://www.factcheck.org/2008/08/born-in-the-usa/, accessed June 28, 2021; Sheryl Gay Stolberg, "Hawaii's Governor Takes on 'Birthers,'" December 24, 2010, http://www.nytimes.com/2010/12/25/us/25hawaii.html, accessed September 8, 2021; Gabriel Winant, "The Birthers in Congress," *Salon*, July 28, 2009, http://www.salon.com/2009/07/28/birther_enablers/, accessed June 28, 2021.

33. On September 12, 2009, Tea Party rally in Washington, see Jeff Zeleny, "Thousands Rally in Capital to Protest Big Government," *New York Times*, September 12, 2009, http://www.nytimes.com/2009/09/13/us/politics/13protestweb.html, accessed June 28, 2021; Asha Beh, "Thousands of Anti-Obama Protestors March in D.C.," *NBCWashington.com*, September 12, 2009, http://www.nbcwashington.com/news/local/Taxpayer-Protestors-Get-Party-Started-Early-59126782.html, accessed June 28, 2021; Toby Harnden, "Thousands of 'Tea Party' Protestors March Against Barack Obama in Washington," *The Telegraph*, September 13, 2009, http://www.telegraph.co.uk/news/worldnews/barackobama/6184800/Thousands-of-tea-party-protesters-march-against-Barack-Obama-in-Washington.html, accessed June 28, 2021. For racist signs, see Ryan Grim and Luke Johnson, "Is the Tea Party Racist? Ask Some Actual, Out-of-the-Closet Racists," *Huffington Post*, October 24, 2013, http://www.huffingtonpost.com/2013/10/24/tea-party-racist_n_4158262.html, June 28, 2021; Justin Berrier and Brooke Obie, "Right-Wing Media Attempt to Erase 'Bigoted Statements' from the Tea Party Movement," *MediaMatters.org*, July 15, 2010, http://mediamatters.org/research/2010/07/15/right-wing-media-attempt-to-erase-bigoted-state/167760, accessed June 28, 2021. See also Anti-Defamation League, "Rage Grows in America: Anti-Government Conspiracies," *ADL.org*, November 2009, http://www.adl.org/combating-hate/domestic-extremism-terrorism/c/rage-grows-in-america.html, accessed June 28, 2021; also Shannon Travis, "NAACP Passes Resolution Blasting Tea Party 'Racism,'" *CNN.com*, July 16, 2010, http://www.cnn.com/2010/POLITICS/07/14/naacp.tea.party/index.html, accessed September 8, 2021.

34. On Obama's cosmopolitan youth and upbringing, see Barack Obama, *Dreams From My Father: A Story of Race and Inheritance* (New York: Crown, 2004); Angie Drobnic Holan, "Obama Attended an Indonesian Public School," *PolitiFact*, December 20, 2007, http://www.politifact.com/truth-o-meter/statements/2007/dec/20/chain-email/obama-attended-an-indonesian-public-school/, accessed August 20, 2020; "Growing Numbers of Americans Say Obama Is a Muslim," Pew Research Center, August 18, 2010, http://www.pewforum.org/2010/08/

18/growing-number-of-americans-say-obama-is-a-muslim/, accessed June 28, 2021.

35. On animosity toward China in the ranks of the populists, see Walter Russell Mead, "The Tea Party and American Foreign Policy: What Populism Means for Globalism," *Foreign Affairs* (March/April 2011), https://www.foreignaffairs.com/articles/united-states/2011-03-01/tea-party-and-american-foreign-policy, accessed September 8, 2021; "Tea Party on Foreign Policy: Strong on Defense and Israel, Tough on China," *Pew Research Center Report*, October 7, 2011, https://www.pewresearch.org/politics/2011/10/07/strong-on-defense-and-israel-tough-on-china/, accessed June 29, 2021; Bruce Stokes and Pew Research Center, "The Tea Party's Worldview," *Politico*, February 12, 2014, https://www.politico.eu/article/the-tea-partys-worldview/, accessed June 30, 2021.

36. On Trump, see Gwenda Blair, *The Trumps: Three Generations That Built an Empire* (New York: Touchstone, 2000); Wayne Barrett, *Trump: The Greatest Show on Earth: The Deals, the Downfall, the Reinvention* (New York: Simon and Schuster, 2016); Jane Mayer, "Donald Trump's Ghostwriter Tells All," *New Yorker*, July 25, 2016, http://www.newyorker.com/magazine/2016/07/25/donald-trumps-ghostwriter-tells-all, accessed June 30, 2021; Michael Wolff, *Fire and Fury: Inside the Trump White House* (New York: Henry Holt, 2018); Bob Woodward, *Fear: Trump in the White House* (New York: Simon and Schuster, 2018); Mary L. Trump, *Too Much and Never Enough: How My Family Created the World's Most Dangerous Man* (New York: Simon and Schuster, 2020); Philip Rucker and Carol Leonnig, *A Very Stable Genius: Donald J. Trump's Testing of America* (London: Bloomsbury, 2020).

37. Bill Carter, "'The Apprentice' Scores Ratings Near Top for the Season," *New York Times*, April 17, 2004, https://www.nytimes.com/2004/04/17/us/the-apprentice-scores-ratings-near-top-for-the-season.html, accessed June 28, 2021; James Traub, "Trumpologies," *New York Times Magazine*, September 12, 2004, https://www.nytimes.com/2004/09/12/magazine/trumpologies.html, accessed June 28, 2021; Patrick Radden Keefe, "How Mark Burnett Resurrected Donald Trump as an Icon of American Success," *New Yorker*, December 27, 2018, https://www.newyorker.com/magazine/2019/01/07/how-mark-burnett-resurrected-donald-trump-as-an-icon-of-american-success, accessed June 28, 2021; Emily Nussbaum, "The TV That Created Donald Trump," *New Yorker*, July 31, 2017, https://www.newyorker.com/magazine/2017/07/31/the-tv-that-created-donald-trump, accessed June 28, 2021; Stuart Heritage, "You're Hired: How the Apprentice Led to President Trump," *The Guardian*, November 10, 2016, https://www.theguardian.com/commentisfree/2016/nov/10/trump-the-apprentice-president-elect-reality-tv, accessed June 28, 2021.

38. One year he contemplated running with Oprah Winfrey on a Democratic Party ticket, the next with Ross Perot's populist Reform Party. His

liberalism on several social issues, including a belief that women had a right to an abortion, inclined others to think that his real affiliation was as a Democrat. In 2005, he invited Democratic royals Bill and Hillary Clinton to his wedding to Melania Knauss; they came. Deborah Orin, "Trump Pumped to Hit Stump—Wants to Run with Oprah on His Ticket," *New York Post* (October 8, 1999), https://nypost.com/1999/10/08/trump-pumped-to-hit-stump-wants-to-run-with-oprah-on-his-ticket/, accessed June 28, 2021; Adam Nagourney, "Reform Bid Said to Be a No-Go for Trump," *New York Times*, February 14, 2000, https://archive.nyti mes.com/www.nytimes.com/library/politics/camp/021400wh-ref-trump. html, accessed June 28, 2021.

39.   Jacob M. Schlesinger, "Trump Forged His Ideas on Trade in the 1980s—and Never Deviated," *Wall Street Journal*, November 15, 2018, https://www.wsj.com/articles/trump-forged-his-ideas-on-trade-in-the-1980sand-never-deviated-1542304508, accessed December 17, 2020; Beth Reinhard and Peter Grant, "How the 1990s Became Donald Trump's Personal Crucible," *Wall Street Journal*, July 20, 2016, https://www.wsj.com/artic les/how-the-1990s-became-donald-trumps-personal-crucible-1469035278, accessed December 17, 2020; Don Gonyea and Domenico Montanaro, "Donald Trump's Been Saying the Same Thing for 30 Years," *NPR.org*, January 20, 2017, https://www.npr.org/2017/01/20/510680463/donald-tru mps-been-saying-the-same-thing-for-30-years?t=1608117553171, accessed December 17, 2020; Timothy Noah, "Trump vs. Clinton Is the 1980s vs. the 1990s," *Politico*, July 31, 2016, https://www.politico.com/magazine/story/2016/07/2016-history-hillary-bill-clinton-donald-trump-1990s-1980s-214125, accessed December 17, 2020. As he would do with the Central Park Five, Trump published a full-page newspaper ad on foreign policy in 1987 expressing his opposition to free trade with Japan and China. The ad was part of a tentative foray into politics. Ilan Ben-Meir, "That Time Trump Spent Nearly $100,000 on an Ad Criticizing U.S. Foreign Policy in 1987," *BuzzFeedNews.com*, July 10, 2015, https://www.buzzfeednews. com/article/ilanbenmeir/that-time-trump-spent-nearly-100000-on-an-ad-criticizing-us, accessed June 28, 2021; Howard Kurtz, "Between the Lines of a Millionaire's Ad," *Washington Post*, September 2, 1987, https://www.washingtonpost.com/archive/politics/1987/09/02/between-the-lines-of-a-millionaires-ad/9c6db9c3-f7d6-4aa4-9ec4-a312feb2639e/, accessed December 17, 2020; Michael Kruse, "The True Story of Donald Trump's First Campaign Speech—in 1987," *Politico*, February 5, 2016, https://www. politico.com/magazine/story/2016/02/donald-trump-first-campaign-spe ech-new-hampshire-1987-213595, accessed December 17, 2020.

40.   Oliver Laughland, "Donald Trump and the Central Park Five: The Racially Charged Rise of a Demagogue," *The Guardian*, February 17, 2016, https://www.theguardian.com/us-news/2016/feb/17/central-park-five-donald-trump-jogger-rape-case-new-york, accessed June 23, 2021; a

reproduction of Trump's ad in the New York tabloids can be found in this article.

41. For the story of the Central Park Five, see Jim Dwyer, "The True Story of How a City in Fear Brutalized the Central Park Five," *New York Times*, May 30, 2019, https://www.nytimes.com/2019/05/30/arts/television/when-they-see-us-real-story.html, accessed June 24, 2021; and Ken Burns, Sarah Burns, and David McMahon, *The Central Park Five* (Sundance Selects/WETA/Florentine Films/PBS/The Central Park Five Film Project, 2012); Sarah Burns, *The Central Park Five: The Untold Story Behind One of New York's Most Infamous Crimes* (New York: Vintage Books, 2012).

42. Michael Cohen, *Disloyal: A Memoir: The True Story of the Former Personal Attorney to the President of the United States* (New York: Skyhorse Publishing, 2020), 107–110.

43. Trump seized headlines by announcing that he had sent his own investigators to Hawaii to determine the truth and that "they cannot believe what they are finding." No evidence of Obama's foreign birth ever appeared. Both PolitiFact and FactCheck.org verified the authenticity of Obama's birth certificate, both the short-form and long-form versions. Obama's decisive victory over Mitt Romney in 2012 finally seemed to quash the birther challenge. Bill Adair, "PolitiFact's Guide to Obama's Birth Certificate," *PolitiFact*, April 27, 2011, http://www.politifact.com/truth-o-meter/article/2011/apr/27/politifacts-guide-obamas-birth-certificate/, accessed June 23, 2021; Lori Robinson, "Indeed, Born in the U.S.A.," *FactCheck.org*, April 27, 2011, http://www.factcheck.org/2011/04/indeed-born-in-the-u-s-a/, accessed June 8, 2016; Adam Caparell, "Show Me! Donald Trump Wants to See President Obama's Birth Certificate with His Own Eyes," *New York Daily News*, March 24, 2011, http://www.nydailynews.com/news/politics/show-donald-trump-presidentobama-birth-certificate-eyes-article-1.118369, accessed June 23, 2021; "Trump on Obama's Birth Certificate: 'Maybe It Says He's a Muslim,'" *Fox Nation*, March 30, 2011, http://nation.foxnews.com/donald-trump/2011/03/30/trump-obama-maybe-hes-muslim, accessed June 23, 2021; Sheryl Gay Stolberg, "Hawaii's Governor Takes on 'Birthers'"; "Obama Releases 'Long Form' Birth Certificate," *BBC News*, April 27, 2011, http://www.bbc.co.uk/news/world-us-canada-13212230/, accessed September 8, 2021; Ta-Nehisi Coates, "Fear of a Black President," *The Atlantic*, September 2012, https://www.theatlantic.com/magazine/archive/2012/09/fear-of-a-black-president/309064/, accessed September 8, 2021; Jeff Greenfield, "Donald Trump's Birther Strategy," *Politico*, July 22, 2015, http://www.politico.com/magazine/story/2015/07/donald-trumps-birther-strategy-120504, accessed June 23, 2021; Joshua Green, "What Donald Trump's Birther Investigators Will Find in Hawaii," *The Atlantic*, April 12, 2011, http://www.theatlantic.com/politics/archive/2011/04/what-donald-trumps-birther-investigators-willfind-in-hawaii/237198/, accessed September 8, 2021.

44.   "Donald Trump 2015 Presidential Candidacy Announcement Speech,"
      June 15, 2015, https://time.com/3923128/donald-trump-announcement-
      speech/, accessed May 26, 2021; Katie Reilly, "Here Are All the Times
      Donald Trump Insulted Mexico," August 31, 2016, https://time.com/4473
      972/donald-trump-mexico-meeting-insult/, accessed May 26, 2021.

45.   Trump's role in railroading the Central Park teenage "rapists" had been a
      lead tabloid story in 1989. His affair with Marla Maples, soon to become
      his second wife, and his divorce from Ivana Trump, his first wife, were
      big tabloid stories in 1990. See, for example, Jamie Ross, "The Real Story
      Behind Trump's Famous 'The Best Sex I Ever Had' Headline," *Daily
      Beast*, April 12, 2018, accessed December 15, 2021. Ross's report includes
      a reproduction of the notorious February 16, 1990 *New York Post* cover
      and headline: "Marla Boasts to Her Friends About Donald: Best Sex
      I Ever Had."

46.   Sidney Blumenthal, "A Short History of the Trump Family," *London
      Review of Books* 39 (February 16, 2017), https://www.lrb.co.uk/the-paper/
      v39/no4/sidney-blumenthal-a-short-history-of-the-trump-family, accessed
      June 23, 2021.

47.   Blumenthal, "A Short History of the Trump Family."

48.   Nick Rogers, "How Wrestling Explains Alex Jones and Donald Trump,"
      New York Times, April 25, 2017, https://www.nytimes.com/2017/04/
      25/opinion/wrestling-explains-alex-jones-and-donald-trump.html,
      accessed June 4, 2021; Shannon Bow O'Brien, *Donald Trump and the
      Kayfabe Presidency: Professional Wrestling Rhetoric in the White House*
      (New York: Palgrave Macmillan, 2020). Also see *YouTube* clips of Donald
      Trump and Vince McMahon performing at WWE's 2007 Wrestlemania
      23 in an event billed as "The Battle of the Billionaires"; the second clip
      contains footage of Trump violently throwing McMahon to the ground
      just outside the ring. https://www.youtube.com/watch?v=5NsrwH9I
      9vE&t=84s, July 20, 2011; https://www.youtube.com/watch?v=jkghtyxZ
      6rc, February 3, 2016; both accessed June 14, 2021. Thanks to Emily
      Charnock and Charlie Laderman for alerting me to Trump's professional
      wrestling links.

49.   Cohen, *Disloyal*, 95. Cohen added: "Fast food, trash TV, leering at
      attractive women—Trump channeled blue-collar white men because that
      was part of how he saw life."

50.   He understood the essence of New York's high-stakes real estate
      industry—namely, that rules and contracts were made to be broken. He
      had a good if ruthless mentor in Roy Cohn, Joe McCarthy's longtime
      aide. Donald J. Trump with Tony Schwartz, *The Art of the Deal* (1987;
      New York: Ballantine Books, 2015). On Trump's association with Roy
      Cohn, see Jonathan Mahler and Matt Flegenheimer, "What Donald
      Trump Learned from Joseph McCarthy's Right-Hand Man," *New York*

Times, June 20, 2016, https://www.nytimes.com/2016/06/21/us/politics/donald-trump-roy-cohn.html, accessed September 8, 2021.

51. Maureen Dowd, "Chickens, Home to Roost," *New York Times*, March 5, 2016, http://nyti.ms/1U27ZJ5, accessed April 27, 2021. See, also, Elizabeth Lunbeck, "The Allure of Trump's Narcissism," *Los Angeles Review of Books*, August 1, 2017, accessed September 15, 2021.

52. Peter Oborne, *The Assault on Truth: Boris Johnson, Donald Trump and the Emergence of a New Moral Barbarism* (New York: Simon and Schuster, 2020); Adam Serwer, *The Cruelty Is the Point: The Past, Present, and Future of Trump's America* (New York: One World, 2021).

53. Mattathias Schwartz, "Pre-Occupied," *New Yorker*, November 20, 2011, https://www.newyorker.com/magazine/2011/11/28/pre-occupied, accessed June 28, 2021; Jamie Lalinde, Rebecca Sacks, Mark Guiducci, Elizabeth Nicholas, and Max Chafkin, "Revolution Number 99," *Vanity Fair*, January 10, 2012, https://www.vanityfair.com/news/2012/02/occupy-wall-street-201202, accessed June 28, 2021.

54. "What Is Our One Demand? #OccupyWallStreet, September 17, Bring Tent," *Adbusters*, Poster (2011), http//upload.wikimedia.org/wikipedia/en/5/57/Wall-Street-1.jpg, accessed June 28, 2021; William Yardley, "The Branding of the Occupy Movement," *New York Times*, November 27, 2011, https://www.nytimes.com/2011/11/28/business/media/the-branding-of-the-occupy-movement.html, accessed June 28, 2021.

55. Schwartz, "Pre-Occupied"; Brian Greene, "How 'Occupy Wall Street' Started and Spread," *USNews.com*, October 17, 2011, https://www.usnews.com/news/washington-whispers/articles/2011/10/17/how-occupy-wall-street-started-and-spread, accessed April 28, 2021; David Graeber, "Occupy's Liberation from Liberalism: The Real Meaning of May Day," *The Guardian*, May 7, 2012, https://www.theguardian.com/commentisfree/cifamerica/2012/may/07/occupy-liberation-from-liberalism, accessed April 28, 2021. On the student debt crisis, see Elizabeth Tandy Shermer, *Indentured Students: How Government-Guaranteed Loans Left Generations Drowning in College Debt* (Cambridge, MA: Belknap Press of Harvard University Press, 2021).

56. David Graeber, *Debt: The First 5,000 Years* (New York: Melville House, 2011); on 1990s protest, see Richard Saich, "Social Movements and Resistance to Neoliberalism in America, 1979–2000" (PhD dissertation, University of Cambridge, 2022).

57. Schwartz, "Pre-Occupied"; Mattathias Schwartz, "Map: How Occupy Wall Street Chose Zuccotti Park," *New Yorker*, November 21, 2011, https://web.archive.org/web/20140405004551/http://www.newyorker.com/online/blogs/newsdesk/2011/11/occupy-wall-street-map.html, accessed April 28, 2021; Brian Greene, "How 'Occupy Wall Street' Started and Spread," *USNews.com*, October 17, 2011, https://www.usnews.com/news/

washington-whispers/articles/2011/10/17/how-occupy-wall-street-started-and-spread, accessed September 9, 2021.

58. On the demographics of the Occupy Wall Street Movement, see Laura Norén, "Occupy Wall Street Demographics," *Thesocietypages.org*, November 17, 2011, https://thesocietypages.org/graphicsociology/2011/11/17/occupy-wall-street-demographics/, accessed June 28, 2021; Jillian Berman, "Occupy Wall Street Actually Not at All Representative of the 99 Percent, Report Finds," *Huffington Post*, January 29, 2021, https://www.huffingtonpost.co.uk/entry/occupy-wall-street-report_n_2574788?rii8n=true, accessed June 28, 2021.

59. Megan Gibson, "Solidarity Saturday: Occupy Wall Street Goes Global," *Time*, October 17, 2011, http://newsfeed.time.com/2011/10/17/solidarity-saturday-occupy-wall-street-goes-global/, accessed April 28, 2021; Michael Levitin, "The Triumph of Occupy Wall Street," *The Atlantic*, June 10, 2015, https://www.theatlantic.com/politics/archive/2015/06/the-triumph-of-occupy-wall-street/395408/, accessed April 29, 2021; Emily Stewart, "We Are (Still) the 99 Percent: Occupy Wall Street Was Seen as a Failure When It Ended in 2011. But It's Helped Transform the American Left," *Vox*, April 30, 2019, https://www.vox.com/the-highlight/2019/4/23/18284303/occupy-wall-street-bernie-sanders-dsa-socialism, accessed April 29, 2021.

60. *Dissent* (https://www.dissentmagazine.org) started publishing in 1954, *N + 1* (https://nplusonemag.com) in 2004, and *Jacobin* (https://jacobinmag.com) in 2011. A middle-aged left/liberal magazine, *The American Prospect*, also revived at this time, staving off bankruptcy in 2012, and then flourished across a second life from 2014 forward: https://prospect.org/. And *The Nation*, of course, remained the left standard-bearer. Thomas Piketty, *Capital in the Twenty-First Century* (Cambridge, MA: Belknap Press of Harvard University Press, 2014) (originally published in French in 2013); Naomi Klein, *No Logo: No Space, No Choice, No Jobs* (New York: Fourth Estate, 2010); David Graeber, *Revolutions in Reverse: Essays on Politics, Violence, Art, and Imagination* (London: Minor Compositions, 2011); Katharine Q. Seelye, "Warren Defeats Brown in Massachusetts Senate Contest," *New York Times*, November 6, 2012, https://www.nytimes.com/2012/11/07/us/politics/elizabeth-warren-massachusetts-senate-scott-brown.html, accessed April 29, 2021; "Bill de Blasio Sworn in as New York Mayor," *The Guardian*, January 1, 2014, https://www.theguardian.com/world/2014/jan/01/bill-de-blasio-sworn-in-as-new-york-mayor, accessed April 29, 2021; Alan Rappeport, "Bernie Sanders, Long-Serving Independent, Enters Presidential Race as a Democrat," *New York Times*, April 29, 2015, https://www.nytimes.com/2015/04/30/us/politics/bernie-sanders-campaign-for-president.html, accessed April 29, 2021; Kate Aronoff, Peter Dreier, and Michael Kazin, eds., *We Own the Future: Democratic Socialism, American Style* (New York: New Press, 2020).

61. Adam Geller, "Bernie Sanders' Early Life in Brooklyn Taught Lessons, Some Tough," *Times of Israel*, July 21, 2019, https://www.timesofisrael. com/bernie-sanders-early-life-in-brooklyn-taught-lessons-some-tough/, accessed June 29, 2021; Jas Chana, "Straight Outta Brooklyn, by Way of Vermont: The Bernie Sanders Story," *Tablet*, August 20, 2015, https:// www.tabletmag.com/sections/news/articles/bernie-sanders-story, accessed June 29, 2021; Mark Leibovich, "The Socialist Senator," *New York Times*, January 21, 2007, https://www.nytimes.com/2007/01/21/magazine/21Sand ers.t.html, accessed June 29, 2021.

62. Leibovich, "The Socialist Senator."

63. Marketwatch, "Text of Bernie Sanders' Wall Street and Economy Speech, January 5, 2016, https://www.marketwatch.com/story/text-of-bernie-sand ers-wall-street-and-economy-speech-2016-01-05, accessed July 19, 2021. See also Transcript of Bernie Sanders-Hillary Clinton Debate, March 6, 2016, *New York Times*, March 7, 2016, https://www.nytimes.com/2016/03/07/ us/politics/transcript-democratic-presidential-debate.html, accessed May 31, 2021.

64. Marketwatch, "Text of Bernie Sanders' Wall Street and Economy Speech."

65. Bernie Sanders, Iowa Caucuses Speech, February 2, 2021, https://www. vox.com/2016/2/2/10892752/bernie-sanders-iowa-speech, accessed June 28, 2021.

66. "Transcript of Bernie Sanders-Hillary Clinton Debate," March 6, 2016; Bernie Sanders, Campaign Speech in Pittsburgh, *WESA*, March 30, 2016, http://wesa.fm/post/super-pacs-paid-speeches-living-wages-take-sand ers-full-pittsburgh-stump, accessed June 28, 2021. For Bernie Sanders's views on trade, see Amy Chozick and Patrick Healy, "Caustic Sanders Pushes Clinton on Trade and Jobs at Debate in Michigan," reprinted in *Anchorage Daily News*, September 30, 2016, https://www.adn.com/nation-world/article/caustic-sanders-pushes-clinton-trade-and-jobs-debate-michi gan/2016/03/07/, accessed September 9, 2021 (originally published in the *New York Times*, March 7, 2016); Nick Corasaniti, "Bernie Sanders Hones Anti-Trade Message for Illinois and Ohio," *New York Times*, March 11, 2016, https://www.nytimes.com/2016/03/12/us/politics/bernie-sanders-hones-anti-trade-message-for-illinois-and-ohio.html, accessed February 24, 2021; Editorial Board, "Jobs and Trade on the Campaign Trail," *New York Times*, April 2, 2016, https://www.nytimes.com/2016/04/03/opin ion/sunday/jobs-and-trade-on-the-campaign-trail.html, accessed February 24, 2021; Bernie Sanders, "Bernie Sanders: Democrats Need to Wake Up," *New York Times*, June 28, 2016, https://mobile.nytimes.com/2016/ 06/29/opinion/campaign-stops/bernie-sanders-democrats-need-to-wake-up.html?referer=https://t.co/ywq46GeMt4, accessed February 24, 2021; Arnie Seipel, "Sanders Centers Platform Fight on Trans-Pacific Trade Deal," *NPR.org*, July 3, 2016, https://www.npr.org/2016/07/03/484574

128/sanders-centers-platform-fight-on-trans-pacific-trade-deal, accessed
February 24, 2021; Jennifer Steinhauer, "Both Parties Used to Back Free
Trade. Now They Bash It," *New York Times*, July 29, 2016, https://www.
nytimes.com/2016/07/30/us/politics/in-time-of-discord-bashing-trade-
pacts-appeals-to-both-parties.html, accessed February 24, 2021.

67.   "Read Donald Trump's Speech on Trade," *Time*, June 28, 2016, https://
time.com/4386335/donald-trump-trade-speech-transcript/, accessed June
22, 2021.

68.   On Clinton Foundation donations, see Paul Lewis and James Ball,
"Clinton Foundation Received Up to $81m from Clients of Controversial
HSBC Bank," *The Guardian*, February 10, 2015, https://www.theguardian.
com/us-news/2015/feb/10/hillary-clinton-foundation-donors-hsbc-swiss-
bank, accessed June 28, 2021; James V. Grimaldi and Rebecca Ballhaus,
"Foreign Government Gifts to Clinton Foundation on the Rise," *Wall
Street Journal*, February 17, 2015, https://www.wsj.com/articles/foreign-
government-gifts-to-clinton-foundation-on-the-rise-1424223031, accessed
June 28, 2021; Rosalind S. Helderman and Tom Hamburger, "Foreign
Governments Gave Millions to Foundation While Clinton Was at State
Dept.," *Washington Post*, February 25, 2015, https://www.washingtonpost.
com/politics/foreign-governments-gave-millions-to-foundation-while-clin
ton-was-at-state-dept/2015/02/25/31937c1e-bc3f-11e4-8668-4e7ba8439ca
6_story.html, accessed September 9, 2021; Carlos Barria, "Many Who
Met with Clinton as Secretary of State Donated to Foundation," *CNBC.
com*, August 23, 2016, https://www.cnbc.com/2016/08/23/most-of-those-
who-met-with-clinton-as-secretary-of-state-donated-to-foundation.html,
accessed June 28, 2021; Jonathan Allen, "Clinton's Charity Confirms
Qatar's $1 million Gift While She was at State Dept," *Reuters*, November
4, 2016, https://www.reuters.com/article/us-usa-election-foundation-
idUSKBN12Z2SL, accessed June 28, 2021.

69.   On Clinton's Wall Street speeches and the controversy they aroused,
see Nicholas Confessore and Jason Horowitz, "Hillary Clinton's Paid
Speeches to Wall Street Animate Her Opponents," *New York Times*,
January 21, 2016, https://www.nytimes.com/2016/01/22/us/politics/in-race-
defined-by-income-gap-hillary-clintons-wall-street-ties-incite-rivals.html,
accessed June 28, 2021; Robert Yoon, "$153 Million in Bill and Hillary
Clinton Speaking Fees, Documented," *CNN*, February 6, 2016, https://
edition.cnn.com/2016/02/05/politics/hillary-clinton-bill-clinton-paid-
speeches/index.html, accessed June 28, 2021; Robert W. Wood, "Hillary's
Wall Street Speech Fees: Hers or Clinton Foundation's?," *Forbes*, February
9, 2016, https://www.forbes.com/sites/robertwood/2016/02/09/hilla
rys-wall-street-speech-fees-hers-or-clinton-foundations/?sh=86b6cf864
407, accessed June 28, 2021; Amy Chozick, Nicholas Confessore, and
Michael Barbaro, "Leaked Speech Excerpts Show a Hillary Clinton at
Ease with Wall Street," *New York Times*, October 7, 2016, https://www.

nytimes.com/2016/10/08/us/politics/hillary-clinton-speeches-wikile aks.html, accessed June 28, 2021; "Hillary Clinton's Wall St Speeches Published by Wikileaks," *BBC News*, October 8, 2016, https://www.bbc. co.uk/news/election-us-2016-37595047, accessed June 28, 2021; Tamara Keith, "Wikileaks Claims to Release Hillary Clinton's Goldman Sachs Transcripts," *NPR.org*, October 15, 2016, https://www.npr.org/2016/10/15/ 498085611/wikileaks-claims-to-release-hillary-clintons-goldman-sachs-transcripts?t=1625134407257, accessed June 28, 2021; Katie Forster, "Barack Obama: Hillary Clinton's Wall Street Speeches Cast Her as an 'Insider' and Helped Her Lose to Donald Trump," *The Independent*, November 18, 2016, https://www.independent.co.uk/news/world/americas/barack-obama-hillary-clinton-lost-insider-goldman-sachs-speeches-a7424476. html, accessed June 28, 2021.

70. On Clinton's political views, see Hillary Rodham Clinton, *Living History* (London: Headline, 2003); Hillary Rodham Clinton, *Hard Choices* (New York: Simon and Schuster, 2014); Hillary Rodham Clinton and Tim Kaine, *Stronger Together: A Blueprint for America's Future* (New York: Simon and Schuster, 2016); Hillary Rodham Clinton, *What Happened* (New York: Simon and Schuster, 2017); Karen Blumenthal, *Hillary: A Biography of Hillary Rodham Clinton* (London: Bloomsbury, 2017); Jonathan Allen and Amie Parnes, *Shattered: Inside Hillary Clinton's Doomed Campaign* (New York: Broadway Books, 2017); Ivy Cargile, Denise Davis, Jennifer Merolla, and Rachel Vansickle-Ward, eds., *The Hillary Effect: Perspectives on Clinton's Legacy* (New York: I. B. Tauris, 2020).

71. African Americans constituted 14 percent of drug users in the United States but "45 percent of those imprisoned for drug crimes." Walter Johnson, *The Broken Heart of America: St. Louis and the Violent History of the United States* (New York: Basic Books, 2020), 422.

72. Lizette Alvarez and Michael Cooper, "Prosecutor Files Charge of 2nd-Degree Murder in Shooting of Martin," *New York Times*, April 11, 2012, http://www.nytimes.com/2012/04/12/us/zimmerman-to-be-char ged-in-trayvon-martin-shooting.html, accessed June 29, 2021; Greg Botelho, "What Happened the Night Trayvon Martin Died," *CNN. com*, May 23, 2012, http://edition.cnn.com/2012/05/18/justice/florida-teen-shooting-details/, accessed June 29, 2021; "The Trayvon Martin Case: A Timeline," *The Week*, July 17, 2012, http://theweek.com/artic les/476855/trayvon-martin-case-timeline, accessed June 29, 2021; David A. Graham, "Quote of the Day: Obama: 'If I Had a Son, He'd Look Like Trayvon,'" *The Atlantic*, March 23, 2012, http://www.theatlantic. com/politics/archive/2012/03/quote-of-the-day-obama-if-i-had-a-son-hed-look-like-trayvon/254971/, accessed June 29, 2021. For the death of Eric Garner, see Joseph Goldstein and Nate Schweber, "Man's Death After Chokehold Raises Old Issue for the Police," *New York Times*,

July 18, 2014, https://www.nytimes.com/2014/07/19/nyregion/staten-isl and-man-dies-after-he-is-put-in-chokehold-during-arrest.html, accessed June 29, 2021; Ken Murray, Kerry Burke, Chelsia Rose Marcius, and Rocco Parascandola, "Staten Island Man Dies after NYPD Cop Puts Him in Chokehold— SEE THE VIDEO," *New York Daily News*, July 18, 2014, http://www.nydailynews.com/new-york/staten-island-man-dies-puts-choke-hold-article-1.1871486, accessed June 29, 2021. For an account of the death of Michael Brown, see "Tracking the Events in the Wake of Michael Brown's Shooting," *New York Times*, November 24, 2014, http://www.nytimes.com/interactive/2014/11/09/us/10ferguson-mich ael-brown-shooting-grand-jury-darren-wilson.html?_r=0#/#time354_ 10512, accessed June 29, 2021. On the killing of Laquan McDonald, see Quinn Ford, "Cops: Boy, 17, Fatally Shot by Officer After Refusing to Drop Knife," *Chicago Tribune*, October 21, 2014, https://www.chicagotrib une.com/news/breaking/chi-chicago-shootings-violence-20141021-story. html, accessed June 29, 2021; Monica Davey and Mitch Smith, "Chicago Protests Mostly Peaceful After Video of Police Shooting Is Released," *New York Times*, November 24, 2015, https://www.nytimes.com/2015/ 11/25/us/chicago-officer-charged-in-death-of-black-teenager-official-says. html, accessed June 29, 2021. On the killing of Walter Scott, see Christina Elmore and David MacDougall, "N. Charleston Officer Fatally Shoots Man," *Post and Courier* April 3, 2015, https://www.postandcourier.com/ archives/n-charleston-officer-fatally-shoots-man/article_4480489f-a733-57fc-b326-bdf95032d33c.html, accessed June 29, 2021; Michael S. Schmidt and Matt Apuzzo, "South Carolina Officer Is Charged with Murder of Walter Scott," *New York Times,* April 7, 2015, http://www.nytimes.com/ 2015/04/08/us/south-carolina-officer-is-charged-with-murder-in-black-mans-death.html?_r=0, accessed June 29, 2021. On the death of Freddie Gray, see Natalie Sherman, Chris Kaltenbach, and Colin Campbell, "Freddie Gray Dies a Week After Being Injured During Arrest," *Baltimore Sun*, April 19, 2015, http://www.baltimoresun.com/news/maryland/fred die-gray/bs-md-freddie-gray-20150419-story.html, accessed June 29, 2021; David A. Graham, "The Mysterious Death of Freddie Gray," *The Atlantic*, April 22, 2015, http://www.theatlantic.com/politics/archive/2015//04/ the-mysterious-death-of-freddie-gray/391119/, accessed June 29, 2021; Jon Swaine, "Baltimore Freddie Gray Protests Turn Violent as Police and Crowds Clash," *The Guardian*, April 26, 2015, https://www.theguardian. com/us-news/2015/apr/25/baltimore-freddie-gray-protests-violence-pol ice-camden-yards, accessed June 28, 2021; Bill Keller, "David Simon Talks About Where the Baltimore Police Went Wrong," *Vice.com*, April 29, 2015, https://www.vice.com/en/article/exq4ep/david-simon-talks-about-where-the-baltimore-police-went-wrong-429, accessed June 29, 2021.

73. Keeanga-Yamahtta Taylor, "Why Should We Trust You? Clinton's Big Problem with Young Black Americans," *The Guardian*, October 21, 2016,

https://www.theguardian.com/us-news/2016/oct/21/hillary-clinton-black-millennial-voters, accessed June 2, 2021.

74. United States Department of Justice, Civil Rights Division, *Investigation of the Ferguson Police Department*, March 4, 2015 (Washington, DC: Government Printing Office, 2015), 1–6; quotes from Jelani Cobb, "The Matter of Black Lives," *New Yorker*, March 14, 2016, http://www.newyorker.com/magazine/2016/03/14/where-is-black-lives-matter-headed, accessed June 29, 2021. See also Elizabeth Day, "#BlackLivesMatter: The Birth of a New Civil Rights Movement," *The Guardian and The Observer*, July 19, 2015, https://www.theguardian.com/world/2015/jul/19/blacklivesmatter-birth-civil-rights-movement, accessed September 9, 2021.

75. Taylor, "Why Should We Trust You?" See also Keeanga-Yamahtta Taylor, *From #Blacklivesmatter to Black Liberation* (Chicago, IL: Haymarket Books, 2016).

76. Tyler Tynes, "Black Lives Matter Activists Interrupt Hillary Clinton at Private Event in South Carolina," *Huffington Post*, February 25, 2016, https://www.huffingtonpost.co.uk/entry/clinton-black-lives-matter-south-carolina_n_56ce53b1e4b03260bf7580ca?ri18n=true; accessed June 1, 2021.

77. Taylor, "Why Should We Trust You?"

78. Relative to Trump, Jackson qualifies more as an insider than an outsider. He had been fighting as a soldier and then as a general for the United States since he had been a boy in the years of the American Revolution. He had long served in Washington, DC, as a senator from Tennessee. He believed deeply in the country's founding ideals and both knew and subscribed to the principles of governance embodied in the US Constitution. Trump had never served in the military nor in Congress or in any other government post. He possessed little knowledge of the US Constitution or the democratic ideals on which the country had been founded.

79. John Cassidy, "James Comey's October Surprise," *New Yorker*, October 28, 2016, https://www.newyorker.com/news/john-cassidy/james-comeys-october-surprise, accessed June 28, 2021; Sarah N. Lynch and Mark Hosenball, "Report Rebukes Comey, but Says No Bias in Clinton Email Case," *Reuters*, June 14, 2018, https://www.reuters.com/article/us-usa-congress-fbi-idUSKBN1JA0D4, accessed June 28, 2021. See also James B. Comey, "Statement by FBI Director James B. Comey on the Investigation of Secretary Hillary Clinton's Use of a Personal E-Mail System," FBI National Press Office, Washington, DC, July 5, 2016, https://www.fbi.gov/news/pressrel/press-releases/statement-by-fbi-director-james-b-comey-on-the-investigation-of-secretary-hillary-clinton2019s-use-of-a-personal-e-mail-system, accessed June 28, 2021.

80. On the 2016 campaign and especially its final month, see Allen and Parnes, *Shattered*.

Chapter 8

1. This portrait of Trump is based on my reading of multiple relevant newspapers, magazines, and websites in the United States and the United Kingdom across a five-year period as well as what I have gleaned from reading the multiple books on Trump that have appeared, including Michael Wolff, *Fire and Fury: Inside the Trump White House* (New York: Henry Holt, 2018); Bob Woodward, *Fear: Trump in the White House* (New York: Simon and Schuster, 2018); Philip Rucker and Carol D. Leonnig, *A Very Stable Genius: Donald J. Trump's Testing of America* (New York: Penguin Press, 2020); Mary L. Trump, *Too Much and Never Enough: How My Family Created the World's Most Dangerous Man* (New York: Simon and Schuster, 2020); Michael Cohen, *Disloyal: A Memoir: The True Story of the Former Personal Attorney to the President of the United States* (New York: Skyhorse Publishing, 2020); Adam Serwer, *The Cruelty Is the Point: The Past, Present, and Future of Trump's America* (New York: One World, 2021); Corey Robin, *The Reactionary Mind: Conservatism from Edmund Burke to Donald Trump*, 2nd ed. (New York: Oxford University Press, 2018), 239–272. Those wanting to review my own thinking about Trump in real time can do so by consulting the many episodes on Trump and American politics I did with David Runciman on his podcast, *Talking Politics*. See *Talking Politics* website, https://www.talkingpoliticspodcast.com, and deploy its search engine to find the episodes in which I was involved.

2. Scott Shane, "The Fake Americans Russia Created to Influence the Election," *New York Times*, September 7, 2017, https://www.nytimes.com/2017/09/07/us/politics/russia-facebook-twitter-election.html, accessed September 28, 2021; Sharon LaFraniere, Mark Mazzetti, and Matt Apuzzo, "How the Russia Inquiry Began: A Campaign Aide, Drinks and Talk of Political Dirt," *New York Times*, December 30, 2017, https://www.nytimes.com/2017/12/30/us/politics/how-fbi-russia-investigation-began-george-papadopoulos.html, accessed September 28, 2021. For the full collection of the *New York Times* articles on Russia, see "Trump and the Russians," https://www.nytimes.com/spotlight/trump-russia. See also Jane Mayer, "How Russia Helped Swing the Election for Trump," *New Yorker*, September 24, 2018, https://www.newyorker.com/magazine/2018/10/01/how-russia-helped-to-swing-the-election-for-trump, accessed September 28, 2021; Marik von Rennenkampff, "There Was Trump-Russia Collusion and Trump Pardoned the Colluder," *TheHill.com*, April 17, 2021, https://thehill.com/opinion/white-house/548794-there-was-trump-russia-collusion-and-trump-pardoned-the-colluder, accessed September 28, 2021.

3. Sharon LaFraniere, Andrew E. Kramer, and Danny Hakim, "Trump, Ukraine and Impeachment: The Inside Story of How We Got Here," *New York Times*, November 11, 2019, https://www.nytimes.com/2019/11/11/us/ukraine-trump.html, accessed September 28, 2021; Lauren Gambino

and Tom McCarthy, "The Inside Story of Trump's Alleged Bribery of Ukraine," *The Guardian*, November 30, 2019, https://www.theguardian.com/us-news/2019/nov/30/trump-ukraine-alleged-bribery-impeachment-inquiry, accessed September 28, 2021.

4. Special Counsel Robert S. Mueller III, "Report on the Investigation into Russian Interference in the 2016 Presidential Election," 2 vols., issued by the Department of Justice, March 2019 (Cambridge, MA: Harvard Bookstore, 2019).

5. Jane Mayer, "The Danger of President Pence," *New Yorker*, October 16, 2017, https://www.newyorker.com/magazine/2017/10/23/the-danger-of-president-pence, accessed September 23, 2021.

6. The phrase "deep state" was appropriated and then deployed by Steve Bannon while he was writing for *Breitbart*. Alana Abramson, "President Trump's Allies Keep Talking about the 'Deep State.' What's That?," *Time*, March 8, 2017, https://time.com/4692178/donald-trump-deep-state-breitb art-barack-obama/, accessed September 23, 2021; Daniel Benjamin and Steven Simon, "Why Steve Bannon Wants You to Believe in the Deep State," *Politico*, March 21, 2017, https://www.politico.com/magazine/story/2017/03/steve-bannon-deep-state-214935/, accessed September 23, 2021. See also Joshua Green, *Devil's Bargain: Steve Bannon, Donald Trump, and the Nationalist Uprising* (New York: Penguin Press, 2017).

7. Tom McCarthy, "Why Has Trump Appointed So Many Judges—And How Did He Do It?" *The Guardian*, April 28, 2020, https://www.theguard ian.com/us-news/2020/apr/28/explainer-why-has-trump-appointed-so-many-judges, accessed September 28, 2021; Kadhim Shubber, "How Trump Has Already Transformed America's Courts," *Financial Times*, September 25, 2020, https://www.ft.com/content/032b3101-9b8b-4566-ace4-67b86 f42370b, accessed September 28, 2021; Anita Kumar, "Trump's Legacy Is Now the Supreme Court," *Politico*, September 26, 2020, https://www.polit ico.com/news/2020/09/26/trump-legacy-supreme-court-422058, accessed September 28, 2021; Sara Reynolds, "Trump Has Appointed Second-Most Federal Judges Through November 1 of a President's Fourth Year," *Ballotpedia News*, November 3, 2020, https://news.ballotpedia.org/2020/11/03/trump-has-appointed-second-most-federal-judges-through-november-1-of-a-presidents-fourth-year/, accessed September 28, 2021; Mark Sherman, Kevin Freking, and Matthew Daly, "Trump's Court Appointments Will Leave Decades-Long Imprint," *AP News*, December 26, 2020, https://apn ews.com/article/joe-biden-donald-trump-judiciary-coronavirus-pandemic-us-supreme-court-c37607c9987888058d3d0650eea125cd, accessed September 28, 2021; John Gramlich, "How Trump Compares with Other Recent Presidents in Appointing Federal Judges," *Pew Research Center*, January 13, 2021, https://www.pewresearch.org/fact-tank/2021/01/13/how-trump-compa res-with-other-recent-presidents-in-appointing-federal-judges/, accessed September 28, 2021.

8. On Trump's stance on NATO, see Julie Hirschfeld Davis, "Trump Warns NATO Allies to Spend More on Defense, or Else," *New York Times*, July 2, 2018, https://www.nytimes.com/2018/07/02/world/europe/trump-nato.html, accessed September 28, 2021; Julian E. Barnes and Helene Cooper, "Trump Discussed Pulling U.S. from NATO, Aides Say Amid New Concerns over Russia," *New York Times*, January 14, 2019, https://www.nytimes.com/2019/01/14/us/politics/nato-president-trump.html, accessed September 28, 2021; Ryan Browne, "Trump Administration to Cut Its Financial Contribution to NATO," *CNN.com*, November 28, 2019, https://edition.cnn.com/2019/11/27/politics/trump-nato-contribut ion-nato/index.html, accessed September 28, 2021. On Trump and Brexit, see "EU Referendum: Donald Trump Backs Brexit," *BBC News*, May 6, 2016, https://www.bbc.co.uk/news/uk-politics-eu-referendum-36219612, accessed September 28, 2021; Justin Wise, "Trump Says He Supports UK Leaving EU Without a Brexit Deal," *TheHill.com* June 2, 2019, https://thehill.com/policy/international/446504-trump-says-he-supports-uk-leav ing-eu-without-a-brexit-deal, accessed September 28, 2021.

9. A 1962 law the permitted such actions—Section 232 of the Trade Expansion Act of 1962. Emily Loftis, "Who Has the Authority to Impose Tariffs and How Does This Affect International Trade?," Yeutter Institute, Institute of Agriculture and Natural Resources, University of Nebraska, May 20, 2019, https://yeutter-institute.unl.edu/who-has-authority-impose-tariffs-and-how-does-affect-international-trade, accessed August 16, 2021.

10. Peter S. Goodman, "Global Trade Is Deteriorating Fast, Sapping the World's Economy," *New York Times*, October 1, 2019, https://www.nyti mes.com/2019/10/01/business/wto-global-trade.html, accessed August 16, 2021.

11. "Trump's 15% Tariffs on $112 Billion in Chinese Goods Take Effect," CNBC, September 1, 2019, https://www.cnbc.com/2019/09/01/trumps-15percent-tariffs-on-112-billion-in-chinese-goods-take-effect.html, accessed September 28, 2021.

12. See, for example, "New Data Show the Failures of Donald Trump's China Trade Strategy," *The Economist*, February 10, 2021, https://www.econom ist.com/graphic-detail/2021/02/10/new-data-show-the-failures-of-donald-trumps-china-trade-strategy, accessed August 16, 2021.

13. Felix Richter, "Has Globalization Passed Its Peak?," *Statista*, May 26, 2020, https://www.statista.com/chart/21821/global-trade-volume-as-a-percentage-of-gdp/, accessed August 16, 2021; Institute of Chartered Accountants in England and Wales, "Global Trade in Decline Long Before the Pandemic," 2021, https://www.icaew.com/technical/economy/economic-insight/global-trade-in-decline-long-before-the-pandemic, accessed August 16, 2021.

14. Marc Levinson, *Outside the Box: How Globalization Changed from Moving Stuff to Spreading Ideas* (Princeton, NJ: Princeton University Press, 2020),

210 and passim; Institute of Chartered Economists in England and Wales, "Global Trade in Decline Long Before the Pandemic."

15. Quoted in Green, *Devil's Bargain*, 9.

16. James Politi, "The Rise and Fall of the Trump Economy in Charts," *Financial Times*, November 4, 2020, https://www.ft.com/content/81264 46c-4959-4e87-8c78-3546bbf2ebc2, accessed September 28, 2021; Jeffrey Kucik, "How Trump Fueled Economic Inequality in America," *TheHill. com*, January 21, 2021, https://thehill.com/opinion/finance/535239-how-trump-fueled-economic-inequality-in-america, accessed September 28, 2021.

17. Josh Dawsey, "Trump Attacks Protections for Immigrants from 'Shithole' Countries," *Washington Post*, January 11, 2018, https://www.washingtonp ost.com/politics/trump-attacks-protections-for-immigrants-from-shith ole-countries-in-oval-office-meeting/2018/01/11/bfc0725c-f711-11e7-91af-31a c729add94_story.html, accessed August 17, 2021.

18. Immigration and Ethnic History Society, Immigration History, "Muslim Travel Ban," Department of History, University of Texas at Austin, https://immigrationhistory.org/item/muslim-travel-ban/, accessed August 17, 2021.

19. Southern Poverty Law Center, "Family Separation Under the Trump Administration—A Timeline," June 17, 2020, https://www.splcenter.org/ news/2020/06/17/family-separation-under-trump-administration-timeline, accessed August 17, 2021.

20. See Gary Gerstle, "Becoming Americans—U.S. Immigrant Integration," Testimony before the U.S. House of Representatives Committee on the Judiciary, Subcommittee on Immigration, Citizenship, Refugees, Border Security, and International Law, 110th Congress, First Session, May 16, 2007, https://www.aila.org/File/Related/07072061b.pdf, accessed September 28, 2021; see also Gary Gerstle, "Minorities, Multiculturalism, and the Presidency of George W. Bush," in Julian E. Zelizer, ed., *The Presidency of George W. Bush: A First Historical Assessment* (Princeton, NJ: Princeton University Press, 2010), 252–281.

21. Gerstle, "Minorities, Multiculturalism, and the Presidency of George W. Bush."

22. "Full Text: Trump's Comments on White Supremacists, 'Alt-Left' in Charlottesville," *Politico*, 15 August, 2017, https://www.politico.com/story/ 2017/08/15/full-text-trump-comments-white-supremacists-alt-left-transcr ipt-241662, accessed September 28, 2021; Michael D. Shear and Maggie Haberman, "Trump Defends Initial Remarks on Charlottesville; Again Blames 'Both Sides,'" *New York Times*, August 15, 2017, https://www.nyti mes.com/2017/08/15/us/politics/trump-press-conference-charlottesville. html, accessed September 28, 2021.

23. Rodrigo Duterte, "Donald Trump, Vladimir Putin and the Lure of the Strongman," *Financial Times*, May 16, 2016, https://www.ft.com/content/

1c6ff2ce-1939-11e6-b197-a4af20d5575e, accessed September 28, 2021; John Gray, "How We Entered the Age of the Strongman," *New Statesman*, May 23, 2018, https://www.newstatesman.com/uncategorized/2018/05/how-we-entered-age-strongman, accessed September 28, 2021; Gideon Rachman, "Donald Trump Leads a Global Revival of Nationalism," *Financial Times*, June 25, 2018, https://www.ft.com/content/59a37a38-7857-11e8-8e67-1e1a0 846c475, accessed September 28, 2021; Tom Parfitt, "Strongmen Flex Their Muscles as Faith in Democracy Withers," *The Times*, December 31, 2019, https://www.thetimes.co.uk/article/strongmen-flex-their-muscles-as-faith-in-democracy-withers-o2xzc9swt, accessed September 28, 2021.

24. Trump had no interest, as Bush had had, in spreading the gospel of free markets and the values of liberal democracy associated with them, to the farthest reaches of the earth. Trump was much more skeptical than Reagan or Bush had been about the utility of deploying the US military in the world. He wanted to end US involvement in ongoing foreign wars in Syria and Afghanistan, to close foreign bases (or require the host nations to pay for them), and to bring US troops home. That Trump was actually less eager for war than his Republican predecessor George W. Bush is an easily overlooked feature of his presidency, an oversight that is understandable given his (Trump's) fascination with the military and with violence.

25. Regulating or breaking up the social media companies was increasingly the battle cry of portions of the Republican Party that saw themselves as being in vanguard of a populist GOP. See, for example, Josh Hawley, *The Tyranny of Big Tech* (Washington, DC: Regnery, 2021). For more on the erosion of the open, global character of the internet and the rise of "cyber sovereignty," see James Griffiths, *The Great Firewall of China: How to Build and Control an Alternative Version of the Internet* (London: Bloomsbury, 2019); Elizabeth C. Economy, "The Great Firewall of China: Xi Jinping's Internet Shutdown," *The Guardian*, June 29, 2018, https://www.theguardian.com/news/2018/jun/29/the-great-firew all-of-china-xi-jinpings-internet-shutdown, accessed September 27, 2021; "China Internet: Xi Jinping Calls for 'Cyber Sovereignty,'" *BBC News*, December 16, 2015, https://www.bbc.co.uk/news/world-asia-china-35109 453, accessed September 27, 2021; Justin Sherman, "Russia and Iran Plan to Fundamentally Isolate the Internet," *Wired*, June 6, 2019, https://www. wired.com/story/russia-and-iran-plan-to-fundamentally-isolate-the-inter net/, accessed September 27, 2021; Matt Burgess, "Iran's Total Internet Shutdown Is a Blueprint for Breaking the Web," *Wired*, October 7, 2020, https://www.wired.co.uk/article/iran-news-internet-shutdown, accessed September 27, 2021; Paul Bischoff, "Internet Censorship 2021: A Global Map of Internet Restrictions," *Comparitech.com*, August 3, 2021, https:// www.comparitech.com/blog/vpn-privacy/internet-censorship-map/, accessed September 27, 2021.

26.   On Justice Democrats and the Sunrise Movement, see Andrew Marantz, "Are We Entering a New Political Era?," *New Yorker*, May 31, 2021, https://www.newyorker.com/magazine/2021/05/31/are-we-entering-a-new-political-era, accessed August 30, 2021. On Momentum, see Tyler Kingkade, "These Activists Are Training Every Movement That Matters," *Vice*, https://www.vice.com/en/article/8xw3ba/these-activists-are-training-every-movement-that-matters-v26n4, accessed August 30, 2021. See also Mark Schmitt, "The American Left Is a Historical Success Story," *Democracy*, July 15, 2021, https://democracyjournal.org/arguments/the-american-left-is-a-historical-success-story/, accessed August 30, 2021. For more on these movements see their websites: https://equitablegrowth.org/ and https://newconsensus.com/, both accessed August 30, 2021.

27.   For more on these organizations, see https://www.opensocietyfoundations.org/; https://omidyar.com/; https://hewlett.org/; https://www.berggruen.org/; all accessed December 9, 2022.

28.   On Warren's policies, see Elizabeth Warren, "Here's How We Can Break Up Big Tech," *Medium*, March 8, 2019, https://medium.com/@teamwarren/heres-how-we-can-break-up-big-tech-9ad9e0da324c, accessed September 24, 2021; Sheelah Kolhatkar, "How Elizabeth Warren Came Up with a Plan to Break Up Big Tech," *New Yorker*, August 20, 2019, https://www.newyorker.com/business/currency/how-elizabeth-warren-came-up-with-a-plan-to-break-up-big-tech, accessed September 24, 2021. Sanders's reform agenda included promoting government programs to make university education free to all Americans, to offer health care to every American ("Medicare for All"), to cancel trillions of dollars in student debt, and to establish a federal minimum wage of $15/hour. Bernie Sanders, "It's Time to Complete the Revolution We Started," *The Guardian*, February 25, 2019, https://www.theguardian.com/commentisfree/2019/feb/25/its-time-to-complete-the-revolution-we-started; Bernie Sanders, "The Foundations of American Society Are Failing Us," *New York Times*, April 19, 2020, https://www.nytimes.com/2020/04/19/opinion/coronavirus-inequality-bernie-sanders.html, accessed September 24, 2021.

29.   Emily Cochrane and Sheryl Ann Stolberg, "$2 Trillion Coronavirus Stimulus Bill Is Signed into Law," *New York Times*, March 27, 2020, https://www.nytimes.com/2020/03/27/us/politics/coronavirus-house-voting.html, accessed August 30, 2021.

30.   Martin Crutsinger, "A New $2.3 Trillion Fed Plan to Aid Localities and Companies," *AP News*, April 9, 2020, https://apnews.com/article/municipal-bonds-jerome-powell-financial-markets-virus-outbreak-business-8508af5848939f715622a71a44d3af20, accessed December 20, 2021.

31.   Rachel Cohrs, "The Trump Administration Quietly Spent Billions in Hospital Funds on Operation Warp Speed," *Stat News*, March 2, 2021, https://www.statnews.com/2021/03/02/trump-administration-quietly-spent-billions-in-hospital-funds-on-operation-warp-speed/, accessed August 30, 2021.

32. Gary Gerstle, "The New Federalism," *The Atlantic*, May 6, 2020, https://www.theatlantic.com/ideas/archive/2020/05/new-federalism/611077/, accessed September 27, 2021.

33. As a young husband and father, Biden lost his wife and daughter in a car crash. He later lost one of the two boys who survived that crash—Beau—to brain cancer. Biden's lone surviving biological offspring, Hunter, struggled with—and almost succumbed to—drug addiction.

34. Fintan O'Toole, "The Designated Mourner," *New York Review of Books*, January 16, 2020, https://nybooks.com/articles/2020/01/16/joe-biden-designated-mourner/, accessed September 27, 2021.

35. In this respect, he resembled a previous Democratic president, Franklin Roosevelt, whom Biden was coming to admire. Roosevelt never spoke publicly of the agony, physical and mental, that he had to endure once polio struck him in the early 1920s, leaving him paralyzed from the waist down for the rest of his life. Nor was this deeply Protestant man of Anglo-Dutch ancestry ever heard reciting verse from Irish-Catholic poets. But, as with Biden, his brush with tragedy, and his resisting the temptation to give into anger and despair, made Roosevelt far more empathetic than he had been, far more able to understand and speak to the losses that others had suffered and to devise a politics to address their pain. On this side of Roosevelt, see Geoffrey C. Ward, *A First-Class Temperament: The Emergence of Franklin Roosevelt, 1905–1928* (New York: HarperPerennial, 1989).

36. "Inflection point" was a phrase that Biden himself began to use. See, for example, his speech to the United Nations in September 2021. Kathryn Watson and Melissa Quinn, "Biden Says the World Stands at an 'Inflection Point' in First Address to U.N.," *CBS News*, September 21, 2021, https://www.cbsnews.com/live-updates/biden-united-nations-general-assembly-speech-inflection-point/, accessed September 28, 2021.

37. "Fact Sheet: President Biden to Announce All Americans to Be Eligible for Vaccinations by May 1, Puts the Nation on a Path to Get Closer to Normal by July 4th," *White House Press Release*, March 11, 2021, https://www.whitehouse.gov/briefing-room/statements-releases/2021/03/11/fact-sheet-president-biden-to-announce-all-americans-to-be-eligible-for-vaccinations-by-may-1-puts-the-nation-on-a-path-to-get-closer-to-normal-by-july-4th/, accessed September 28, 2021; "President Biden Announces American Rescue Plan," White House Press Release, January 20, 2021, https://www.whitehouse.gov/briefing-room/legislation/2021/01/20/president-biden-announces-american-rescue-plan/, accessed September 28, 2021; Jim Tankersley, "Biden Details $2 Trillion Plan to Rebuild Infrastructure and Reshape the Economy," *New York Times*, March 31, 2021, https://www.nytimes.com/2021/03/31/business/economy/biden-infrastructure-plan.html, accessed September 28, 2021; Maegan Vazquez, Kate Sullivan, Tami Luhby, and Katie Lobosco, "Biden's First 100 Days: What

He's Gotten Done," *CNN.com*, April 28, 2021, https://edition.cnn.com/2021/04/28/politics/president-biden-first-100-days/index.html, accessed September 28, 2021; Desiree Ibekwe, "The Daily: Biden's First 100 Days," *New York Times*, April 28, 2021, https://www.nytimes.com/2021/04/28/podcasts/joe-biden-infrastructure-stimulus-congress.html, accessed September 28, 2021.

38. Bill Dupor, "How Recent Fiscal Interventions Compare with the New Deal," *Regional Economist* (a publication of the Federal Reserve Bank of St. Louis), July 13, 2021, https://www.stlouisfed.org/publications/regional-economist/third-quarter-2021/how-recent-fiscal-interventions-compare-new-deal, accessed September 2, 2021; Michael Schuyler, "A Short History of Government Taxing and Spending in the United States," *taxfoundation.org*, February 19, 2014, https://taxfoundation.org/short-history-government-taxing-and-spending-united-states/, accessed September 2, 2021.

39. This collaboration was a world away from the antagonistic way in which the Clinton and Sanders teams had approached each other in 2016. Marantz, "Are We Entering a New Political Era?"

40. Marantz, "Are We Entering a New Political Era?"; Schmitt, "The American Left Is a Historical Success Story"; J. W. Mason, "The American Rescue Plan as Economic Theory," *Slackwire*, March 15, 2021, https://jwmason.org/slackwire/the-american-rescue-plan-as-economic-theory/, accessed September 2, 2021; Saahil Desai, "Joe Biden's Man on the Left," *The Atlantic*, October 29, 2020, https://www.theatlantic.com/politics/archive/2020/10/jared-bernstein-joe-biden-progressive-personnel/616861/, accessed September 2, 2021; Zachary Warmbrodt, "'Radical' Biden Nominee Faces Backlash from Banks," *Politico*, September 24, 2021, https://www.politico.com/news/2021/09/24/radical-biden-nominee-faces-backlash-from-banks-514189, accessed September 28, 2021; Stephanie Kelton, *The Deficit Myth: Modern Monetary Theory and the Birth of the People's Economy* (New York: PublicAffairs, 2021); Lina M. Khan, "The Amazon Anti-Trust Paradox," *Yale Law Review* 126 (2017), 710-805, https://www.yalelawjournal.org/pdf/e.710.Khan.805_zuvfy yeh.pdf, accessed December 17, 2021; Saule T. Omarova, "The People's Ledger: How to Democratize Money and Finance the Economy," October 20, 2020, Cornell Legal Studies Research Paper No. 20-45, *Vanderbilt Law Review*, forthcoming, available at SSRN: https://ssrn.com/abstract=3715735 or http://dx.doi.org/10.2139/ssrn.3715735, accessed September 27, 2021. See also K. Sabeel Rahman, *Democracy Against Domination* (New York: Oxford University Press, 2017), and Ganesh Sitaraman, *The Great Democracy: How to Fix Our Politics, Unrig the Economy, and Unite America* (New York: Basic Books, 2019).

41. Evan Osnos, "Can Biden's Center Hold?" *New Yorker*, August 23, 2020, https://www.newyorker.com/magazine/2020/08/31/can-bidens-cen

ter-hold, accessed September 28, 2021; Daniel Strauss, "Biden Bids to Placate the Left as He Builds Centrist Transition Team," *The Guardian*, November 29, 2020, https://www.theguardian.com/us-news/2020/nov/29/joe-biden-transition-left-centrists-democrats, accessed September 28, 2021; Lisa Lerer and Reid J. Epstein, "How Biden United a Fractious Party Under One Tent," *New York Times*, February 9, 2021, https://www.nytimes.com/2021/02/09/us/politics/joe-biden-democratic-party.html, accessed September 28, 2021.

42.   On the centrality of the cheap, fossil-fuel strategy of the New Deal, see Matthew Owen, " 'For the Progress of Man': The TVA, Electric Power, and the Environment" (PhD dissertation, Vanderbilt University, 2014). On energy politics more generally, see Helen Thompson, *Oil and the Western Economic Crisis* (London: Palgrave Macmillan, 2017), and Helen Thompson, *Disorder: Hard Times in the 21ˢᵗ Century* (Oxford: Oxford University Press, 2022).

43.   Evan Hill, Ainara Tiefenthäler, Christiaan Triebert, Drew Jordan, Haley Willis, and Robin Stein, "How George Floyd Was Killed in Police Custody," *New York Times*, May 31, 2020, https://www.nytimes.com/2020/05/31/us/george-floyd-investigation.html, accessed September 28, 2021.

44.   Derrick Bryson Taylor, "George Floyd Protests: A Timeline," *New York Times*, June 2, 2020, https://www.nytimes.com/article/george-floyd-protests-timeline.html, accessed September 28, 2021; Audra D. S. Burch, Amy Harmon, Sabrina Tavernise, and Emily Badger, "The Death of George Floyd Reignited a Movement. What Happens Now?," *New York Times*, April 20, 2021, https://www.nytimes.com/2021/04/20/us/george-floyd-protests-police-reform.html, accessed September 28, 2021; Larry Buchanan, Quoctrung Bui, and Jugal K. Patel, "Black Lives Matter May Be the Largest Movement in U.S. History," *New York Times*, July 3, 2020, https://www.nytimes.com/interactive/2020/07/03/us/george-floyd-protests-crowd-size.html, accessed September 28, 2021; Mariame Kaba, "Yes, We Mean Literally Abolish the Police," *New York Times*, June 12, 2020, https://www.nytimes.com/2020/06/12/opinion/sunday/floyd-abolish-defund-police.html, accessed September 28, 2021.

45.   Jonathan Martin, Alexander Burns, and Thomas Kaplan, "Biden Walks a Cautious Line as He Opposes Defunding the Police," *New York Times*, June 8, 2020, https://www.nytimes.com/2020/06/08/us/politics/biden-defund-the-police.html, accessed September 28, 2021.

46.   Ta-Nehisi Coates, "The Case for Reparations," *The Atlantic*, June 15, 2014, https://www.theatlantic.com/magazine/archive/2014/06/the-case-for-reparations/361631/, accessed September 27, 2021; Ta-Nehisi Coates, "Ta-Nehisi Coates Revisits the Case for Reparations," *New Yorker*, June 10, 2019, https://www.newyorker.com/news/the-new-yorker-interview/ta-nehisi-coates-revisits-the-case-for-reparations, accessed September 27, 2021.

47. Marantz, "Are We Entering a New Political Era?"

48. Pete Williams and Nicole Via y Rada, "Trump's Election Fight Includes over 50 Lawsuits. It's Not Going Well," *CNBC*, November 23, 2020, https://www.nbcnews.com/politics/2020-election/trump-s-election-fight-includes-over-30-lawsuits-it-s-n1248289, accessed September 28, 2021; Kadhim Shubber, "Lawsuit Tracker: Donald Trump's Legal Battle Runs into Repeated Dead Ends," *Financial Times*, December 11, 2020, https://www.ft.com/content/20b114b5-5419-493b-9923-a918a2527931, accessed September 28, 2021.

49. Michael Wolff offers a good journalistic (and panoramic) account of these months in his book *Landslide: The Final Days of the Trump Presidency* (New York: Henry Holt, 2021). See also Dan Barry and Sheera Frenkel, "'Be There. Will Be Wild!': Trump All but Circled the Date," *New York Times*, January 6, 2021, updated July 27, 2021, https://www.nytimes.com/2021/01/06/us/politics/capitol-mob-trump-supporters.html, accessed September 28, 2021; Dan Barry, Mike McIntire, and Matthew Rosenberg, "'Our President Wants Us Here': The Mob That Stormed the Capitol," *New York Times*, January 9, 2021, updated September 25, 2021, https://www.nytimes.com/2021/01/09/us/capitol-rioters.html, accessed September 28, 2021. See, also, Select Committee to Investigate the January 6th Attack on the United States Capitol, *The January 6th Report* (New York: Celadon Books, 2022).

50. On the sense of a democratic crisis gripping the United States and the world, see David Runciman, *How Democracy Ends* (London: Profile, 2018); Steven Levitsky and Daniel Ziblatt, *How Democracies Die* (New York: Penguin Press, 2017); Nadia T. Urbinati, *Democracy Disfigured: Opinion, Truth and the People* (Cambridge, MA: Harvard University Press, 2014); Thompson, *Disorder;* see also Eugenio T. Biagini and Gary Gerstle, eds., *A Cultural History of Democracy in the Modern Age* (London: Bloomsbury Academic, 2021).

51. For work outlining the contours of a post-globalization political economy, see Rana Foroohar, *Homecoming: The Path to Prosperity in a Post-Global World* (New York: Crown Publishing, 2022); Dani Rodrick, "The New Productivism Paradigm," *Project Syndicate*, July 5, 2022, https://www.project-syndicate.org/commentary/new-productivism-economic-policy-paradigm-by-dani-rodrik-2022-07, accessed March 1, 2023; Adrian Wooldridge, "Globalization Isn't Making a Comeback at Davos," *Bloomberg UK*, December 22, 2022, https://www.bloomberg.com/opinion/articles/2022-12-20/don-t-be-fooled-at-davos-globalization-as-we-knew-it-won-t-be-coming-back?leadSource=uverify%20wall, accessed December 24, 2022.

52. H.R. 4346 Chips and Science Act of 2022, 117th Congress (2021–2022), https://www.congress.gov/bill/117th-congress/house-bill/4346, accessed March 1, 2023; and H.R. 5376 Inflation Reduction Act of 2022, 117th

Congress (2021–22), https://www.congress.gov/bill/117th-congress/house-bill/5376/text, accessed March 1, 2023.

53.   On the contours of Biden's industrial policy, see "Progressive Industrial Policy: 2022 and Beyond," Roosevelt Institute Conference, Washington D.C., October 7, 2022, https://rooseveltinstitute.org/event/progressive-industrial-policy-2022-and-beyond/ and https://rooseveltinstitute.org/wp-content/uploads/2022/10/RI_IP_Forum_Agenda.pdf, accessed March 1, 2023; Todd N. Tucker, "Industrial Policy and Planning: What It Is and How to Do It Better," *Roosevelt Institute*, July 30, 2019, https://rooseveltinstitute.org/publications/industrial-policy-and-planning/, accessed February 28, 2023; Todd N. Tucker and Steph Sterling, "Industrial Policy and Planning: A New (Old) Approach to Policymaking for a New Era," *Roosevelt Institute*, August 10, 2021, https://rooseveltinstitute.org/publications/a-new-old-approach-to-policymaking-for-a-new-era/, accessed February 28, 2023; Gary Gerstle, "Are US Politics Starting to Turn Towards a More Hopeful Future?," *The Guardian*, November 15, 2022, https://www.theguardian.com/commentisfree/2022/nov/15/are-us-politics-starting-to-turn-towards-a-more-hopeful-future, accessed February 27, 2023.

54.   The anti-abortion decision was U.S. Supreme Court, *Dobbs v. Jackson Women's Health Organization*, No. 19-1392, 597 U.S. _____ (2022).

55.   Biden and the Democratic Party would have to pull off this sweep in an electoral system that systematically undervalues the votes of urban dwellers among whom the Democrats are traditionally strong and against a Republican Party that in multiple states seems to be doing everything in its power to make it harder for Democratic-leaning citizens to cast their votes.

56.   The phrase "ruins of the neoliberal order" is from Wendy Brown, though I see progressive as well as reactionary possibilities lying among the neoliberal ruins. Wendy Brown, *In the Ruins of Neoliberalism: The Rise of Antidemocratic Politics in the West* (New York: Columbia University Press, 2019).

57.   Katie Johnson, "Earnings Rising Faster for Lower-Wage Workers," *Boston Globe*, December 10, 2021, https://www.bostonglobe.com/2021/12/09/business/first-time-decades-earnings-are-rising-faster-lower-wage-workers/?et_rid=1773137024&s_campaign=todaysheadlines:newsletter, accessed December 10, 2021; Dee-Ann Durbin and Carolyn Thompson, "In a First for Starbucks, Workers Agree to Form Union," *Boston Globe*, December 9, 2021, https://www.bostonglobe.com/2021/12/09/business/first-starbucks-workers-agree-union-buffalo/, accessed December 10, 2021.

58.   See, for example, Saule Omarova's proposal to shift consumer deposit accounts from private banks to the Fed as a way of democratizing finance. Omarova, "The People's Ledger." See also Charles Lane, "Joe Biden Isn't a Socialist but His Nominee to Regulate Banks Has Pretty Radical Ideas

About the Fed," *Washington Post*, October 13, 2021, https://www.washing tonpost.com/opinions/2021/10/13/joe-biden-isnt-socialist-his-nominee-regulate-banks-has-pretty-radical-ideas-about-fed/, accessed October 13, 2021. For other interesting analyses of the Fed, and how it does (and does not) exercise power, see Greta R. Krippner, *Capitalizing on Crisis: The Political Origins of the Rise of Finance* (Cambridge, MA: Harvard University Press, 2012); and Lawrence R. Jacobs and Desmond King, *Fed Power: How Finance Wins* (2016; New York: Oxford University Press, 2021).

59. There are some indications that momentum for such a movement is building. See, for example, William Davies, "The Reaction Economy," *London Review of Books*, March 2, 2023, 3–8; Michelle Goldberg, "Don't Let Politics Cloud Your View of What's Going On with Teens and Depression," *New York Times*, February 24, 2023, https://www.nytimes.com/2023/02/24/opinion/social-media-and-teen-depression.html?searchResultPosition=2, accessed February 24, 2023; and Christopher Booker, "Social Media Companies Face Legal Scrutiny Over Deteriorating Mental Health Among Teens," *PBS News Hour*, February 14, 2023, https://www.pbs.org/newshour/show/social-media-companies-face-legal-scrutiny-over-deteriorating-mental-health-among-teens, accessed March 3, 2023.

INDEX

For the benefit of digital users, indexed terms that span two pages (e.g., 52–53) may, on occasion, appear on only one of those pages.